How to Build a Speech Recognition Application

Second Edition

D1744041

A Style Guide for Telephony Dialogues

$10

Send this coupon in today and receive $10 back on the purchase of this book. To find out more about EIG's professional services, workshops and other publications call **1-888-EIG-4 IVR** or visit our web site at **www.eiginc.com**

First Name (please print)   Middle Initial   Last Name

Company Name

Mailing Address   City   State   Zip

E-mail   Telephone Number   Fax Number

www.eiginc.com

ENTERPRISE
INTEGRATION
GROUP

 ENTERPRISE
INTEGRATION
GROUP

BUSINESS REPLY MAIL
FIRST-CLASS MAIL   PERMIT NO. 126   SAN RAMON, CA

POSTAGE WILL BE PAID BY ADDRESSEE

ENTERPRISE INTEGRATION GROUP
2410 SAN RAMON VALLEY BLVD., SUITE 225
SAN RAMON, CA 94583-9625

How to Build a Speech Recognition Application

Second Edition

A Style Guide for
Telephony Dialogues

Bruce Balentine
David P. Morgan

EIG Press

ISBN 0-9671278-2-3

Published by Enterprise Integration Group, Inc.
2410 San Ramon Valley Blvd., Suite 225
San Ramon, California 94583

1-888-344-4487 (U.S.A.)
+ 925-362-1700 (outside U.S.A.)
http://www.eiginc.com

If you have comments, write to the above address or send e-mail directly to:
styleguide@eiginc.com

To our families

Patti, Beth, and Leslie

Christine, Michael, and Ryan

Contents

CHAPTER 1   THE TELEPHONY USER INTERFACE 1

  1.1   A STYLE GUIDE FOR USER INTERFACES 2
    1.1.1   Target Audience   3
    1.1.2   Style Guide Versus Standards   7
    1.1.3   Goals and Objectives   9
  1.2   BASIC SPEECH INTERFACE CONCEPTS 10
    1.2.1   Unique Characteristics of Speech   11
    1.2.2   Moving Through States   12
    1.2.3   Turn Taking   15
    1.2.4   Additional Concepts   16
  1.3   TERMINOLOGY 19
    1.3.1   Understanding Rejection   20
    1.3.2   Speech Recognition Errors   25
    1.3.3   Barge-In and Other Terms   26
  1.4   HOW THIS BOOK IS ORGANIZED 27
    1.4.1   Formatting Conventions   27
    1.4.2   Chapter Summaries   28

CHAPTER 2   SPOKEN MACHINE OUTPUT 33

  2.1   PHYSICAL PROPERTIES OF MACHINE SPEECH 33
    2.1.1   Loudness and Noise   33
    2.1.2   Sound Quality of Spoken Output   34
    2.1.3   Synthesized Versus Digitized Spoken Output   38
    2.1.4   Minimum and Maximum Timing Values   39
    2.1.5   Proportions of Speech and Silence   40
    2.1.6   Rhythm and Rate of Speech   41
  2.2   WORDING OF SPOKEN OUTPUT 41
    2.2.1   Types of Spoken Output   41
    2.2.2   Voice, Person, Tense, and Mood   42
    2.2.3   Opening Greetings   44
  2.3   PROMPTS 45
    2.3.1   Prompt Design   45
    2.3.2   Yes-No Interrogative Prompts   47
    2.3.3   Other Interrogative Prompts   49
    2.3.4   Implied Interrogative Prompts   49
    2.3.5   Imperative Prompts   51
    2.3.6   Verbatim Prompts and Data Prompts   51

2.4 FEEDBACK **54**
   2.4.1 Types of Feedback   *54*
   2.4.2 Relationship Between Feedback and Prompts   *55*
2.5 INSTRUCTIONS **57**
   2.5.1 Wording and Construction   *57*
   2.5.2 Grammatical Forms for Instructions   *59*
   2.5.3 Mnemonic Consistency   *61*
2.6 HELP **61**
   2.6.1 When to Offer Help   *61*
   2.6.2 Help Mode   *64*
   2.6.3 Tutorials   *65*
2.7 APPLICATION DATA **65**
   2.7.1 Digit-String Grouping   *65*
   2.7.2 Timing and Inflection of Digit Strings   *67*

CHAPTER 3 SELECTING THE VOCABULARY **71**

3.1 THE RECOGNIZER'S IMPACT ON VOCABULARY SELECTION **72**
   3.1.1 Analyzing the Recognizer's Behavior   *73*
   3.1.2 Strategies to Improve Recognition   *78*
   3.1.3 Word-Pair Discrimination   *86*
3.2 CONSISTENCY IN VOCABULARY SELECTION **92**
   3.2.1 Voice/Keypad Equivalents   *92*
   3.2.2 Parallel Structure and Consistency   *93*

CHAPTER 4 BARGE-IN AND TURN TAKING **97**

4.1 IMPLEMENTING BARGE-IN **98**
   4.1.1 What Is Echo Cancellation?   *98*
   4.1.2 Basic Problems with Echo Cancellation   *99*
   4.1.3 User Interface Issues with Barge-In   *101*
   4.1.4 Three Approaches to Stopping Prompts   *106*
4.2 CHOOSING A TURN-TAKING PROTOCOL **110**
   4.2.1 Full Duplex or Half Duplex?   *110*
   4.2.2 Creating Speaking Opportunities   *111*
4.3 IMPLEMENTING FULL-DUPLEX DESIGNS **116**
   4.3.1 Timing and Implementation of Barge-In   *116*
   4.3.2 Techniques for Stabilizing Barge-In   *117*
   4.3.3 Suppressing Barge-In for Legal Reasons   *119*
4.4 IMPLEMENTING HALF-DUPLEX DESIGNS **120**
   4.4.1 Managing Turn Taking   *121*
   4.4.2 Recovering Spoke-Too-Soon Errors   *122*

CHAPTER 5   TONES **127**

  5.1   NON-SPEECH AUDIO **127**
    5.1.1   Classes and Functions of Tones   *127*
    5.1.2   Attributes of Non-Speech Audio   *130*
  5.2   WHEN TO USE TONES **132**
    5.2.1   Without Barge-In   *133*
    5.2.2   With Barge-In   *134*
  5.3   PROMPTING TONES **135**
    5.3.1   Single-Tone Prompts   *135*
    5.3.2   Logos as Prompting Tones   *136*
    5.3.3   Announcing Hidden Menus   *136*
  5.4   FEEDBACK/CONFIRMATION TONES **137**
    5.4.1   Why Use Post-Recognition Tones?   *137*
    5.4.2   Tension/Release Patterns   *139*
  5.5   CONTEXT TONES **140**
    5.5.1   Menu Announcements   *140*
    5.5.2   Help, Waiting, and Other Contexts   *141*

CHAPTER 6   DIALOGUE DESIGN **143**

  6.1   DIALOGUE MODELS **144**
    6.1.1   Command and Control Dialogues   *147*
    6.1.2   Form-Filling Dialogues   *148*
    6.1.3   Searching Dialogues   *149*
  6.2   MENUS **150**
    6.2.1   Speech Versus DTMF Menus   *151*
    6.2.2   Number of Selections per Menu   *159*
    6.2.3   List Interruption   *159*
    6.2.4   Two-Way Branching and Quasi-Menus   *162*
    6.2.5   Hidden Menus   *163*
  6.3   YES-NO QUERIES **166**
    6.3.1   Yes-No Dialogue Design   *166*
    6.3.2   Yes-No Error Recovery   *168*
    6.3.3   Implicit Yes-No Windows   *170*
    6.3.4   Stabilizing Dialogues with Yes-No   *172*
    6.3.5   One-Shot Yes-No   *176*
  6.4   REUSABLE DIALOGUE COMPONENTS **179**
    6.4.1   Designing Dialogue Components   *179*

CHAPTER 7   MIXED MODALITIES: SPEECH AND DTMF **183**

  7.1   SWITCHING BETWEEN SPEECH AND DTMF **183**
    7.1.1   Coupling the Two Modalities   *184*
    7.1.2   Switching Modalities   *187*

7.2   MIXING SPEECH AND DTMF 190
   7.2.1   *The "Press or Say" Construct*   *190*
   7.2.2   *Prompt and Feedback Interruption*   *191*
   7.2.3   *Navigation Through n-Best*   *193*
   7.2.4   *Legal Obligations*   *195*

CHAPTER 8   NATURAL LANGUAGE INTERFACES 197

8.1   WHAT IS NATURAL LANGUAGE? 197
   8.1.1   *NL Technology Components*   *198*
8.2   REACHING TERMINALS IN THE HIERARCHY 199
   8.2.1   *DTMF Menu Navigation*   *199*
   8.2.2   *NL Speech Recognition*   *200*
8.3   NL PROMPT DESIGN 203
   8.3.1   *NL Prompting*   *204*
   8.3.2   *NL Feed-Forward Prompts*   *208*
8.4   NL ERROR PREVENTION AND RECOVERY 213
   8.4.1   *NL Feedback*   *213*
   8.4.2   *Yes-No and Ambiguity Recovery*   *215*
   8.4.3   *New User and Transition Tutoring*   *216*
8.5   CHALLENGES IN IMPLEMENTING NL SYSTEMS 217
   8.5.1   *User Skill and User Learning*   *217*
   8.5.2   *The Convergence Problem*   *228*
   8.5.3   *Designing Well-Balanced Grammars*   *236*
   8.5.4   *Statistical Language Models*   *239*

CHAPTER 9   PERSONIFIED INTERFACES 245

9.1   ISSUES WITH PERSONIFICATION 245
   9.1.1   *Anthropomorphism*   *246*
   9.1.2   *Personalization*   *246*
   9.1.3   *Personification*   *246*
   9.1.4   *Social and Professional Issues*   *248*
   9.1.5   *Persona Versus Personality*   *251*
9.2   CHOOSING PERSONALITY TRAITS 254
   9.2.1   *Personae, Names, and Gatekeepers*   *254*
   9.2.2   *Machine/User Relationship*   *258*
9.3   THE HANC APPLICATION PERSONA 261
   9.3.1   *Initiative and User Knowledge*   *262*
   9.3.2   *Vocabulary Selection*   *268*

CHAPTER 10   ERROR RECOVERY AND PREVENTION 271

10.1   DETECTING AND HANDLING ERRORS 271
   10.1.1   *Distinguishing Error Types*   *272*
   10.1.2   *Giving Up and Disconnecting*   *276*
   10.1.3   *Avoiding Repeated Mistakes*   *277*

10.2   USER-INITIATED ERROR RECOVERY 278
  10.2.1   Approaches for Barge-In   278
  10.2.2   Approaches for Half-Duplex Systems   280
10.3   MACHINE-INITIATED CORROBORATION OR RECOVERY 282
  10.3.1   Yes-No Queries   282
  10.3.2   Digit Strings   283
  10.3.3   Resolving Ambiguities   289
10.4   ERROR PREVENTION 290
  10.4.1   Expecting, Preventing, and Detecting Rejections   290

CHAPTER 11   USABILITY TESTS AND PERFORMANCE REPORTS .. 293

11.1   INTRODUCTION TO USABILITY TESTING 294
  11.1.1   Types of Usability Tests   294
  11.1.2   Reductionist Testing Strategies   299
11.2   LABORATORY TESTS 301
  11.2.1   Physical Laboratory Setup   301
  11.2.2   General Test Design Principles   302
  11.2.3   OOG Post-Test Interviews and Questionnaires   306
11.3   WIZARD OF OZ AND PROTOTYPE TESTING 307
  11.3.1   What Is Wizard Testing?   307
  11.3.2   Wizard Methodologies   308
11.4   LOGGING AND REPORTING 309
  11.4.1   What to Log and Measure   309
  11.4.2   Analyzing Logged Data   312
  11.4.3   Voice Logging   313
11.5   SUMMARY 314

APPENDIX A NL HARDWARE PROVISIONING 317

A.1   WIZARD TESTS ESTIMATE HARDWARE REQUIREMENTS 317
A.2   COMPUTING THE REQUIRED NUMBER OF LICENSES 318
A.3   HARDWARE PROVISIONING 321
A.4   OTHER ISSUES TO CONSIDER 323
A.5   THE CONSEQUENCES OF INSUFFICIENT PROVISIONING 324

APPENDIX B VOICE PORTALS 325

B.1   WHAT IS A VOICE PORTAL? 325
  B.1.1   Voice Portal Utility   327
  B.1.2   Portal Architecture   328
  B.1.3   Comparing Voice Portals and VRU Systems   329
  B.1.4   Enterprise Portals   329
  B.1.5   Consumer Portals   331

B.2 VOICE WEB GUIDELINES 332
B.2.1   *Relationship Between the Voice Browser and Web Browser*   *334*
B.2.2   *Presenting a Web Page*   *337*
B.2.3   *Style and Personality Issues*   *340*
B.2.4   *Search and Negotiation Issues*   *341*

APPENDIX C VOICE TALENT AND RECORDING 343

C.1 VOICE RECORDING 343
C.1.1   *Subtleties of Voice Files*   *343*
C.1.2   *Preliminary Test Recordings*   *348*
C.1.3   *Selecting and Coaching Voice Talent*   *349*
C.2 RECORDING IN FOREIGN LANGUAGES 353
C.2.1   *Selecting Foreign Language Voice Talent*   *353*
C.2.2   *Coaching Foreign Language Voice Talent*   *354*

BIBLIOGRAPHY 356

OTHER STANDARDS 363

GLOSSARY 365

INDEX 386

List of Figures

Figure 1.1—EXAMPLE STATE ERROR 14

Figure 2.1—DIGIT INFLECTIONS 68

Figure 2.2—INFLECTIONS AND PAUSES AT GROUPINGS 69

Figure 3.1—REJECTION LOGIC FOR TOGGLE WORDS 91

Figure 4.1—SOURCES OF ECHO 99

Figure 4.2—STOPPING THE PROMPT ON ENERGY DETECTION 107

Figure 4.3— STOPPING THE PROMPT ON WORD DETECTION 108

Figure 4.4— STOPPING THE PROMPT BASED ON THE FIRST SYLLABLE 109

Figure 4.5—POINT AND SPEAK FEATURE 113

Figure 4.6—FULL DUPLEX POINT AND SPEAK 114

Figure 4.7— HALF DUPLEX POINT AND SPEAK 115

Figure 5.1—OPENING AND CLOSING TONE PAIRS 138

Figure 6.1—YES-NO BARRIER 174

Figure 7.1—SEPARATE DIALOGUE SOLUTION 184

Figure 7.2—MODAL SOLUTION 185

Figure 7.3—DTMF CONSTRAINED SOLUTION 186

Figure 7.4—SEAMLESS SPEECH-CENTRIC SOLUTION 186

Figure 8.1—DTMF MENU HIERARCHY 200

Figure 8.2—NATURAL LANGUAGE INTERFACE 202

Figure 8.3—USER SKILL REQUIRED TO USE NL EFFECTIVELY 218

Figure 8.4—NATURAL GRAVITATION OF NL DIALOGUE 230

Figure 9.1—ROUGH PRECISION TIME 264

Figure 10.1—FOUR DIGIT INFLECTIONS 286

Figure 10.2—INFLECTED DIGIT PLAYBACK 288

Figure 10.3—HANDHELD TELEPHONES 291

Figure 11.1—USABILITY LABORATORY 302

Figure 11.2—ANALYSIS BASED ON TIME LAGS 313

Figure B.1—AN INTERNET VOICE PORTAL 326

Figure B.2—ENTERPRISE PORTALS 330

Figure B.3—TYPICAL WEB PAGE 333

Figure B.4—CALL ROUTING VOICE PORTAL 341

List of Tables

Table 1.1—ISSUES AFFECTING DIALOGUE DESIGN 16

Table 2.1—TYPES OF SPOKEN MACHINE OUTPUT 42

Table 2.2—TYPICAL CLASSES OF NUMERIC DATA 66

Table 3.1—WORDS ASSOCIATED WITH CONSUMER TECHNOLOGIES 77

Table 3.2—UNSTRESSED SYLLABLES 85

Table 3.3—WORD PAIRS WITH SHARED SYLLABLES OR VOWELS 87

Table 3.4—WORDS WITH DROPPED SYLLABLES FORM WORD PAIRS 88

Table 6.1—DIALOGUE DESIGN MODELS 146

Table 7.1—REASONS FOR USING DTMF 189

Table 7.2—BACKUP FUNCTIONS WITH DTMF 193

Table 8.1—TYPES OF SPOKEN MACHINE OUTPUT 214

Table 8.2—TYPICAL RESPONSES TO TWO- AND THREE-WAY BRANCHES 221

Table 8.3—STATISTICAL LANGUAGE MODEL 241

Table 9.1—NAMES OF APPLICATION PERSONAE 255

Table 9.2—DISCRETE GATEKEEPER STATE 256

Table 9.3—NL GATEKEEPER 257

Table 11.1—USABILITY TESTING IS CONFOUNDED 295

Table A.1—EXAMPLE OF PROVISIONING PROCESS 319

Table A.2—NUMBER OF SPEECH RECOGNITION LICENSES needed 321

Table A.3— NUMBER OF SPEECH RECOGNITION LICENSES FREEING UP 321

Table C.1—VOICE WARM-UP 351

Foreword

William S. Meisel, Ph.D.
President, TMA Associates
Publisher & Editor, Speech Recognition Update

There is little question about the value of using speech recognition over the telephone. The telephone's evolution has been limited by the current user interface—the touch tone keypad. Speech recognition improves that interface to such an extent that it creates significant new ways to use the telephone. This includes interacting with automated systems, personal assistants, and web sites via the telephone.

The change in the telephony interface from a touch tone to a voice user interface will rival in importance the creation of the graphical user interface (GUI) for personal computers (PCs). The GUI expanded the use of the PC from the technology hobbyist to the general public. Likewise, the telephony voice user interface will result in the availability of a personal assistant on every existing telephone (wired or wireless)— without a hardware or software upgrade!

If electronic commerce is defined by cost-effective, satisfying customer *self-service*, then telephone automation should be viewed as a second leg of e-commerce. There are many transactions where it is more convenient to pick up a telephone, be connected quickly, ask for information, a product or service, and get immediate results. As the cost of telephone service continues to decline (and it will), economic costs associated with the telephone will be equivalent to those of the Internet. (In many cases, subscribers will obtain telephone and Internet services from the same provider over the same wire, cable or wireless connection.) Moreover, Web designers will simply add scripts for voice browsers to enable their sites for telephone access.

If telephone speech recognition does not become ubiquitous, it will be because application developers deploy terrible dialogues. Just as there can be a poor GUI on the PC, there can be poor implementations of the voice user interface. Poor dialogues are no better than a badly designed series of touch tone menus—they can be confusing, frustrating, and ultimately create errors.

How can developers avoid this pitfall? We can learn from the evolution of the PC. Intel's and Microsoft's de facto hardware and software standards gave developers a single platform for their applications. This was a critical element of PC growth because it allowed PCs to be sold in volume at low cost for multiple applications. But, if this were the only element, then why is the Macintosh still viewed as one of the easiest PCs to use? The fact is that—within an application—the GUI is consistent for different types of PCs. The key element in making the PC *usable*, as opposed to *affordable*, was the consistency in the implementation of the GUI. Even today, software reviewers are critical of a new software product that has an unusual GUI.

Now for the key point. Successful PC software applications are designed for what users have come to expect from the GUI—a certain style. Users learn from one application and apply it to the next. Consistency eliminates much of the need for extensive training and manuals. A GUI style may have been originally formulated with a style guide developed by Apple. It evolved as PC developers copied each others' good ideas. Bad or inconsistent styles disappeared as buyers voted against them with their wallets. If telephone speech recognition developers do not similarly establish a consistent style, then every time a caller interacts with a voice user interface, he or she will encounter a different style. Callers will not be able to learn from one application and apply it to the next. *Dialogues should have a consistent style to speed the adoption of the voice user interface.*

In a nutshell, the concepts of style and consistency are why this book is so important. Bruce Balentine and Dave Morgan have labored to distill what is known about the telephony voice user interface into a style guide. This is not, and cannot be, a standard. It is a guide. The authors realize that, like style in writing, there is an exception to almost every rule. But dialogue writers who adhere to these principles will design highly predictable and usable voice user interfaces that will result in higher user acceptance.

The quality of this book comes from two sources: (1) extensive research into what we already know about man-machine dialogue, particularly over the telephone; and (2) the substantial personal experience of the authors in working with telephone speech recognition. Despite the scarcity of relevant material from which to draw, the authors have found the truly relevant information and distilled it, while avoiding the overly theoretical. The glossary and bibliography alone are invaluable to readers who want to peruse the literature or who want to quickly learn the jargon of this new field.

The writers have first hand experience in speech recognition dialogue design from different viewpoints. Bruce Balentine has been a pioneer in understanding how to make speech recognition work at a time when the dialogue often had to compensate for the inadequacies of the technology. He worked from the viewpoint of a technology vendor trying to satisfy a wide range of customers. Dave Morgan was an early adopter of the technology at a major financial institution. He had to understand what would work with customers and how the technology was *not* "just like talking to a person."

Anyone who is serious about developing or implementing telephone speech recognition should have this book handy and well thumbed. It is fun to read because it reveals so many fascinating insights about how humans communicate with machines. It is also an essential reference for resolving many development issues by clarifying the options, revealing what has been proposed and what has worked. Dialogue designers using this book will eliminate many design iterations and will be more likely to implement a design that is familiar to the caller, as other designers will be doing likewise.

Standards determine the platform. Styles determine if the platform is usable. The telephone voice user interface could fall apart in a tangle of conflicting styles. If so, it will be in spite of Balentine's and Morgan' s wonderful book.

William S. Meisel
April, 1999

About the Authors

Bruce Balentine has over sixteen years experience designing and developing speech, audio, and multimodal user interfaces. As Vice President of Speech Technologies for Enterprise Integration Group, he provides research, usability testing, and interface design consulting services worldwide. His expertise includes user interface design for telecommunications, desktop multimedia, entertainment, language training, medical, and home automation products.

Mr. Balentine earned a Bachelor's and Master's Degree from the University of North Texas with interdisciplinary work in electronic music, computer music, and intermedia composition. Prior to specializing in speech, he devoted more than ten years to work in audio recording, stage lighting, and other performance and production media. Mr. Balentine is also the author of "The GoodListener Cookbook," and "A Practical Guide to Phonetic Recognition," as well as several articles and publications related to spoken user interfaces.

 David Morgan has over fifteen years experience with speech recognition and related voice technologies. As Vice President of Technology Planning for Fidelity Investments Telecommunications, he helps plan and design voice and data network infrastructure for both internal and customer facing applications. He has been involved in all the major deployments of speech recognition at Fidelity. Dr. Morgan's previous work experience includes digital signal processing chip design, directory assistance systems, and voice and communications surveillance systems.

Dr. Morgan received his Ph.D. in Electrical Engineering from Brown University. He is also the author of "Neural Networks and Speech Processing." In addition, Dr. Morgan has published over twenty papers in the speech processing field and has taught a graduate course entitled, "Digital Signal Processing of Speech" at Northeastern University.

Acknowledgements

Many people have generously contributed to the production of this book. First and foremost, we would like to thank our reviewers—Harry Hersh at Fidelity Investments, Bradley Witteman at Arabesque Communications, Brian Scott at Universal Interface, Caroline Pappajohn at CAP/Tech, and Kevin Erler at Nuance Communications—all of whom read draft material that was fragmented and incomplete and yet provided thoughtful and informed edits. Harry in particular not only gave a detailed and constructive review of the early manuscript, but also contributed valuable usability lab observations and expertise.

Additional reviewers focused on portions of the manuscript, providing specialized expertise. Judith Markowitz at J. Markowitz, Consultants gave brief but incredibly helpful advice regarding the organization of the material. Martha Lindeman of Users First assisted with writing style and first impressions. Matt Yuschik of Comverse Network Systems gave a detailed read of several sections and followed up with his usual rigor and insight. Thanks also to Bill Meisel, Lauren Hodgson, Mike Cohen, Daryle Gardner-Bonneau, Steve Kaufman, Wayne Lea, Bonnic Thomson, and Gary Wright.

We also wish to thank Rex Stringham and Doug Devine at Enterprise Integration Group for their help in publishing the book. Steve Greenwood, Gaugarin Oliver, Tom Schalk, and Sam Weber of Voice Control Systems made suggestions for improving terminology and commented on technical details. Thanks also goes out to Dick Rosinski at Periphonics and Jeff Picone at E-Trade for their viewpoints on both contents and marketing of the book. We owe a special thanks to Nuance Communications for allowing us to use several examples from their *TickerTalk*™ application, to VCS for the windowing examples, and to Mike Glynn of Caremonitor and The Codman Research Group for permission to reproduce the HANC dialogues.

For the barge-in diagrams of Figure 4.2, Figure 4.3, and Figure 4.4 of Chapter 4, we wish to thank Comverse Network Systems, Inc., which allowed us to rework the three original illustrations. The diagrams are Copyright 1998 Comverse Network Systems, Inc. and reprinted with its permission.

Thanks to Blattner and Muller for the illustrations in Figure 4.5, Figure 4.6, and Figure 4.7, which are adapted from the following: edited by M. Blattner/R. Dannengerg, MULTIMEDIA INTERFACE DESIGN, (figure 1.9 from page 30 – chapter

1 written by M. Muller/R. Farrell/K. Cebulka/J. Smith). ©1992 ACM Press. Reprinted by permission of Addison Wesley Longman.

For contributions to the second edition, thanks to David Thomson of Lucent Technologies for the natural language illustration in Figure 8.3, which is adapted from his original, and to Dr. Jim Larson, Chairman of the W3C Voice Browser Working Group, for the illustration of VoiceXML and portal architecture in Figure B.1, which is adapted by permission of Pearson Education, Inc., Upper Saddle River, N.J., from VOICEXML: INTRODUCTION TO DEVELOPING SPEECH APPLICATIONS by Larson, ©2002, a forthcoming Pearson Education publication.

Thanks to Dr. Holger Stoltze and Dr. Kate Dobroth for their reviews of the second edition, and to Dr. Jerry Duncan of Deere and Company for our many discussions on design and design philosophy. We are also deeply grateful to David Attwater of BTexact Technologies for discussions and guidance on natural language, statistical language models, and voice portals. David's knowledge and experience have been especially helpful.

We owe special appreciation to Dr. Ralph Melaragno for his many contributions to the natural language research documented in [EIG00]. The illustration in Figure 8.4 is Ralph's, and much of the success of the entire research project can be attributed to his skills, insights, and guidance.

Also, in the hope of righting an unintended wrong, a belated thank you goes to Marvin Preston for his many contributions over the years. Marvin's brilliance has raised the bar on clarity of thought and integrity of design for more than a decade.

Finally, we would like to thank the many people we have worked with at Fidelity Investments who have shown a keen interest in this technology and who helped motivate us to write this style guide.

Bruce Balentine
David P. Morgan
April, 1999
December, 2001

Comments on the Second Edition

Although this style guide has stood up fairly well over the two and a half years since it was first published, the voice user interface subject area has continued to expand and mature. In this edition we have taken more time to address voice portals and we have added an appendix on selecting and training "Voice Talent." It has become obvious over the past few years that selecting the talent for the application can have as much impact on the end user as the design itself. Furthermore, the application designer and the talent must work together to create a satisfying user experience.

We have also rewritten and expanded on Chapter 11, "Usability Testing and Performance Reporting." Most of the new material summarizes our experiences since the first edition was published. In addition, we have added a major section to Chapter 8 on "Challenges in Implementing Natural Language Systems"—new material that has been compiled since the first edition. We have also updated the yes-no discussion in Section 6.3 with a description of some recently-proven methods for handling mixed-initiative replies. Other improvements in this edition include updated dialogue examples, more copious cross references, and improvements to the index and glossary.

Since this book was published, many speech vendors and application developers have conducted formal studies and/or focus groups to learn more about design decisions and to provide guidelines for future voice user interface development. In all of the studies we are aware of, our empirical observations have been validated. Hence none of the guidelines in the first edition have been overturned or found to be in error. In several cases, we have upgraded our guidelines from "Good Practice" to "Recommended" or to "Required" based on these results.

Finally, we tried not to make any structural changes to this text. None of the section numbers have been changed except in Chapter 11, Appendix A, and the beginning of Chapter 9. So if people on your design team have copies of both the first and second editions, you should be able to cross reference them easily.

Enjoy the second edition!

Bruce Balentine
David P. Morgan
December, 2001

Chapter 1
The Telephony User Interface

A user interface is that component of any product, service, or application, that interacts directly with the human user. The job of the interface is twofold. First, it must present information to the user—information about the task at hand as well as information about the interface itself. Second, it must accept input from the user—input in the form of commands or operations that allow the user to control the application.

A *spoken user interface* is one in which both machine presentation and user input take the form of human speech. Speech replaces the video display, indicator lights, buttons, and knobs of the more traditional user interfaces. The machine presents output through digitized or synthesized speech—in effect, "reciting" information to the user—and accepts and interprets spoken user input through the use of speech recognition technology.

The *telephony user interface* is, of necessity, becoming a spoken user interface. The machine that hosts the application is remote from the user, typically residing at a call center or other service provider site. The user has access to a telephone, an instrument that was originally designed for human-to-human conversation. Through this very limited "terminal," the user must interactively send and receive all information required by the application. Tasks performed through telephony interfaces include: remote banking, travel reservations, information inquiry, stock, mutual fund, and other financial transactions, international calling, credit card verification, and a myriad of other transaction-oriented services.

The unique application design issues that relate to the use of the telephone as the user interface for verbal interaction with automated products and services are the motivation and the subject of this style guide.

1.1 A Style Guide for User Interfaces

User interface design is particularly resistant to rigid methodologies that attempt to define it simply as another branch of engineering. One reason is that design goals may readily change—leading to moving targets and ill-conceived functional elements. Another reason is basic lack of knowledge about the broad range of users and the motivations and assumptions that they bring to the interaction. Perhaps the most important reason of all, however, is that we are dealing with **human** perception and **human** performance; and humans are notoriously varied, interesting, unpredictable, and creative. This means that human users invent all kinds of new and unexpected ways to interact with our designs.

The unique constraints of the telephony interface make it especially sensitive to the human factors and usability challenges that are so important to user interface design. "Especially sensitive" means that design flaws that might be tolerated in, for example, a desktop computer application or an automatic teller machine become insurmountable when the sole method of communication is via the telephone.

With telephony interfaces, we have to do an especially good job to achieve even mediocre results. Thoughtless sentence constructions confuse. Unnecessary friendliness irritates. Careless error messages cause new errors. Lengthy instructions cause loss of context. Tutorials fail to teach. Poor designs fail.

With telephony interfaces, there is no margin of error. Unlike the computer screen that we can revisit when we're lost; unlike the bookmark that returns us to our previous position; unlike the simple restaurant menu that confines our choices, the words transmitted across the telephony interface have no persistence.

Because telephony interfaces are especially sensitive to design flaws, we must exhibit rigorous discipline in both design and implementation. And yet—because the medium is new—there are no clearly established "rules" that ensure success. Instead we must navigate without a map, establishing directions after traveling down dead ends and making wrong turns.

This challenge is similar to another creative human endeavor—the craft of writing. And as students of that craft well know, one of the most effective aids is the style guide. Of course, there are no rules which—even applied rigorously—guarantee that one writer will succeed while another fails. But there are general principles of good expression that seem to work reliably. There are underlying patterns of language that resonate with readers. There are, indeed, **guidelines**, which can be extracted from examples of effective writing—guidelines that point toward clarity and professionalism in communication.

Style guides provide solutions for specific writing problems. These problems appear spontaneously as the writer thinks through and constructs her work. Equally important, however, style guides establish **conventions**—of capitalization, punctuation, page layout, and outlining—which are important for the unimpeded flow of thoughtful information. The ultimate choice of convention is not so important; in many cases, one solution works as well as another. But it is essential that they be applied consistently throughout, as whimsy or carelessness in the use of style conventions leads to noisy, sloppy, and mentally taxing reading.

As an analog of the writer's handbook, this style guide aims to give speech recognition practitioners the groundwork for the basic elements of style that have the most impact on the effectiveness of telephony interfaces. This includes the same principles of expression important to the written word—the proper use of tense and mood, the placement of keywords in prompts, the effects of person, gender, number, the declaration of fact without prejudice and, perhaps most importantly, the clear and simple expression of the here and now. It also expands on these basic principles to organize and codify the **dynamic** aspects of spoken dialogues—the interactive control over whose turn it is to speak, the communication of state changes that leads the user to construct a meaningful utterance, and, perhaps most importantly, proper management of the users' ability to accomplish their goals.

1.1.1 Target Audience

This style guide is designed specifically for those involved with developing Voice Response Unit[1] (VRU) applications. Within that group, these guidelines should appeal to a number of different readers:

- Interface designers,
- Product and Project Managers,
- Developers,
- Product Marketing Managers, and

---

[1] A "Voice Response Unit" is any product that communicates automatically with human users via telephone. Some references [EIG96] differentiate between VRU hardware and Interactive Voice Response (IVR) application software—a distinction not emphasized here. In this style guide, the acronyms VRU and IVR are treated synonymously.

- Application testers.

The book will also be of interest to those who have a stake in the success of VRU applications, including Account Managers, Call Center Managers, and Customer Service personnel of all kinds.

There will be readers who have worked extensively with DTMF[2] applications, but who have not experienced the hands-on design and development of systems that employ speech recognition. Although prior experience with DTMF is not required, it is also not particularly useful. The reason is that speech recognition includes a number of unique concepts which are difficult and cannot be skimmed over or brushed aside.

Several key concepts are introduced in this chapter, and novice readers are encouraged to master the terms here. As an additional aid, the glossary at the end of the book provides further detail on the core concepts that define the speech recognition domain. Finally, a bibliography provides a sampling of books on the subject. Our hope is that these guidelines will help the reader across the divide that separates DTMF applications from speech applications.

1.1.1.1 Help for Designers

By drawing on a common set of guidelines, application designers are able to understand and therefore reuse design solutions that are common to speech-enabled applications. By "designer," we are referring here not just to professional human factors engineers or user interface specialists. The term applies to anyone who is charged with the task of determining what the spoken telephony interface will **do**—a task identified variously as "script writing," "call-flow layout," or "dialogue design."

The practical realities of today's workplace encourage the need for these guidelines. Those who are leading the application design may not necessarily come from a specific background—whether software, telephony, human factors, or otherwise. This book strives to provide these designers with a cogent, organized, and reductionist approach to the spoken telephony interface. This means, unfortunately, that there is not a lot of "handholding" for the reader who is new to speech recognition technology. Designers are encouraged therefore to explore the material here, acquire additional material via the bibliography, identify those areas most applicable to their indi-

---

[2] Dual Tone Multiple Frequency—the so-called "touch tones" of the telephone keypad. DTMF as used in this text applies to keypress input of all kinds. Note that, although mobile (wireless) telephones do not communicate keypresses via DTMF, the term has become widely adopted and is used throughout this text.

vidual circumstances, and—most important of all—think for themselves regarding application goals and design specifications.

Designers can expect to learn the following:

- How to craft effective prompts,
- How to predict and manage social user-behaviors,
- How to exploit the capabilities of speech recognition technologies,
- How to use time to the advantage of both user and application,
- How to keep a consistent "look and feel"[3] to the interface,
- How to balance tradeoffs when selecting recognition vocabulary,
- How to approach the problem of application "personality,"
- How to prevent errors from looking like errors, and
- How to choose between competing technologies and competing dialogue design structures to create the most parsimonious solution to user needs.

The most important message to designers is to resist relinquishing control to the speech technology. Excessive reliance on recognition "accuracy" does a disservice both to the user and to the technology itself. The goal is to make the two converge— even in the presence of uncertainty—and the designer must handle the errors that are certain to occur. Good design raises the accuracy of even poor recognizers; bad design reduces the accuracy of even the best.

1.1.1.2   Help for Developers and Testers

Reuse of designs—even reuse of the code itself—benefits application developers. Programming becomes more efficient when interactive behaviors draw on a common library of standard functions. By relying on repeatable design principles for voice interaction, application developers can optimize software architecture and reuse software functions.

Code reuse impacts testing as well. For example, by observing common procedures when developing a yes-no query interaction, each instance of this query relies on the same code. Testers can exercise the query thoroughly, knowing that special-case errors or exotic conditions will not find their way into every dialogue branch.

---

[3] The term "look and feel" refers to the subjective reaction of users and observers as they interact with systems. VRU applications, of course, exploit the senses of speech and hearing as opposed to sight and touch—making the terms "look and feel" metaphorical rather than literal.

Developers and testers can expect to learn the following:

- How to reduce the application to a collection of reusable **dialogue components**, [4] such as yes-no queries, menus, list navigation, name-capture strategies, digit entry, large-vocabulary list interactions, and many other "standard" interactions,

- How to minimize the amount of spoken machine output by devising well-constructed messages that are reusable in a number of contexts,

- How to reduce the total number of machine states by generalizing behaviors and understanding them from a user's perspective,

- Why synonyms and other variety in design seem like a good idea but only compound the complexity, reliability, and succinctness of the overall dialogue,

- How to select a dialogue structure that best fits the task and the users' prior knowledge and skill, and

- How to trap and handle errors within a given dialogue component reliably—with minimum impact on the rest of the application—in order to reduce the number of error recovery conditions that must be handled in software.

When building a speech recognition application, it is impossible to predict or test everything that a user will say. Therefore, the most important message to developers is to resist thinking about what the user will say, and to focus instead on what the application can do to move the task forward—regardless of recognized results. Excessive reliance on recognition leads to dialogues that spend more time confirming what the user said than reaching the user's goal. Under bad conditions, the application's look and feel becomes feeble and uncertain—constantly asking if the course is correct, always suggesting help, permanently nagged by doubt. Under good conditions, the application's look and feel becomes plucky and over-confident—leading the user down the "primrose path" with bravura, only to slam unsuspecting into the first error. By focusing on effective ways to move forward in the face of uncertainty, on the other hand, developers can generate a more appropriate look and feel—a competent and professional interface that performs reliably in all conditions.

1.1.1.3   Scope of Material

Spoken interaction is a very broad field of study. These guidelines are restricted to the use of speech recognition in telephone-based audio-only dialogues. The book is tightly limited in scope to this subject. It specifically avoids the following areas:

---

[4] This has become the industry-accepted term for reusable ASR software modules. See the glossary and Chapter 6 for a description of "dialogue components."

1. DTMF (touch tone) interfaces except as they impinge on speech recognition,

2. Speaker verification or speaker identification technologies,

3. Speech synthesis (text-to-speech) technologies, except as they may serve as the spoken machine output in a speech recognition interface,

4. Speech recognition in desktop, multimedia, or other non-telephone interactions,

5. Speech recognition over the telephone in conjunction with screen phones, video-phones, or other telephony-based devices that use non-audio modalities, and

6. A review or competitive comparison of any speech recognition products currently on the market.

These are all very important areas, and the reader should take note of the many sources that address them. A selected sample of reference documents appears in the bibliography.

1.1.2 Style Guide Versus Standards

This is a style guide and by no means intended to serve as a standard. The difference is important, as it affects the reading and interpretation of the information presented in this book. A standard, by definition, incorporates known principles into a collection of rules, providing the designer with explicit recommendations aimed at compliance. Such principles are known in one of two ways: either empirical data have resulted from rigorous research, or common practices have emerged from a large body of similar and successful applications in the field. Regardless of derivation, known principles must precede and cannot follow standards.

1.1.2.1 Empirical Data

Usability research has generated a large body of data that are useful to designers. Such data describe measurements of short-term memory and data organization [Miller56], human turn-taking behaviors [Heins97], word-selection [Baber97], audio-reinforced feedback [Brewster97], anthropomorphism [Shneiderman97], the social response to media [Reeves96], and many other aspects of human perception and performance. These data are important and the reader is encouraged to become familiar with them. However, it cannot be argued that an adequate collection of scientific measurements exists from which clear standards for the design of spoken telephony interfaces can be created.

1.1.2.2   Common Practices as De Facto Standards

The mere existence of a practice does not itself endorse that practice. While it is true that certain common practices—if applied in a variety of settings with some degree of success—become de facto standards simply through frequent use, it cannot be argued that such are the circumstances of contemporary speech recognition design principles. Even successful applications—those that match user interface to user need—experience significant and anomalous usability problems. It is clear that the effectiveness of basic speech recognition technologies currently outstrip designers' ability to exploit them.

This style guide includes a number of design methods commonly used in speech applications. Where practices are common and non-controversial, they are tagged as "required"—a convention that allows designers to apply the guidelines in a useful and practical way. Such tags should not be misconstrued as "standards" in the rigorous sense of the word. Standards by their nature are developed and critiqued by a broad body of specialists, reviewed by an even larger body of practitioners, and then refined by formal consensus. It is too early in this industry to begin such a process.

On the other hand, this style guide does attempt to satisfy certain specific needs related to the issue of standards, in effect to:

- Provide raw working material to standards committees now incorporated,
- Suggest workable solutions to designers in the absence of firm standards, and
- Raise appropriate questions that must be addressed by future standards.

1.1.2.3   Current Standards that May Be Applicable

Many user interface standards originally developed for visual media apply equally well to spoken interactions. Others must be slightly modified but are still useful and should be taken under advisement. One of these standards is the ISO 9241 standard for graphical interfaces.[5] Designers are encouraged to acquire this and related documents. Pertinent information is only briefly touched upon here.

The 9241 standard posits that interfaces should fulfill the following criteria, in order of importance:

1. Effectiveness,
2. Efficiency, and

---

[5] A selection of ISO and other standards organizations can be found in the bibliography.

3. User satisfaction.

These three general points mean that first and foremost a user interface must work (that is, get the task accomplished). After that, it is important that a user interface accomplish its task as productively as possible. Finally, a user interface that is already effective and efficient can be improved by focusing on user satisfaction as measured with questionnaires and other user feedback.

The American National Standards Institute (ANSI) develops guidelines, procedures, and standards that reflect agreements among companies and other organizations. The Human Factors and Ergonomic Society (HFES) is currently developing the HFES-200 standard, *Ergonomics of Software User Interfaces*. These and other documents are made available through their respective organizations.

In addition, the military and other government agencies have developed their own standards for user interface design and development, standards that are used for quality control and procurement decisions. The bibliography contains a separate section on standards organizations and other sources including web sites. Designers should locate and acquire these standards.

1.1.3   Goals and Objectives

This style guide consolidates design concepts and practices into a collection of guidelines, thereby facilitating effective integration of speech recognition technology with Voice Response Unit (VRU) applications. Such consolidation assists the application developer with rapid development, testing, and user acceptance of new applications employing speech recognition.

The goal of this book is to streamline integration and maximize usability of speech recognition technologies in VRU applications. These guidelines should facilitate the evolution of a consistent and predictable look and feel for VRU applications that make use of one or more speech recognition technologies. Predictability in the look and feel of VRU applications benefits designers, developers and end-users.

1.1.3.1   Benefits to End Users

End-users benefit from a predictable look and feel in several ways. A well-designed interface tends to evoke spontaneous user-behaviors that are productive—thereby decreasing error rates and raising user satisfaction. Users also learn a given application faster. In addition, consistency between similar applications allows transfer of learning—the user is able to apply skills already learned in one application to the productive use of another.

1.1.3.2   Benefits to the Service Organization

Besides the obvious advantages of streamlined development and more productive users, organizations deploying VRU applications benefit from a consistent look and feel in the design of their customer-service applications. By helping users recognize an application as a member of a family of products, style consistency often enhances corporate identity. In addition, by keeping users productive and satisfied, style consistency increases customer loyalty.

1.1.3.3   How to Approach this Book

Speech recognition is an emerging technology, and ongoing changes in technical capabilities as well as design options can therefore be expected. This style guide is a snapshot of a technology that to date has only a few early adopters. As it becomes more widely accepted, the industry's collective knowledge may change as concepts are tested and lessons learned.

Guidelines represent a formal restatement of knowledge and experience within a complex area. As such, they may not be universally applicable, appropriate, or additive. In fact, in places they may even be contradictory. This is one reason why design is as much art as science.

Designers and developers are therefore cautioned to avoid two complementary errors. The first is to second-guess these guidelines—either refusing to implement with the argument of irrelevance or obsolescence, or finding implementation difficult and therefore "bending the rules." The second error—equally captious—is to apply these guidelines literally in a churlish spirit, even when a better solution or legitimate special case exists. Both errors violate the intent of this style guide, which is aimed at guiding application design to its most stable and useful form.

1.2 Basic Speech Interface Concepts

This style guide is not a primer on speech recognition. Nevertheless, certain basic concepts are important to understand the guidelines and the examples that underscore them. The following discussions provide a high-level view of these concepts.

1.2.1 Unique Characteristics of Speech

Speech recognition input is a unique and specialized human interface medium that differs considerably from the traditional media of DTMF, computer-console, and other visual-mechanical interfaces. These unique attributes should be well understood when approaching telephony interface design.

1.2.1.1 Serial Information

Speech is sequential (serial) in nature. The parallel presentation of information—in the form of menus, the data fields on a form, or the GUI widgets that users take for granted in a visual interface—is lacking with audio. Rather, the user must hear and comprehend all information one element at a time.

Similarly, spoken input must be supplied one command or datum at a time, requiring that the user remember and order information in a way that is more taxing than it is with visual and mechanical interfaces.

This simple fact—speech interactions are time-consuming—has significant ramifications for design. The challenge is to accomplish as much as possible in as little time as possible. However, using spoken machine output that is too terse sometimes confuses users—leading to wasted time detecting and correcting errors. Similarly, spoken machine output that is too verbose taxes user memory and causes loss of context and distraction from the task. It is very difficult to find the best tradeoff between too much and too little machine presentation. Instead, the designer must encourage the user to construct a mental model of the task and the interface that serves it, thereby creating and sustaining an illusion of forward movement that exploits time by managing and responding to user goals.

1.2.1.2 The Persistence Problem

Visual displays have the powerful advantage of persistence. That is, once presented, data remain on the display until replaced by new data or cleared by the user. This addresses a fundamental aspect of user interfaces—memory. By remembering for the user, persistence in a visual display allows the user to:

- Return to a task after interruption,
- Review—by scanning back and forth—among several possible menu choices,
- Eliminate or minimize the effects of time by scrolling freely between the past and the present, and
- Maintain context—even when confronted with multiple tasks.

When the machine presents data via spoken machine output, there is no persistence. This places the burden of remembering machine output on the user.

1.2.1.3   Temporal Characteristics

The enemy of the spoken user interface is time. This is because the persistence problem is only overcome by frequent data presentation by the machine. Frequent presentation in turn increases the memory burden on the user.

In addition to the lengthy amount of time required by a spoken interface, certain short-term rhythmic effects dominate human speech. These short-term timing problems lead to conflicts, user anxiety, and social considerations that cause frequent interaction breakdown.

1.2.1.4   Social Qualities

It is often argued that speech recognition is a powerful user interface medium because it is **natural** (i.e., humans already know how to talk, engaging in spoken interactions frequently, spontaneously, and effortlessly). This point is misleading, as the common shared experience of humans is in talking to and with each other—sentient, self-aware beings that share a common cultural heritage and possess certain assumptions about the reality of the world in which they live.

Humans have no precedent for verbal interaction with non-sentient devices that are not self-aware. Indeed, human speech is dependent on a powerful set of social techniques that derive from a fundamental assumption—when a human being talks to another, that other human presumably has some stake in the outcome of the interaction. This assumption collapses when the partner is a machine.

The result of this expectation of social awareness that is built into human speech is that structured and goal-oriented protocols become necessary to steer the user away from social speech behaviors and toward work-oriented, task-oriented interactions. Even users conforming to such protocols may feel estranged from original expectations of "naturalness," and thus remain uncomfortable with the interface.

1.2.2   Moving Through States

Many VRU applications are built as state machines [Lewis81]. Even those that are not implemented in a classic state-machine architecture tend to take advantage of state-machine concepts and terminology. In this model, a machine adopts a certain **starting state**—consisting of various settings and parameters. Events from the outside world then cause **transitions** from one state to the next. The telephone rings, for example, and the application goes to the off-hook state. Only off-hook applications can interact with users.

Similarly, once in its off-hook state, the machine presents auditory information to the user. The user in turn presents commands to the machine—in the form of DTMF or speech. Some input causes the machine to remain in its current state after performing some action—say presenting a help message. Other input causes the machine to transition from the current state to some new state.

In many speech recognition applications, a major dependency of a given state is its **active vocabulary**[6]—that is, the words that a user is allowed to say. Transitions from one state to the next—for example between menus, yes-no questions, and numeric data capture—entails changing this set of allowable user responses. Notifying the user of this change in expected input is a major aspect of interface design.

The foregoing discussion is necessarily simplified. The reader may wish to consult any of a large number of references on the subject of state machines.

1.2.2.1   State Errors

There are circumstances in which state transitions occur incorrectly. The machine may misrecognize or misinterpret user input. If such a circumstance leads to a state transition, then the machine is in a different state than the one anticipated by the user. This is called a **state error**.

A similar state error occurs when the user presents what he considers a valid command. The machine, however, misses the input. With speech recognition technology, this can happen when rejections of user speech occur due to spoke-too-soon errors, false rejections, or other conditions.[7] In this type of state error—the reverse of the first—the machine remains in the same state while the user mentally "moves forward," assuming that the machine has made a state transition. An example of this state error is shown in Figure 1.1 for a common DTMF function.

---

[6] A "vocabulary" is the set of utterances known to the recognizer. The "active" vocabulary is that subset of all possible utterances that a user may speak in a given state.

[7] These terms will be defined and discussed in detail shortly—see Section 1.3.

In either case—the machine leaves the user behind, or the user leaves the machine behind—state errors cause the user and machine to possess different expectations regarding the next legal input.[8]

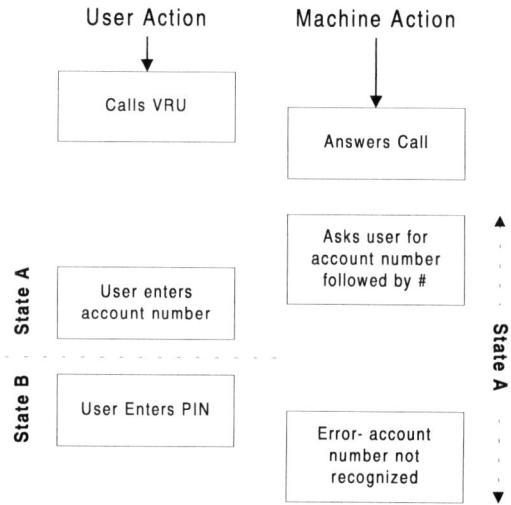

Figure 1.1—**EXAMPLE STATE ERROR** is based on a typical DTMF interaction in which the user forgot to use the pound key to terminate an account number. Instead, the user keys ahead and continues with the PIN. In the example, the user has made a mental transition from state A to state B, while the machine remains in state A.

1.2.2.2   Error Amplification

A single state error—caused perhaps by a speech recognition rejection—can often lead to subsequent errors. This phenomenon is known as **error amplification**. A user, for example, speaks a word that is appropriate for a given menu—the assumed state of the machine. If the machine, in fact, is expecting different words—has either made a transition to a new menu or has failed to transition when the user has moved on—then correct user behavior leads to recognition of incorrect words.

This type of state error often occurs in complex menu hierarchies, when users "end up in the wrong menu." In such a case, the next user utterance is likely to result in a new error: since the user thinks she is in a different state, she chooses words relevant

---

[8] Speech technologies, like people, can only recognize words that they know—that is, words that they have been programmed to recognize. Use of such words is considered "legal."

to that state. In many cases, the next several speech events become confused, a degree of amplification that can be fatal.

The potential for error amplification is one reason why error-prevention and error-recovery methods are so important in spoken dialogues. The same circumstances occur frequently with humans, of course, but recovery is much more effective. Machine anticipation of error is thus critical for design.

> In person-to-person conversations, error rates are [also] quite high, but people don't realize it because error recovery is so effective. How much simpler it would be if systems were so forgiving [Hersh99].

Since the range of possible errors with speech recognition technologies is far greater than with DTMF VRU applications, error-amplification problems are much more common when speech is the primary input modality.

1.2.3   Turn Taking

One type of state error that is especially common and difficult to manage with speech recognition is associated with turn taking [Heins97]. Users speak when they think it is their turn. Machines then respond, reclaiming the turn. When the protocol for turn taking breaks down, either the user or the machine makes a transition to a new state. Faulty turn taking thus leads to state errors that are difficult to detect and repair.

1.2.3.1   Without Barge-in

Half-duplex interactions—systems without **barge-in**[9]—often use tones to hand over the dialogue to the user [Balentine97a]. The tones become turn-taking cues in an artificial protocol. Users that speak before or during the tone cannot be heard by such applications.

Turn-taking errors with tone-based half-duplex protocols must be recovered immediately or the errors inevitably amplify themselves. Short prompts or tones are usually incorporated into these applications, making them highly interactive.

1.2.3.2   With Barge-in

Full-duplex interactions—systems that use barge-in—allow the user to "speak through" the spoken machine output. The user thus has direct control over turn taking—users simply interrupt the machine whenever they are ready to speak. Most cur-

---

[9] The ability for the user to interrupt spoken machine output. Barge-in will be discussed in more detail shortly—Section 1.3.3—as well as throughout Chapter 4.

rent technologies, however, prevent the application from knowing what part of the message was playing at the moment of user interruption. For this reason, the application has less control over time, making it somewhat less interactive.

1.2.4 Additional Concepts

Other important terms and concepts affect design goals and objectives.

1.2.4.1 Issues Relevant to Design

The social relationship between the application and the user is one of several style decisions that are dependent on five closely related but distinctly different issues, summarized in Table 1.1.

Table 1.1—**ISSUES AFFECTING DIALOGUE DESIGN** are similar but not identical. A clear distinction between these closely related issues can reduce conflict among members of the development team. Rigorous attention to these issues also allows priority decisions on conflicting features.

Issue	Examples
Marketing	company image, user comfort & acceptance, brand recognition & loyalty, buyer impressions, perceived value
Design	technology capability & limitations, tasks allowed & supported, architecture, error recovery, "personality" of application
Productivity	speed, ease of use, range of functions and options, accessibility, complexity versus flexibility, documentation
Aesthetics	look and feel, user familiarity, professional image, user impressions, persona
Ergonomics	cognitive load, memory, turn taking, reaction time, reach envelope, attention issues

Designers should keep track of these distinctions. It is not unusual to come across arguments related, for example, to marketing as though they applied to fundamental ergonomic issues. Similarly, perfectly compelling aesthetic descriptions of a certain design proposal often find themselves at odds with equally compelling productivity requirements. Whenever conflicts appear, they can often be traced to the differences in goals represented by these closely related issues.

1.2.4.2   Conflicts Between DTMF and Speech Recognition

Particular note should be taken of the DTMF component of typical IVR[10] interfaces. In some cases, certain standards [Schwartz93], studies [TARP97], or analyses [EIG96] have appeared that are well tested and thoroughly validated for dialogues that present spoken machine output and accept DTMF input. These standards—aimed primarily at the wording of prompts—rarely apply to speech recognition enabled systems. This means that a properly-worded prompt for DTMF systems is rarely appropriate for a speech-enabled application. While DTMF applications are based on highly structured hierarchies, speech recognition is more flexible and adaptable.

This fact is unfortunate for two reasons:

1. Although strongly desired, designing applications that use both DTMF and speech recognition effectively is difficult—either as parallel modalities or as single-mode input mechanisms used in alternating parts of the dialogue.

2. Existing DTMF-IVR systems tend to resist simple upgrading to speech recognition without considerable restructuring. Typically, converting such systems requires significant changes to most spoken machine output (prompts), as well as a restructuring of the call-flow and overall dialogue architecture.

This book sidesteps the conflict between speech and DTMF by limiting its scope to speech recognition. To the degree that guidelines can help with the distinction, recommendations appear in Chapter 7.

1.2.4.3   Cost-Saving Versus Value-Add Speech Applications

There are two generic business models for speech applications. The business model has a great impact on how success is measured and which user interface issues are the most important to address.

A **cost-saving** application is one in which the enterprise—a business or government agency—automates a service with the goal of reducing the cost of delivering that service to its users. The most typical method for delivering full customer service is via the call center, a labor-intensive enterprise. Most call centers today use a VRU front end to intercept incoming calls, offering the opportunity for customers to first engage in self-service—answering their questions or completing their transactions automatically. Those callers who cannot or will not accept self-service are then transferred to live answer by human representatives, who then deliver full service.

---

[10] Interactive Voice Response. Refer to the glossary for the distinction between IVR and VRU.

Because self-service is less expensive than full service, the enterprise can cost justify its investment in the VRU system. In many cases, the return on investment is several hundred percent, and payback can be achieved in a very short time.

Self-service comes at a customer satisfaction price, however. Users report that automated systems—whether DTMF or speech-enabled—often stand between them and their goals. Such users express resentment that the enterprise does not value their call enough to make full service readily accessible. For this reason, the cost-saving business model must make tradeoff decisions between two competing goals: reduced cost associated with self-service versus reduced customer satisfaction associated with the fact that self-service is inferior to full service.

In the worst tradeoff, the enterprise develops a poorly-designed VRU and then closes its call center. Although self-service rates reach 100%, customer satisfaction drops and the enterprise loses callers (customers). Conversely, the enterprise may avoid automation, delivering full service to all customers on demand. Although customer satisfaction rates are high, the enterprise is unable to compete due to high prices.

In the ideal tradeoff, the enterprise identifies an acceptable decrease in customer satisfaction—automating those transactions that lend themselves well to self-service and designing a VRU that is simple and effective—and then retains a professional call center to deliver full service for all other areas.

Cost-saving business models have the following attributes:

- The user does not choose to use speech recognition,
- The VRU is not a product or service that the user pays for directly, and
- The user is calling for a reason, and therefore has some stake in the outcome of the dialogue.

These attributes imply that the caller will tolerate a certain degree of inconvenience or anxiety, provided the application is well-designed, and that full service is available in the event of failure.

Value-add applications are based on a completely different set of assumptions about the business. In such an application, the speech recognition technology is viewed as a feature of the product, one desired by the user and one that increases the perceived value of the product or service. Examples include voice-activated features on mobile telephones, enhanced services such as ASR-enabled voicemail or e-mail, personal assistants, and consumer voice portals.

Value-add business models have the following attributes:

- The user chooses to use or not use speech recognition,
- The user pays for the product or service directly, and
- The user therefore has a real stake in the performance of the system.

Because of the above attributes, value-add products must meet performance expectations within the price requirements of the buyer. Human users have very high expectations for speech recognition—speech is very simple and natural for humans—and users do not feel much obligation to change their behaviors for products that they have purchased. What's more, ASR-enabled systems often provide limited functionality—users may perform operations that they already can do now (e.g. dialing the telephone), but in a way that is presumably more convenient. Buyers typically value such convenience at prices that are quite low.

This is why value-add speech applications have often been derided as an "ever-receding imminent bonanza" among businesspeople in the speech industry. Callers expect 100% accuracy and zero cost before they will embrace the product—a business model that is less than appealing to developers of these systems.

Most ASR telephony applications fielded today are cost-saving business models. An emerging collection of value-add systems—primarily in the form of voice portals—require care in design and development to ensure that they deliver true value with high performance at low cost.

1.3 Terminology

Speech recognition is a complex subject. It is impossible for any book on interface design to provide the technical background that is required to understand and apply speech technologies. Those who are new to the subject are strongly urged to acquire not one but several of the popular references that explore the subject.[11]

With that strong caveat in mind, however, it is essential that a basic set of terms be identified and defined. We have done our best to be clear and simple, but the following terms are essential if the designer is to approach the telephony interface in a reasonable way. These are therefore the **minimum required terminology** for understanding the guidelines in this book, and the reader is encouraged to return to them repeatedly. These terms will occur throughout this book.

---

[11] For example, [Rabiner93], [Schmandt94], [Markowitz96], and [Young96].

1.3.1 Understanding Rejection

Rejection is the single most important concept to master. There is no corresponding DTMF correlate—it is unique to speech recognition—and application designers almost universally mishandle it. The following definitions provide background on rejection: where it came from, how it is measured, and what it means. The designer should become comfortable with these terms, returning frequently to this discussion.

Confidence   Speech recognition systems typically report one or more values—sometimes called recognition "scores," but more often referred to as "confidence." The value reports the likelihood that a candidate word reported by the recognizer is correctly classified. Different technologies present different versions of this value, including raw (absolute) scores, relative (normalized) scores, and confidence as a percentage. A recognizer often returns one or more words that are candidates for recognition along with their confidence values. Speech recognition errors can sometimes be detected by interpreting these confidence values.

Rejection   A condition in which the recognizer has detected input but confidence is low. The input may be an utterance[12] produced by the user, or it may some kind of speech or noise from the environment. What the recognizer hears may resemble one or more candidate words in its vocabulary. Most recognizers report the condition and then leave it to the application to decide whether and how to reject the input.

1.3.1.1 Reasons for Low Recognition Confidence

The confidence value for a given user input may be low for a number of different reasons. The user may speak with a dialect or accent. The telephone connection may be of poor quality. The user may be in a noisy environment. In many cases, there is no obvious reason why a given utterance is recognized with low confidence. Playback of recorded sessions often reveals no discernible difference between one utterance of high confidence and another that is rejected. It is also not important to speculate on the cause of the condition. Instead, commit the following to memory:

---

[12] A single user-input event—from silence to silence—is known as an "utterance." The utterance may contain a single word, a string of words, or it may encompass an entire sentence. The utterance may also be meaningless, as in a cough, grunt, or mumble. Because of its generality, the term is preferred over more meaningful terms such as "word" or "sentence."

- Every example of user speech is different from every other example.

- Think of a user utterance as an **instance** of an idealized class.

- Although the class—for example a word like "yes"—may seem like a real and tangible object, each instance of it varies in many ways.

- The challenge of a recognizer is to analyze an utterance, comparing it against its vocabulary (collection of classes), and to decide which one is "closest" to this unique instance.

- The recognizer uses a scoring method to determine the "closeness" of the input utterance to these ideal classes: the better the score, the closer the two are to each other; the worse the score, the more distant they are.

- Scores are then used to calculate the confidence, which represents "how sure" the recognizer is that the unknown utterance is an authentic instance of the closest class. Confidence is often (though not always) expressed as a percentage.

- Because of the variability in human speech, the recognizer is never 100% certain that it has classified the input correctly.

- Because every instance differs from the ideal in many ways, the confidence value that is associated with each recognized class fluctuates from instance to instance, sometimes by quite a lot.

- Confidence can be viewed as a statistical measure: input that is statistically similar to a given class will fall close to that class—resulting in high confidence. Input that is statistically dissimilar will be more distant from one class, and perhaps closer to another incorrect class. This occurrence is the source of speech recognition errors.

- Low confidence therefore alerts the application that the recognizer's reported classification may be in error.

A rejection is not necessarily an error—it simply indicates that the response **might** be in error because the confidence is low. These points may seem overly complex, but the concept of rejection is exceptionally important.

1.3.1.2 Purpose of Rejection

The term rejection has a historical legacy. Laboratory experiments in speech recognition rely on a database of recorded speech samples. A human listener transcribes each recording. Imagine, for example, that a database consists of several thousand recordings of different people saying the digits zero through nine. A given recording may be labeled as "seven," for example, because a human listener has played the recording and determined that "seven" is the class which corresponds to the spoken sample.

Most of these recordings are "clean" recordings—that is, there is no disagreement among humans over whether the class is correct. This judgment is based on the recording alone. Of course, as we all know, every recording sounds different: Some are male and some are female; some are fast, some slow; some Southern pronunciations like "fav" or "nan" differ significantly from Northern pronunciations; some people say "zero" as though it were "Sarah." But one person fluent in English, listening to each recording in isolation, would classify these "clean" recordings the same as another person.

Some recordings, however, are not "clean." Many may be mixed with background noise—in some cases, enough noise to obscure the word. Other recordings may be devoid of noise, but are quite distorted in other ways: A native German speaker may pronounce the /v/ in "seven" as an /f/; some recordings may be so low in volume that the word "one" sounds almost identical to the word "nine"—sort of an indistinguishable nasal grunt; some recordings may include recorded breath noise, or a loud inhalation prior to speech, or clicks and pops throughout the recording.

Speech scientists—listening to these atypical examples of recorded speech—decided early in the industry to **reject** some of them as candidates for classification. The argument is a convincing one: If humans cannot agree that a given sound belongs to a specific class, then we should not expect the speech recognition technology to do so. Recordings that are not "clean" examples of a given class should be excluded from the classification process.

Later, technology evolved to allow the automatic "rejection" of such examples—in this case, by setting thresholds that permit the technology to "throw away" or "refuse to recognize" those examples that are statistically unusual. Rather than classifying the input, the recognizer would return a "rejection" notice to the application—indicating that the input is ambiguous in some way.

With today's technologies, it has become clear that rejection is a user interface decision that should be performed at a much higher level than represented by the speech recognizer. So most recognizers attempt to return some recognized result—along with scores and/or confidence information—allowing the application itself to make an informed decision about whether to trust and what to do with the result. This means that "rejection" is determined by the application, thereby confusing the original intent of the term.

The rejection rate can be adjusted by tuning confidence thresholds or scoring parameters.[13] The goal is to "pass" all input that is confident (i.e., above some threshold). This makes the dialogue move quickly with minimum risk of error. Even occasional errors can be tolerated provided they don't occur too often. Thresholds are set empirically to ensure that substitutions occur, on average, less than 2% of the time.

What this means is that ambiguous speech input is usually rejected—that is, the recognition confidence is below the threshold—allowing the application to trap and handle those utterances that are more likely to be in error. The application either asks the user to repeat the input, or uses a yes-no query to confirm what was spoken. This takes more time, slowing the dialogue, but only occurs for ambiguous recognition results. In general, for a well-trained vocabulary, thresholds require a 10% rejection rate to achieve a substitution rate under 2% in field conditions.[14]

1.3.1.3   Types of Rejection

The term rejection has come to have several interpretations and context-dependent implications. They all derive from the basic premise of ambiguous spoken input. False rejection and correct rejection refer to the accuracy of the action taken by the application. Inter-word rejection and out-of-grammar rejection are recognition conditions in which information is returned to the application to be processed.

False Rejection   The user speaks a legal word. The recognizer returns the correct word, but confidence is low so the word is rejected. Because classification is correct, the input should not have been rejected. It is impossible, however, for the application to differentiate between a false and a correct rejection. The application may attempt to recover the rejection in one of two ways. It may ask the user—using a yes-no question—if the recognized word is correct, or it may prompt the user to repeat the word. If the application simply discards correctly recognized input—either ignoring it or requiring repetition—the false rejection is called a **deletion** error.

---

[13] These parameters vary from technology to technology. Refer to a specific vendor's reference documentation for specific settings and examples.

[14] A substitution is worse than a rejection, as it cannot be detected by the machine. In practical terms, rejections will result in asking the user to repeat—or to answer "yes" or "no" in response to some question—perhaps once for every ten input utterances. Sometimes the proposed word will be wrong—requiring a "no" response. But the user can expect, on average, to avoid having to correct an outright error more than once or twice per lengthy session.

23

Correct Rejection

The user has spoken an illegal[15] word or has produced such a distorted version of a legal word that it cannot be considered a correct instance of that word. The recognizer rejects the input by returning low confidence. Rejection of an out-of-vocabulary word or out-of-grammar[16] utterance is the correct response of the recognizer to illegal input. Specifically, there is no error if the user or background actually presents illegal input. The recognizer has performed correctly, preventing illegal input from being falsely accepted as a vocabulary word.

Inter-Word Rejection

The user says a legal word. The recognizer returns two (or more) different candidates with roughly the same recognition scores. For example, the user says the digit "five" and the recognizer returns two words—*five* and *nine*. Although the input is probably one of the two words, the recognizer cannot choose between them. An inter-word rejection thus points toward a small distance[17] between in-vocabulary words. Because the recognizer cannot "make the call" due to the similarity of scores, both words may be rejected.

OOG Rejection

An illegal utterance or noise has been detected by the recognizer. The input may be words the recognizer is unprepared to recognize—conversational speech, proper nouns, words outside the scope of the task, foreign words and phrases—or it may be non-speech events such as grunts, breath sounds, or background noises. Common terms for correct OOG detection include the following:

- Out-of-grammar (OOG) input,

- Out-of-vocabulary word (OVW),[18]

- Out-task speech,

- "Garbage," or

- Correct rejection

---

[15] When users present input that is not part of the recognizer's vocabulary, it is considered "illegal" by convention.

[16] A "grammar" is the complete set of all possible legal sentences—ordered sequences of words—that a user may speak at a given moment.

[17] Some recognizers use scores that represent "distance" in a literal, geometric sense. Others rely on "probabilities" or "likelihoods." We use "closeness" or "distance" as a conceptual tool because it is easy to visualize.

[18] Refer to the glossary for the distinction between OOG and OVW.

OOG is the preferred term for natural language technologies. OVW is applicable to discrete and continuous-digit recognizers.

1.3.2 Speech Recognition Errors

This text uses the following definitions for speech recognition errors:

Deletion
In continuous recognition, user input is incorrectly segmented, resulting in the deletion of a legal word. For example, the user says the five-digit number "one-two-three-four-five" and the recognizer returns the four-digit number *one-three-four-five*. The digit "two" has been deleted.

False Acceptance
An error in which a noise or illegal utterance is recognized as a legal vocabulary word. This is also called **insertion** and, occasionally, an **intrusion** error. For example, the user says, "What was the question?" and the recognizer returns *yes* with high confidence. The recognizer has accepted the OOG phrase "What was the question?" rather rejecting it as illegal.

False OOG Rejection
A legal user utterance is incorrectly rejected as OOG. For example, the user says "Help" and the recognizer returns a null response or an explicit OOG recognition. This is also called **deletion**, although that term is usually reserved for segmentation errors.

Insertion
In continuous recognition, user input is incorrectly segmented, resulting in the deletion of a legal word. For example, the user says the four-digit number "one-two-three-four" and the recognizer returns the five-digit number *one-two-three-six-four*. The digit *six* has been inserted into the digit string.

Substitution
The user speaks a word. The recognizer returns a different word. Recognition confidence is high, preventing the error from being detected. For example, the user says, "Take a message" and the recognizer returns *Make an appointment* with high confidence. One utterance has been substituted for another.

Spoke-too-Soon
This occurs when barge-in is not enabled. After playing a prompt the application engages the recognizer. Speech is detected immediately. Either the user began speaking too soon or background noise was detected as speech. The recognizer, unable to know how much speech may have been missed, stops recognition and returns

a spoke-too-soon error to the application.

Spurious Error A spurious error is any condition in which the recognizer does not return a recognized legal result. Spurious errors include:

- Spoke-too-soon,

- OOG rejection,

- NULL response, and

- Silence timeout.

The term is not standard in the industry and should be avoided. Instead, the designer should refer to the specific condition that is returned from the recognizer. The one attribute that is shared by all spurious responses is the absence of any recognition hypothesis. This means that—unlike the case of inter-word rejection—the application cannot use a yes-no query about a hypothetical candidate to correct the error.

1.3.3   Barge-In and Other Terms

Barge-in is an ancillary technology that is incorporated into the front-end processing of many speech recognizers. It has important ramifications for spoken dialogues, and the following terms are important in understanding it.

Barge-In The ability of the user to speak at any time and have the system recognize the utterance. Barge-in relies on echo cancellation and speech endpoint detection to allow the user to interrupt an outgoing machine message by speaking. In most cases the machine stops playback of the outgoing message as soon as the endpointer detects speech onset. In other cases, the machine waits until speech is confidently recognized before stopping playback. See Chapter 4 for details.

The following synonyms are commonly used for the generic term "barge-in." Some of these terms have finely-shaded differences in meaning, but can be considered synonyms in the context of this style guide—which uses barge-in throughout.[19]

---

[19] Some technology vendors use their own trademarked designations for barge-in and other speech-processing products. Such proprietary terms are avoided here.

- Cut-through,

- Talk-over,

- Talk-through, and

- Prompt interruption.

Full Duplex   A VRU application that uses barge-in. Both the user and the machine may speak at the same time.

Half Duplex   A VRU application that does not use barge-in. The recognizer is turned off during spoken machine output, and will not "hear" a user who speaks when the machine is speaking.

Utterance   This book uses "word" freely throughout to mean "any spoken user input." Speech scientists use the term "utterance" as a broader and more rigorous reference. The term encompasses words, phrases, sentences, and colloquialisms—as well as unintended user input such as coughs or mumbling.

1.4   How this Book Is Organized

1.4.1   Formatting Conventions

1.4.1.1   Symbols Legend

The following conventions are used throughout this text:

<u>Underlined Numbers</u>   Design guidelines are individually numbered and underlined for quick access.

Italics   Machine output is italicized.

"Quotation Marks"   Examples of user input are quoted.

<u>Underlined Bold</u>   Important points within free-running text are occasionally underlined in boldface for emphasis.

1.4.1.2   Requirement Conventions

This text provides three levels of guidelines.

√   **Required** items have strong evidence to support their use and specify standard practice. Applications must conform to required guidelines to be compliant with this style guide.

+ **Recommended** items are guidelines that are not required, but which are backed by enough evidence that they represent desired actions. Recommendations should not be violated without explicit, good, and defensible reasons.

≈ **Good Practice** items are guidelines which are more specific to certain cases, which appear to be common sense but are not supported by any evidence, or which seem to work in practice but are easily missed by designers. These guidelines should be taken under advisement and applied where appropriate.

Starting with Chapter 2, a running header provides this legend at the top of each right-hand page, allowing a quick view of requirement levels.

1.4.1.3   Style Conventions and Structure

Each guideline is written in the imperative, as though a command to the reader. This style guide does not use the "shall, must, or should" forms common in many standards documents. Where guidelines are conflicting, the reader should rely on the requirement level as described in Guideline 1.4.1.2 above.

Most guidelines are at the fourth heading level, as indicated by the underline. Outline levels above the fourth level are organizational.

Occasional sub-guidelines appear at the fifth level in the document structure. Sub-guidelines are specific only to their fourth-level parent, and are aimed at detailing that guideline only. Fifth-level sub-guidelines are indented for clarity.

1.4.2   Chapter Summaries

This style guide is organized in roughly the order in which designers may proceed with dialogue design. Early chapters cover the basics, giving an overview of methods for designing spoken output and input. Subsequent chapters go into increasingly specialized detail about various dialogue structures, architectures, and look and feel issues. The final chapters address error recovery and testing, including an appendix that assists system planners with hardware provisioning for VRU architectures, and two appendices that address special issues that are related to design.

As a roadmap for speech recognition dialogue design, readers will find it useful to read through the book in order. However, those who wish may skip some material, as each chapter is—to the degree practicable—a standalone discussion of its subject.

After first reading, this style guide is designed to be used as a reference. The table of contents provides information to the third-level heading. The index allows direct access to material. In addition, a comprehensive glossary provides a detailed definition of all concepts that are discussed in the book.

Chapters 2 through 5 cover basic information—guidelines on machine presentation and subsequent user input. These basic principles represent the core behaviors of a typical spoken telephony interface. The next four chapters address structure and architecture, suggesting methods for assembling individual components into a coherent whole. Chapters 10 and 11 and Appendices A, B, and C round out the book with discussions of error recovery, testing, provisioning, understanding voice portals and the voice web, and selecting and coaching voice talent.

Chapter 2	**Spoken Machine Output** is the single most important machine behavior, as it is the part of the application over which designers have complete control. Wording and construction of machine speech directly affect users' perception of both the machine and its relationship to user tasks and goals. This chapter describes specific methods for presenting speech to the user. The reader is encouraged to return to this chapter frequently.
Chapter 3	**Selecting the Vocabulary** is the complement of spoken machine output. In this chapter, the designer considers what the user may say in response to machine prompts—that is, the input side of the interface. The challenges are more difficult, as the designer does not have control over user behaviors. Likely utterances must therefore be considered, as well as the technical issues that underlie recognition accuracy. Methods for imbuing the application with a consistent and predictable look and feel are also discussed.
Chapter 4	**Barge-In and Turn Taking** are closely related subjects that are often neglected by designers. Barge-in is a technology that allows the user to interrupt machine speech. Turn taking is the method whereby the machine and user trade opportunities to speak, moving in alternation toward a common goal. Barge-in has a number of misunderstood attributes, and a detailed discussion therefore exposes the designer to those technical issues that must be understood if barge-in is employed for the turn-taking protocol. Simple and inexpensive alternatives to barge-in are then discussed, providing the designer with a range of options for interactivity.
Chapter 5	**Tones** offer a natural counterpoint to spoken machine output, and

can be used for turn-taking cues, to provide feedback, or as announcements that declare changes of application context. This chapter provides guidelines for applying tones to telephony interfaces. It also points the reader toward some of the research that is currently underway on the subject of auditory icons, earcons, and music as applied to information presentation.

Chapter 6 **Dialogue Design** is a big subject—too big for one chapter. So the subject is introduced here, with an emphasis on six types of dialogue models. The menu, command and control, form filling and searching dialogue models are discussed in detail. Two of the more sophisticated models—natural language and personified interfaces—are introduced briefly but are discussed in detail in their respective chapters. Other topics in this chapter include yes-no queries and reusable dialogue components.

Chapter 7 **Mixed Modalities: Speech and DTMF** is a subject that is treated only briefly. In this case, guidelines for how and when to switch from speech recognition to DTMF are discussed, along with methods for relying on keypress input to satisfy legal requirements and for consistency between DTMF and speech versions of the same application. Alternate architectures for relating speech and DTMF input, as well as some general advice for migrating from DTMF to speech recognition are also introduced.

Chapter 8 **Natural Language** is a sub-class of speech recognition aimed at complex applications with flexible spoken interfaces. Users present complete sentences of their own construction, enjoying user-initiated dialogues with minimum machine guidance. If properly exploited, this ability enhances the user's perception of simplicity and power, but comes at a price: users must experiment to learn what to say and when to speak. This creates new challenges for the design of prompts, help routines, and feedback.

Chapter 9 **Personified Interfaces** are becoming popular in the form of so-called "virtual assistants." These applications provide unified messaging and personal information management (PIM) features to subscribers who rely on them for appointments, follow-me tracking, call-management, and contact functions—just as they would a human executive assistant. In addition to these basic functions, however, personified interfaces exhibit traits associated with anthropomorphism—the attribution of human-like characteristics to the application. This means they have names, are imbued with "personalities," and play certain social roles. Such interfaces are fraught with controversy, and—by stepping into the human social arena—are susceptible to user attitudes that may backfire, producing results contrary to design intent. This chapter argues against such designs, but—in the event the designer is determined to design a personified interface—it also provides guidelines aimed at maximizing benefit and minimizing risk.

Chapter 10   **Error Recovery and Prevention** draws on material from earlier chapters. The focus is on preventing errors from occurring, and on avoiding error-oriented messages and problem-centered dialogues that are an easy trap in speech-based designs. For cases in which errors do occur, this chapter provides guidelines for presenting the facts to the user in a way that reduces error amplification. A sample dialogue for capturing and recovering errors within digit strings serves as a detailed example that summarizes both the philosophy and the methods discussed in other chapters.

Chapter 11   **Usability Testing and Performance Reporting** summarizes several types of usability tests that can be performed as the application design and development process unfolds. These usability tests include focus groups, wizard tests, prototypes, dialogue component tests, and integration tests. The objectives and expected learnings of each of these tests, as well as how to instruct the participants, construct the usability environment, and observe their behavior are described. This chapter also emphasizes the importance of application logging and how to use logging to measure application effectiveness.

Appendix A   **Hardware Provisioning** is a subject, somewhat ancillary to user interface design, which should be addressed sooner rather than later. There are two reasons. First, the initial cost of hardware and the incremental cost associated with features such as natural language or barge-in must be known when "look and feel" decisions are being considered. Second, fundamental decisions about software architecture and dialogue components—decisions that directly impact design—depend in large part on system architecture issues associated with hardware provisioning. This discussion is specific to client/server architectures and may not apply to the specific requirements of a given speech technology.

Appendix B   <u>**Voice Portals**</u> is a new appendix that addresses telephone-based access to multiple services. A voice portal is an entry point into a knowledge domain, including corporate databases, information aggregators such as Internet access sites, and enhanced services.

Appendix C   <u>**Voice Talent and Recording**</u> addresses what has become an art in itself—realizing the persona design for the application. It describes best practices and processes for developing human voice recordings. It includes guidelines for deploying multiple voices and recording in other languages. It also describes the value of the voice coach, who works with the talent and is intimately familiar with the dialogue design and goals.

Chapter 2
Spoken Machine Output

The design of spoken machine output must consider three aspects of speech:

1. The sound quality of the spoken output.

2. The wording of the spoken output.

3. How the spoken output fits into the dialogue structure.

This chapter is devoted to the first two aspects. See Chapter 6 for details on dialogue structure and design.

2.1   Physical Properties of Machine Speech

This section addresses the physical properties of spoken machine output. Characteristics such as rhythm and pacing, sound quality, and intelligibility—as well as the perceived professionalism of machine speech—contribute significantly to user understanding of application intent.

Some information in this section is based on the Ameritech Guidelines document [Schwartz93], which in turn references the HFES-HCI Standards Document dated 1993. Certain standards—such as ensuring that signals may be carried over the telephone network—are absent here because they are obvious.

Note that there are many more sources of information about these issues, and that guidelines presented here touch briefly on the subject. The reader should become acquainted with the many documents that specify telephone signal levels, signal-to-noise ratio, equal loudness, and other physical and perceptual quality attributes.

2.1.1   Loudness and Noise

The following are self-explanatory and therefore presented without discussion. They should be viewed as required, non-controversial guidelines.

2.1.1.1 √ Minimize Background Noise in Recorded Output

This includes both acoustical noise from the room—in which an open microphone is capturing recorded speech—and electrical noise such as hum.

2.1.1.2 √ Do Not Peak Clip

Recordings should be made so that the peak amplitude of the speech signal falls within the dynamic range of the recording device.

2.1.1.3 √ Keep Volume at or Below 85 dB

Volume of spoken machine output should conform to telephony standards. This guideline is from Ameritech [Schwartz93].

2.1.2 Sound Quality of Spoken Output

The "quality" of spoken machine output is a multi-dimensional issue. Attributes of intelligibility, pleasantness, professionalism, and social appropriateness depend on the application context and the targeted user. Although this is a subjective judgment, the end result can and should be tested with a representative sample of users.

2.1.2.1 √ Ensure that Recorded Voices Sound Clear and Intelligible

Digital audio recording is a mature technology. Applications that do not exhibit the highest audio quality are rejected by users as amateur. If the development team does not possess studio-recording skills—and if the development environment does not support recording capabilities—then the recording of spoken messages must be out-sourced to an appropriate specialist.

2.1.2.1.1 √ Professional and Well-Recorded

This guideline is self-explanatory.

2.1.2.1.2 √ Maintain Consistency in Prompt Recordings

Sudden changes in the sound quality of prompts are distracting to users and should be avoided. Variations—in microphones, microphone placement, room ambiance, and other conditions—cause such changes from one recording session to the next.

Note that this guideline also applies to more subtle variations—including rate of speech—caused by the time lag in recording some prompts. If several days or weeks pass between recording sessions, the voice talent loses her context. It then becomes important to review the previous recordings and, whenever possible, to have the voice talent interact for a time with the application. This reduces variations in speaking style between old and new prompts.

2.1.2.1.3   √ Equalize Recordings for Target Environment

Recorded speech may be played to the user through headphones, open-air loudspeakers, or telephone handsets or headsets. All such channels require a different spectral tilt—known as "equalization" or simply "EQ"—to effect maximum perceived speech intelligibility and quality. Developers that are not experts in such matters should seek assistance.

2.1.2.2   + As a General Rule, Use One Voice

The "voice of the application" is the primary look and feel component of the application. Once this voice is selected and trained, it is important to maintain its consistency across and within applications. Although mixing voices arbitrarily during test phases is perfectly acceptable—practical considerations dominate when making "quick and dirty" assessments of dialogues—the final fielded application should make careful use of a single professional voice.

This style guide does not take a stand on the preference of male versus female voices, as various industry sources adopt different views on the subject. The issues probably vary from culture to culture. The following are not guidelines but observations—noted here simply to ensure that they are on record. Sources for them are vague and the observations should be taken with a grain of salt. Any reader who is aware of real data on this subject is encouraged to apply them cautiously.

Note that roughly three out of four DTMF-based IVR applications in America use female voices for spoken machine output [TARP97].

2.1.2.2.1   ≈ People Tend to Perceive Male Voices as More Authoritative

This observation is from the Ameritech standard[1] that in turn references HFES-HCI and so is reprinted here. The guideline is marked as "recommended" and goes on to say, "… a male voice is recommended in an emergency situation." Note that such perceptions probably reflect cultural trends that may vary with time.

---

[1] See Section 4.2.2.2a page 38 of [Schwartz93].

2.1.2.2.2   ≈ Users Often Perceive Female Voices as "The Operator"

This is an anecdotal observation. Participants in focus groups and usability studies often refer to the female voice as an "operator." This is probably because over-the-telephone applications bear general resemblance to customer-operator interactions of many kinds. The tendency of callers to think of receptionists at businesses as "operators"—in the sense that they receive and then route calls within the company—may contribute to this perception. Traditionally—at least in American culture—those employed as operators and receptionists have been primarily female.

2.1.2.2.3   ≈ Some Studies Report Male Voices as More Intelligible

The fundamental frequency and range of formants[2] in male voices are ostensibly better suited to the bandwidth of telephone networks and instruments according to certain studies. Such conclusions are not compelling given that females have little difficulty communicating with each other via telephone.

2.1.2.3   √ If Using Mixed Voices, Design with Care

There may be good reasons for mixing male and female voices. It may also become necessary to mix digitized with synthesized speech. Although highly subjective, this guideline specifies that the reason for mixing voices—as well as a position on rules for managing the resulting change in look and feel—must be formulated in advance if such mixing is to be compliant with this style guide.

The following sub-guidelines describe several situations in which mixing voices can be effective. They are drawn from the Ameritech document and other sources.[3]

2.1.2.3.1   + Consider Using Different Voices to Signal Different Modes

Using a male voice in one mode and a female voice in a different mode can help reinforce the user's mental model of application structure. For example, a "Help Coach" might have a different voice than the main prompting voice of the application, thereby cueing users that they are in the "help" as opposed to the "application" mode. Such a coach may even provide training commentary concurrent with the regular service prompts.

---

[2] Formants indicate high-energy frequency regions in the speech signal, and are caused by resonances in the vocal tract as it changes in shape and volume.
[3] See Section 4.2.2.2.a page 37 of [Schwartz93].

Some DTMF-based applications switch from one voice to another to call attention to important information. In one example, the application "... uses primarily a female voice and then switches to a male voice (to get the customers [sic] attention) when the customer makes an error and the computer is providing additional help. They found usability was higher with the female/male option vs. all female voice" [TARP97].

2.1.2.3.2   + Consider Using Different Voices for Different Languages

Most multilingual systems adopt either one or the other language according to user selection at the beginning of the dialogue. Once a language is selected, the "One Voice" Guideline 2.1.2.2 then applies. Note that if the application is to allow interspersing of prompts in different languages, the designer may wish to create individual agents—one for each language—each with its own voice.

2.1.2.3.3   ≈ Consider Using Different Voices for a "Team" of Agents

In complex applications, the design challenge often becomes one of "chunking" functions appropriately [Miller56]. Many applications use a menu hierarchy to accomplish this [Balentine99]. An alternative is to use a separate personal assistant for each functional area of the application [Balentine94]. Each assistant has a unique voice, thereby providing cues to the user regarding function and context. In a PIM[4] application, for example, one voice handles faxes, another manages voicemail messages, while a third keeps track of appointments. The user thinks of himself as interacting with a "team" of specialized agents rather than with a single complex agent.

Note that this approach—using distinctive human voices to establish context— is likely to lead to anthropomorphism on the part of the user, calling for a personified interface. Such designs are difficult to control and the designer is cautioned to understand the implications of personified designs.

2.1.2.3.4   ≈ Consider Creating a "System Operator/Model User" Duality

In simple applications that employ discrete speech recognition, the user is expected to select from a small set of commands. Such applications—usually menu-driven designs—must present such commands clearly to the user in the form of a list. Such designs may benefit from two-voice presentation methods. The female voice serves as the "system" voice, presenting all instructions and

---

[4] Personal Information Manager. Some Virtual Assistants offer these capabilities.

prompts. The male voice presents discrete vocabulary, usually in the form of spoken lists.

The following example is from an early demonstration prototype [Balentine92a] and [Balentine92b]:

Female Voice:	*Please select one of the following...*
Male Voice:	*News ... Sports ... Weather ...*
User:	"Sports."
Female Voice:	*Today's sports...*

In the example, all spoken machine output relies on a female voice except for the listing of vocabulary words, which are spoken in isolation by a male voice. The male character serves as a "model" user—exemplifying speech that is expected of the user, who in turn emulates this model. The method tends to reduce the occurrence of out-of-vocabulary words (OVW).

2.1.3   Synthesized Versus Digitized Spoken Output

2.1.3.1   + Use Digitized Speech Whenever Possible

Although this guideline varies with application and targeted users—as well as the current state-of-the-art of speech synthesis—it remains true as of this writing that users still express resistance to hearing synthesized speech over the telephone. The issue of presenting unconstrained text may only be overcome using synthesized speech. But unless synthesis is required, it is generally easier and more effective to create digitized recordings for all spoken machine output.

Note that new synthesis technologies—some based on the concatenation[5] of digitized phonemes and syllables—are making good progress. As designers acquire control over prosody[6] and other aspects of synthetic speech, these new technologies may gradually open new areas of applicability. Until then, the discipline and fine control over spoken machine output that is achievable with existing digitized methods makes

---

[5] Concatenation is the technique of joining together two or more objects into a single larger object. In the context of synthesis, prerecorded phones are concatenated and smoothed to create intelligible syllables and words. See the glossary and index entries for concatenation, phonemes, and phones to learn more.

[6] Prosody includes inflection, pitch contour, and other non-semantic aspects of speech. See the glossary for a definition of "prosody."

the use of digitized speech the preferred technique for presenting system messages and prompts that rarely change.

2.1.3.2   + Use Synthesized Speech for Unbounded Information

In general, synthetic speech is appropriate for machine-readable, unbounded information. This includes yellow and white pages, encyclopedia read-back, rapidly-changing information (such as news), HTML streams, and electronic mail. Synthetic speech is less appropriate for dialogue navigation, menu prompting, or list presentation.

2.1.3.3   + Avoid Synthesis for Single Isolated Words

Users become accustomed to synthetic speech in the same way that they do foreign accents. As with such accents, intelligibility is lowest at the single-word level—where context and grammar cannot help with meaning. For this reason, users have the greatest difficulty understanding synthesized machine output when it consists of single isolated words—such as menu selections or single-word feedback of recognized discrete vocabulary words.

2.1.4   Minimum and Maximum Timing Values

2.1.4.1   + Maximum of 100 ms Delay After Prompt

No more than 100 milliseconds should elapse between the end of a prompting message or tone and the acceptance of user speech as input to the recognizer. This value depends on system latency and certain parametric settings within the recognizer itself. It also requires that audio recordings be trimmed aggressively, as extraneous silence at the end of prompts must be included in this delay.

2.1.4.2   √ Edit (Trim) Prompts if Barge-In Is Not Used

When the application does not take advantage of barge-in, users may unintentionally preempt the tone, causing "spoke too soon" turn-taking errors.[7] Such errors are minimized (although never eliminated) when the tail end of all prompts are aggressively trimmed. This means eliminating all silence (at the least), and removing a significant fraction of the ending phoneme (best). Long noisy phonemes—an ending /s/ for example—can often be excised with no perceptible change. The goal is to activate the recognizer as soon as "triggering information" from the prompt causes the user to begin speaking.

---

[7] See Section 1.2.3 and Chapter 4 for discussions of turn taking.

2.1.4.3   + Communicate Errors Within 0.5 to 5.0 Seconds

No more than a few seconds should elapse between the occurrence of a speaking error and the communication of that error to a user. Note that this is a general timing guideline and therefore may have many exceptions. The lower value (500 milliseconds) applies to short-term errors such as turn taking stumbles, while the higher value applies to various state errors (including recognition errors, such as those that land the user in the "wrong" menu). Two or three interactions may be required before a state error can be detected and reported—hence the longer value. See Section 1.2.2 for a discussion of state errors.

2.1.5   Proportions of Speech and Silence

Machine output typically occupies more time than user speech. Care must be taken that the timing of all spoken machine output is appropriate for the interaction.

2.1.5.1   √ Organize Spoken Machine Output into Simple Clear Sentences

Avoid long cumbersome discourses—even if barge-in is available to allow user interruption. Users rarely listen to, integrate, or retain complex verbal information.

2.1.5.2   √ Keep Sentences Short

A typical machine sentence should last no more than two or three seconds.

2.1.5.3   + Provide Ample Pauses Between Phrases and Sentences

On average, there should be one second of interspersing silence for every two seconds of spoken machine output.

This guideline is true whether barge-in is permitted or not. When speaking, users often take their turn at natural syntactic junctures [Heins97]. This makes "prompt-interruption" a very different behavior when compared to DTMF applications, in which users press keys at arbitrary times during the outgoing machine speech. Frequent silences encourage the user to interrupt gracefully at such syntactic junctures, leading to a more natural dialogue and less strain on the part of the user—who is trying to be heard over machine output. It is also likely that user speech that falls within one of the pauses will suffer less from substitution and rejection errors.

2.1.6   Rhythm and Rate of Speech

2.1.6.1   √ Roughly 150 Words per Minute

Avoid speaking rates that are too fast or too slow. In general, speaking rates between 140–160 words per minute represent a good average pace.

2.1.6.2   + Slightly Faster for Synthesized Speech

Use a rate of about 150–180 words per minute for synthesized speech. This is from the Ameritech guidelines [Schwartz93], which in turn reference [Marics88].

2.1.6.3   √ Maintain Consistent Speaking Rate

Throughout the application, all spoken machine output should adopt the same rate of speech. Note that certain exceptions may exist. For example, the definition of difficult concepts or the presentation of important information may require somewhat more deliberate (i.e., slower) machine speech. Even in such cases, it is important to avoid speaking too slowly. Instead, interspersing silences should be elongated, allowing users to digest the information as it is presented.

2.2   Wording of Spoken Output

The wording of prompts and other spoken machine output determines the user's understanding of the intent of a message and of the application's expectations for subsequent user input. As the machine's only externally-observable behavior, spoken machine output is thus the cornerstone of dialogue design. This section focuses on general principles for constructing effective spoken output.

2.2.1   Types of Spoken Output

When machines speak to users, the spoken machine output serves five purposes or functions, as shown in Table 2.1. These types are discussed in detail in Sections 2.4 through 2.7 respectively. In addition to the specific terms shown, other more generic terms are used in the industry with varying meanings. The word "announcement," as well as "message" and sometimes "recording" are used to mean "spoken machine output." The word "prompt" is also used in a generic sense, implying that all spoken machine output serves the purpose of prompting. Such confusion of terminology leads to a number of common design flaws. For this reason, specific terms here are preferred over vague and general terminology.

2.2.2   Voice, Person, Tense, and Mood

An understanding of the basic elements of English grammar is a good place to start when crafting spoken machine output. A brief definition of each grammatical term appears with its associated guideline. For readers not well versed in English grammar, see any of a number of English style guides such as [Merriam-Webster91].

2.2.2.1   √ Use Active Voice

Avoid passive voice. Instead, use active voice to construct strong, imperative prompts in which the user is expected to perform the action represented by the verb.

Active voice is a sentence construction in which the subject performs the action represented by the verb. In the sentence, "John is throwing the ball," for example, the subject of the sentence—John—is the one doing the throwing. With passive voice constructions, on the other hand, the subject receives the action represented by the verb, e.g., "The ball is being thrown by John."

Avoid: *Your account number is requested.*

Use: *Please enter your account number.*

Table 2.1—**TYPES OF SPOKEN MACHINE OUTPUT** are listed according to function.

Type	Function
Prompts	A prompt indicates it is time for user input. The prompt thus serves as a turn-taking cue.
Feedback	Feedback presents the application state that results from user input, allowing the user to compare original intent with final result.
Instructions	Instructions give information to the user about operating the user interface or understanding the task.
Help	Help instructions often adopt a separate mode or state aimed at coaching the user.
Application Data	Application data represents information—for example, weather, stock information, or travel arrangements—that the machine presents to the user as part of the application task itself.

2.2.2.2   √ Use Second Person

Unless the interface is specifically personified as an anthropomorphic design, spoken machine output should avoid first person (either in the form "I" or "we"). Similarly, in the absence of compelling arguments to the contrary, spoken machine output should avoid the third person (he, she, they, and them). Instead, spoken machine output is best when the user is addressed directly. Users easily understand second person imperative or indicative prompts and instructions.

Exception: The first person plural "We" can occasionally serve to imply collaboration between machine and user in which the user has the power:

Use: *Let's start over.*
        Shall we go ahead?

2.2.2.3   + Use Present Tense

Avoid the past or future. Instead, use present tense.

Avoid: *You will be asked for your card number.*
        Your response was not recognized.

Use: *When you are prompted, please speak your card number.*
        Say that again?

Exception: Reference to an immediately preceding event in an error-recovery dialogue may sometimes take advantage of past tense:

Use: *Was that a yes?*
        Did you say…?

2.2.2.4   + Avoid Subjunctive Mood

According to the *Concise Handbook for Writers*:[8]

> Mood indicates manner of expression. The indicative mood states a fact or asks a question (He *is* here. *Is* he here?). The subjunctive mood expresses condition contrary to fact (I wish that he *were* here). The imperative mood expresses a command or request (*Come* here. Please *come* here) [Merriam-Webster91].

---

[8] [Merriam-Webster91] This reference is a very helpful and easy-to-use aid for understanding basic English grammar, expressions, and the principles of clear writing.

Words such as "would," "were," "could," and "should" represent a hypothetical manner of expression that is rarely appropriate for goal-oriented, task-oriented activities. Subjunctive mood should be replaced with imperative or indicative.

Avoid: *You could …*
         Should the city name be incorrect, you may backup by saying "Cancel."

Use: *You can …*
         If the city name is wrong, say "Cancel."

2.2.3   Opening Greetings

2.2.3.1   √ Let Users Know They Are Interacting with a Computer

Users should know that they are not talking to a real person. For example:

Avoid: *Acme, Incorporated. May I help you?*
         Welcome to Acme.

Use: *Welcome to the Acme speech recognition system.*
         You have reached Acme's automated travel system.

This guideline is based on the Ameritech document.[9]

2.2.3.2   √ Identify the System Immediately

Users should hear the name of the service-providing company in the first sentence of the greeting message. This allows wrong number callers to exit immediately, and reinforces correct callers that they have reached the service they want. This guideline is based on the Ameritech standard.[10]

2.2.3.3   ≈ An Audio Logo Makes an Excellent Greeting

Where possible, corporate logos that are well known to users can fulfill both of the above guidelines. In such logos, a musical fragment—such as the three well-known NBC tones, the Southwestern Bell "pixie dust" sound, or the "Intel inside" melody—or a musical sound mixed with a speaking voice such as the AT&T greeting, is used to identify the company. Such short logos may also serve as prompts to speak. See Chapter 5 for details.

---

[9] See Section 4.1.4.3.b of [Schwartz93] which in turn references [Deffner92].
[10] See Section 4.2.1.a of [Schwartz93] which in turn references Voice Processing Corporation, 1991, [VCS91].

2.3 Prompts

Prompts represent a specific type of audio message that should conform to certain principles of construction. Since prompts are the **turn-taking cues** within spoken dialogues, they are inherently related to issues of interactivity and throughput. A prompt has two purposes:

1. Cause the user to speak.

2. Optionally, convey to the user what may be spoken.

Because of this dual requirement, prompts should be as distinguishable as possible from instructions and other non-interactive components of the dialogue.

2.3.1 Prompt Design

2.3.1.1   √ Make Prompts Short

Prompts are turn-taking cues. They should accomplish this purpose quickly and then give the turn to the user. The following sub-guidelines assist with the problems of instructing prior to prompting.

2.3.1.1.1   √ Precede Prompts with Instructions

An extremely terse prompt is sometimes not enough to convey input require-ments to the user. A complete "machine turn" should therefore consist of any instructions in compliance with Section 2.4, followed by the prompt.

Avoid combining prompts and instructions together into long cumbersome structures that cannot be separated.

2.3.1.1.2   √ Repeat Only the Prompt

If error recovery requires a repetition, repeat only the short prompt. Do not re-peat instructional messages prior to the prompt.

Avoid:

App: *Your plan requires that you select a PIN to use the system.*
      The PIN must be 5-9 digits in length.
      At the tone, please say your PIN.

User: "One Seven…." (spoke-too-soon occurs)

App: *Be sure to wait for the tone before you speak.*

Your plan requires that you select a PIN to use the system.
The PIN must be 5-9 digits in length.
At the tone, please say your PIN.

This is a common design mistake. In the example, the user committed a simple turn-taking error—as evidenced by the spoke-too-soon—and knows what to do next. However, the application has incorporated instructions as well as the prompt into a single long recording. The machine therefore repeats unnecessary information—instructions that the user already knows. This increases the likelihood that the behavior will repeat itself [Balentine97].

Use:

App: *Your plan requires that you select a PIN to use the system.*
The PIN must be 5-9 digits in length. Please say your PIN.

User: "One Seven…." (spoke-too-soon occurs)

App: *Be sure to wait for the tone.*
Please say your PIN.

In the improved version, instructions and prompt are separate recordings. On errors, only the prompt is repeated. This simple design approach goes a long way toward addressing the issue of expert versus novice users.

2.3.1.2   √ Deposit Key Information Immediately Before Expected User Speech

The purpose of a prompt is to cause the user to speak. The prompt conveys to the user what to say either directly or indirectly. Certain "key information" embedded within the prompt can be thought of as triggering a clear understanding in the user's mind of what the machine expects. The prompt should be constructed such that this key information appears just before the moment when the user is expected to begin speaking. Note that this moment is different for full- and half-duplex systems, as described by the following sub-guidelines.

2.3.1.2.1   √ Place Key Information Before Tone if Not Using Barge-In

When there is no barge-in, follow the prompt immediately with a tone. Ensure that there is no trailing silence following the key information at the end of the prompt. Invoke recognition immediately after the tone.

2.3.1.2.2   √ Place Key Information at Phrase Boundary if Using Barge-In

When barge-in capability allows the user to interrupt, place key information early in the prompt—but at the end of a natural phrase boundary. Add silence after the phrase to allow the user to take her turn and to capture speech during this natural pause. If user speech begins during the pause, wait until there is a response from the recognizer before presenting any new speech output.

2.3.2   Yes-No Interrogative Prompts

Yes-no responses are often the last line of defense in error recovery. Therefore they must be worded clearly and unambiguously.

2.3.2.1   √ Use Interrogative Form

The interrogative form asks a question directly, and is generally better than the imperative for constructing yes-no questions. Interrogative is usually shorter, and tends to evoke spontaneous "yes" or "no" responses.

Avoid: *If this is correct, please say "yes" now.*
For another transaction, say "yes."
If you want a quote on <fund name>, say "yes." Otherwise, say "no."

Use: *Is this correct?*
Do you want another transaction?
Did you say <fund name>?

If the response to the corrected examples are eliciting OVW, for example, the user responds "Correct," then play *"Please respond 'yes' or 'no,'"* and re-prompt. See Section 6.4 for more details on recovering yes-no errors.

2.3.2.2   √ Include the Verb on Interrogative Yes-No Prompts

Avoid: *Correct?*
Use: *Is this correct?*

Users are often observed answering the first question with "Correct" rather than "yes" or "no." The second form evokes "yes" or "no" more reliably. Contrast this with Guideline 2.3.4.1.

[handwritten note: ✱ What's accuracy of Correct vs other?]

47

2.3.2.3 √ Reserve Imperative Form for Recovery

If the user fails to provide a legal "yes" or "no" response to an interrogative, the error-recovery prompt may adopt an imperative tone:

Use: *For more quotations, say "yes" now.*

Please answer "yes" or "no."

2.3.2.4 √ Avoid Compound Questions

Avoid: *Are you traveling alone and will you need a rental car?*

Are the name and address correct?

Yes-no questions must be very clear and simple, addressing only a single subject. Combining multiple questions into one is common in casual human-to-human discourse because the interrogator can understand an unbounded set of replies. Yes-no questions in human-to-machine discourses should be more structured.

Another version of this same problem is the question that may be answered with "yes" or "no," but which may also be viewed as a two-way branching inquiry (see Quasi-Menus in Section 6.2.4). The following example is seen repeatedly in order entry and transaction dialogues.

Avoid: *Do you want to cancel or change your order?*

Use: *To process your order, say one of the following ...*

Confirm ... Change ... Cancel...

In the first example, the user is not certain whether "cancel" is the same thing as "change order," or if a change may be an alternative to canceling. Depending on the context, as well as the inflection of the question, users may answer "yes" or "no," or may provide wordy responses such as, "I want to change my order." Although grammars may be designed that will capture such responses, ambiguity is built into the question. Such ambiguous interrogative prompts should be avoided or reformulated into a menu construct.

2.3.3   Other Interrogative Prompts

2.3.3.1   + Use the Interrogative for Constrained Numeric Data

Certain numeric data types are well-constrained, allowing user input of this data to be reliably predicted. In such cases, the interrogative is a convenient and fluid form filling construction.

Avoid: *Please state the sell price now.*
         Speak the number of shares you want to buy.

Use: *Sell at what price?*
         How many shares?

2.3.3.2   + Avoid Interrogative (Use Imperative) for Unconstrained Data

Avoid questions that are likely to evoke a widely varying response. Such questions have too many logical and apparently appropriate answers to constrain with reasonable grammars:

Avoid: *When were you born?*
         What is your age?

Use: *Please provide the following personal information...*
         The year that you were born.
         The month?
         The date?

The top two questions tend to evoke sentence responses ("I was born …" or "I'm … years old.")—as well as free-form answers ("September the 21st" or "in 1964")—making user responses difficult to bound and therefore to predict. Bear in mind that grammars in contemporary speech recognition technologies are based on prediction of user responses. When user responses are difficult to predict—or when the range of predictable responses is great—the prompt should be redesigned. In the corrected example, a typical form filling sequence prompts the user for one piece of unambiguous information at a time.

2.3.4   Implied Interrogative Prompts

Some prompting strategies take the form of single words or short phrases that are recorded with an upward inflection. Such prompts represent implied interrogative prompts. The inflection increases the tendency to respond, as the user perceives the upward (interrogative) inflection as a turn-taking cue.

2.3.4.1   √ Drop the Verb when Interrogative Is Implied

Implied interrogatives do not require long and complete sentences. Rather, they should be used only in those circumstances where short, simple, upward-inflected cues are likely to be unambiguous. In such circumstances, the "sentence" is implied and the verb is not needed. Contrast this with Guideline 2.3.2.2.

Avoid: *What is the security you want quoted?*
         What is your PIN number?

Use: *Security name?*
         PIN number?

The full-sentence constructions are too long. Instead, drop the verb and use the short-noun forms. The dropped verb is what makes the implied interrogative prompt effective as the shortest useful prompt.

2.3.4.2   √ Use Short Nouns for Implied Interrogative

Since implied interrogatives should be used only in unambiguous circumstances, a single noun that serves as a keyword or key phrase is usually sufficient.

Avoid: *What is the name of the fund?*
         What is your PIN number?
         What is the name of the person you would like to call?
         Which command would you like to perform?

Use: *Fund name?*
         PIN number?
         Name?
         Command?

2.3.4.3   √ Use Implied Interrogative with Digitized Speech Output Only

Single words are the most difficult to understand with synthesized speech. For short and clear prompting, use digitized speech for implied interrogatives. See Guideline 2.1.3.3.

2.3.5   Imperative Prompts

The imperative implies "you" as the subject, as in "[You] say your credit card number." The implied "you" is understood to be the user, and such prompts take the form of a command to the user to engage in action. Imperative prompts are thus clear and unambiguous.

2.3.5.1   ≈ Optional "Please"

Some guidelines argue that a preceding "Please" before a prompt creates an expectation that user action is impending. Others argue against it as likely to trigger similar extraneous social courtesy fillers on the part of the user.

This style guide posits that "Please" and "Thank you" fillers are optional and usually benign. They should be monitored during **usability testing**,[11] but are allowed unless proven detrimental during testing.

2.3.5.2   + Reserve "Enter" and "Press" for DTMF Actions

Some style guides recommend the verb "Enter" for multiple-action entries and "Press" for single-action entries:

Please enter your account number.
For an account balance, press two.

Avoid using these verbs to prompt for user speech.

2.3.6   Verbatim Prompts and Data Prompts

Verbatim prompts are common in DTMF applications and instruct the user explicitly to "say" a specific word or phrase:

App: *Say, "At the market."*

Data prompts, on the other hand, use a structure that is aimed at conveying to the user what types of data are required—without giving verbatim phrases:

App: *Please enter a limit price.*

In the example, the user is expected to say a dollar amount, not the phrase "a limit price." The user understands this because the prompt does not begin with the word "Say" as do verbatim prompts.

---

[11] Refer to Section 11.1 for a discussion of "usability testing."

2.3.6.1   √ Use "Say" for Verbatim Prompts

When a prompt commands the user to say a specific datum—as represented by the presence of a direct object—the verb is said to be transitive. "A *transitive* verb acts upon a direct object" [Merriam-Webster91]. Such transitive prompts should use the word "say" rather than "speak" or "state."

Avoid: *Please speak that again.*
            Please state one of the following: Boston, Massachusetts or Austin, Texas.

Use: *Say that again?*
            Please say either "Boston, Massachusetts" or "Austin, Texas."

2.3.6.2   √ Use "State" for Data Prompts

When a prompt instructs the user to enter specific data, use "state" as the verb form. This will reduce confusion on the part of the user, who frequently parrots back the direct object of the verb phrase.

Avoid: *Say the stock name*
            Say your PIN.

Use: *State the stock name*
            State your PIN

In the top example, the user could become confused and say "the stock name" or "your PIN." This can be a common behavior for users who are not familiar with the application. In the corrected version the user is instructed to provide specific data.

2.3.6.3   √ Avoid Mixing Verbatim Prompts and Data Prompts

When verbatim and data prompts are combined, mimicking behaviors often lead to errors:

App: *How many shares would you like to buy?*

User: "Seventy-five shares."

App: *Say, "At the market." Or enter a limit price.*

User: "Enter a limit price."

App: *I'm sorry, I didn't understand.*

In this example, the user interpreted the prompt as follows:

App: *Say, "At the market," or "Enter a limit price."*

As a result of the misinterpretation, the user expected a subsequent prompt for the limit price itself. Instead, the speech recognizer rejected the input phrase, requiring a re-prompt. Note that the "wrong" interpretation is reasonable given the distribution of commas and quotation marks. These visual cues are missing in the audio prompt, while the word "*Say*" at the front is a strong but misleading instruction.

Note that an alternate solution is to reverse the two verb phrases in the prompt. This allows the verb "*enter*" to stand in contrast with the verb, "*say.*"

App: *Enter a limit price. Or say, "At the market."*

App: *State a limit price or say, "At the market."*

2.3.6.4   ≈ Optional "Answer" or "Speak" for Alternative Speech Cues

Although "Say" is the preferred verb in transitive prompts, certain prompts or error-recovery instructions may also use "answer" and "speak" as verbs that apply exclusively to spoken (not DTMF) entries. Use the verb "speak" when the prompt is intransitive (no direct object). Use the verb "answer" when the prompt refers specifically to interrogative constructions.

Use: *Please answer "yes" or "no."*

        Please answer the following questions.

        Speak now.

        You may speak at any time.

2.3.6.5   √ Eliminate Extraneous Words Between "Say" and the Actual Command

Avoid: *Please say either the word "yes" or "no."*

Use: *Please say "yes" or "no."*

This is a modified (unambiguous) version of the Ameritech standard.[12]

---

[12] See Section 4.1.4.3.e of [Schwartz93] which in turn references [Gellman88].

2.4 Feedback

Feedback is a type of spoken machine output that is aimed specifically at informing the user of the result of some action or operation. In speech interfaces, feedback is critical, as it conveys directly or indirectly what was recognized. Improper feedback designs may lead to error-amplification conditions.

2.4.1 Types of Feedback

There are several different ways that an application can notify the user of various states and conditions. These include spoken machine output, non-speech audio (tones, etc.), and withholding machine output when it's expected.

2.4.1.1 + Avoid Literal Feedback

Speech recognition is an errorful medium, sometimes unpredictable. Presenting data to the user for confirmation should be graceful and unpresuming. Avoid feedback prompts that literally interpret the recognizer's response as "what the user said."

Avoid: *Your entry was not 7 digits.*
  You said 1234967...
  You entered 1234967...

Instead, use statements of fact, followed by interrogative or imperative prompts:

Use: *The PIN must be exactly seven digits. Please repeat your PIN.*
  1234967—Is that correct?

In the examples, the idea is to get at what the number **actually is** not what the user **said**. In the first example, the user probably did say a 7-digit number—the recognizer has simply experienced a deletion error. Similarly, any substitution results in a false machine statement when the feedback is presented as, *"You said...."*

Users become confused when the machine declares that they "said" something that they in fact didn't say.

2.4.1.2 ≈ Consider Using Tones as Feedback

Tones do not have to serve only as prompts. They can also be very effective forms of feedback. Details appear in a number of journal articles [Blattner89]. See Chapter 5 for examples.

2.4.1.3   + Replace Apology and Blame with Prompts

Avoid apologizing for problems or inadvertently blaming the user for them. Instead, simply move forward by prompting for the next appropriate user action. There are two motivations for this. First, the application can never be certain of the underlying error, so descriptions of the problem may be incorrect or misleading. Second, explaining the problem does not necessarily influence the user in a constructive way. Rather than dwelling on the condition that has led to a problem, it is better to describe what action is now expected of the user.

Avoid: *Sorry, I didn't understand.*
          You <did something wrong>.

Use: *Please repeat.*
          Do you want help?

Exception: A phrase such as *"Sorry for the confusion …"* prior to being passed to a help desk or operator appears to be interpreted by users as a simple social protocol that is not prejudicial.

2.4.2   Relationship Between Feedback and Prompts

2.4.2.1   + Use Embedded Confirmation On High Confidence

Where possible, the prompt for input should also serve as feedback for the immediately preceding input. This example is from a voice-dialing application:

User: "Call."

App: *Name to call?*

User: "John Doe."

In the example, the prompt for a speaker dependent name—*"Name to call?"*—also serves as feedback for recognition of the command "Call." In this way, the user is assured that the dialogue is on-track. The method is called **embedded confirmation** because feedback aimed at confirming a past recognition is embedded in a prompt aimed at causing future user speech.[13]

Note that this "chaining" approach to feedback and prompting only works when confidence is very high that the recognized command is correct. The designer is encour-

---

[13] Contrast this with explicit and implicit confirmation.

aged to use both rejection thresholds and n-best[14] hypotheses to ensure that substitutions or rejections are extremely unlikely. If confidence is low, use the following guideline.

2.4.2.2 √ Uncouple Feedback from Prompts if Confusing

Guideline 2.4.2.1 should be ignored if the attempt at combining a prompt with feedback is confusing to the user. For example, feedback of a spoken name combined with a prompt for a number fails if there is a misrecognition.

Good Example (correct recognition):

App: *Stock name?*

User: "Microsoft."

App: *Shares of Microsoft to sell?*

User: "Five thousand."

Failed Example (recognition error):

App: *Stock name?*

User: "Texaco."

App: *Shares of PepsiCo to sell?*

User: "… umh … No, that's wrong …"

It may also be the case that embedded feedback is unnecessarily redundant. Food-ordering menus, for example, may offer the same "ingredients" for every item. In this case, including the feedback with the prompt wastes time:

Avoid: *What ingredients would you like on your hamburger?*
        What ingredients would you like on your pizza?
        What ingredients would you like on your salad?

Use: *What ingredients would you like?*

---

[14] It cannot be over-emphasized that n-best and rejection are important concepts. Designers should be intimately familiar with both OOG and inter-word rejections, as well as the use of n-best to detect and recover these conditions. See Section 1.3.1.1 and the glossary.

2.5   Instructions

When the machine provides factual information to the user about the interface itself, the audio output is considered instructional. This includes menu listings, statements about when to speak, and similar factual information. Instructions differ from prompts in that they are not intended to be immediately followed by user speech.

2.5.1   Wording and Construction

The purpose of instructions is to convey factual information to the user. This information should be useful and relevant. Note that users do not need more information than is absolutely essential for holding up their end of the conversation, so less is more when it comes to instructions. It is better to under-explain—allowing the user to take more turns—than to over-explain, keeping the turn and lecturing the user.

2.5.1.1   √ Avoid Embedding Instructions Within Prompts

Where possible, it is best to let users explore an interface, learning on their own. All audio output that is instructional should be judged—emphasizing brevity and clarity—and treated as a separate class of message. In particular, instructions should not be confused with or combined with prompts. As a goal, it is best to remove all non-essential instructions from the normal call-flow, either moving them to a help dialogue or eliminating them altogether.

Avoid: *Please say the name of the fund that you are interested in inquiring about.*
         Please speak naturally and wait for the tone before speaking.
Use: *Please state the fund name.*

In the top example, the two sentences confuse the need to prompt the user with the need to provide amplifying instructions. The designer has added clarification to what is meant by "*name of the fund*"—it is not just "any" fund, but the one the user is "*interested in inquiring about.*" After this parenthetical comment, the prompt then continues with instructions about how and when to speak—instructions that should be moved to another location in the dialogue.

In the succinct corrected example, the message is designed to prompt the user quickly and then immediately let the user take a turn. Users that already know what is meant by fund name—as well as how and when to speak—are thus not penalized by unnecessary embedded instructions.

2.5.1.2   + Re-Use Instructions with Amplification for Help

Re-use the same audio messages in different contexts—treating them as simple, individual factoids in help sequences and elsewhere. Instead of rewording messages, add to them with additional, clarifying information. This allows an inverted pyramid[15] format for quick help.

Avoid: *When you're listening to your messages, you may say words like, "Save" to save your messages, or "Delete" to delete your messages. You may also say "Play" or "Skip" if you want to hear the message again or if you want to skip to the next message without acting on the current one. You do not have to wait until the message is over, but ... instead ... you may speak at any time while the message is still playing.*

Use: *Your commands are...*
    Play ... Save ... or Delete?
    You may speak at any time.

In the top example, the tutorial or help sequence is an unstructured running collection of arbitrary material. Such sequences take the form of a "lecture"—written as one might write an essay. Most sentences are so specific to the context of the lecture that the wording and inflection would be inappropriate elsewhere in the dialogue. Such sequences bloat the collection of audio messages that must be recorded, tested, archived, and maintained. They also confuse users.

In the corrected example, specific factoids are recorded in isolation, allowing them to be reused in a number of different contexts. For example, the first two sentences may be concatenated[16] to create a logical help instruction, *"Your commands are ... play, save, or delete."* The second sentence alone, however, makes a good menu prompt, *"Play, save, or delete?"* Note that—although printed here with different punctuation—the same inflection implied by the question mark applies to both. Say the sentences out loud to understand this principle. The last sentence, *"You may speak at any time,"* functions well as one of several sentences in a tutorial, and yet also serves as a turnaround prompt after timeouts or similar errors.

---

[15] The "inverted pyramid" is a form of writing, such as that used in journalism, in which the most important information appears first while less important details are progressively disclosed in order of importance.

[16] Concatenation is the technique of joining together two or more objects into a single larger object. In the context of audio messages for IVR, two or more prerecorded phrases are played in sequence to create meaningful sentences. See the glossary and index to learn more.

This principle of **reusability** establishes structural discipline, makes repeated information easier to learn, and represents parsimonious use of design elements.

2.5.1.3   √ Avoid Telling the User How to Speak

Although it seems reasonable to encourage users to avoid "strained" and artificial-sounding speech, such behaviors are the result of talking to a machine that they perceive is not very bright—or otherwise discomforting to communicate with.

Avoid: *Please speak naturally.*

   Try to speak clearly and with a firm voice.

The fact is, users think they **are** speaking "naturally." If instead they are producing stilted or wooden input, it is because of the context of the interaction; such users will prove unable to willfully change their speech. Instead, they will become self-conscious and aware of talking—usually exhibiting even more unusual and unnatural behaviors. Observing untrained children or adults who are asked to read aloud in public—or in a school play, for example—exposes this phenomenon.

2.5.2   Grammatical Forms for Instructions

There are four general forms that English sentences may adopt:

1. Declarative,
2. Interrogative,
3. Exclamatory, and
4. Imperative.

A declarative sentence expresses a statement. Unless there are good reasons to the contrary, instructions should use simple declarative sentences.

An interrogative sentence asks a question, while an exclamatory sentence expresses an exclamation—an "outcry or an emphatic or ironic comment" [Chicago93]. There are occasions in which interrogative or even exclamatory messages may be appropriate for instructions.

The imperative sentence expresses a request or command. Because it implies a direct command to the user—thereby leading to user action—the imperative form is best reserved for prompts and should be avoided in instructions.

2.5.2.1 √ Use Declarative Sentence Structures for Instructions

Imperative and interrogative forms imply strongly that the user is expected to speak. By definition, only prompts should create this expectation. Instructions should therefore use declarative constructions.

Avoid: *Read one of the fund names from your reference card.*

Choose from the following list.

Check the form: how many digits are in the PIN? The answer is seven.

Use: *The fund names are printed on your reference card.*

You may choose one of these.

A PIN must be at least seven digits long.

2.5.2.2 √ Make Declarative Sentences User-Centered

Where possible, make all statements of fact relevant to the action that will be expected of the user. Avoid statements that are "about" the dialogue or application structure.

Avoid: *The menu consists of five items.*

Use: *You may choose from one of the following.*

2.5.2.3 ≈ Consider Replacing Ambiguous Instructions with Questions

Avoid open-ended or ambiguous directions. If necessary for clarity, replace directions with questions. Although this will introduce an additional interaction into the dialogue, it will ensure that the user is ready to provide the necessary spoken input.

Avoid: *Please have your credit card ready.*
Use: *Do you have your credit card ready?*

2.5.2.4 ≈ Reserve Exclamatory Sentence Structures for Certain Error Messages

Occasionally, a statement of error may require an exclamatory sentence. Note that this is rare, and should be used with caution.

Use: *Too much background noise!*

2.5.3   Mnemonic Consistency

If speech and DTMF are cross-referenced due to mnemonic relationships between words and keys on the keypad, then such mappings should be reinforced. See Chapter 7 for more guidelines on the mixed use of DTMF and speech.[17]

2.5.3.1   + Ensure that the Mnemonic Is Consistently Reinforced

Avoid: *For _tips_ on speaking fund names, press _Star H_ at any time.*
Better: *For _help_ with speaking fund names, press _Star H_ at any time.*

In the first example, the word "*tips*" is substituted for "*help*." Although the word is useful and would represent good variety in writing, it waters down the mnemonic value of *H as the path to getting help. It is better to repeat the word "*help*," thereby reinforcing the mnemonic for the *H key combination.

2.5.3.2   + Keep Mnemonic Equivalents Adjacent

Better: *For _help_ with speaking fund names, press _Star H_ at any time.*
Best: *For _help_, press _Star H_ at any time.*

The word "*help*" and its mnemonic equivalent should be as close together in time as possible, allowing one to be easily associated with the other. This principle is more important than any enhancing or clarifying information such as, "*speaking fund names.*" Such information, if required, should appear after the user invokes the function—in the example, by pressing *H.

2.6   Help

Help messages are similar to instructions, and may in fact use the same audio files as those targeted for instructions. The difference is that help appears within a different context or mode: the user has explicitly asked for help or the machine has automatically transferred the user to a help sequence. The latter may occur if error frequency or severity is such that the interaction is unlikely to succeed.

2.6.1   When to Offer Help

The following guidelines are common to all help approaches.

---

[17] Note that the use of mnemonics for DTMF is a bad practice [EIG96]. It is better to avoid mnemonics altogether. This guideline applies only to systems that use mnemonics for legacy or other reasons.

2.6.1.1   + Empower the User with Help Availability

User-selected help is generally more beneficial than machine-activated help.

2.6.1.1.1   + Let the User Know that Help Is Available

Present an instruction at the beginning of the dialogue, or in an error-recovery procedure. Occasionally, it's appropriate to ask explicitly:

Do you want help?

Do you need help?

2.6.1.1.2   + Let the User Know How to Get Help

For help, press Star H at any time.

You may say "Help" at any time.

2.6.1.1.3   + Once Help Is Declared Available, Keep it Available

If help is a feature, then every recognition or DTMF input opportunity must handle this feature. This may include states in which the application is expecting only a yes-no response from the user.

2.6.1.2   + Return to a Logical Starting Point After Help

Whether the user asked for help or the machine automatically initiated help, return to the interaction immediately preceding the point of departure when the help sequence is complete.

2.6.1.3   + Use Examples for Help

Users can mimic an example dialogue more quickly than they can understand instructions about how and when to speak. Where possible, present examples during help sequences:

<interrupting help chime>

Help Coach: *State the date like this …*

Prompt Voice: *Date of birth? <prompt tone>*

Male Voice: *Six-eighteen-forty-nine*

Help Coach: *Now you try it.*

<closing help chime>

Prompt Voice: *Date of birth? <prompt tone>*

The user speaks here, mimicking the male voice presented in the example.

In the example, three different voices are used.[18] The "Help Coach" interrupts the dialogue at a strategic point. She presents the example, which plays a quick example interaction between the prompting voice used throughout the application and an "example user," represented by a distinctively different male voice. Immediately after hearing the example, the help sequence is over. The coach returns control to the dialogue with a parting instruction to the user. Distinctive tones help cue the beginning and ending of the interruption.

2.6.1.4   √ Ensure that Help Is Helpful

Well-meaning design and development teams often intend to create clear and unambiguous context-sensitive help at each decision-making juncture within an application. As the reality of schedules and project pressures appear, however, such help does not always find its way into the product. Instead, help routines simply repeat—perhaps with some additional detail—those facts that the user already knows. The following example exaggerates the problem to make its point, but is not facetious. The designer may recall similar examples from existing applications.

App: *Please say one of the following...*

Create a New Entry ... Reply to Current Posting ... Calibrate Gridgeon...

User: "Help."

App: *If you want to create a new entry, say "Create a new entry."*

To send a reply to the current posting, say "Reply to current posting."

To setup or calibrate your Gridgeon record, say "Calibrate Gridgeon."

Please make your selection now.

This help routine is not helpful. The user has asked for help in order to understand what a "Gridgeon" might be, and why she might want to calibrate it. The help routine, in turn, only repeats the same information already presented in the menu. Although "context sensitive," the routine is not helpful. It is important to understand that users often need help with the task rather than with the interface. Indeed, it could be argued that help with the task is the more common user need—especially with well-designed

---

[18] Contrast this with Guideline 2.1.2.3.4 (System Operator/Model User).

interfaces. Help routines that simply repeat boilerplate information, possibly sprinkling in a few additional modifiers, do not get to the heart of the user's problem.

2.6.1.5   + Help with Only One Fact at a Time

Avoid trying to tell the user everything all at once. Instead, present the most important fact required for the user to surmount the next obstacle in the interaction. Then continue to coax the user forward by unfolding these facts as they are needed.

2.6.2   Help Mode

If help is offered as a separate activity within a separate "mode," the following additional guidelines apply.

2.6.2.1   + Differentiate Between Help and Application Mode

Introductory audio cues, a different voice, or a background sound that is constantly present may be used to indicate to the user that a different mode is now active.

2.6.2.2   + Let the User Exit the Help Mode

Give the user an immediate way to exit help mode at any time. This may include a spoken exit word (if the system supports barge-in) or DTMF entry.

2.6.2.3   + Without User-Exit, Keep Help Mode Short

If the user is unable to willfully exit the help mode, ensure that frequent junctures appear for exit.

Either provide frequent, fact-by-fact exit points:

App: *Do you want to return to the application?*

Do you want more help?

Shall we continue?

Or automatically return to the application after presenting a single, specific fact or instruction to the user via help mode:

App: *<"Help Wizard" logo>*

Remember, when you hear a list of options … [some instructional fact]

Now, here's the menu …

<"Price Menu" logo>

In the first examples, the user has just heard a single fact in the context-sensitive help dialogue. After each fact, the system offers an exit via a yes-no question. In the second set of examples, a context-sensitive wizard has been activated—either by user command or automatically as the result of some specific machine condition. After presenting its fact, tip, or elucidation, the wizard automatically returns to the menu or state from which it was activated.

2.6.3   Tutorials

Tutorials can sometimes be useful as a kind of help.

2.6.3.1   + Let the User Practice "Safely"

If the user is told that no action will be taken, then it is easier and less threatening to experiment. Tutorial modes that allow users to "buy shares" or to "schedule appointments" are therefore effective methods for non-destructive practice sessions. Note that such complicated tutorials are generally useful only when applications are already extremely complex.

2.6.3.2   + Use a Different Voice for Tutoring

The user may confuse the tutoring session with the real application unless a different voice or audio cue conveys that the tutorial is a separate mode.

2.7   Application Data

2.7.1   Digit-String Grouping

Many interactions require the playback of numeric data, as shown in Table 2.2. One example is the digit string, an ordered set of digits that must be presented to the user by speaking each digit. Such strings have several attributes that affect the user's ability to understand the string and to organize it into a meaningful whole. The following guidelines are specifically aimed at digit-by-digit playback of these strings. The designer should note that there are many classes of numeric data besides digit strings.[19]

2.7.1.1   + Apply Groupings with Pauses to Digit Strings

When reading back digit strings, place short pauses at appropriate points according to natural digit groupings. For example, where digit groups printed on a card or reference are separated by hyphens, spaces, or other separators, insert pauses between

---

[19] See the glossary entries for "digit string," "natural numbers," and "super-numeric."

each group during playback. These pauses may be incorporated directly into the "intermediate inflection" recordings of Guideline 2.7.2.3.

When machines simply play digits one after the other, some users become confused, reporting that the application is "barking numbers" at them. The problem is exacerbated when each digit has a slightly different duration, leading to a ragged and disjointed rhythm. In such designs, the pace of playback must often be slowed to allow users to hear and integrate the digit string. By adding pauses, the application "chunks" the data more effectively [Miller56], thereby allowing the user to integrate each group individually.

Table 2.2—**TYPICAL CLASSES OF NUMERIC DATA**. Note that some data may be represented by more than one class with varying degrees of complexity (e.g., telephone numbers). This section addresses only the digit-string presentation.

Numeric Data	Examples	When Spoken As
Digit Strings	• Social Security Numbers	• one two three—four five—six seven eight nine
	• Telephone Numbers	• one eight zero zero—five five five— one two one two
Natural Numbers	• Telephone Numbers	• one eight hundred—five fifty five— twelve twelve
	• Quantities	• six hundred and fifty
Super-Numeric	• Dates	• March thirty-first; the third of August
	• Times	• five PM; six o'clock; twelve noon
	• Money Amounts	• thirty-six dollars and fifteen cents

2.7.1.2   + Avoid Arbitrary Groupings

There are certain digit-strings for which no standard groups apply. Many non-U.S. telephone numbers, for example, exhibit arbitrary numeric grouping. In such cases, it is helpful to "read" the number the way the user spoke it, (see Guideline 10.3.2.4). If this is not possible, it is probably best to avoid digit grouping altogether. The reason is that "illogical" grouping—that is, organizing the number into groups that do not correspond to the user's natural grouping—is likely to hurt more than help.

As an exercise, the designer may wish to speak personal numeric data aloud with alternate groupings. For example, a U.S. Social Security number, spoken with unusual groupings, takes on a very different character.

Example: *123-45-6789*

Read As: *1234-567-89*

For best results, substitute a real number for the one shown. During this exercise, make note of the increase in concentration required to recognize the digit string.

2.7.2   Timing and Inflection of Digit Strings

2.7.2.1   + Record Digits with Equal Duration

When playing a digit string, each individual digit is typically a separate digitized recording. Some digits tend to be shorter (6) or longer (7) than others, leading to ragged playback as various digits are concatenated together.[20] To avoid this, each digit should be recorded and then edited to ensure that all recordings are the same duration. This means, of course, that words such as "seven" must be spoken somewhat more quickly. It also means that each recording must be edited to ensure that silences before and after each digit are properly proportioned.

If speech synthesis is the method for digit-string playback, then timing and rate-of-speech parameters should be tuned to allow an appropriate pace for the digits.

2.7.2.2   ≈ Apply Metered Rhythm to Digit-String Playback

The digit plus its following silence at the end of a group should be twice or three times as long as the embedded and number-ending digit, establishing a well-metered[21] rhythm. The decision of which multiplier to use depends on the overall pace of digit playback.

If, for example, each digit is 300 milliseconds in duration—a good quick pace for numeric playback—then the silence following a digit group should be exactly 600 milliseconds in duration. The digit plus its following silence thus becomes 900 milli-

---

[20] Concatenation is the technique of playing multiple recordings of individual digits one after the other to create the appearance of complete number strings. See the glossary and index entries for concatenation to learn more.

[21] In music, speech, and verse, meter is a type of rhythmic organization based on periodicity. A regular repetition of events that occurs according to durations or time divisions that have integer relationships is said to be metrical.

seconds, resulting in periodicity. Similarly, if each digit is 400 milliseconds in dura-tion—an average pace for numeric playback—then the silence following a digit group should be exactly 800 milliseconds. The digit plus its following silence then becomes 1200 milliseconds, also resulting in periodicity.

Organizing time periodically is known as **meter**, and leads to expectations on the part of the user. These expectations may be exploited to control both when the user pre-dicts a machine event and when the user is likely to speak to interrupt the machine. Meter is organized by an underlying pattern of **beats**—the same pattern that makes a listener tap his foot "in time" to music. The act of bringing down the foot represents a prediction on the part of the listener. When foot and music coincide, the two are syn-chronized.

This guideline, of course, does not posit that the user will literally tap his foot while listening to digit playback. Rather, the implicit beats that organize metered playback are expressed in other ways—specifically in the timing of interruptions and in the lowered concentration required to understand, organize, and comprehend numeric data. Section 10.3.2 describes an algorithm for playing digit strings in a barge-in en-abled system. The design is based on expectations associated with metrical time.

2.7.2.3   + Apply Inflection Patterns to Digit Strings

When reading back digit strings, create at least three versions of each digit—one with an upward inflection, one with an intermediate (contoured) inflection, and one with a downward inflection, as in Figure 2.1.

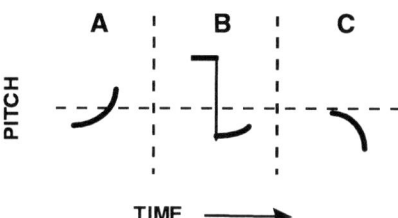

Figure 2.1—DIGIT INFLECTIONS allow the user to hear the organization of a digit-string. The verti-cal axis shows pitch and the horizontal axis shows time.

Use the downward inflection for the last digit of the entire number. Use the interme-diate inflection at the end of each digit group—for example as the third and fifth digit of a standard nine-digit social security number. Use the upward inflection for all other (embedded) digits. Refer to Figure 2.1 for a schematic diagram of these inflected patterns. Each example in the figure represents the pitch[22] variation (inflection) for a single spoken digit.

The upward inflection at point A should not be confused with the similar inflection associated with questions. The pitch is not as high, nor is the range as great. Instead, the word begins at a medium pitch and then rises by about a third. It is recorded with the natural prosodic curve that implies there is "more to follow." The intermediate inflection pattern at B starts at a high pitch and then immediately drops to a pitch that is about a fifth lower. The pitch then rises at the end of the word. The overall pitch contour sounds and looks complex in print, but is in fact quite natural and simple. The designer is encouraged to speak digits out loud until the intermediate inflection is understood. The final downward inflection (C) is spoken with finality—conveying, "this is the end."

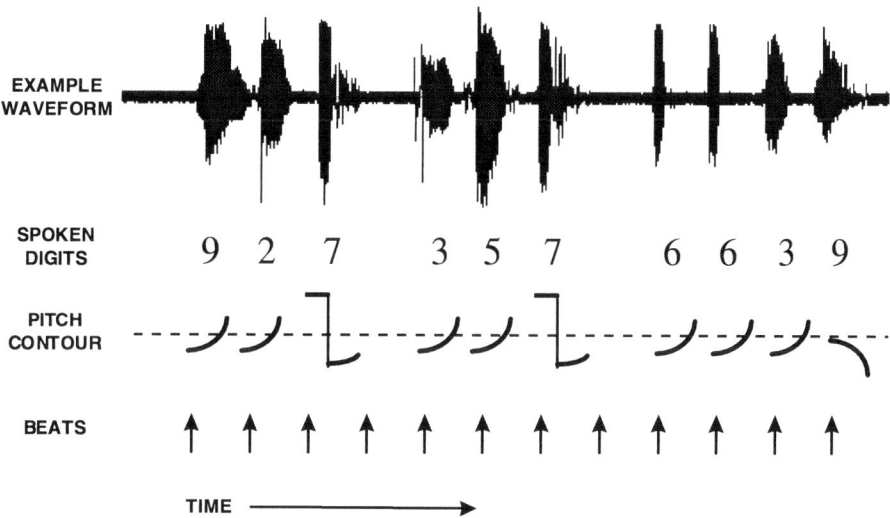

Figure 2.2—**INFLECTIONS AND PAUSES AT GROUPINGS** clarify machine playback of a typical U.S. telephone number. The three-digit groups end with the digit *seven* by coincidence only. All digits except those that end a group are spoken with the upward inflection described in Figure 2.1. The first two groups end with an intermediate inflection followed by a silence of equal duration. The final digit is presented with a downward inflection. The entire number thus consists of 12 300 ms beats, two of which are silent. The result is a metered and inflected number—presented in 3.6 seconds—that users are most likely to hear, integrate, and recognize.

---

[22] Pitch is the subjective perception of frequency [Schiffman82].

Figure 2.2 shows a typical waveform with the inflections described in Figure 2.1. Below the waveform is the digit sequence spoken. The figure shows the pitch contour for each digit in the string, which is a U.S. telephone number. Note that the intermediate inflection ends each of the three-digit groups. Each group is then followed by a silence of equal duration (the fourth and eighth beat). The downward inflection concludes the entire number.

Note that the inflections shown in these illustrations and examples are only some of the ways that inflection and rhythm may be applied to application data. Such techniques also have effect in error-recovery dialogues (see Chapter 10).

Chapter 3
Selecting the Vocabulary

This chapter focuses on spoken user input that is allowed by the speech recognition vocabulary. When selecting vocabulary, designers must often consider tradeoffs between human-factors issues—including the "naturalness" of the words which may be spoken by the user—and technical issues such as raw accuracy, memory, and latency concerns. In addition, the kinds of errors committed by recognizers are often confusing and counterintuitive, making vocabulary selection something of an art. Guidelines in this chapter are aimed at helping the designer make effective tradeoff decisions when selecting the vocabulary.

This chapter uses the terms "word," "phrase," or sometimes simply "input" to imply a single utterance in an attempt to provide generally-applicable guidelines to vocabulary selection across different speech recognition technologies.[1] An application using discrete recognition, for example, may use the phrase "Play Messages" as a vocabulary entry. This single utterance will be referred to as a "word"—even though it consists of two English words. Similarly, natural language technologies rely on grammars to support a combinatorial approach to spoken input. That is, individual words may be combined into phrases and sentences that can become quite complex.

There are so many approaches to speech recognition that to distinguish between them would confuse rather than clarify the approaches. Note that there are several components of speech processing, each with its own unique error types and each dependent upon a different set of criteria when choosing words that are the most likely to perform well. From a functional point of view, these components include:

- Speech detection,

---

[1] See the glossary for distinctions between speech recognition technologies, such as continuous and discrete recognition.

- Word capture and time alignment[2],
- Statistical models to account for speaker variability, and
- Confusable word (word-pair) discrimination.

What this means is that speech detection and capture—including time alignment—produce specific errors in discrete recognizers. Detection and capture alone—independent of time alignment—exhibit different behaviors in continuous and natural language recognizers. All recognizers must address the anomalies introduced by statistical artifacts that are used to develop vocabularies. Finally, there are often difficulties with certain word pairs. It is important to understand the source of these errors, as it aids with vocabulary-selection decisions.[3]

3.1 The Recognizer's Impact on Vocabulary Selection

Speech recognition technologies are generally based on pattern-matching algorithms that attempt to classify varying instances of similar patterns—regardless of the speaker. Classification is based on those features of the input that are the most statistically significant and the least variant across the range of expected input. This means that recognition technologies must detect and normalize the salient input features of speech while ignoring noise, vocal quality, dialect, and other non-salient features.

Variation from utterance to utterance is almost universally represented in contemporary speech technologies through some sort of statistical representation and analysis. The result is a statistical model[4]—of phonemes, words, or phrases. Such models contain statistical-processing artifacts that bear no direct relation to human hearing, and consequently speech recognizers often make mistakes that humans would not make. The aim of this section is to anticipate these mistakes and to compensate for them—to the degree possible—through vocabulary selection.

---

[2] Words vary in duration from one instance to the next. Time alignment is the process of adjusting for variations in duration by stretching or compressing the phonetic elements of the input to produce the "best fit" for comparison with word models.

[3] Speech vendors have the tools and the experience to analyze proposed vocabularies prior to development—and to test them after development. Designers should work closely with the vendor on these vocabulary-selection issues.

[4] A model based on statistical estimates, for example the phonetic makeup of a word or the prior probabilities of someone speaking an equity from a list of 12,000 equities. Statistical processes are often used to analyze or model complex systems—such as human speech—that exhibit great variability. They can be thought of as mathematical descriptions of both the average value and the typical range of the elements within such systems.

3.1.1   Analyzing the Recognizer's Behavior

There are certain general guidelines that apply to most VRU applications and speech technologies. Although necessarily broad, these guidelines can be expected to help focus the designer on effective vocabulary selection.

3.1.1.1   √ Rely on User Testing Rather than Analysis Where Possible

This is the single most important guideline in this chapter. It is difficult to resist the urge to "second-guess" a speech recognizer, and many style documents argue that vocabularies should not include "sound-alike" words. The problem is that what sounds "alike" to a human does not necessarily sound "alike" to a recognizer—and vice versa. This means that—despite the guidelines in the rest of this chapter that derive from the field experience and linguistic knowledge of many experts—rigorous testing is the only way to really know which words perform reliably in the context of a specific recognition technology and user environment.

A good procedure is as follows:

1. Make a first pass at selecting vocabulary words according to the guidelines in this chapter.

2. Use Wizard of Oz testing[5] and other methods to acquire input from potential users as early as possible.

3. Prototype the vocabulary as soon as possible—even on a recognizer other than that targeted for final deployment.

4. Use the prototype to experiment and to learn about the performance of each vocabulary word. For example, make note of those attributes that affect endpointing, and learn to distinguish them from phonetic characteristics. Observe the behavior of stressed and unstressed syllables,[6] and especially note word pairs that tend to be competitive.

5. Share these observations with the speech vendor.

Do not put too much emphasis on absolute accuracy percentages—such numbers will vary with the precision of data collection and threshold tuning. Instead, make note of coarse performance, including which words tend to recognize most-frequently on background noise (candidates for false acceptance), which words fail to trigger when

---

[5] Refer to Section 11.3 for a complete description of Wizard of Oz (WoZ) or "wizard" testing.
[6] See Guideline 3.1.2.4.1 for a description of unstressed syllables.

spoken normally (candidates for deletions), and which word pairs tend to appear to-gether in first and second place (candidates for false rejection and substitution).

This procedure will accomplish two things. First, it will expose obvious word-selection problems before too much time and expense has been devoted to vocabulary development. Second, the designer will develop a good ear and practical experience that is based on speech recognition technology rather than instincts about what "sounds similar."

3.1.1.1.1   + Note False Acceptance Errors

Every vocabulary has its noisiest component—the word that appears most commonly as a false acceptance error.[7] To test a given vocabulary, simply ex-pose it to random occurrences of foreground and background noise.[8] Most vo-cabularies will consistently reject such noise, but occasional out-of-vocabulary word (OVW) insertions are inevitable. The word that most consistently ap-pears as a false acceptance is the "noisiest" word in the vocabulary. If a given vocabulary tends to experience an abnormally high false acceptance rate for a given word, then that word is a candidate for replacement.

Be aware that the more common form of insertion—the introduction of an ad-ditional word into a continuous string of words—is the result of a segmenta-tion error and is more difficult to understand and manage. One cause of this might be using a very short word, such as the letter "E." The speech vendor can help with this class of error.

3.1.1.1.2   + Note False Rejection Errors

Words with a high percentage of noisy fricatives—unvoiced consonants[9] such as /h/, /f/, and /s/—tend to experience high false rejection rates. This is particu-larly true of short words, but can be surprisingly high with longer words as well if they contain a number of noisy phonemes. Words that experience a large number of false rejections are candidates for replacement.

---

[7] This error is also known as an **insertion** or an **intrusion**. Words that are statistically noisy (and therefore intrusive) are sometimes the underlying cause of inter-word rejection or even outright substitution problems in a given vocabulary. Eliminating the former fixes the latter.

[8] Foreground noise occurs adjacent to the handset (e.g., chewing gum) while background noise occurs in the user's environment (e.g., in an airport terminal).

[9] Unvoiced speech is produced by exhaling (forcing air) while the mouth, teeth, and tongue (articulators) are in a specific position. [Rabiner93] has a good discussion of voiced and un-voiced speech production.

Be aware that rejections may result from a number of underlying causes. Words that don't trigger the endpointer—either because they are short, soft, or both—result in silence-detection timeouts. If this problem occurs often, the parameters that control the endpointer may be the underlying problem. More commonly, certain words are detected but subsequently rejected, resulting in OOG responses from the recognizer. These rejections are sometimes reported as null responses, and occasionally as consistent inter-word rejections. The application has the power to manage these responses under many circumstances as discussed later in this chapter.

3.1.1.1.3 + Note Substitution Errors

Substitutions often do not make sense to end users,[10] as they have nothing to do with words that "sound alike." Rather, they are a by-product of statistical variations and their distribution across the vocabulary. It is therefore important to minimize their occurrence.

3.1.1.2 √ Use Words that Are Likely to Be Spoken

Certain vocabulary words are non-negotiable. If users are likely to use a certain word, then it is better to have that word in the vocabulary—even if simply to reject it or to correct the user's behavior. Some "common" words have poor acoustical characteristics, but if the word is likely to be spoken, then the designer must insist on its inclusion.

The following is a list of "unfortunate" words—that is, words that speech scientists and application designers wish would go away, but are common in automated interactions (e.g., your ATM machine) and often must be used.

Help   This is a short word. The /h/ is lost in the telephone transmission channel, so the speech recognizer often decides that the beginning of the word is the vowel. The /p/ is sometimes stopped and sometimes aspirated—with the result that endpoint "jitter" is appreciable. The above attributes conspire to cause false rejections. Consider using "instructions" instead.

Cancel   This is a noisy word. The embedded /s/ is lost in the telephone channel, and sometimes is long enough that it exceeds the allowed time for an embedded silence. In addition, the final syllabic is un-

---

[10] Some substitutions even evoke a good laugh. It is a good idea to test the vocabulary with laughter to avoid "laughter amplification." ;)

stressed, and often so low in energy that it is not picked up by the endpointer. Although rarely deleted, the word experiences substantial variation in scores and is a candidate for rejection and substitution. Consider using "start over" instead.

Six   This is a short word—in fact the shortest digit in the English language. The surrounding /s/ is not detected by the endpointer and the vowel can be as little as 60–80 milliseconds in duration. The digit is therefore commonly deleted—both in discrete and continuous recognizers.

These examples were chosen to provide some assistance in understanding what causes false rejections and other recognition errors. Commonly used words are shown to emphasize that designers cannot always eliminate words that are likely to exhibit errors. Understanding the error is the key to making good decisions.

Most words that are likely to be spoken for a given task will often appear in **usability testing**.[11] Users will be predisposed to words they use when interacting with a person or technology. Table 3.1 provides a list of technology-related words that most people have some level of familiarity and comfort. When these words are used in the vocabulary, users bring previous learning and expectations. Avoid introducing a new word in the context of one of the words listed in the table.

3.1.1.3 √ Keep Vocabularies as Small as Possible

This guideline applies specifically to discrete speech recognition that is word-specific but is relevant generally to all technologies. The guideline is especially important in high-noise or distracting[12] environments. It is less applicable to designs that are intrinsically large-vocabulary oriented (e.g., stocks or city names). Even so, designers often fall into the trap of "thinking of every way users might say something," adding synonyms and grammatical expressions heedlessly. Such designers are encouraged to understand that such variety increases rather than diminishes complexity, and that tradeoffs are exactly that—a balance between opposing solutions. It is best to avoid getting carried away when it comes to synonyms.

---

[11] See the glossary and Section 11.1 for a description of "usability testing." "Wizard of Oz" tests in particular are an important part of vocabulary selection.

[12] Distractions that are notorious for limiting the user's full concentration on tasks include driving, calling from meeting rooms where others may interact with the user, and calling from noisy public places such as airports. The user's ability to remember available options decreases appreciably under distracting conditions.

3.1.1.4   + Consider Barge-In and Turn-Taking Issues When Selecting Vocabulary

Tradeoffs associated with barge-in are based on the specific implementation of barge-in chosen by the designer (see Chapter 4). In general, consider the following:

*   Short (one- or two-syllable) words decrease the stuttering effect.[13]

*   Short words are more susceptible to false rejection.

*   Long (multi-syllable) phrases are more likely to recognize well.

*   Long phrases are more susceptible to the stuttering effect and make it more difficult to implement recognition windowing[14] in half-duplex applications.

Table 3.1—**WORDS ASSOCIATED WITH CONSUMER TECHNOLOGIES** that will be readily understood and spoken. Words in bold show different ways to say the same thing; words in italics have low energy and should be avoided.

Technology	Associated Words
Telephone	*hold*, *flash*, redial, *mute*, speed dial, transfer, star, pound
Voicemail	*play*, delete, user options, ***make***, **exit**, greeting, **passcode**, **attendant**, *keep*
Voice Response Unit	Main Menu, *help*, **representative**, **PIN**
Word Processor	*cut*, *paste*, select all, edit, undo, *find*, replace, open, ***close***, *save*, properties, *help*, *tools*
Email	subject, *send*, receive, ***save***, **compose**, *view*, *help,* forward, reply, *from*
Automatic Teller Machine	**cancel**, enter, OK
Computer	logon, folders, **password, reboot**
CD Player	*pause*, *stop*, *play*, record, **repeat**
Video Game	*start*, **start over**
Automated Directory Assistance	city name, listing, **operator**

---

[13] See Guideline 4.1.3.4 for a discussion of the stuttering effect.

[14] Windowing applies to half-duplex systems in which a window of silence (typically one second or less) is inserted between prompts and the recognizer is turned on. See Guideline 4.2.2.2 and the glossary for a more detailed description of "windowing."

The above contradictions demonstrate that barge-in decisions affect word selection. The designer must base her decisions on the goal of striking the most effective balance between these opposing principles. The best procedure is this: select a turn-taking protocol and choose the form of barge-in that best serves that protocol. Then examine the (preliminary) vocabulary and analyze each word with respect to its performance with the selected barge-in implementation. Change words that are likely to perform poorly with the specific turn-taking solution.

3.1.2 Strategies to Improve Recognition

Although only live testing can determine the scoring distance between words in a given vocabulary, the designer can make some good approximations by observing certain phonetic features. This analysis requires a good "ear" for the sound of language, and also benefits from field experience and the analysis tools that speech labs have accumulated over the years. For this reason, the designer is encouraged to work closely with the speech vendor to ensure that effective decisions are made. The purpose of this section is to equip the designer with a basic knowledge of "what to listen for" in the early stages of vocabulary selection.

3.1.2.1   + Use Multi-Syllable Words or Phrases Where Possible

Longer words that are rich in phonetic features tend to be captured more reliably by the endpointer and also tend to be more distinguishable from other words in the vocabulary. All else being equal, long phrases are better than short ones from a raw accuracy perspective. Note that some long phrases tend to experience endpoint errors (those with extended regions of embedded low energy), making this guideline dependent on the selected phrase. See Guideline 3.1.2.4.2 for examples of endpointing errors associated with long phrases.

3.1.2.2   + Understand and Consider Statistical Artifacts and Noise

Vocabulary models are designed to tolerate variation. Some words are more variant than others, making the statistical process that is at the core of most speech recognizers difficult to manage. This is because highly-variant words must be prevented from causing errors.

Example Substitution (Speaker Dependent)

User: "Call."

App: *Name to call?*

User: "Melchior Hakane."

App: *Calling Jonathan Brown...*

The example is from a voice-dialing application. The user has spoken a name. The speaker-dependent recognizer has made an error. The question is, which word model is at fault? Jonathan Brown or Melchior Hakane? Certainly the two do not seem to sound at all alike—an aspect of speech recognition that has always bemused designers, developers, and users alike. How is it possible for the recognizer to "confuse" such disparate names?

The answer is that the recognizer is not "hearing" the speech in terms of what sounds alike and what does not. The machine is simply performing a search through a sequence of numbers. The numbers include statistical information about how much "weight" to give to various acoustical components of the word. The resulting scores are sorted, and the best score is the winner. The second-best score is in second place, and so on through the vocabulary. The machine has no idea about the "sound" of the words. Some words consistently score well, not because the acoustics are similar to the input, but because the weighting information increases their chances of winning. This statistical effect of weighting is what is meant by "statistical artifacts and noise." The principle is tough to grasp at first, so here are some additional examples.

Example Insertion (Digits)

App: *Please say your PIN.*

User: "One-three-seven-five."

App: *One-three-six-seven-five.*

In the example, the digit "*six*" has inserted itself incorrectly into the recognized number. The input has been segmented incorrectly, dividing the end of "three" and the beginning of "seven" into an additional segment. The inserted digit is commonly "six" because that digit is highly variant. Scores for "six" tend to be anomalously high after being adjusted for statistical variation—the word "likes to be recognized" and it can appear easily within the string.

Example Rejection (Natural Language)

User: "Buy 500 shares of General Motors Class E."

App: *Did you say Cisco Systems?*

User: "No, General Motors Class E."

App: *500 shares of General Motors Class E ...*

In the example, *"Cisco Systems"* appeared in first place (incorrectly). The correct "General Motors" security name appeared in second place (not shown) with very similar scores. The existence of the inter-word rejection triggered the yes-no query. Because the subsequent user input matched the second-place candidate from the first input, the rejection was recovered (see Guideline 3.1.3.5).

These kinds of errors—substitutions, insertions, and rejections, among others—occur apparently at random. It is important to understand that any word can recognize in place of another under various conditions. However—and this is the point of this discussion—some words tend, on average, to experience better recognition scores than is appropriate when the user says something other than those words. These words tend to appear in first place incorrectly more often than others do.

It is impossible to determine in advance which words will exhibit this statistically noisy trait. But during vocabulary testing, these tendencies will show up. If statistical artifacts are the source of the three errors described in this discussion, then the "correct" word did not misbehave—there is no problem with the models for Melchior Hakane, three, seven, or General Motors Class E. Rather, the error was committed by the inserted words— Jonathan Brown, six, and Cisco Systems.

One final comment. Do not infer from this guideline that somehow certain words should not be used. Rather, this discussion is to help the reader understand and consider the phenomenon, which is one explanation for recognizer behaviors that don't make sense according to what we hear. The following sub-guidelines provide some applicability in specific cases.

3.1.2.2.1   + Avoid Noisy Words if Possible

Certain consonants—such as the unvoiced fricatives /f/ and /s/—consist almost exclusively of random noise. Since instantaneous measurements of noise are highly variant from one instance to the next, statistical models of noise tend to accumulate large statistical variances. In other words, noisy regions are statistically random (or nearly so) across large numbers of training samples, so these regions score consistently low during recognition.

Speech recognizers compensate for this and similar statistical artifacts with a number of normalization techniques, striving to equalize recognition scores across the vocabulary and across the population—regardless of the mix of voiced and voiceless components. Despite such attempts at normalization, however, certain noisy words tend to experience a higher number of recognition errors. If possible, they should be avoided.

3.1.2.2.2   + Avoid Low-Energy Words if Possible

Certain voiced phonemes—such as the nasals /m/ and /n/—are inherently low in energy. This is also true of many consonants. Words that contain a large percentage of low-energy regions tend to perform poorly (e.g., sent, loan). Such words should be replaced with higher energy words if possible.

3.1.2.3   + Do Not Force Users to Make Decisions Based on Recognition

As described above, speech recognizers use statistical processes that are quite unlike the way humans recognize and understand speech. The errors made by such statistical processes are often confusing. Designers often "hear" in their minds a sample dialogue that is based on words that "sound alike." Usually, this means rhyming words, and the assumption leads the designer astray.

A common case revolves around speaker-dependent speech recognition. In this technology, the user creates the vocabulary himself—by twice or thrice reciting a given word to "train" the system.[15] The technology remains popular with inexpensive voice-activated dialing applications, as the user may select the names for his personal phonebook without prior planning.

A typical dialogue goes something like this:

User: "Add."

App: *Name?*

User: "John Doe."

App: *Again?*

User: "John Doe."

App: *Number?*

User: "555-1212."

App: *Adding ...* [user's voice] *<John Doe>*

---

[15] Training requires that the user present an example of a new class to the machine. Also called "enrollment," the process represents a form of machine learning and applies to speaker dependent recognition, speaker verification, and other classification technologies that can learn from the users.

In the example, the user is required to speak the new name twice. These so-called enrollment passes[16] capture two instances of the word—the minimum for statistical variation—and also create a digitized recording of the user speaking the new word. This recording "tags" the new name—in this case "John Doe"—allowing the user to hear the name associated with the phonebook entry.

The problem is that certain names may become confused with others already in the phonebook, resulting in inter-word rejection or substitution errors when the user later places calls to names in the phonebook. In an attempt to prevent this, many designers add logic to the enrollment process, aimed at checking for potential errors when the user adds each new name. The designers imagine a dialogue like this:

User: "Add."

App: *Name?*

User: "John Doe."

App: *Similar to ...* [user's voice] *<Jon Lowe>*

         Please choose another name.

User: "Jonathon Q. Doe."

The designer has imagined a circumstance in which the user's phonebook already contains a name—in this case, Jon Lowe—that sounds like John Doe. The two names appear likely to cause rejections whenever the user refers to one or the other. To prevent this, the designer adds some logic. When the user provides a sample for enrollment of the new name, a recognition match is concurrently performed against the existing phonebook. If a match that is "too close" occurs, then the condition triggers a dialogue aimed at requiring the user to choose an alternate name.

The scheme seems perfectly plausible. But it is based on an invalid assumption—that the user will agree with the application and will then understand how to choose another name when such sound-alike coincidences occur.

A more typical scenario, unfortunately, is as follows:

User: "Add."

App: *Name?*

---

[16] Most speaker dependent recognizers require more than two passes—examples of a new word—for optimum performance. Such technologies often capture additional examples during normal application use, a process called **adaptation**.

User: "John Doe."

App: *Similar to ...* [user's voice] *<Susan at Work>*

          Please choose another name.

User: "mmm... how 'bout Johnny?"

In the example, the existing name doesn't sound like the new name. This rejection may be an anomalous one—caused by background noise or endpoint problems—or there may be statistical artifacts at work. Regardless of the explanation, however, the user is now stuck with the problem of figuring out how to choose another name for John Doe that doesn't sound like "Susan at work."

In studies of voice dialers, one of the most telling observations is that users forget the names in their phonebook [Damhuis97]. The error-prevention scheme described above is one of the reasons. In the preceding examples, the user will almost certainly never remember the phrase, "mmm... how 'bout Johnny?" Even "Jonathon Q. Doe" is a stretch from the user's first spontaneous utterance.

Although it may seem perfectly reasonable to prevent the user from adding names that sound similar, it turns out that the better solution is the simpler one: let the user resolve the problem later. The logic goes like this:

1. Make it easy for the user to add and delete names quickly.

2. Never require that the user choose a different name.

3. As a result, the user is most likely to remember the names in the phonebook, because whatever "spontaneously occurred" to the user during training is what is likely to spontaneously occur during recognition.

4. If two names really are competitive—for whatever reason—then the problem will turn up whenever the user calls one or the other name. The symptom will be that the machine queries more often about one name than about the others.

5. If this becomes an irritant to the user, let the user decide to change the name—later, after the problem proves to be consistent, and at whatever time is convenient for the user. Ensure that the user can delete the old name and add a new one quickly—without allowing any intervening error-prevention dialogues to get in the way.

The key message is to design dialogues based on the broad and general events that occur with speech recognizers. The assumption that errors make any kind of sense biases the designer, and by extension the user, who should never be required to change her behavior based on recognition issues such as sound-alike words.

3.1.2.4 + Understand and Consider Endpointing Issues

The endpointer is responsible for detecting the onset and offset (coda) of user speech and is not immune to mistakes. The following guidelines are aimed at taking word-detection performance into account when considering vocabulary. The designer should be aware of the following:

• Endpointers vary across speech technology.

• Endpointers are **parametric**. Correct setting of parameters that tune the end-pointer to the target environment is critical when assessing performance.[17]

• Working with the speech vendor is essential for understanding the detailed operation and performance of the endpointer and other related components of the speech recognizer.

Because there are so many exceptions to rules about endpointing and other technology-affected signal processing, all of the following sub-guidelines are marked at the lowest level of recommendation ≈ (Good Practice).

3.1.2.4.1 ≈ Consider the Effects of Unstressed Syllables

Words that begin or end with schwa[18] are often poorly endpointed. The end-pointer deletes the unstressed syllable before the recognizer even gets a chance to begin its match. The result is inter-word rejection or substitution with words that share acoustical patterns with the stressed portion of the word. Words that end in syllabics[19] experience similar problems.

Table 3.2 shows some examples of words with unstressed syllables and the effect that syllable deletion has on the word.

As shown in the table, the word "erase" sometimes experiences syllable deletion. To understand this, say the word aloud—do not pronounce the first "e"

---

[17] A parametric system changes its behavior according to the setting of various parameters. Endpointing parameters include thresholds to distinguish speech from silence, timing parameters that determine how long to wait for various events, and filter parameters that measure the spectral components of the input.

[18] Schwa is the most common vowel in English. It is the unstressed "uh," such as the *a* in *about* or the *e* in *linen*. Variants include the back schwa, which sounds like "ih," such as the *i* in *debit*, and the retroflex schwa, which sounds like "er," as in *enter*.

[19] A syllabic is a short unstressed vowel-consonant syllable, such as the *on* in *button*.

long or with stress; instead, pronounce it like "a" in "alone." The short schwa is easily lost. When this happens, the stressed syllable—"rase"—is much closer to words such as "play" or "save," and the rate of substitutions and rejections increases. The same is true for the other words shown in the table.

Table 3.2—**UNSTRESSED SYLLABLES** such as schwa and syllabics are sometimes lost in the background noise when spoken over the telephone channel. The partial word that remains is the stressed portion of the word, as that portion is what the endpointer captures and delivers to the recognizer.

Syllable	Examples	Result of Deletion
Schwa	"Erase"	"... rase"
	"Reply"	"... ply"
	"Repeat"	" ... peat"
Back Schwa	"Credit"	"Cre ..."
Retroflex Schwa	"Enter"	"Ent ..."
Syllabic	"Cancel"	"Canc ..."
	"Transfer"	"Tran ..."

3.1.2.4.2   ≈ Consider the Effects of Embedded Silences

Polysyllabic words tend to exhibit superior recognition (see Guideline 3.1.2.1), but there is a downside as well. Words or phrases that have low-energy regions in the middle are more difficult to endpoint consistently. The phrase "Next Screen," for example, contains an embedded stop[20] followed by /s/ and another embedded stop, producing a region of low energy in the middle of the phrase. If the phrase is spoken quietly or slowly—or if the telephone channel is especially noisy—the endpointer will sometimes interpret the embedded silence as the end of the phrase. The result is that only a fragment of the input[21] is matched against the vocabulary, leading to illogical recognition results that are difficult to recover.

---

[20] A stop consonant—such as /t/ or /k/—temporarily stops airflow through the vocal tract.

[21] Utterances truncated by the endpointer are commonly referred to as "speech fragments."

3.1.2.4.3   ≈ Consider the Effects of Input-Channel Artifacts

Most of us have experienced the "breakup" of voice that occasionally occurs with mobile phone calls. A temporary loss of signal or variation in signal strength causes us to lose a portion or all of the caller's conversation. Similar events occur when cells[22] hand off the call, or when "squelch" circuits built into the telephone or the hands-free car kit cause temporary loss of speech. Such events affect the endpointer and all subsequent recognition, and the application is ill equipped to distinguish these events from other results returned from the recognizer.

The three preceding sub-guidelines are short introductions to endpointing errors.[23] The discussion is aimed at conveying an understanding of the subject that allows the designer to consider these issues, to the degree possible, when selecting vocabulary. It is not necessary to labor the subject, but it is true that some vocabulary words or phrases are more sensitive to endpointing errors than others. By understanding that endpointing is a separate process from recognition and can exhibit its own errors, the designer may be able to correct problems by changing the vocabulary.

3.1.3   Word-Pair Discrimination

A substitution error occurs when one word in the vocabulary is substituted for another. It is the most commonly measured form of speech recognition error. Indeed, the term "accuracy" is often interpreted as "raw substitution rate." Substitution errors have less to do with the acoustical discriminability of each word than with phonetic and statistical similarities between and across words. For this reason, the substitution rate varies greatly with vocabulary. Word pairs are often the culprit.

3.1.3.1   √ Avoid Word Pairs with Excessive Syllable- or Vowel-Sharing

The easiest word similarities to hear are those that involve shared syllables between words within the proposed vocabulary, as shown in Table 3.3. This is because consonant/vowel patterns across large time-scales are easier for humans to discern than are the minimal phonetic differences within syllables.

---

[22] Cellular telephone coverage areas are called "cells." When mobile phone subscribers move from one coverage area to another, their connection is handed off from one cell to another.

[23] Be aware that endpointing problems are exacerbated in mobile environments.

Words that share syllables do not necessarily exhibit severe recognition problems. The more important premise is that the word pair tends to exhibit similar recognition scores on average. This will result in an increase in inter-word rejection rates.

Table 3.3—**WORD PAIRS WITH SHARED SYLLABLES OR VOWELS** tend to experience higher inter-word rejection rates. Such pairs should be handled carefully, and one word of the pair should be replaced if tests indicate a problem and a replacement can be identified.

Word 1	Word 2
"Del<u>ete</u>"	"Rep<u>eat</u>"
"Back<u>up</u>"	"Hang-<u>up</u>"
"S<u>a</u>ve"	"Pl<u>ay</u>"

If the application is structured so that the user repeats the input whenever it encounters an inter-word rejection, then word pairs become a severe problem—even repeated instances of a given word will cause its counterpart to score closely as well. On the other hand, applications that use yes-no queries to resolve inter-word rejections fare better: the correct word is usually in first place and evokes a "yes" from the user. Even so, dialogues get bogged down if there are too many such queries.

3.1.3.2   + Consider Syllable-Dropping When Assessing Word Pairs

The discussion in Guideline 3.1.2.4.1 describes the conditions leading to the loss of unstressed syllables. Although it is not necessary to predict every possible condition, there are certain word pairs that suddenly materialize when unstressed syllables are dropped. Understanding this phenomenon allows these apparently inexplicable misrecognitions to make sense.

For example, many designers like to include the word "Cancel" in a yes-no question. The solution allows the user to back up on errors, turning the query into a three-way branch. The word seems to be very different from either "yes" or "no," and should not cause inter-word rejections or substitutions. However, as illustrated in Table 3.4, the endpointer will occasionally drop the syllabic "el" from the word "Cancel." The resulting speech fragment "Canc..." now shares a common vowel and /s/ with the word "yes." The result is an apparently random inter-word rejection between "Cancel" and "yes."

3.1.3.3 + Consider Using Asymmetrical Word Pairs

Avoid: "Go to beginning" and "Go to end"

"Turn on" and "Turn off"

Use: "Start over" and "Go to end"

"Activate" and "Turn off"

The first example uses the words "Go to beginning" and "Go to end" as a symmetrical word pair. This may be easier for the user to remember. But the pair experiences syllable sharing, thus violating Guideline 3.1.3.1. The corrected word pair introduces the most common synonym for one of these words—"Start over" replaces "Go to beginning." By using the asymmetrical alternative, the two words are much less likely to be confused.

Table 3.4—**WORDS WITH DROPPED SYLLABLES FORM WORD PAIRS** that increase inter-word rejection. Although the vocabulary words are dissimilar, when the unstressed syllable of one word is dropped, the two converge.

Word 1	After Syllable-Dropping	Word 2
"Erase"	"... rase"	"Paste"
"Cancel"	"Canc ..."	"Yes"
"Correct"	"... rect"	"Next"

Note that by violating the principle of parallel structure, this guideline may produce a net decrease rather than an increase in recognition performance—at least in some cases. This is because users may say, "Go to beginning" due to learning effects after using "Go to end."

Only testing can uncover problems with word pairs. So this guideline may be amended: "Where substitution errors exist, certain word pairs may benefit from an asymmetrical relationship." If there are no problems with a word pair, then this guideline is irrelevant.

3.1.3.4   + Keep Similar Pairs if They Are Likely to Be Spoken

OVW is typically a bigger problem than substitution. Error rates rise quickly if users say words that are not in the vocabulary. Because of this, any word that users are likely to speak must be in the vocabulary—even if that word has unfortunate capture or discrimination attributes.

Note that simple declarations of "likely to speak" are easy to make and hard to prove. The designer is encouraged to avoid such declarations. Rather, the designer should consider studies of this problem [Baber97b]. In addition, Wizard of Oz tests are good at uncovering user preferences and spontaneous speech behaviors.

3.1.3.5   √ Apply Back-End Information to Recover Substitutions

It may not be necessary to distinguish a confusable word pair as soon as it is detected. Sometimes context, history, and other extraneous information can gracefully disambiguate inter-word rejection. Thus inter-word rejection can be allowed to happen more frequently—meaning that the words can be allowed to remain in the vocabulary—if back-end logic can reliably resolve these rejections. Back-end logic refers to logic applied after the speech recognizer returns its results to the application. This logic may be based on the following questions:

- Is the function associated with either of the two words a destructive function that requires a yes-no question?
- Is one function more common than the other?
- Has one of the words been refused in the recent past?
- Does the user tend to select one choice more frequently than the other?

By relying on the answers to these and similar questions, a series of rules can sort through many instances of inter-word rejection. The result of these rules is to trigger yes-no questions, query on one choice preferentially before the other, or accept one choice outright.

The designer should be cautious about starting down this "expert system" path. There are many approaches to adding intelligence to speech applications. The goal is to make the application more responsive to what the user wants by considering more than the acoustically ambiguous information in the speech signal alone. However, adding intelligence brings its own risks, not the least of which is distinguishing between the sources of errors in a complex system.

3.1.3.5.1 √ Use *n*-Best to Determine When to Query

The *n*-best list contains two, three, or more recognition candidates. Back-end logic should look at these candidates along with extraneous contextual information to resolve inter-word rejections.

3.1.3.5.2 + Use Frequency-of-Use Data to Devise Querying Strategies

To the degree possible, accumulated statistics can be brought to bear when the application must incorporate word pairs that are acoustically similar. This includes how frequently certain functions can be expected, which functions tend to follow others, and similar statistics.

3.1.3.6 + Allow Toggling Word Pairs to Coexist

Certain word pairs constitute **toggles**—binary operations that switch the application into one of two states:

"On/Off"

"Start/Stop"

Understandably, speech scientists are uncomfortable with the acoustical similarities of these pairs. From a design point of view, however, these toggling pairs rarely constitute a problem. The reason is that the application is keeping track of the state of the system. It is therefore not important to distinguish between the two words—only to detect that one or the other has been spoken given the current state. Once one is detected, the application has only to toggle between states. Absolute performance in discriminating between the two words is irrelevant.

Note that these toggle words are often included in different active vocabularies. The assumption is that the word "On" should only be active if the state is "Off" and vice versa. The logic is faulty, however, as it assumes that the user will keep track of the current state. It is not unusual for users to turn something "On" that is already on—or to "Stop" something which is currently stopped.

For this reason, it is best to keep both words active. If the user says "On," then the recognizer may return either "On" or "Off" as its first choice. Even if illogical—that is, the word "On" has a higher score when the application state is already "On"—it is not necessary to query the user to recover the "error." The word "Off" is likely to appear as the second choice in the *n*-best list—and moreover, the confidence level for both words is likely to be low. After all, the purpose of inter-word rejection is to report "closeness" of recognition scores between two words.[24] Correct machine behavior is to toggle the state based on the detection of this word pair. Figure 3.1 shows pseudocode for this for word-pair toggling logic.

If it does become necessary to query the toggle state, it is important to avoid asking the user "what she said." As shown in the pseudocode, the user may have said another word. What matters is not so much what she said as it is what she **wants**. The query should be about the state of the application desired by the user:

Avoid: *Did you say, "On?"*
          Was that "Stop?"

Use: *Turn on call screening?*
          Do you want to stop the timer?

This principle is discussed in more detail in Guideline 6.2.3.4.

```
IF toggle-word appears in first place THEN
    IF toggle-word partner appears in second place THEN
        ignore recognition confidence /* rejection doesn't matter */
        accept input as unambiguous command
        toggle the application state;
    ELSEIF high confidence THEN   /* unrelated word in second place */
        accept input as unambiguous command /* word doesn't matter */
        toggle the application state;
    ELSE query on toggling action /* low confidence */
    ENDIF;
ENDIF;
```

Figure 3.1—**REJECTION LOGIC FOR TOGGLE WORDS** handles the word pair as a meaningful unit. Distinguishing between words is not so important if the task is well structured. Recognizers that do not return detailed rejection information cannot make these kinds of judgments.

Words such as "On" and "Off" are often used as gatekeeper words.[25] The user perceives that she is "turning the recognizer on or off." Obviously, the recognizer can

---

[24] Return to Section 1.3.1 if this is not clear.

[25] See Guideline 9.2.1.2 for a description of the "gatekeeper" function.

never actually be turned off, as it would then not hear the user's command to turn it back on. Instead, the application enters an attention or gatekeeper state, listening for the "On" command and discarding all other recognition results. In this case, additional logic must be added to the query shown above to determine if the application should respond to the toggle command. If the current state is a listening state, then rejected toggle words should be acted upon or queried. Alternatively—if the current state is a non-listening state—then the input should be ignored.

Some recognizers reject inter-word score violations automatically—without returning the *n*-best list to the application. The logic described in this guideline cannot be implemented with these recognizers. Rejection is a decision that should be made at levels higher than the current recognition state, and simple queries such as the ones described here are a strong argument for why the recognizer should never be allowed to make unilateral rejection decisions.

3.2   Consistency in Vocabulary Selection

3.2.1   Voice/Keypad Equivalents

Speech recognition interfaces often enhance and eventually replace DTMF keypads. This means that users have typically acquired DTMF skills and are then transitioned to speech technologies in a series of steps. To the degree possible, there should be a transfer of learning among existing users from their keypad experience to interacting with speech recognition.

3.2.1.1   + Choose Words that Map Mnemonically to Existing Keypad Commands

For many VRU applications, the 0 key is reserved for "operator," the 6 key or the *M key combination for "Main Menu," the H key or the *H combination for help, and other keypad commands are based on a mnemonic[26] reference to a meaningful word. If the pre-existing (legacy) system uses mnemonic keypad commands, it is important to ensure that spoken words correspond to the previously-learned mnemonics. Note that these considerations may be at odds with recognition accuracy considerations. Careful attention must be paid to the tradeoffs between the "best" word from a human factors or legacy user-skill perspective, and the "best" from a recognition accuracy perspective.

---

[26] A shortcut that's designed so that it's easy to remember. See the glossary and Section 2.5.3 for a more detailed description of "mnemonic."

3.2.1.2   + Avoid Key-Emulation Vocabularies

One of the values of using speech recognition is that the words have meaning. The meaning directs the user toward the end-goal of a task, presumably easing the burden of mapping functions onto actions. "Key emulation" words defeat this, leading to unnecessary difficulties for the user.

Avoid: "Star-Zero"
          "Enter" or "Return"
          "Star," "Asterisk," "Pound," or "Hash"

Use: "Operator"
          "Go ahead" or "Continue"
          "Play," "Record," "Redial," "Login," and "Start Over"

3.2.1.3   + Change Vocabulary When Accuracy Tests Expose Flaws

Usability labs often expose problems with vocabulary words. For example, the word "Return" was shown to perform poorly on Asian speakers in one such lab.[27] Similarly, the word "Next" has proven difficult for users to say consistently after a few repetitions, leading to recognition failures [Balentine87].[28] If such usability problems appear during testing, then recognition performance usually takes precedence over other considerations.

3.2.2   Parallel Structure and Consistency

Parallel structure and consistency principles—both within lists and from one part of a dialogue to another—attempt to simplify and organize the user's conception of available options. Note that this is easier said than done. There is a compelling case against user interface consistency as a design principle [Grudin89].[29] The designer is cautioned to avoid thoughtless consistency for its own sake. Rather, consistency guidelines represent a default design principle—reasonable in the absence of compelling arguments otherwise. Such arguments should be made through informed deci-

---

[27] This is an anecdotal report. Perhaps the problem was the production of the letter "R" by native Japanese in the test group.
[28] The word "Next" was used to move from state to state in a desktop multimedia spoken-language training application. Once its frequency of use was reduced, it became easily produced and useful again.
[29] The [Grudin89] article provides an engaging discussion on how assumptions about words that are charged with "good" connotations such as *consistency* often lead us away from, rather than toward, effective design.

sion, however, as the disregard for parallel structure leads to vocabularies that seem arbitrary or unpredictable to the user.

3.2.2.1 + Maintain Parallel Structure in Lists

As a general rule, lists should contain either all verbs or all nouns. Avoid mixing user input items. For example, consider the following menu list:

Account Balance

Fund Prices

Help

Return

Transfer

The first two menu items are nouns. The third item, *"Help"* could be viewed either as a verb—*"Help [me, please]"*—or as a noun—*"[give me] Help."* The last two items are verbs, as in *"Return [to the Main Menu],"* or *"Transfer [me to a Service Representative]."*

In this example, all items can be defined as nouns, replacing the last two items with the nouns *"Main Menu"* and *"Service Representative."*

In the following example—taken from the *WildFire*™ application—user input is sometimes an imperative instruction to the machine:

"Call."

"Remind me to call."

"Take a message."

At other times, user input is a statement of future actions:

"I'll take it."

"I will be …"

Note that parallel structure is a basic principle of strong writing, and, by logical extension, to effective speaking. Users presumably hear and comprehend parallel lists with less effort, enhancing understanding and clarifying machine intent. Nevertheless, it should be noted that this assumption has not been rigorously quantified experimentally. For this reason, style guidelines such as this are similar to other general rules for clear expression.

94

3.2.2.2   √ Maintain Consistency Between Input and Output Styles

When the machine presents spoken output, the user often adopts a similar structure and speaking style to respond to the machine prompt. This phenomenon is known as **convergence** [Baber97a].[30] The structure of valid input should take into account the wording of machine output prompts, as well as feedback and instructions. The following three sub-guidelines clarify this principle.

3.2.2.2.1   √ Avoid Unnecessary Use of "Synonyms" in Output

Avoid: *To <u>turn on</u> this service, say "Activate call waiting."*

Use: *To <u>activate</u> this service, say "Activate call waiting."*

In this example, the spoken machine output complicates the function unnecessarily by using "*turn on*" as a synonym for "*activate*."

Consider the following voice-dialing dialogue:

User: "Call."

App: *Name?*

User: "John Smith."

App: *Dialing …*

In the example, the user command verb "Call" is properly recognized and leads to a correct machine action. However, the application makes the mistake of presenting feedback with a different word—"*Dialing*" instead of "*Calling*"—thereby watering down the positive reinforcement that comes from success. The user is in danger of using the word "Dial" in subsequent interactions.

3.2.2.2.2   + Ensure the Recognizer Can Handle User Speech that Mimics the Style of the Machine's Output Speech

Many VRU applications today use colloquial or "lighthearted" spoken machine output aimed at personifying a glib and friendly agent. These applications provide feedback or confirmation messages like:

Sure.

You Bet!

---

[30] More commonly this manifests itself as the user mimicking or "parroting" the spoken machine output.

Yep.

Got it!

Such messages encourage the user to speak with similarly gay abandon when responding to the machine. Once the user presents this type of speech to the machine, many recognizers exhibit poor accuracy. When failures happen, the user may be understandably confused that the machine has different standards for machine output than for allowed user input.

3.2.2.2.3   + Avoid Output Speech that, if Mimicked by the User, Will Cause Recognition Problems

This guideline, similar to Guideline 3.2.2.2.2, is written in inverted form to ensure that the designer understands that decisions on spoken input vocabulary and spoken machine output are complementary and interdependent. Once the former results in final vocabulary decisions, then the latter must be adjusted to conform to the constraints established by speech recognition. Another way to put it is as follows: the machine must play by the same rules that it specifies for its user.

Chapter 4
Barge-In and Turn Taking

The term "barge-in" refers to the user's ability to speak while a prompt (or more precisely any spoken machine output) is being played. To make this possible, barge-in
employs echo cancellation technology that permits the recognizer to be active during
playback. Echo cancellation is accomplished by subtracting the returning machine
output (echo) from the input signal. In user interface terms, barge-in allows the user
to interrupt the prompt. Systems with and without barge-in exhibit very different
"look and feel" characteristics with regard to interface design. In particular, turn-
taking protocols differ fundamentally.

Applications that use barge-in are **full duplex**—that is, both the machine and user
may listen or speak at any given time. The turn-taking protocol in full-duplex interactions has the following characteristics:

- A long turn is taken by the machine.
- The user claims a turn arbitrarily by interrupting the machine.
- Because turns change infrequently, there are fewer interactions.
- It is easier for novices to learn.
- It is not subject to timing constraints.

Applications that do not employ barge-in are **half duplex**—that is, the machine and
user must listen and speak in alternation. The turn-taking protocol in half-duplex interactions has the following characteristics:

- Short turns are taken by both the machine and user.
- It requires quick recovery of turn-taking errors.
- If properly designed, turns can change frequently, resulting in more interactions.
- It is harder for novices to learn.

• It tends to be fastest for experts.

4.1 Implementing Barge-in

For barge-in to work, the user's speech input must be separated from the spoken machine output.[1] However, the speech signal received by the VRU is a combination of the user's speech, the machine prompt, the echo from the user, and the echo from the machine. Consequently, there are a number of technical considerations associated with barge-in that affect interface design.

4.1.1 What Is Echo Cancellation?

Echo is inherent in a communications network whenever speech is transmitted over a two-wire link. Typically the link that connects the user at home to the Local Exchange Carrier (LEC) has just two wires. Four wire links are used between central office switches and carry both sides of the conversation independently. A "hybrid" is used to connect the two wire and four wire links. The hybrid attempts to balance the impedance at this connection for each new call. When the impedance is not accurately matched, energy from the original signal is reflected back on the line, albeit highly attenuated.

The distance from the speech signal origin to the point of its conversion dictates the latency of the echo. If the conversion takes place within a nearby metropolitan area, the delay is typically under 8 ms. For rural areas, it can be as high as 30 ms. For a cross country analog circuit, the delay can be 120 ms. For a point to point four wire digital circuit there will be no echo.

Figure 4.1 shows some of the connections that might be present in the connection between a user and a VRU. The user typically has a two wire analog line (labeled A) to the local exchange carrier (LEC). Toll free numbers are typically serviced by an inter-exchange carrier (IXC), but may be serviced by the LEC if they terminate within that area (LATA[2]). The LEC usually provides echo cancellation to the user, while the toll free service provider will always provide echo cancellation when bringing the call on its digital network. Echo cancellation at the user's end of the circuit is called **far-end** echo cancellation (from the perspective of the VRU).

---

[1] Machine "prompts" and "spoken output" will be used interchangeably in this chapter.
[2] Local Access and Transport Area. A LATA is the geographic area assigned exclusively to each Baby Bell prior to the Telecommunications Act of 1995.

The call can be passed from an IXC to a competitive access provider (CAP), shown at points 3 and 4, and then to the VRU (at 5). With or without the CAP, line B is typically a digital T1 connection. If line B is a two-wire analog connection, it will create an attenuated echo of the machine output on the **near end**. In order for the speech recognizer to work, both near end and far end echo must be removed. It should be noted that this echo is not something that can be audibly detected, but it can have disastrous effects on the recognition performance.

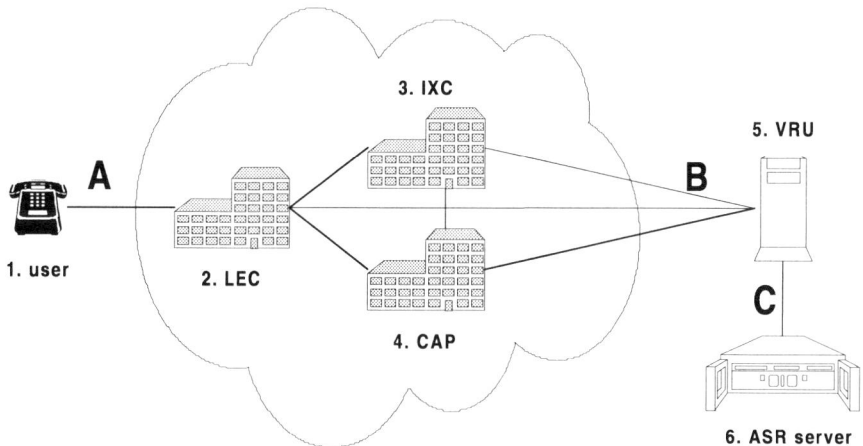

Figure 4.1—SOURCES OF ECHO in the public telephone network. Connection A from the user (point 1) to the local exchange carrier (LEC) is usually a two-wire analog circuit. The Local Exchange Carrier (LEC) (point 2) may pass the signal to an inter-exchange carrier (IXC) at point 3 and/or a competitive access provider (CAP) at point 4. Connection B from the network to the VRU is typically a T1. The VRU (5) then passes digitized speech to the recognizer (6) via LAN or T1 connection C.

4.1.2   Basic Problems with Echo Cancellation

The manner in which the user interacts with the machine from a turn-taking perspective is vastly different when barge-in is present or absent. This difference leads to significant look and feel differences between applications. The following are some of the important issues that must be addressed when considering full-duplex speech recognition interfaces.

4.1.2.1   Echo Cancellation Is Expensive

Echo cancellation is an expensive and difficult feature to implement for the following three reasons:

1. It consumes MIPS,[3] thereby requiring extra hardware,

2. It increases duty cycle,[4] thereby lowering channels-per-port density, and

3. It requires access to both incoming and outgoing speech samples.

Calculating the delay of the echo is a computationally intensive process. It requires significant MIPS from the host processor, or requires that special purpose hardware be associated with each voice channel. It also requires access to both the incoming and outgoing speech samples. The machine output must be accessible to compare it to the incoming voice channel to calculate the echo delay.

Echo cancellation is also expensive in that it requires speech recognition be active for a larger percentage of the call, and in most cases the entire call. Therefore more MIPS must be available for barge-in enabled applications. Stated another way, it results in a lower recognition channel-per-port density.

4.1.2.2   Certain Architectures Impede Echo Cancellation

Client/server architectures sometimes have a problem with accessing both incoming and outgoing speech samples. Specifically, architectures in which the VRU cannot perform echo cancellation and in which the recognizer relies on a client/server configuration present more challenges to accomplishing accurate echo cancellation. Referring again to Figure 4.1, line C between the VRU and ASR server is used to pass digitized speech. In this architecture the ASR server does not know when the machine output was played, and hence cannot effectively cancel the inbound echo. Such architectures often result in latency, causing a sloppy sense of time and rhythm during user interaction.

An alternative is to bridge line B into the ASR server using a digital T1 connection. However, the echo cancellation calculation will still be tainted by the fact that the ASR server does not know the exact instant in which the machine output was placed on the T1. This is masked by the length of the connections and any delay imposed by the physical bridge. It is therefore highly recommended that the echo cancellation calculation take place on the VRU. If that is not an option, then there are external

---

[3] Machine Instructions Per Second—a measure of computing power.
[4] See the glossary for a more detailed description of "duty cycle."

echo cancellation devices that can be placed between the VRU and the network connection to remove near end echo.

4.1.3   User Interface Issues with Barge-In

Problems associated with barge-in and turn taking impact menu design and vocabulary selection, requiring that the application designer adopt an explicit position on turn-taking protocols. Otherwise, the starting and stopping that constitute turn taking will be interpreted by the user and machine according to their own respective rules. When these rules conflict—particularly rules that govern timing and rhythm—it is not unusual for the two to battle over control of the dialogue. For example, the following dialogue is extracted from a usability lab that was acquiring baseline data for a demonstration stock trading system [Hersh98].

User: "Umm, I'd like to know, ahhh… "

App: *I'm sorr...*

User: "I'd like to know … the number of sh… "

App: *I'm...*

User: "I want to sell half my shares of Motorola. "

App: *I didn't understand.*

User: "I'd like to SELL … half my shares… "

App: *I didn ...*

User: "… of Motorola. "

App: *I didn't under...*

User: "I'd like to SELL … Motorola."

App: *I didn't understand.*

In this example, the user injects pauses in her speech. Some are the result of uncertainty and some are caused by the "stuttering effect" (explained below). Needless to say, the application did not stop the machine output quickly enough to suit the user. In each instance, the machine begins to respond, "*I didn't understand*"—aimed at conveying that the recognizer has rejected the input. The machine, of course, has no knowledge that the input is only part of a more complex request and that the user is pausing because of uncertainty regarding who has the turn. The user perceives this error-recovery message as a new machine turn, subsequently pausing. The machine meanwhile has heard the user's ongoing speech, and responds by interrupting with its own error message.

In an attempt to make herself more clearly understood, the user begins emphasizing the keyword "sell" (indicated by capital letters), perhaps assuming that the machine will hear and adjust. The recognizer in turn rejects this exaggerated user speech, leading to a runaway condition typical of error amplification. This example dialogue highlights many of the problems addressed in the following guidelines.

4.1.3.1   False Prompt Cutoff Due to Endpointer Errors

One inherent problem with barge-in is the false acceptance of sounds or unintentional speech as though it were legal speech. In this context, the user makes a sound that is not aimed at the recognizer. Alternatively, the recognizer detects a random background noise. Either way, the speech endpointer is triggered and reports the occurrence of the sound and the application immediately stops the machine output.

One problem with stopping machine output whenever the endpointer determines that the user may be speaking is that users lose their place in the dialogue when this "speech" input is not intentional.

False prompt cutoff typically results from the following:

- Background noises,
- Breath noises (breathing on the telephone handset),
- Coughs and throat clearings,
- Speech directed toward others in the vicinity, and
- Unconsciously muttering to self.

When the problem is background noise, the starting and stopping of machine speech is very confusing to the user, who doesn't understand why the machine "thinks that I said something," or worse, "suddenly stopped talking for no reason." Note that false prompt cutoff is more likely to occur when the caller is using a hands-free telephone in a noisy environment such as a car. Prompt cutoff also increases when the caller is using a public telephone or in public places such as airports.

When the problem is user speech that is not directed toward the machine, the user becomes confused that the machine cannot distinguish between willful intentional speech on the one hand and irrelevant speech on the other. In human factors terms, barge-in requires an **unnatural level of user attention** to remain silent when not intentionally speaking to the application. This requirement is difficult for the application to convey and equally difficult for the user to observe.

The speech endpoint detection algorithm is controlled with various thresholds:

- Thresholds that control loudness[5] sensitivity, and
- Thresholds that determine recognition confidence.

The former is aimed at minimizing prompt cutoff caused by distant sounds or low-energy noise. The latter is aimed at rejecting low confidence speech and out-of-vocabulary speech.

4.1.3.2   False Rejection of Valid Speech

When threshold parameters are not met, the speech recognizer rejects the input. Most of the time, this allows the machine to continue with its spoken output in the face of noise or illegal speech—that is, it prevents false acceptance. However, if the input is a legal vocabulary word then the opposite problem occurs—false rejection. In this condition, the machine refuses to recognize a legal utterance. This makes the machine appear to be "hard of hearing" or "deaf."

Users react by speaking loudly and exaggerating their speech when talking to a "deaf machine." Anger and extraneous speech often follow. Such speech is unlikely to be recognized, leading to a runaway condition known as **error amplification**.

4.1.3.3   Rejection Tradeoffs and Error Amplification

Threshold parameters represent tradeoffs between false acceptance and false rejection. There is no optimum setting that will eliminate both. If false acceptance of noise or illegal speech is a major problem, the thresholds should be "raised." This results in an increasing number of false rejections. If the thresholds are "lowered," the result is a reduction in false rejection at the expense of false acceptance.

Note that both conditions amplify user confusion and subsequent error. False acceptance terminates machine output and leaves the users in unknown states. These users tend to mutter or say words that are not legal for the current state. Conversely, false rejection causes users to repeat words. Presuming that the machine "didn't hear" or "didn't understand," the users speak more loudly, elongate their speech, or add syllables to the front and back of commands. This speech is even more likely to be rejected, leading to the appearance of failure on the part of the recognizer.

----

[5] Loudness or volume is a function of the energy of the received speech signal.

4.1.3.4   The Stuttering Effect

When the user is ready to interrupt the machine, she begins speaking. At this point the machine should stop speaking. If it does not, the user sometimes concludes that the machine "missed" part of the input. This causes the user to stop and then start again. By this time, the machine may have stopped the prompt. However, the user's starting-and-stopping is likely to be rejected by the recognizer as illegal speech. The machine then starts speaking again—perhaps to present an error message. However, the user has started again as well, causing the machine to stop again.

The effect of this user turn-taking behavior is the appearance of stuttering, in which the interrupting user starts and stops speech with the goal of synchronizing with the machine. The effect increases when the time required to stop the prompt exceeds 300 milliseconds or so. This means that single-syllable commands are relatively immune to stuttering input, while longer words or phrases begin to exhibit this problem. Natural language systems, in which the user is able to present entire sentences to the recognizer, are especially vulnerable to stuttering.

4.1.3.5   Lombard Speech

When people speak in a noisy environment, they distort their speech in certain predictable ways. Pitch goes up, certain syllables are stressed with greater energy, and the overall loudness is greater. A somewhat subtler version of this distortion occurs when the user speaks through machine output. If the telephone is handheld, the user must speak loudly enough to hear himself over the incoming prompt. If the telephone is hands-free, then the user speaks loudly enough (in the user's opinion) for the machine to "hear" through the background noise.

The specific distortions of the vocal tract—and hence the resulting acoustical signal—caused by speaking while concurrently hearing speech, noise, or both is known as Lombard speech.[6] The effect is pronounced in extremely noisy environments, but can influence speech recognizers in a more subtle manifestation when users speak while hearing a prompt. The user who is thinking about "stopping the prompt" does the same thing as humans do when interrupting each other—increasing the loudness of stressed syllables to "get the attention" of the interlocutor.[7] Although the effect is

---

[6] A detailed discussion of Lombard speech is beyond the scope of this book. See [Markowitz96], [Stanton88], or [Schmandt94] for more complete technical discussions.

[7] Note that many users speak at syntactic junctures, which may be viewed as natural turn-taking junctures [Heins97]. Such users do not exhibit this Lombard effect because they do not perceive themselves as interrupting. Rather, they perceive that the machine is yielding its turn

not as great when interrupting in normal-volume environments as it is when the user is speaking in high background noise, this version of the Lombard effect is still enough to impact recognition performance. Note that the user returns to a normal speaking style once the machine prompt stops playing—presumably because the user perceives that the machine has yielded the turn. This means that long input phrases such as those used in natural language sentences exhibit Lombard effects for the first few syllables only.

4.1.3.6   Discouraging "Talk Ahead"[8] Behavior

Talk ahead allows the user to provide spoken input for current and subsequent machine states. Users familiar with the "key ahead" feature[9] in DTMF applications might expect talk ahead to be available in speech-enabled applications. For example, when using key ahead, users can key in their account number and then their PIN without waiting for the prompt to enter the PIN. When using talk ahead, the user may try to enter multiple pieces of information (tokens),[10] and be thwarted.

App: *Please state your six-digit account number.*

User: "123456 ... 1234."

App: *Your account number must be six digits.*

Please repeat your account number.

There are several reasons why talk ahead should not be supported. Most recognition technologies have an optimized grammar for each machine state. The recognition results from the user's spoken input then trigger the next machine action and subsequent grammar. When the user talks ahead and combines input from two states, this introduces several problems.

The first problem is that the end of spoken input is determined by an endpointer that detects a silence interval, usually less than a half second. Pauses between spoken input intended for two states may or may not trigger the endpointer, as shown in the following example.

---

and that they are accepting this proffered change of turn.

[8] The ability to provide spoken input for the next state before the application has requested it. See the glossary for a detailed description of "talk ahead."

[9] The ability to enter DTMF for the next state before the application has requested it. See the glossary for a detailed description of "key ahead."

[10] A term used in this book to refer to the smallest unit of input that is meaningful to the application. See Chapter 8 for details.

App: *Please say your six-digit account number.*

User: "123456 ... 12."

App: *Please ...*

User: "34."

App: *Your PIN must contain at least four digits.*

  Please repeat your PIN.

The second problem is that recognition applications incur latency after the end of spoken input and while the recognizer is making its decision. In the worst case this should be no more than two seconds.[11] While the recognizer is processing the current input, the application may not be listening for subsequent input. It might be technically feasible to do so, but any new user input will have to be queued and processed after the recognizer returns its results and proceeds to the next state. Care must be taken when creating queues of spoken input, as a user could create a very large queue, intentionally or otherwise, which could seriously degrade system performance.

Finally, if the application designer wishes to allow talk ahead, then the complexity of the grammar will increase, and recognition accuracy is likely to be compromised. Therefore, the best approach to allowing multiple token input is to reformulate the application using natural language (NL). This will flatten the menu structure and allow both single token and multiple token input, as described in Chapter 8.

4.1.4 Three Approaches to Stopping Prompts

There are three approaches for detecting user input and deciding to terminate the machine prompt. They are based on energy detection, speech detection and word detection. Energy detection is the simplest approach, but is more susceptible to false acceptance. Speech detection analyzes the user input to determine if it has speech-like properties, typically waiting for one or two confident syllables before concluding that the input is legal. Word detection relies on the final decision of the speech recognizer, waiting for the user to finish speaking and then stopping machine output only after confident recognition of legal speech. The advantages and disadvantages of each approach are discussed below.

---

[11] See the Appendix for a detailed discussion of how to provision sufficient hardware to ensure a reasonable recognition latency.

4.1.4.1   Option 1: Stop Prompt on Energy Detection

It would seem appropriate to stop the prompt immediately after the endpointer detects energy above some required threshold, as shown in Figure 4.2. Such machine behavior has the best chance of properly recognizing user input. This is because the input signal is likely to suffer the least from distortions induced by barge-in and by user interruption effects such as Lombard speech. This option is also the most responsive of the solutions, as the machine stops speaking as soon as the user starts.

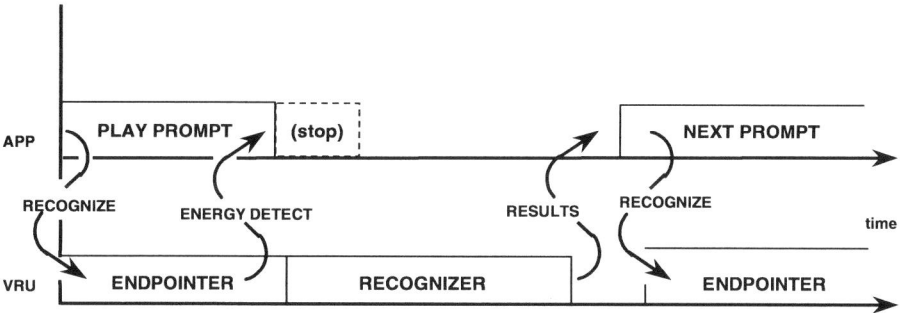

Figure 4.2—**STOPPING THE PROMPT ON ENERGY DETECTION** is the simplest approach. After initiating prompt playback, the application activates echo cancellation and endpointing. When the endpointer detects energy—presumably the onset of user speech—it reports this fact to the application, which immediately stops prompt playback. Upon conclusion of user speech the recognized result is reported to the application which then interprets it and presents the next prompt in the dialogue.

However, this solution increases false acceptance, as the machine stops speaking whenever it hears a noise and before it can determine recognition confidence. As shown in Figure 4.2, the prompt stops immediately—well before the speech recognizer can distinguish between noise, illegal speech, and confident legal results. This false rejection is fatal if it occurs often, for example in harsh environments.

Advantages:

• Increases recognition accuracy by limiting the distortion caused by barge-in to the first syllable of user speech (in most cases).

• Minimizes exaggerated user speech caused by the Lombard effect.

• Minimizes the stuttering effect.

Disadvantages:

- Increases false acceptance of background noise, as the recognizer does not have time to make a confident decision before the prompt is stopped.

- It is too sensitive to false starts, user coughs, and disfluencies.[12]

- Requires an increase in the number of yes-no queries in order to recover rejections (near-misses) aimed at avoiding false acceptance. This impedes the dialogue flow.

4.1.4.2   Option 2: Stop Prompt on Confident Word Detection

An alternative solution is to allow the recognizer to match a word (or sub-word) before deciding to stop the machine prompt. This is an especially attractive option if the application targets noisy environments—expecting, for example, a large number of wireless calls including hands-free calls within an automobile. Noisy environments make Option 1 unacceptable.

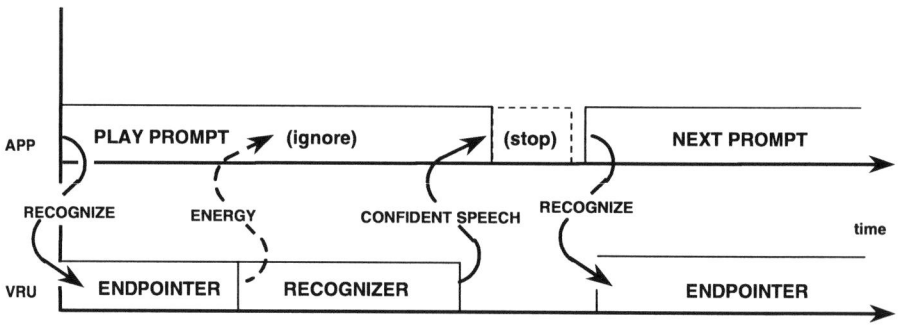

Figure 4.3—**STOPPING THE PROMPT ON WORD DETECTION** is the most reliable method for eliminating extraneous noises while responding to legal speech.

Advantages:

- Minimizes false acceptance problems, making the system more robust in noisy or uncontrolled environments.

- Reduces the need for yes-no questions to recover rejections, making the dialogue flow more effectively with fewer annoying user interruptions.

Disadvantages:

- Increases false rejections, leading to error amplification.

---

[12] "Umh" and "er." Such utterances appear more often at the beginning of the input phrase. Refer to the glossary to contrast the similar terms *disfluency* and *back channel*.

- Reduces recognition accuracy due to barge-in distortions, Lombard speech, and user-interruption stress.

- Increases the stuttering effect on multiple word utterances.

4.1.4.3   Option 3: Stop Prompt After Speech Detection

Many recognition technologies offer an improved "speech detection" enhancement that is aimed at ameliorating the problems described above. These enhancements attempt to distinguish background noise from speech during the first syllable or so of input—sometimes relying on features that are used for recognition to test against various noise models. Once the input passes these initial tests the VRU reports this to the application, which in turn stops the prompt. The speech detection algorithm may be implemented in either the endpointer or in the recognizer.

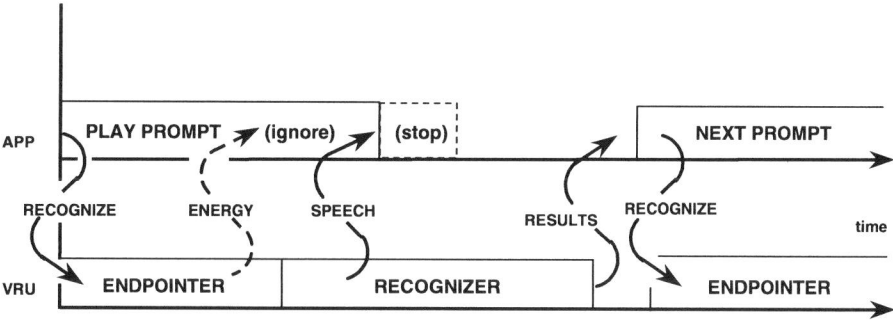

Figure 4.4—STOPPING THE PROMPT BASED ON THE FIRST SYLLABLE or so of input is an effective compromise for barge-in.

The process usually makes a speech detection decision within 150 to 300 milliseconds, quickly enough to minimize or eliminate the stuttering effect. However, the time required to decide between speech and noise—that is, the latency between onset of user speech and the stopping of machine playback—is variable. In addition, the technique is not very effective at rejecting disfluencies and illegal speech; so the application will still be sensitive to false acceptance of conversational background and other non-user speech.

Advantages:

- Minimizes false acceptance problems caused by non-speech background noise.

- Reduces but does not eliminate the stuttering effect.

Disadvantages:

- Still sensitive to illegal speech.

- Latency in stopping machine playback makes the turn-taking behavior between user and machine less predictable, slowing the dialogue.

4.2 Choosing a Turn-Taking Protocol

Using barge-in is not an "automatic" decision: there are sound reasons for deciding against a full-duplex turn-taking protocol. Many designers choose instead to rely on a well-designed half-duplex solution. Their reasons may include simplicity, stability, and lower cost. It is a popular misconception that barge-in—perhaps because it is an advanced and sophisticated technology—is intrinsically superior and should always be incorporated into spoken interfaces. In fact, as with all technologies, barge-in is one element in the designer's palette—appropriate only under certain conditions and only when properly applied.

After choosing a turn-taking protocol, it is equally important to implement the solution effectively. This means understanding the ramifications of when the user is allowed to speak, and designing the interface in such a way that this protocol is a well-understood and useful feature rather than an awkward and arbitrary annoyance that holds the user back.

4.2.1   Full Duplex or Half Duplex?

The following guidelines provide suggestions for deciding whether to use barge-in to manage turn taking. Be aware there are many exceptions to these "rules," so none of the guidelines are required. They are here to assist the designer in this important and complex decision.

4.2.1.1   + Use Barge-In if Most Users Are One-Time Callers

The spontaneous turn-taking behavior of most users is to interrupt the machine prompt—not at arbitrary points, but as a dovetailing[13] action toward the end of phrases at natural syntactic junctures [Heins97]. Half-duplex protocols do not support this behavior, and therefore tend to be more formal. As such they require more skill

---

[13]When one speaker begins just as another is finishing, there is a moment when both are speaking. This "dovetail" (after the term used for interlocking joints in woodworking) is a graceful part of conversation and is not considered interruption in the same sense as DTMF key through.

to navigate. If the application tends to receive a high proportion of first-time/only-time callers, then there is no opportunity to acquire and practice this skill. Such applications should probably use barge-in.

4.2.1.2   + Use Barge-In if Spoken Machine Output Is Unavoidably Long

There are certain cases when it is not possible to dictate the duration of spoken machine output. One obvious example is the voicemail system that plays messages that have been recorded by an outside caller. Synthesized speech presenting e-mail or web browsing text is a similar example. These messages may be minutes in duration. If possible, all applications that present unavoidably long spoken machine output should use barge-in, allowing user interruption of the audio.[14]

4.2.1.3   + Avoid Barge-In in Noisy Environments

High background noise—especially intermittent noise that varies in intensity—causes frequent false interruptions of full-duplex dialogues. In cases where the noise is always present, such interruptions occur so often that the turn-taking benefits of barge-in are lost. The user is constantly hearing prompts, followed by inappropriate pauses, yes-no queries, false recognitions, or declarations that the machine "didn't understand" (an all-too-common result of out-of-grammar (OOG) responses to the noise). Rarely can the user find a reasonable rhythm for interacting with a full-duplex system in noise. Applications that expect to be exposed consistently to noisy environments should implement half-duplex methods, which tend to be more robust in noise.

4.2.2   Creating Speaking Opportunities

4.2.2.1   √ Use Short Phrasings for Spoken Machine Output

It is a common design mistake to allow the presence of barge-in to justify verbose and unstructured machine speech. Spoken machine output should <u>always</u> be crafted with short, clear sentences—and should include frequent intervening pauses to encourage the user to speak at natural turn-taking junctures—regardless of whether the application is half or full duplex.

---

[14] See Guideline 4.4.1.4 for an alternative method of interrupting long machine output in the case of half-duplex turn-taking protocols.

4.2.2.2 ≈ Make Use of Recognition Windows

A specific method—just beginning to appear in some speech applications—is called **windowing.**[15] In this method, the user is given a turn via the presence of a "window" of silence. Expert users speak at this juncture to speed up the application. Users that don't speak are then prompted with the customary commands.[16]

If there is sufficient use of windowing, then more users will tend to take their turn during a window rather than during a spoken machine prompt. This will likely increase the percentage of correct first-attempt recognition and reduce false rejection in full-duplex systems. It will provide "breakout" capabilities for jumping ahead or moving back in half-duplex systems.

Because users get to take their turns more frequently, they will also—on average— tend to speak less often during prompts. This will decrease the frequency of false acceptance. In addition, with more frequent short prompts, false acceptance and subsequent prompt termination will be less offensive.

It is also possible to add a short prompt to the front of each recognition window, thereby encouraging formal turn taking. The predicted effect of these recommendations is to relegate barge-in to its more natural utility—supporting the dovetailing of machine and user speech while discouraging aggressive user interruption of long prompts.

Note that these windows are sometimes silence pauses embedded within a prompt— the echo cancellation algorithm is still running—while at other times they are explicit opportunities to speak with no echo cancellation in operation. Choosing between the two and understanding the human dynamics of spoken turn taking is a major design challenge and should be addressed quite early in the design and development process. With care, the functional differences between full- and half-duplex interactions can be minimized.

---

[15] Windowing applies to half-duplex systems in which a window of silence (typically one second or less) is inserted between prompts while the recognizer is turned on. See the glossary for a detailed description of windowing.

[16] See Guideline 6.2.1.3 for details. For a discussion of the application of windowing for implicit yes-no confirmations, see Section 6.3.3. For details on hidden menus, see Section 6.2.5. For a discussion of windowing in the context of landmarks, see Sections 5.3.3 and 6.2.1.3.

112

4.2.2.3   + Avoid the "Now" Word

Although some application designers prefer to use the word "now" to trigger user speech, it has little or no effect at reducing spoke-too-soon errors.[17] There are better solutions—so the value of the "now" word is not great enough to justify the resulting incompatibility between half- and full-duplex systems. Because it is a turn-taking cue, the "now" word can be thought of as a "beep in speech clothing."

4.2.2.4   + Support "Point and Speak" Features

There are cases in which a user may wish to indirectly select an item from a list. This is accomplished by speaking a word that refers to list elements previously presented by the machine. As shown in Figure 4.5, such demonstrative words "point at" specific list elements.

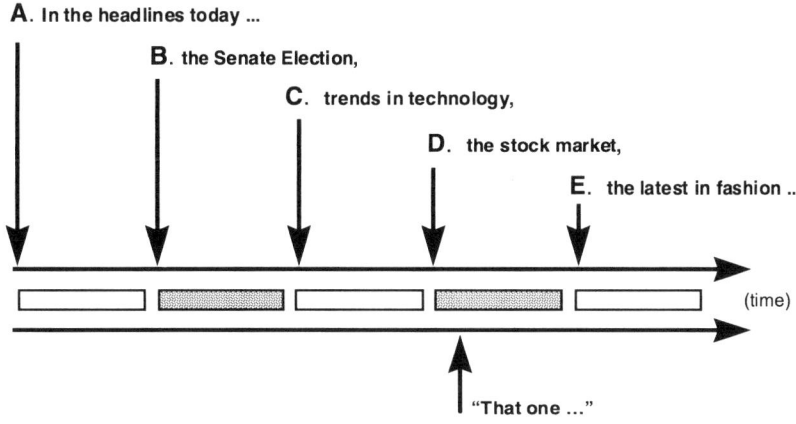

Figure 4.5—POINT AND SPEAK FEATURE requires attention to the timing of both machine output and user input. Although the application keeps track of the beginning and ending of each element in a sequence of choices—much like in menu designs—the user's decision and subsequent utterance may lag the prompt. In the example, the user's utterance "that one" misses its target. The user may have selected item C, but speech appears during the early part of item D.

Pointing words may include:

"That one."

"I'd like to know more about that."

---

[17] Section 1.3.2 discusses spoke-too-soon errors.

"OK."

The following example is from an early demonstration prototype:[18]

Female Voice:	*Please select one of the following...*
Male Voice:	*News ... Sports ...*
User:	"That one."
Female Voice:	*Do you want sports?*
User:	"Yes."
Female Voice:	*Today's sports...*

In the example, all spoken machine output relies on a female voice except for the listing of vocabulary words, which are spoken in isolation by a male voice. The principle of using an alternate voice as a "model user" is discussed in more detail in Guideline 2.1.2.3.4. Both examples are from the same prototype, and both move the user to the same sports selection. In the previous example, however, the user repeats the vocabulary word—"Sports"—and moves directly to the sports menu. In this example, the user points at the selection with a demonstrative reference—"That one"—requiring that the application infer which of the menu selections is intended. Figure 4.5 shows a timeline that demonstrates the relationship between machine speech and user reaction times.

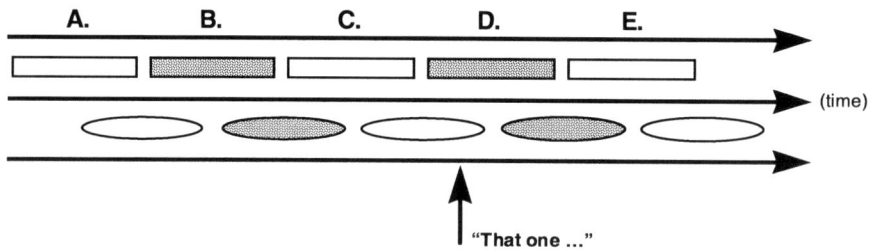

Figure 4.6—FULL DUPLEX POINT AND SPEAK compensates for delayed selection decisions represented by the illustration in Figure 4.5. In this example, the user has heard, chosen, and then selected item C. Although item D is currently being presented, the lagged temporal window (ovals) correctly determines the user's selection. This approach necessitates barge-in.

---

[18] See Guideline 2.1.2.3.4 for the citation.

It is important to understand that the recognizer need not recognize the phrase, "That one." The reason is that no useful information is contained in the **meaning** of the phrase—rather, it is the **timing** that matters. Even a human, upon hearing the phrase, "That one," would have to search backward for an antecedent to understand what the user wants. By noting the moment of speech onset, on the other hand, the application can respond appropriately to a number of otherwise meaningless responses, including OOG, spoke-too-soon, and inter-word rejections. This means that the application can make intelligent decisions about user intent without having to recognize all possible inputs.

Like the "point and click" user behavior supported by WIMP interfaces,[19] the use of spontaneous utterances to select elements in a running list can be viewed as a "point and speak" action. The method requires that the application keep track of time—both the time at which the machine speaks each list element and the time at which the user responded to machine output. The problem of delayed responses is shown in Figure 4.5. A full duplex solution—shown in Figure 4.6—uses lagged response windows to compensate for the delay. A half-duplex solution that is almost as effective is shown in Figure 4.7.

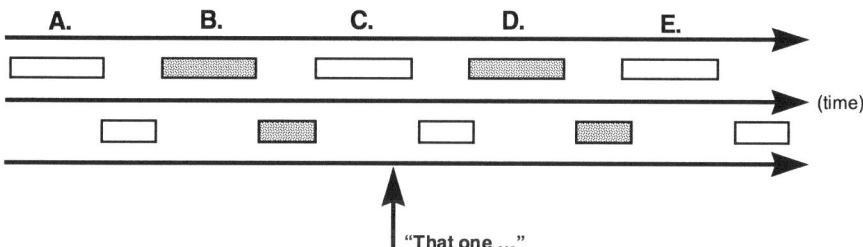

Figure 4.7—**HALF DUPLEX POINT AND SPEAK** replaces the overlapping (lagged) windows of Figure 4.6 with slightly elongated delays between each list element. The method is most effective when spoken choices (top row) are short. The bottom row shows recognition windows of roughly one-second duration. User speech typically produces spoke-too-soon conditions or speech that does not conclude before the window is closed. Such occurrences are no problem, however, as the application can query on the preceding element—in this case item C. The design allows a half-duplex interface to simulate the interruption capabilities of barge-in.

---

[19] Windows, Icons, Menus, and Pointing device.

4.3   Implementing Full-Duplex Designs

Given the problems discussed above, several tradeoffs become important when implementing a barge-in system. These tradeoffs impact vocabulary selection and other design issues.

4.3.1   Timing and Implementation of Barge-In

The following are technical issues associated with adaptive echo cancellation that have relevance to port densities, user behaviors, and other application issues.

4.3.1.1   + 8 ms Window Sufficient for Local Delay

An 8-millisecond window is sufficient to calculate delays due to near end echo. This specification may be applied to calculations regarding the number of taps in the inverse filter constructed to remove the echo and other compute-resource decisions.

4.3.1.2   √ Estimation of Near End Must Be Dynamic

Network components are responsible for dynamically canceling network delay. The network continually adjusts the echo parameter for these far-end echo cancellation processes—an adaptive method that allows maximum attenuation of the changing routing conditions within the public switched telephone network. Whatever the residual delay—even if it's just two to four milliseconds—that echo impacts the echo observed on the near end.

The implication of this effect is that estimation on the near end must also be performed dynamically—the network keeps changing so it is not as simple as measuring the delay once and then keeping that calculation throughout a given call. This is especially true for mobile users, whose call will be rerouted after each cell handoff.

4.3.1.3   √ Prompt Cutoff in Under 300 ms

Users that begin speaking do so with the intention of interrupting the machine—and therefore speak with the expectation that the machine will yield to this turn-taking interruption. When user speech is detected the prompt must stop playing, as discussed in Section 4.1.4.

The maximum delay from the start of user speech to the cutoff of the machine prompt should be under 300 milliseconds. If spoken machine output continues beyond this delay, the user is likely to stutter—starting and stopping speech in an attempt to synchronize turn taking with the machine.

It is therefore obvious that the recognizer must process speech in increments far smaller than 300 ms. This implies that the VRU must collect and analyze speech at these smaller increments. Care should be taken to ensure the VRU can handle this data transfer rate and that machine output can be stopped by an external process.

4.3.2   Techniques for Stabilizing Barge-In

The most appealing choice for stopping the prompt is to wait until the recognizer is confident in its results. This means that the application must be stabilized through additional techniques aimed at minimizing the disadvantages for each option discussed above.

4.3.2.1   √ Design Prompts that Encourage Natural Turn Taking

There are several techniques associated with prompt design that control the user's behavior regarding when to begin speaking. The specific guidelines are discussed in Chapter 2, cross-referenced here for convenience. Techniques include but are not limited to the following:

- Phrase prompts in such a way as to deposit "key information" at appropriate locations in the prompt (Guideline 2.3.1.2). The goal is to cause users to speak just as the prompt is ending. This will result in a natural dovetailing between machine and user.

- Organize prompts into short and meaningful phrases that encourage interaction (Guidelines 2.1.5.2, 2.3.1.1, and 2.5.1.2), causing users to speak frequently.

- Add pauses at natural locations within a given prompt sequence, encouraging the user to gracefully interrupt during silences (Guidelines 2.1.5.3 and 2.7.1.1).

- Manage prosody (stress and inflection) of prompts to increase the clarity of turn-taking cues (Sections 2.3.4 and 2.7).

- Control machine verbosity with various intelligent algorithms (e.g., more talkative for novices and less talkative as users become expert).

- Attend carefully to the progressive disclosure of information (Guideline 2.6.1.5).

4.3.2.2   + Bias Parameters Against False Acceptance

Raise threshold parameters to bias barge-in in favor of rejecting rather than accepting speech. Occasional false rejection is more likely to be recovered when the user encounters a pause and speaks more naturally. This should "damp" error amplification.

False acceptance, on the other hand, is more likely to result in confused users and subsequent error amplification due to state errors.[20]

4.3.2.3 √ Test Explicitly for Turn-Taking Problems

It is important to develop usability tests for turn taking as early as possible in the application design to uncover barge-in problems. Note that these timing behaviors may not appear in Wizard of Oz[21] testing and therefore are not usually discovered until field trials.

4.3.2.4 Predicted Result if Guidelines Are Followed

The following are **assumptions** that represent the predicted effect of the preceding guidelines. These behaviors can and should be measured. The application developer is encouraged to institute procedures aimed at testing these predictions as early as possible in the development cycle.

1. By the time a user begins speaking, the prompt will already be ending.[22] Users will perceive that it is their natural turn to talk.

2. Users will not perceive that they are claiming their turn arbitrarily by interrupting the prompt. They will therefore not perceive that they must "speak up" to be heard by the machine.

3. The beginning of user speech will thus naturally dovetail with the ending of machine speech.

4. On average, user speech will be more natural, falling more often within the vocabulary training statistics. Out-of-vocabulary word (OVW) and OOG utterances will go down. Recognition accuracy will go up.

5. Because prompts are short—and because users are given ample opportunity to speak—users will feel less impatient to "get on with it" by brusquely interrupting the prompt. Non-speech breath noises and sighs, as well as OVW muttering and "asides" will decrease, reducing false acceptance.

6. Users will tend to listen rather than make noise during short prompts.

7. The statistical likelihood that a spurious background noise will appear during machine output will decrease if the percentage of time the machine spends talk-

---

[20] See Section 1.2.2 for a discussion of state errors.

[21] Wizard of Oz testing enables the developer to test a potential application with a user without having to build the application. See the glossary for a detailed description of this so-called "WoZ" testing.

[22] This follows inevitably if prompts are kept short and succinct.

ing is significantly reduced.

8. Throughput will go up if the percentage of time that the user spends talking is significantly increased.

4.3.3   Suppressing Barge-In for Legal Reasons

There are two machine actions that might be required for legal reasons. The first is forcing playback of certain messages to ensure that the user has heard them. This means in effect turning off barge-in to prevent the user from interrupting these messages. The second is confirming certain transactions with DTMF rather than speech. Both such forced actions have the same goal—either to eliminate error or to protect against the future claim of misunderstanding or not hearing the intended message.

4.3.3.1   + Consider Accepting Interruption and Explaining Legal Obligation

This guideline is aimed at helping with the turn-taking problem caused by playback of legally obligatory data. Such behavior causes a negative learning effect in the user, who is suddenly incapable of interrupting prompts. This in turn discourages prompt interruption at future turn-taking junctures, and leads to superstitious assumptions. The user understands, "Sometimes the machine can hear me and sometimes it can't," but doesn't really understand why. Such users may speak more loudly or aggressively.

In the example below, the application is presenting obligatory data when the user begins speaking. The machine has two options. It can either accept input or ignore it. If it ignores it—turning off barge-in—the following may transpire:

Avoid:

App: *<extended explanation of some obligatory item>*

User: "I need a … I need a quote on Microsoft options … I said QUOTE ON MICRO …. HELLO?"

App: *<still continuing with obligatory output>*

In the example, the machine ignores the user. The user stutters after the first phrase due to the expectation that the machine prompt will stop. When it doesn't, the user proceeds with spoken input. This behavior then amplifies unproductively.

Note that the goal of forcing the user to hear legally obligatory data has not been achieved—the user has not heard the message due to preoccupation with getting the machine's attention.

119

An alternative approach allows the user to interrupt the machine at all times. Certain conditions then require that the machine reclaim its turn and continue with the legally obligatory data:

Use:

App: *<extended explanation of some obligatory item>*

User: "I need ...."

App: *<stop output>*

User: "... a quote on Microsoft options."

App: *Thank you. But before we continue, you must hear this message ...*

Other phrasings may include:

Regulations require that you hear this information in its entirety.

Please wait until this important legal message is complete.

4.3.3.2   ≈ Consider Relying on DTMF for Legal Responses

See Guideline 7.2.4.1 for details on DTMF confirmations.

4.4   Implementing Half-Duplex Designs

In half-duplex designs, the machine takes a turn and then the user takes a turn—the recognizer cannot be active during spoken machine output. This means that alternating between machine speech and user speech is necessarily more formal. Turn-taking errors often dominate half-duplex interactions, making turn taking a major design consideration.

Half-duplex designs are often a requirement in small, high-density VRU applications for which barge-in is too expensive to consider. They are also a cost-effective solution for embedded applications such as voice-dialing or other applications that are built into local car kits or telephones. Finally, designers may wish to consider falling back on a half-duplex design when excessive noise is causing false acceptance problems in a full-duplex application.

4.4.1   Managing Turn Taking

4.4.1.1   √ Give the User Frequent Turns

When the machine is presenting information in a half-duplex application, then by definition the user is powerless to claim a turn. This means that the VRU can easily dominate the conversation, preventing the user from correcting even well understood and simple errors. It is therefore up to the machine to give speaking opportunities to the user. This should happen frequently.

4.4.1.2   + Use Tones as Turn-Taking Cues

The most common cue for turn taking is a tone or "beep." It is easily heard, and represents a protocol that is easily learned and followed. See Chapter 5 for more suggestions.

4.4.1.3   √ If Tones Are Not Available, Use Caution with Prompt Timing

Some applications cannot or choose not to use tones. In such cases,

* The turn-taking cue may not be obvious, and

* Spoke-too-soon recovery prompts have difficulty explaining the timing problem.

These two problems mean that spoke-too-soon conditions will be more difficult to recover, and therefore must be aggressively prevented. There are three particularly important techniques for handling this circumstance. These guidelines appear elsewhere but are here cross-referenced for convenience.

1.   Keep prompts short (Guideline 2.1.1.1 and 2.3.4.2).

2.   Put key information at the end of the prompt (Guideline 2.3.1.2).

3.   Trim prompts aggressively (Guideline 2.1.4.2).

4.4.1.4   √ Consider DTMF Interruption if Extended Output Is Unavoidable[23]

There are certain cases when it is not possible to control the duration of spoken machine output. One obvious example is the voicemail system that plays messages that have been recorded by an outside caller. Synthesized speech presenting e-mail or web browsing text is a similar example. Such messages may be minutes in duration. In a half-duplex interface, the user is powerless to interact during this message playback.

---

[23] See Section 7.2.2 for a detailed discussion of DTMF interruption methods.

If the application must be half duplex and there is no control over message duration, then the user should be provided with an alternate modality—keypress, DTMF, or similar input—that allows interruption. After pressing a key to interrupt, the application should then present a menu or similar message that returns control to the user. Note that another more complex alternative is to design a "Message Player" interface that inserts interruption windows into the message itself.

4.4.2   Recovering Spoke-Too-Soon Errors

4.4.2.1   √ Recover Spoke-Too-Soon Errors Quickly

A spoke-too-soon error is a short "stumble" that is a natural consequence of user turn taking. It should not be treated as a complex problem that requires extensive coaching. In fact, the user should be allowed to speak again as soon as possible after the spoke-too-soon.

Avoid:

App: *Is the number correct? <beep>*

User: (interrupting the beep) "Yes."

App: *I'm sorry, I didn't understand.*
         Please wait for the tone, and then say "yes," "no," or "cancel."
         Is the number correct? <beep>

User: "Yes."

In the example above, the user replies—correctly—to a yes-no query. Although the spoke-too-soon indicates a turn-taking error, the application presents additional, irrelevant information. Specifically, the application "helps" the user with the vocabulary—a problem that the user does not have and that a spoke-too-soon condition does not imply.

Better:

App: *Is the number correct? <beep>*

User: (interrupting the beep) "Yes."

App: *Remember to wait for the tone.*
         Is the number correct <beep>?

User: "Yes."

In the second example, the application helps only with the problem at hand—a reminder that the tone is the cue to speak. This is better because it is shorter.

Best:

App: *Is the number correct? <beep>*

User: (interrupting the beep) "Yes."

App: *<beep> <beep> <beep>*

User: "Yes."

In the third example, the application uses non-speech audio to cue the user that the machine was not ready. This solution is even shorter than spoken feedback. Users learn to respond to such cues quickly—within their first-use session [Balentine97]. In the example, the user repeats "yes" after hearing the triple beep.[24]

4.4.2.2   √ Have Re-Prompt Focus on Repetition

A turn-taking error is just that—the user took her turn before the machine was ready. There is no reason to assume that any other error exists. For this reason, the user should be encouraged to repeat exactly what was just said. This repetition should occur while the input remains in the user's short-term memory and before any other speech appears. By focusing on repetition, most turn-taking stumbles can be recovered quickly and gracefully—repetition is an easy thing for a user to do.

Here is an example turnaround[25] prompt from a voice dialing application:

User: "Call."

App: *Name? <beep>*

User: (interrupting the beep) "John Smith."

App: *Again? <beep>*

User: "John Smith."

Such "repetition" prompts include:

---

[24] The beep need not be offensive. A triple beep—much like the "time is up" cue on the television game show *Jeopardy*™—is quite effective. Other sounds include short buzzers or simply repetitions of the prompting tone itself. See Chapter 5 for a more detailed discussion of sound qualities and types.

[25] This is called a *turnaround* prompt because the machine must quickly go back and pick up something that it has missed. Failure to do so will result in a state error.

Again?

Say that again?

One more time...

What was that?

Once more...

Please repeat.

In the special case of yes-no questions, the turnaround prompt must encourage repetition of the "yes" or "no," not a repetition of the datum being queried:

Was that a yes?

The answer to the question is "yes" if the previous response was "yes." The answer is "no" if the previous response was "no." Either way, the prompt causes the user to repeat "yes" or "no" with minimum distraction.

This solution is better than other common turnaround prompts.

Avoid:

User:	"Delete."
App:	*Do you want to delete the message? <beep>*
User:	(interrupting the beep) "Yes."
App:	*Say that again? <beep>*
User:	"Delete."

The prompt is ambiguous. Say **what** again? In the example, the user responds with "Delete" rather than repeating the "yes." This causes a state error—the active vocabulary at this state is expecting "yes" or "no" and cannot recognize "Delete." The error has been amplified by the turnaround prompt.

Use:

User:	"Delete."
App:	*Do you want to delete the message? <beep>*
User:	(interrupting the beep) "Yes."
App:	*Was that a yes? <beep>*

User: "Yes."

In the improved version, the turnaround prompt disambiguates machine expectation. Both user and machine are synchronized and the dropped "yes" is quickly recovered. The same is true for a dropped (rejected) "no:"

User: "Cancel."

App: *Do you want to save the message for later? <beep>*

User: (interrupting the beep) "No."

App: *Was that a yes? <beep>*

User: "No."

4.4.2.3   √ Ensure that the Re-Prompt Is Shorter than the Prompt

If the user has anticipated the prompt, speaking before the recognizer is ready, then this rhythm must be disrupted on the re-prompt. For this reason, the prompt to repeat the input should be shorter than the original prompt. This is another good reason why a tone makes a good spoke-too-soon cue—tones are shorter than prompts, making it unlikely that the user will repeat the error a second time.

4.4.2.4   ≈ Consider Using Tones for Spoke-Too-Soon Alerts

Double beeps, buzzers, or other auditory cues make good indicators for turn-taking (spoke-too-soon) errors. Note that the timing of subsequent recognition windows must be well managed. See [Balentine97] for the description of a complete algorithm for managing half-duplex turn taking through such tones.

4.4.2.5   √ Track Spoke-Too-Soon Errors Separately from Other Speech Errors

The spoke-too-soon is a natural consequence of the half-duplex turn-taking protocol. Human interactions often including dovetailing—in which the new talker begins just as the old talker is finishing. This "overlapping" turn-taking behavior is perfectly normal for human speech and can therefore be expected to occur often when interacting with a speech-enabled application.

For this reason, spoke-too-soon errors should not be blown out of proportion. If a quick re-prompt captures a user repetition, then the error does not seriously impede the flow of the dialogue. The application should be tolerant of this stumble.

Bear in mind that spoke-too-soon conditions—unlike most speech errors—can be expected to increase as users become expert and comfortable with the application.

This is because they come to anticipate machine prompts and queries, and because they become interested in moving more quickly toward goals. This phenomenon can be a feature if spoke-too-soon recovery methods are quick and graceful. Conversely, it can be a problem if such methods are clumsy and slow. Poor spoke-too-soon recovery tends to slow down users as they become experts, causing them to adopt a turn-taking rhythm that diminishes their preferred (natural) pace. This increases anxiety and irritation, and distracts users from their primary goal.

Chapter 5
Tones

In most cases, time is the real enemy of the spoken interface. Not only does speech itself occupy time; the difficulty to remember and comprehend spoken machine output often leads to repetition of time-consuming information. In other words, the application presents information through spoken machine output, and to the degree that such information must be presented again—simply because the user does not remember it—severely limits the ability of the application to accomplish anything complex. This is one area in which tones become useful. Tones convey information quickly, provide rapid feedback to the user, and can also serve as "landmarks"[1] regarding the current state of the application.

5.1   Non-Speech Audio

5.1.1   Classes and Functions of Tones

Designers should develop an opinion on the use of non-speech audio, applying that opinion in a rigorous and organized way. All tones are not equal and "any old tone" won't do. Because users are able to perceive, remember, and associate different tones with different functions, effective design requires that psychoacoustic principles and the elements of good design should be considered when mixing tones with speech.

5.1.1.1   Tones, Beeps, Chimes, and Blips

The four terms commonly used for non-speech audio in telephony—tones, beeps, chimes, and blips—are generally viewed synonymously but have subtle distinctions. A "tone" or "beep" is usually a simple sound: sinusoidal, short, and unvarying in pitch, with a simple energy envelope.[2] "Tone" is more typically used as a generic

---

[1] Landmarks are feedback given to users to indicate their current menu, mode, or state.

[2] The envelope is the **loudness contour**, from the beginning of the tone to its ending. A simple

reference to any synthesized sound, while "beep" specifically refers to a prompting tone—the user is expected to speak after a beep.

"Chimes," as the term implies, tend to be more colorful, with a bell-like timbre and an interesting envelope. Chimes need not be extremely realistic, but tend to resemble real-world sounds more often than not. The audio can be generated through a number of techniques, including FM synthesis and wave synthesis,[3] but is usually a digitized recording of either synthetic or natural chimes. Chimes are more useful for announcing changes in state or context or for landmarking than they are for prompting.

A "blip" is an especially short tone that may be used for prompting or feedback. Blips are often complex tones rather than sinusoids—sometimes approaching a metallic or wooden timbre. Occasionally a blip is so short that it loses its pitch, becoming instead a sort of "tick" or pitched click. The minimum duration at which a sound changes from a tone pitch to a click pitch ranges from 5 ms to 20 ms [Josephs67]. Clicks and ticks can be useful for marking audio segments and for indicating progress.

5.1.1.2   Found Sounds Versus Signature Sounds

Audio specialists distinguish between found sounds and signature sounds. A found sound, as its name implies, is a recorded natural sound that is removed from its original context. The term is usually used to refer to a sound that has lost its connection to the real world—taking on an abstract character with no intrinsic external associations. Certain exotic animals, for example, make sounds that are not recognizable as such once removed from a known context. Various machine sounds, amplified recordings of normally soft sounds, and sounds transformed by an unusual acoustical environment are other examples. Found sounds are usually valued for their auditory "interestingness" without regard to utility.

A signature sound is a found sound or other class of non-speech audio that has become associated with a specific theme, idea, function, or object. The association is often obvious—for example the storybook that uses a mooing cow to represent the countryside and a jackhammer to represent the city. Typically, however, the association is more abstract. A popular example is the signature sound for "light sabers" in the well-known *Star Wars*™ films. Since light sabers do not exist, it is up to the

---

envelope is simply on and then off. More complex tones exhibit transient attacks, followed by a decay to some steady-state energy, which then ends with a final decay to silence that takes place in some specified release time. This *attack, decay, sustain, release* (ADSR) contour defines many of the perceived attributes of the sound.

[3] See [Kientzle98] for a detailed treatment of these audio principles.

imagination of the sound designer to locate an appropriate signature sound. The *Star Wars™* solution was recorded by attaching a contact microphone to the steel cables of a suspension bridge and then striking the cable, causing sound waves to reflect up and down its length. Although unrelated to light, the fixed-frequency fundamental and its phase-varying harmonics produce an almost synesthetic[4] perception—the appearance and sound of the light saber have a compelling similarity.

In telephony applications, signature sounds make effective landmarking cues; they are also useful for announcing state changes or context switches.

5.1.1.3   Audio Logos

A logo is a symbol that represents a company or product. An audio logo often consists of a short melodic "tune," but may also be an abstract sound—a "whoosh" or "sparkling" sound—that is tied to a visual animation and associated clearly in the listener's mind with its brand. In this sense, an audio logo is a specific instance of the more generic signature sound. Some commonly known examples include the four-note AT&T tune, the similar four-note "Intel Inside" logo, or the Southwestern Bell "pixie dust" sound. Audio logos are sometimes mixed with speech, in which a foreground voice announcement is concomitant with a distinctive background non-speech audio signature.

5.1.1.4   Auditory Icons and Earcons

Gaver developed the term "auditory icon" in his *SonicFinder* [Gaver89] and other designs. The term refers to practical, representational signature sounds. Real-world auditory icons in various applications have included the sound of a closing trashcan lid whenever the user throws away a file, the sound of opening and closing doors as the user moves between "audio rooms"—an alternative to folders or directories as a metaphor for navigating branching structures—and the sound of a letter landing in a mailbox.

Blattner and her colleagues coined the term "earcon" as a memorable way of referring to sounds that take on specific and distinguishable meaning in much the same way that "icons" represent functions or objects in the visual domain [Blattner89]. In fact, an earcon can be viewed as an auditory icon. The term is usually reserved, however, for a more structured and formal set of relationships between a set of auditory cues. In other words, the earcons not only specify the current object, event, or state—

---

[4] Synesthesia is the subjective response to one sense with sensations that belong to another, as when certain sounds can be "seen" as color [Kreitler72].

they also bear relationship to each other, marking the current position within a larger whole. Because of its syntactic power, music is usually the medium of choice for earcons.

In their seminal 1989 paper, Blattner et al. described the use of earcons to show position in a hierarchy. First, a basic tune exhibits certain rhythmic properties that make it memorable. As the user traverses the hierarchy—for example a file system—melodic components become more varied, but the rhythmic component retains its basic identity. Earcons, like musical themes, thus survive considerable development, transformation, and embellishment without losing their inherent similarities—what Blattner calls "perceptual equivalencies."[5]

5.1.2 Attributes of Non-Speech Audio

The following are attributes of non-speech audio that can be exploited for user interface purposes.

5.1.2.1 Tones Are Shorter than Speech

Tones are meaningful and yet very short—inherently shorter than speech. To the degree that a design can exploit this attribute of non-speech audio, the intrinsic time limitations of the speech interface can be reduced.

5.1.2.2 Tones Are Audible Through Noise

The user can detect and recognize tones in environments that might obscure recorded or synthetic speech into unintelligibility. If the application is targeted toward users in noisy environments, then tonal cues can become useful "anchors" that keep the user synchronized in cases where spoken machine output may neither be heard nor understood.

Such environments include:

- Car phones (handheld or hands-free),
- Land-line phones in public place (airports, restaurants, roadside payphones), and
- Mobile phones in many environments.

---

[5] Although this is an oversimplification of a complex subject, the basic flavor is represented. A designer interested in earcons is encouraged to review the literature. As a basic definition, a **representational earcon** is an auditory icon—a digitized recording of a real-world sound— while an **abstract earcon** usually relies on formal musical structures.

5.1.2.3   Tones Are Memorable

Some of the earliest work in Gestalt psychology was based on studies of the human perception of music—specifically musical melodies [Kreitler72]. The question was why musical melodies are so easily remembered and recognized, even when distorted significantly. The answer is that musical melodies are made of short fragments—musical gestures or, more precisely, **motives** [Blattner89]—that fuse into a **gestalt**. A gestalt is a form or structure that is perceived as a single indivisible unit. In other words, the whole (gestalt) is greater (simpler, more easily processed) than the sum of its component parts.[6] Because of this perceptual phenomenon, non-speech audio that conforms to certain gestalt principles is easily remembered.

Speech recognition applications can take advantage of this mnemonic attribute to provide landmarking and context cues to users. The user spontaneously (and unconsciously) learns to recognize a distinctive musical or other non-speech audio through repetition. The user further comes to associate this non-speech audio with a location, function, or condition of the interface. The audio thus tends to "trigger" similar behaviors automatically—without any conscious effort on the user's part.[7]

5.1.2.4   Musical Structures Are Syntactically Complex and Multi-Leveled

The structural characteristics of tonal music—which share certain attributes with spoken language—have been explored by several investigators and applied to interface design in a number of sophisticated ways. Blattner has worked with earcons in many contexts—using musical structures, for example, to communicate the flow in a turbulent liquid. Brewster has designed earcons specifically for telephone-based interfaces [Brewster98] and has also worked extensively with sonification—using non-speech audio to reinforce graphical widgets in visual interfaces [Brewster97].

The important characteristics of music in interface design are its richness in variety and the universality of certain archetypal elements such as "direction" and "distance." Recent experiments have demonstrated that users can recognize musical descriptions of graphical objects, including shape and position in a graphical space. In these experiments, subjects were able to estimate size of objects accurately to within 10%

---

[6] The fact that musical melodies are integrated as a gestalt is one reason why melodies are used as mnemonic devices for remembering complex information. A case in point is the "alphabet song," sung by children and still remembered by adults.

[7] The most popular example of this so-called "secondary reinforcement" is the experiments by Pavlov in which dogs were conditioned to expect food when a bell was rung. After the conditioning, ringing the bell caused the dogs to salivate—even when food was not present.

[Alty98]. Operations such as expanding and contracting were considered completely intuitive, and users required no training to recognize the operations.

5.1.2.5   Non-Speech Audio Mixes Well with Speech

Both speech and non-speech can be played at the same time—allowing concurrent presentation of two or more layers of information without confusion. This is useful not only in simple cueing functions, but can be sustained in the presentation of "environmental" sounds that remain at the periphery of the user's attention. Mynatt and her colleagues have developed a number of systems based on "awareness cues" and augmented reality, most recently in the Audio Aura project at Xerox PARC [Mynatt98]. The work shows that a rich body of peripheral cues can create implicit dialogues between mobile users and their computers.

Secondary information about the state of the application, occurrences in background tasks, and similar context information is easily presented by adding a background layer of sound. For example, a light "warbling" sound—very soft—may be mixed with the spoken machine output whenever a Help Wizard is coaching the user. As the coach enters the dialogue, the current task is temporarily suspended. Throughout the coaching session, which could last several seconds, the background sound indicates the presence of the wizard and, by inference, the change of context to a tutoring mode. After presenting the tip, the wizard disappears in a puff and the warbling sound stops. In this way, the user understands changes in context and is less likely to be confused when the suspended task resumes.

5.2   When to Use Tones

Half-duplex interactions require that the user wait for the machine to finish speaking before taking his turn. Since the application cannot respond to spoken user input during spoken machine output, tones become an effective method for managing turn taking by cueing the user when it is his turn to speak.

Conversely, full-duplex interactions allow both the user and machine to speak at any time. Since the user can interrupt spoken machine output at will, tones are not useful as a cue for him to speak.

These two very different turn-taking protocols imply that, as a general rule, tones are required for applications without barge-in, while they are optional for applications that use barge-in.

5.2.1   Without Barge-In

When the application does not use barge-in, then turn-taking problems tend to dominate the interface. Almost by definition, a "natural" change of turns is impossible, as described in Chapter 4. This means that a more structured and formal method for passing the turn to the user is indicated. Tones are very effective in this capacity, as they are both distinctive and short.

Note that many designers are adamant about avoiding tones, even in half-duplex interfaces, for reasons that range from perceptions of "artificiality" and "unnaturalness" to assumptions that users dislike tones due to association with answering machines and prior experience with poor IVR design. This style guide takes no stance on the subject, assuming that the decision to use tones is both a look and feel and a design decision that can be viewed as a matter of taste and opinion. For those who choose to use tones, the following principles are intended to provide some guidance on when and how to apply them.

5.2.1.1   √ Use a Prompting Tone to Cue Every Required User Input

Avoid using tones sporadically. Instead, present a prompting tone every time the user is required to speak. Ensure that spoken messages refer to the tone. Enforce the tone protocol firmly.

Note that one exception to this guideline is the "hidden" menus (see Section 6.2.5). Such input opportunities represent **optional** rather than required user turns. Hidden states are for experts, and therefore the application should avoid announcing their presence with tones or other turn-taking cues.

5.2.1.2   ≈ Consider Using Multiple Tones for Varied Meaning

Once tones are in use, it is often effective to allow them to carry additional meaning. This may depend on the way the machine handles tones, and also requires an extensive theoretical framework within which musical gestures or auditory icons can flourish.

Note that context has an important influence on users' understanding of musical objects. Alty and Rigas, describing a tool called AUDIOGRAPH, comment:

> The UNDO command was represented by the playing of a tune with a "fault" in it followed by the "correct" tune. At first hearing users were baffled by this, but on hearing the explanation they understood it immediately and had no further trouble recognizing it [Alty98].

Details are beyond the scope of this style guide, but the designer is encouraged to explore the literature.[8]

5.2.1.3 ≈ Consider Using Tones for Confirmation and Feedback

If tones are used to cue the user to speak, different tones are often effective to signal the successful capture of user speech. This allows the tones to cue turn-taking changes in both directions. The user comes to expect the machine confirmation, often speaking again if it is not forthcoming.

The principle is one of **secondary reinforcement**.[9] If, for example—whenever the user speaks—a dual tone appears as confirmation, then the user comes to expect the dual tone. In cases in which speech is not detected—where speech levels are too low, for example—this conditioned expectation is thwarted. When the users don't hear the expected dual tone, they simply repeat what they said—reporting that the "machine didn't hear me."

5.2.2 With Barge-In

5.2.2.1 ≈ Avoid Tones if the Speaking Style Is Conversational

Many large-vocabulary user-driven applications aim for natural and conversational interaction. Such applications might predispose users to reject the use of tones as detrimental or annoying.

5.2.2.2 ≈ Consider Using Tones for Feedback or Landmarking

Even though barge-in allows the user to speak at will, thereby making the prompting tone unnecessary, tones may continue to serve other purposes according to design goals. These may include:

- Identify menus or contexts by name (landmarking),
- Indicate application states,
- Identify "ideal" moments to speak,
- Identify the end of the machine turn,

---

[8] Blattner has explored the use of music in a number of different contexts. In the sophisticated designs at Xerox PARC, Mynatt et al. created sets of auditory cues called "ecologies." The designer is encouraged to study the literature from Georgia Institute of Technology, MIT Media Lab, Stanford University, Xerox PARC, and the important work at universities in the U.K. and elsewhere for more information.

[9] From behavioral psychology [Kreitler72].

- Tag elements in lists that are especially important,

- Indicate the beginning and/or the successful conclusion of tasks,

- Indicate that the machine is processing user speech and is not listening, and

- Convey error conditions.

5.3   Prompting Tones

A prompting tone is a cue aimed at causing the user to speak. As such, the tone "turns over" control to the user. A prompting tone typically appears immediately after a spoken machine prompt.

5.3.1   Single-Tone Prompts

In many applications there is only one prompting tone used throughout the application. The tone should conform to the following guidelines.

5.3.1.1   √ Short

The tone should be a blip rather than a beep. The tone duration should be in the range of 75-150 ms. This makes the tone a "point" rather than a "line," ensuring that the user hears a temporally precise turn-taking cue.

5.3.1.2   √ Medium to High Pitch

Low-pitched tones can get lost in speech and background noise. Prompting tones should generally range in the three octaves from C4 (middle C, 261.63 Hz) to F7 (2793.8 Hz).[10] The most useful range is narrower—roughly 1.5 octave centered around 1kHz. The designer should be aware of the equal loudness curve [Josephs67] with regard to pitch. If pitches are used musically, then the designer should ensure proper tuning [Kientzle98]. Regardless of other considerations, pitches higher than 3KHz should not be used over the telephone due to bandwidth limitations.

5.3.1.3   √ Not Too Loud

Tones command attention and penetrate background easily. They may also occur quite frequently within an application. Care should therefore be exercised to minimize fatigue associated with tones. It is better to err on the side of soft than loud. Tones may be at or near the threshold of perception and remain effective.

---

[10] U.S. system of musical pitches. See [Tufte97] for an excellent illustration by Pierce.

5.3.1.4   + Pleasing

Interfaces that use tones consistently must pay close attention to auditory fatigue. Users will tire rapidly of tones that are aggressive or irritating. The definition of "pleasing" here is deliberately left open. The term should not be confused with "entertaining" or "interesting." Indeed, tones that call attention to themselves are probably inappropriate in a speech interface. Rather, the tones should be gentle on the ear and composed well given the surrounding speech context.

5.3.2   Logos as Prompting Tones

Sound logos can have dual uses, serving as very good prompting tones as well as providing branding for company, product, and service identity.

5.3.2.1   ≈ Enforce Clear Ending

If a logo is to be used as a prompting tone for hidden menus or other special states, it should end in a clearly discriminable way. It should not be surrounded by echo or reverberation. Fade (decay) time should be 150 ms or less. This is especially true with half-duplex applications. Sounds with "spongy" and ambiguous endings tend to cause spoke-too-soon conditions in such applications.

5.3.2.2   ≈ Make Music/Voice Logos Concurrent

Logos that consist of music and voice should be mixed such that both occur concurrently. Avoid playing music followed by a voice announcement (or vice versa). If the music or voice is ever used independently of the other for prompting, then ensure that the mixed version ends together—that is, neither voice nor music trails the other. This is because ambiguous cues can lead to sloppy turn-taking behaviors.

5.3.2.3   + Avoid Overuse

Logos are special and distinctive symbols. They should not be overused.

5.3.3   Announcing Hidden Menus

A hidden menu is an optional input state. Note that expert users are the ones expected to take advantage of hidden states. See Section 6.2.5 for a more extensive discussion of what is meant by hidden menus, including how to structure them and when to use them.

5.3.3.1   + Use Alternate Tones or No Tones for Hidden Menus

Avoid using the same beep used elsewhere. Users should think of hidden menus as places where users **may** speak—not as places where users **must** speak. A hidden menu is optional and should be perceived as such.

5.3.3.2   + Use Logos to Announce Hidden Menus

For hidden menus placed at the start of a dialogue, logos make especially good introductory prompts. Placing a logo at the very beginning of a dialogue provides a good short cue to expert users without confusing novice users. Similarly, "handoffs" from one service to another may be announced by logos and then be followed by hidden input windows.

5.3.3.3   + Consider Playing Chimes with, Before, or After Spoken Landmarks

Landmarks are used to announce menus, as well as specific contexts in natural language dialogues. Landmarks can be reinforced with unique non-speech audio symbols, encouraging user recognition and speech response to the landmark.

5.4   Feedback/Confirmation Tones

5.4.1   Why Use Post-Recognition Tones?

Using tones for feedback or confirmation means that the machine is presenting tones for more reasons than merely prompting the user to speak. Such reasons may include corroborating that speech was heard and accepted, reminding the user of her location within the structure of the dialogue, and relating the currently completed user input to a larger scale of recent and forthcoming events.

In the following two guidelines, the terms **tonic** and **dominant**,[11] as well as the concept of complementary tone pairs may be more thoroughly understood by examining a general reference on musical terms and concepts [Ottman61].

5.4.1.1   ≈ Make Prompting/Confirmation Tones Complementary in Sound

If the prompting tone "opens" the interaction with a dual tone that moves from tonic to dominant, the confirmation tone might be a dual tone that moves from dominant

---

[11] In tonal music, keys are based on major or minor scales. The tonic—the name of the key—is the first step of the scale. The subdominant (4th scale step) and dominant (5th scale step) lead naturally one to the other to produce the sensation of progressive motion. These tonal relationships can be viewed as musical corollaries of syntax and grammar in language.

back to tonic—thereby "closing" the interaction. This structure allows the user—unconsciously—to associate the two sets of tones as related in some intuitive way. The effect is the auditory equivalent of open-and-close parentheses (or brackets, or curly braces).

In one design [Balentine90], for example, a digit-string capture and corroboration procedure is aimed at collecting telephone, credit card, ZIP code, or other numeric data from the user. In this procedure, there are two parts to the interaction—the collection of digits from the user, and the playback of those digits for corroboration. During the course of these dialogue components, numerous errors may occur, including rejection recovery, partial string capture, and even outright substitution error (which requires repetition of the number by the user). Considerable time may elapse between the start and successful conclusion of the task.

In the procedure, tones are pitched in the key of C. The opening prompt tone is a dual descending tone that moves quickly from A to G—the dominant of C. Interspersing events including errors and various yes-no responses from the user are prompted with G (one octave higher) or other notes that remain within the G Major triad. Errors are cued with a short buzzer pitched at F# (the dissonant tritone in the key of C). Upon successful completion of the task, the interaction is closed with a rising dual tone that moves quickly from B to C—an authentic cadence[12] that "resolves" the tension by moving from dominant to tonic. In usability tests and demonstrations, users were observed to respond physically after hearing this resolution, reporting afterwards that they felt a sense of "closure" or "completion" as a result of the rising tone pair.

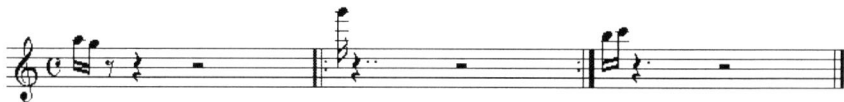

Figure 5.1—**OPENING AND CLOSING TONE PAIRS** create a sense of anticipation followed by a sense of "release" or closure. The first measure represents a prompt to speak, cueing the user to say, for example, a credit card number. The second measure remains on the dominant, and appears as a prompt each time the dialogue engages in "embedded" interactions such as yes-no queries aimed at recovering rejections. This middle unresolved tone delays completion and repeats as many times as there are interactions. The final tone pair (third measure) closes the interaction after successful numeric capture and corroboration.

---

[12] An authentic cadence is a progression from dominant to tonic in tonal music [Ottman61].

Note that the opening pair—A to G—serves as the prompting tone, and is somewhat like an open parenthesis. The closing tone pair—B to C—is not a prompt to speak, but rather is a confirmation tone, serving as the closing parenthesis that ends the musical tension that has been established by the original tone pair. This tension/release pattern—an archetypal and universal attribute of tonal music—serves both to bracket the task across long time scales and to reward the user for successful task completion. By making them complementary in direction and in harmonic progression, the tone pairs serve several purposes at once.

5.4.1.2   ≈ Reinforce Complemented Tone Sequences

Where a tone pair or musical figure uses complementary pitch patterns to bracket spoken user input—the first for prompting and the second for confirmation—then this complementary characteristic should be reinforced with other parameters of music and sound. Such parameters include loudness, timbre (spectral attributes), tempo, interval, direction of motion, etc. The goal is to maximize the user's perception of the two tones and how they are related.

5.4.2   Tension/Release Patterns

Although a detailed discussion of music is beyond the scope of this style guide, it should be noted that all music uses certain patterns—based primarily on pitch and rhythm—that create tension or expectation in the mind of the listener. Other related patterns resolve that tension, producing a pleasurable sensation that is based on the thwarting or fulfillment of a previously created expectation on the part of the listener [Kreitler72].

There are well-known theories that take advantage of this principle of tension and release. These theories may be applied to the design of a spoken user interface, to guide the user's speech behaviors. For details, see any freshman-level textbook on music theory and functional harmony.

5.4.2.1   + Use Tension-Producing Tone Patterns as Cues to Speak

There are a number of two- and three-note figures that produce the sensation of incompleteness and an attendant expectation that some fulfilling action needs to occur. These short tone patterns represent good prompting tones. Note that the rhythmic character of the pattern is as important is the pitch [Blattner89].

5.4.2.2   ≈ Use No Tone, or Tension- Sustaining Tones for Errors

Where errors occur after user speech—errors in loudness, recognition confidence, or synchronization—the interaction is "not complete." Certain tones or tone patterns can convey this condition to the user by sustaining the tension associated with lack of completion. Use tones that are pitched on the dominant of the key, real or implied leading tones such as 7th chords, or dissonant intervals such as the tritone as prompts for these embedded interactions.

5.4.2.3   ≈ Use Tension-Releasing Tone Patterns for Confirmation

Certain well-known tone patterns are used to "close" musical figures, providing a sense of completion and finality to the listener. Such patterns represent excellent confirmation tones, and include both plagal[13] and authentic cadences. Arpeggiated chords that are pitched on the tonic, or progressions that imply a seventh which in turn resolves to the tonic can also be effective and are already understood (intuitively) by users—who have heard these musical patterns all their lives.[14]

5.5   Context Tones

5.5.1   Menu Announcements

5.5.1.1   ≈ Use Distinctive Tones to Identify Menus

Landmarking announcements that identify menus by name are effective identifiers, allowing users to respond more quickly when they arrive at a known state. Such landmarks may be enhanced by mixing a unique sound—abstract or representational earcons—with speech to reinforce user recognition. In some cases, sounds alone may be able to announce menus without recourse to spoken landmarks.

5.5.1.2   ≈ Use Related Tones for Sub-Menus Under Menus

See the discussion of earcons [Blattner89] for details on hierarchical relationships among tones. Such a discussion is beyond the scope of this text. Briefly, one ap-

---

[13] A plagal cadence moves from the subdominant—the 4th step of the key's scale—to the tonic. The well-known "amen" at the end of hymns and chorales is an example.

[14] It could be argued that harmony is Western European, and that claims of universality are chauvinistic. The rise of popular music, however, has generalized equal temperament—the core prerequisite of harmony—through standardization on keyboard instruments. Popular music has thus spread the common experience of harmonic progressions worldwide.

proach uses rhythm. Present a single beep at the Main Menu. Use a double-beep one level down, a triple-beep two levels down, and so forth.

5.5.1.3   √ Test User Acceptance of Tones Thoroughly

Some designers reject the use of tones automatically, declaring that the audio will "annoy people." Others choose tones arbitrarily, without regard to the relative merits of particular pitches, intervals or rhythms. Both of these knee-jerk reactions are wrong, as they are based on the personal tastes and opinions of one person. A better solution is to ask users directly, and to measure tone acceptability and effectiveness in usability labs.

The use of non-speech audio is still experimental. Exhibit caution when committing to tonal menu relationships, and ensure that expected results are thoroughly understood before proceeding.

5.5.2   Help, Waiting, and Other Contexts

Non-speech audio is useful for indicating a number of conditions. Note that there are not many fielded applications that take advantage of such utility, so these guidelines are marked with the lowest level (≈) of recommendation.

5.5.2.1   ≈ Provide Auditory Cues for Wait Times of a Few Seconds or More

Many applications must access other computers to acquire information to present to the user. Such external communications sometimes require long and unpredictable delays before the information is available. There should always be some way to mask or fill long wait times. Non-speech audio in the form of a low-level "ticking" or similar sound can convey to the user that the system is still active and that the user has not lost the connection.

App: *Which information would you like?*

User: "News."

App: *Please hold.*
        <tick … tick … tick …> [15 seconds or more]
        Thank you for holding. In today's headlines …

In this example, the VRU must connect to a server to get the information requested by the user. Such connections entail variable wait times—depending on data traffic, amount of data, and type of connection. Because the time may be somewhat long, the user needs a cue that indicates the action is proceeding. Otherwise, he may conclude that the machine has "hung up."

Although many auto-attendants or help-desk applications use music or spoken advertisements to fill this "dead time," there are cases in which this is not possible or desirable. In such cases, non-speech audio is a suitable alternative. Designers may consider the above "ticking" (which reminds the user of clocks and similar time-passing associations), pitched "wait-tones," or—if the expected wait time is known—an audio "progress meter" that moves toward a predictable goal to indicate the percentage of time that has expired. In this latter example, a changing beep that moves toward a fixed reference frequency is a good way to convey the "distance" from current position to goal. This translates into the perception of "time remaining."

5.5.2.2 ≈ Announce Help Sequences with Chimes

Help coaches or wizards may insert themselves into a dialogue and then exit gracefully after presenting tips, yes-no queries, coaching tutorials, or other helpful guidance. Such sequences may announce their appearance with a distinctive non-speech audio indicator. Upon completion, the user returns to the state just preceding the moment of interruption. This return may itself be announced by a similar audio indicator. In this way the user understands that the help sequence is a parenthetical interjection, allowing time before and after the interruption to be reconnected.

Chapter 6
Dialogue Design

This chapter explores the architectural, organizational, and navigational issues associated with the high-level structure of spoken telephony applications. It is the dialogue as a whole that exhibits the emergent properties we refer to as the "look and feel" of the interface.

Speech recognition design is often conceived as a passive process. The application plays a prompt and then turns on the recognizer. The user speaks. If the recognizer understands what the user says, then we're done—no additional design is required. If the recognizer fails, then somebody should fix it. After all, how can we design an application if the most important subsystem keeps misinterpreting the input?

This bias is deep-seated. The implication is that speech recognition *replaces* design by simply knowing what the user wants. This bias is based on the false assumption that the words and sentences of spoken language are somehow real physical objects that are fixed and knowable, and that decoding the acoustical signal is a deterministic process that will give us the information we seek—information about what the user wants and needs.

In fact, speech recognition is fuzzy and indeterminate—not because the technology is flawed but because the input signal itself does not and cannot contain consistently unambiguous information. Only part of what a user is expressing makes its way into the acoustics of the speech. The rest is inside the user's head; conveyed with facial expression; implied by gesture; and—most importantly—shared by the listener in an unspoken and complex social covenant. This all-important **context** includes so much unconscious information that we cannot begin to understand it ourselves, let alone codify it into machine thinking.

Because so much speech information resides in a human context, there are some practitioners who insist that we must find a way to reduce humanity to software and then shoehorn it into our machines. These researchers seek to model world knowledge, social experience, multi-leveled human discourse—even the subjective affect[1] that underlies emotion—in an effort to decrease the experiential gap between human users and machines. Although understandably motivated, such efforts make it easy to become distracted. It is therefore important to maintain a focus on the primary goal of the user interface—getting the user's *work* done—and to remain cautious when allowing unrelated issues to interfere with that goal. [2]

Instead of getting lost in society, intelligence, or feeling, we must do what all good interface designs strive toward. Focus on the user and the work that she must accomplish. Study that user. Understand her work better than she does. Break it down into tasks. Define those tasks explicitly. Connect them with her understanding, reflex actions, and natural behaviors. Create from them a sense of simple order. Take on the hard problems and make those problems transparent—the little details that are so tricky for the user to master—freeing her mind so that it can stay focused on the big problems. This, more than "friendly" or "polite" dialogue is the key to usability.

With the above principles in mind, this chapter discusses the simple and common guidelines that apply to most applications—directed dialogues, menus, yes-no questions, and reusable dialogue components. More complex dialogues involving natural language and personified interfaces are discussed in later chapters. Designers are encouraged to master these simple interactions before wrestling with the more advanced linguistic and personality issues discussed in those chapters.

6.1 Dialogue Models

The word **call flow** is often used to refer to the logic of the VRU application. It implies not only the spoken output and intent of machine prompting, but also the method adopted by the designer for moving from state to state and for recovering errors during the course of the interaction. In a sense, the word is a good one, as it implies that the dialogue "flows forward in time" according to some coherent pattern of rules and internal organization. On the other hand, the term oversimplifies the problem of dialogue structure by implying that the most important architectural issue

---

[1] Affect is a noun that refers to the physiological and psychological attributes of emotion and subjective perception. It should not be confused with the verb "affect" or the noun "effect." The word is pronounced with stress on the first syllable, which sounds like "a" as in "bat."

[2] The principle that "simple and robust" is superior to complex artificial intelligence is beginning to be embraced as a philosophy by the speech community [Rosenfeld01].

is the "ordering" of the turns that alternate between user and machine rather than the underlying exchange of information at the heart of the interactive system.

For this reason, the following discussion eschews the term call flow in favor of more specific dialogue models that focus the developer on clarity and purposefulness in application organization. The criteria for choosing the best model include the knowledge brought by the user to the interaction, the attention span and understanding of users, and the overall complexity of the task.

Table 6.1 summarizes these criteria and the impact they have on dialogue structure. The left column shows six different dialogue models. Many of these are fairly common; others are just beginning to appear. There is overlap between them, and similar interactions may be realized using different or multiple dialogue models. There are other more exotic dialogues, but those discussed here are the most common.

These dialogue models are similar to Shneiderman's five primary interaction styles for user interface design: menu selection, form filling,[3] command language, natural language, and direct manipulation [Shneiderman97]. Of these, direct manipulation is an interaction style for visual interfaces with no direct correlate in speech. Certain devices allow direct manipulation of audio information—devices that support scrolling through, selection of, and operations upon segments of audio—but tend to fall more into the command and control style of input. Shneiderman's other styles share a rough correspondence with the dialogue models shown in Table 6.1.

The fourth column introduces the term "initiative" to describe the source of knowledge and power in the relationship between interlocutors as they exchange spoken information. The idea can be summarized in the vernacular as, "who does the driving." Each dialogue model in Table 6.1 describes whether user or machine has the initiative. When the user initiates most of the individual turns in the dialogue—in other words, when the dialogue is "user-driven"—then the human user controls the pace and direction of the dialogue.[4] The user must therefore understand the goals of the interaction and must have knowledge of actions that are required to achieve them. The machine takes a passive ("responsive") role in the interaction. User-initiated dialogues achieve the highest duty cycles,[5] because the user spends more time presenting speech to the machine than awaiting machine instructions.

---

[3] [Shneiderman97] uses "fillin" instead of "filling."

[4] User initiated and user-driven are synonymous. See the glossary for details.

[5] A metric to determine the percentage of time the user is speaking relative to the call duration. See the glossary for a detailed description of "duty cycle."

Table 6.1—DIALOGUE DESIGN MODELS are based on differences in the prior knowledge of targeted users, the complexity of tasks supported by the application, and assumptions about who should initiate each interaction.

Dialogue Model	Required User Knowledge	User Behaviors	Initiative	Comments
Command and Control	Novice must learn both task and user interface to be productive.	commanding, directing, operating	user initiated; machine passive but responsive	hard to learn task; easy to learn interface; fast once mastered
Form Filling	User must possess data. No knowledge of task or interface required.	responding, answering questions	machine initiated	easy to learn and to use; little or no advantage to becoming expert
Searching	User must possess goals and some knowledge of paths or keywords for reaching them.	searching, hunting, surfing	user initiated	hard for user to learn; hard for designer to bound; requires extensive feedback (slow)
Menu	Novice must know functions. Task and interface are progressively disclosed.	selecting, choosing	machine initiated; expert may benefit from shortcuts	easy to learn; limit to complexity of tasks that can be supported
Natural Language	User must possess knowledge of task. Interface disclosed progressively but indirectly.	describing, interacting	mixed initiative; most effective when user-driven	learning depends on complexity and user understanding of task; very fast for experts
Personified Interface	User must possess goals. User must share social/cultural assumptions.	conversing, interacting	mixed initiative	Social effects are good or bad depending on design goals.

If the machine initiates most of the individual turns in the dialogue—in other words, when the dialogue is "machine-driven"— then it is the machine that controls the pace and direction of the dialogue.[6] The application must progressively disclose the task to users, who in turn respond to prompts with data or navigation commands relevant to

---

[6] Machine initiated and machine-driven are synonymous. See the glossary for details.

their goal. When the machine uses the dialogue to guide users through tasks, it is called a **directed dialogue**. Both form filling and menus are directed dialogues.

When a design involves both user and machine initiative, it is called a **mixed-initiative** dialogue. These dialogues contain branches or modules that are either user- or machine-driven. Often, the main information-exchanging dialogue may be user initiated, while help and error recovery states remain machine initiated.

This chapter provides a discussion of the most common user initiated and machine initiated dialogues shown in Table 6.1. The discussion is aimed at conveying a deep understanding of these simple and ubiquitous designs. Mixed-initiative dialogues, including natural language and personified interfaces, are more complex paradigms that warrant dedicated in-depth treatment. Natural language (Chapter 8) is dependent on a mix of enabling technologies and a philosophy of interaction that are very different from the simple deterministic dialogues discussed in this chapter. Personified interfaces (Chapter 9) are based on design methods that imbue the dialogue with human-like traits, including a name, personality, and social awareness.

6.1.1   Command and Control Dialogues

In a true command and control (C&C) application, the user is typically an operator or decision-maker who gives direct commands to the application. In this context, the task itself may be quite complex—for example speech control in cockpits, process control consoles, or monitoring systems. Once the user understands the task, however, the spoken actions required to manage the task are usually quite easy to learn and remember. A typical telephony application that conforms to the C&C model is voice-activated dialing (VAD).

Some C&C systems may be organized into separate states that provide different command sets. If the sets are small, they may be presented to the user as lists. In other words, command and control designs may use menus. Bear in mind that this is only one of many approaches to organizing a C&C dialogue. Command and control differs from menus in that the user is actively directing rather than passively selecting. The purpose of the menu—or more accurately the presentation of lists of commands—is to remind the user of the current state and the available actions. Although similar to menus, a command-and-control dialogue tends to be more user-driven. That is, the user takes more turns, spends more time engaging in actions rather than passively listening, and is more aggressively focused on completing tasks.

Table 6.1 shows the issues related to a user initiated C&C dialogue. The user is "commanding" the device, so he must know both what commands to give and what to expect when the commands are properly executed. In other words, the user must be familiar with the task. Command and control approaches are therefore inappropriate for a novice user with respect to the task. Users that are task-knowledgeable but interface-naïve must learn the interface. This is best accomplished via external documentation, or through tutoring or progressive disclosure methods such as menus. Users that know neither the task nor the interface are not well served by C&C dialogues.

6.1.2　Form-Filling Dialogues

As shown in Table 6.1, form-filling dialogues represent a machine-driven method for extracting information from users that have no need to know the structure and details of the interface. As the name implies, the user is filling in the individual fields of a form. The following example is typical of an order-entry application.

App:　*What kind of credit card will you use?*

User:　"Master Card."

App:　*Card Number?*

User:　"1155-5511-1155-5511."

App:　*Expiration Date?*

User:　"Six-oh-three."

App:　*Normal or Special Delivery?*

User:　"Normal."

App:　*Please confirm the order... <machine reads order back for confirmation>*

6.1.2.1　√ Break Complex Fields into Multiple Simple Fields

Form filling requires that machine and user alternate in a chaining sequence toward closure. Each required fact should be individually self-explanatory. In one study, users made mistakes on the machine prompt, *"Starting date of employment?"* because the application wanted only the month and the year. Many users responded instead with day, month, and year. Asking for the month and year separately would have avoided this problem [Hersh99].

6.1.2.2   + Capture All Fields Before Corroborating

Corroborating once at the end of the form filling exercise is less time consuming than corroborating each individual entry, especially if all the entries are correct. If the user indicates there is an error, ask which entry is incorrect or offer to start over.

6.1.2.3   ≈ If Corroborating Field-by-Field, Capture Critical Data Early

Nothing is more irritating to a user than to get well into a dialogue only to fail on a particularly complex form filling activity. It is therefore important that the likelihood of success go up as the duration of the dialogue increases.

App: *Matinee or evening performance?*

User: "Evening performance."

App: *Balcony or floor?*

User: "Balcony."

App: *Credit card number?*

User: Oh … just a minute. It's, umh …

App: *Confirming, oh, six, eight, nine, six, one…*

In this example, the easy questions come first. Each form-filling question offers a small number of options, and the user can parrot back the response without keeping track of the overall transaction.

Capturing the credit card number is the real challenge. In the example, the user is not ready and presents an out-of-grammar (OOG) response to the recognizer, which in turn commits a false acceptance error—recognizing the OOG as a digit string. The design may have benefited by starting with the credit card interaction, delaying the input of simple data fields.

6.1.3   Searching Dialogues

Searching dialogues are used when the desired information is too long to present as a list or menu. Some examples of searching dialogues include finding a phone number using automated directory assistance, finding a stock symbol, and finding the weather in a U.S. city. In the stock symbol example, the user is searching for a mapping between the information he possesses—the stock name—and the symbol that is required by the application.

In these examples it is easy to see that the burden of guiding the user to the desired information is placed squarely on the designer. If the user asks for a phone number for *Pizza Hut*™ in Dallas, the application will likely come back and ask for a street address. If the user response is out-of-grammar[7] (the user doesn't know the address), the application must ask for additional information to select among the multiple *Pizza Hut*™ franchises in Dallas.

A more challenging example of a searching dialogue is "web surfing." In this activity, the user doesn't necessarily know what information is being sought, but instead is moving from location to location in a sort of free association mode. She selects the next jump based on what is present in her current context. The appeal of web surfing is frequent and copious feedback, in contrast to a voice version that may be painfully slow. Although there are a number of developers pursuing web browsing, too little is known about searching dialogues to codify any style recommendations. This text therefore does not address this dialogue model in detail.[8]

6.2 Menus

Menu-driven dialogues are the most common dialogue design in VRU applications, and they exhibit a number of useful properties. A menu is a dialogue model that consists of three parts:

1. Presentation of a list of items from which the user may choose.

2. One or more opportunities for the user to choose one of the items.

3. Additional follow-on interactions to recover ambiguous selections, correct errors, or corroborate destructive functions.

Menus organize application tasks into a hierarchy of small individual lists. Each list represents a bounded set of possible actions, options, choices, or data. The key value of menus is that the user need not possess extensive prior knowledge of either the task or the interface itself. Rather, the application offers the user opportunities to choose and presents a list of choices whenever requested by the user.

In essence, a menu-driven dialogue is a **list manager**. When the machine takes a turn, it spends most of its time offering a list of options from which the user is expected to select. "Selecting" as a behavior is intrinsically easier for the user than "command-

---

[7] Out-of-grammar (OOG) is the preferred term for illegal speech when the technology uses natural language grammars. See Section 1.3 and the glossary.

[8] See Appendix B for a discussion of voice portals and related web-based information services.

ing," "directing," "operating," or "conversing." This is because the act of selecting is somewhat more passive, making menus the device of choice for beginners and casual users who are performing simple and untaxing operations.

6.2.1   Speech Versus DTMF Menus

DTMF and spoken input differ in user psychology and timing [Balentine92b]. List presentation and selection methods that are appropriate for one modality do not necessarily perform well with the other [Balentine99]. Because designers are often well acquainted with DTMF menus, however, existing methods can be viewed as a lowest common denominator for dialogue designs. The following guidelines are therefore aimed at migrating DTMF menu designs into speech solutions without making fundamental changes to the basic menu dialogue model.

The implication of this straightforward migration is that simple and inexpensive discrete recognition technologies[9] benefit the most from slight changes to DTMF menus—allowing designers to exploit them with minimum impact on existing user and developer skills. There are two cautions. First, more sophisticated recognition technologies (e.g., natural language) may be organized into menus, and might benefit from methods other than those that follow. Second, be aware that as the general population becomes experienced with voice menus—and as developers acquire expertise with alternate structures—the designer may wish to move away from this basic dialogue model and toward more user initiated dialogues.[10]

6.2.1.1   + Avoid the *For ... Say* or *To ... Say* Construct

DTMF menus have adopted the method of presenting a function, followed by the expected user action required to select that function. This "function/action" paradigm is quite effective for DTMF menus. Good examples are:

To obtain prices on funds you own, press 1.

To change your PIN, press 2.

This paradigm allows the user to understand the function, form a decision, and then execute that decision with a button-press action. The user is mapping information from the modality of speech onto an action that uses a different, mechanical modality.

---

[9] Both speaker-dependent and -independent. See the glossary for a definition of both terms.

[10] See Chapter 7 for distinctions between DTMF and speech modalities. See Chapter 8 for guidelines specific to natural language dialogue designs.

When the desired user action is spoken, however, the user must not only understand the function—he must also extract an action from the prompt in the form of which word(s) to say. This is more difficult and can lead to errors. In the following examples, the user is expected to understand the prompt and extract the desired action:

Avoid: *To obtain prices on funds you own, say "Funds."*
        To change your PIN, say "PIN."

Use: *Please say one of the following ...*
        Funds ... PIN ...

In the first example, keywords such as *"prices"* and *"you own"* mislead the user. Although the function is clear, the action of speaking the discrete word "Funds" is not obvious. The same is true in the second example, in which the user may wish to change his PIN. Upon hearing the prompt, the word *"change"* resonates with the action but is not included in the spoken command.

A function/action paradigm may seem benign for applications that use barge-in. By allowing the user to repeat a given keyword immediately, barge-in makes it easier to tolerate prompt flaws. But half-duplex systems expose the design flaw—experiencing higher error rates due to users forgetting the keywords. After hearing the list in its entirety, users remember most of the functions but forget the exact wording required to make a selection. Note that both full- and half-duplex systems suffer from the keyword contamination problem shown in the first (Avoid) example. The second (Use) example—in which the machine recites the legal vocabulary—is therefore more effective regardless of the turn-taking protocol.

6.2.1.2   √ Use Landmarks for Navigational Feedback

A landmark is a speech or non-speech cue that marks a specific location within the dialogue. The most common landmark is a menu name—declared at the entry to each menu. Another type of landmark relies on metaphors that encourage the user to visualize different application areas as "devices" or desktop objects. Landmarks are also commonly used to keep the user oriented within a sequential body of data such as voicemail messages. Some systems use earcons[11] as short and distinctive landmarks.

Avoid: *You have reached help, please listen to the following. You may say ...*
        Please say your command.

---

[11] See Chapter 5 for a discussion of tones as prompts, feedback, landmarks, or other tools.

Use: *Help. You may say ...*

         Main Menu. Please state your command.

The function of the landmark is to provide feedback to the user—telling him "where he is" in the dialogue. Landmarks are especially useful for letting the user know that the machine state has changed. This prevents speech errors, incorrect selections, or machine transitions from giving the user the impression that he is in a different state—a condition that tends to generate additional errors.[12]

6.2.1.2.1   + Use Menu Names as Landmarks

Main Menu

Listen to Message List

Help

System Options

The first example is the most typical. The machine simply declares the name of the menu at the point of entry. The inflection is usually downward, with finality. The second example is more verbose. This approach is sometimes used on entry to a help routine, establishing a context for help. The third example is the least verbose—dropping the implied "Menu." The fourth example is a reminder that some menu names may contain more than one word.

6.2.1.2.2   + Use Data Objects or Devices as Landmarks

Message Player

Calendar

Your appointment book is now open.

In the first example, the voicemail component that plays messages is viewed as a "device" called the "Message Player." The user thinks of it as a mechanical object—with "buttons" for rewind, fast forward, play, and pause. In the second example, the user refers to a "Calendar" as a physical calendar. The user can "open" this and other book-like data sources. Both of these examples use the name of the object as the landmark. The user perceives the identifying label as a title—as though printed on a remote control, appliance panel, or book.

---

[12] Specifically, this condition is called a state error, as described in Guideline 1.2.2.1.

The third is a more verbose example of the same type of landmark. The user has just spoken a sentence that a natural language subsystem—in this case for a personal assistant application—has interpreted as a request associated with scheduling appointments. In addition to performing the request, the system "moves to" the appointment book for two reasons. First, the design anticipates that subsequent user operations are more likely to revolve around appointments. Second, the "opening and closing" of these data objects reinforces the user interface metaphor—in this case, of a "desktop" or "virtual office."

6.2.1.2.3   + Use Landmarks as Feedback for Sequencing Through Data

Next message ...

First new message ...

Message Three of Seven ...

Some applications present long intervals of spoken data. In voicemail systems, for example, the user may spend a considerable amount of time within a particular message. Many of these systems therefore re-synchronize the user with landmarks each time she emerges from one of the data elements.

In the first example, the landmark simply delimits each voicemail message. The second and third examples show that landmarks can be informative at multiple levels. In the second example, ordinal numbers allow the user to keep track of messages completed. In the third example, the user is given three facts—the landmark as a delimiter, the number of messages completed, and the number remaining. As a result, users have an instinctive feel for their position in the sequence of data elements, making for high information density in a reasonably short landmark.[13]

6.2.1.3   √ Let the User Go First

DTMF dialogues present the list at the beginning of each menu. The user then interrupts when he hears his choice, or waits until the end of the menu to enter his selection. This paradigm is not as effective with spoken interfaces—particularly half-duplex systems. It is better to offer a speaking opportunity to the user in the form of

---

[13] This third option has the added advantage of using cardinal rather than ordinal numbers, thereby simplifying the quantity and complexity of spoken machine output. See the glossary for a detailed description of "cardinal" and "ordinal."

an initial recognition window.[14] The window should be immediately after the land-mark but before the presentation of the menu list.

The following sub-guidelines describe menu behaviors that are based on the assumption that the user is an expert.[15] Designers that follow these guidelines are encouraged to design dialogues that are tolerant of novice user behaviors—using spurious errors to trigger the menu list in the absence of legal user speech.

6.2.1.3.1   + Present Speaking Opportunity at the Beginning of Each Menu

To let users know they can go first and take a turn, start with a landmark or short prompt and then wait a second or two in anticipation of user input.

Use: *Main Menu <optional beep>*

        Options Menu

        Command please ...

        <unique tone>

In the first two examples, the expert user may speak immediately after hearing the landmark, resulting in rapid navigation through the menu hierarchy. The landmark is all that is required for the expert to remember the commands. In the third example, the application only has one mode—as might be the case in a voice-activated dialing (VAD) application—so identifying the Main Menu by name is not necessary. In the fourth example, a unique tone is the shortest and quickest way to give the turn to the user.

In addition to speeding up the dialogue, the application should make note of the appearance of legal speech during this short window as a good detector of expert users. Conversely, the absence of legal speech is what triggers the presentation of the menu list and identifies the less-experienced user. The simplest menu designs modulate their behaviors—switching from machine-driven to user-driven—according to this type of expert/novice detection.

6.2.1.3.2   √ Present the Menu List on Timeouts

Rely on timeouts or rejection errors following the landmark to trigger spoken machine output that clarifies expected user action. Avoid treating timeouts as

---

[14] Recognition windows are discussed in Guideline 4.2.2.2.

[15] If most users are first-time/only-time callers, and if this circumstance is not likely to change during the life of the application, then these guidelines may not be applicable.

errors. If the user does not speak first, the appropriate machine behavior is to take back the turn—presenting the list of menu choices without prejudice.[16]

Avoid:

App:	*Main Menu <beep>*
User:	<two-second timeout without speech>
App:	*I didn't hear you. Please make a selection or say "Help."*

In this example, the timeout is considered an error, and the application engages in error-recovery. This design presents a dissonance between the expert—who is well served by the shortened menu prompt—and the novice—who is forced to commit an "error" to hear his choices.

A better solution treats the error—the failure to speak—as an opportunity to present more detailed information. Timeouts thus become an automatic trigger for the menu list without requiring error-recovery:

Use:

Female Voice:	*Main Menu <beep>*
User:	<two-second timeout without speech>
Female Voice:	*Please say one of the following …*
Male Voice:	*Arrivals and Departures … Reservations … Vacation Packages … Help … Operator …*
User:	"Reservations."

6.2.1.3.3 √ Present the Menu List When OVW[17] Is Detected

The same principle used for menu timeouts can be applied to automatic list presentation when the user speaks words that are not in the vocabulary:

---

[16] This principle of "errorless" timeout handling has been deployed in a number of applications since publication of the first edition of this style guide. The principle is becoming generalized to a number of dialogue devices, and goes beyond menus. The requirement level is therefore raised in this edition.

[17] Out-of-vocabulary word. See the glossary and Section 1.3 for the distinction between OVW and OOG. The term OVW is preferred for menus, as the required technology is either discrete or single-token continuous ASR.

Avoid:

Female Voice:	*Domestic Reservations <beep>*
User:	"I don't know what to say here ..."
Female Voice:	*I didn't understand you. Please wait for the tone and then repeat your choice. Options Menu <beep>.*
User:	"I didn't say a choice, because ..."
Female Voice:	*I didn't understand you...*

In the example, the application spends too much time talking to the user about what did **not** happen. The statement, "*I didn't understand you*" is unnecessary, as it pointlessly declares an error condition that doesn't exist.

Use:

Female Voice:	*Domestic Reservations <beep>*
User:	"I don't know what to say here ..."
Female Voice:	*Please choose a destination ...*
Male Voice:	*Boston... Cincinnati... Denver .... <list continues>*

In the improved version, the user has again said something that is illegal—so-called out-task speech [Baber97].[18] But in this case, the application simply proceeds with presentation of the menu list. Rather than wasting time recovering the error, the design assumes that the user does not remember—or has never encountered—the selections in this menu. By presenting the list immediately, the novice user receives pertinent information, reducing the likelihood that the error will be amplified by subsequent error-recovery interactions. This is a form of "point and speak."[19]

6.2.1.3.4   √ If Possible, Make the List Interruptible

Menu presentation styles are much more tolerant when the user is allowed to speak immediately after hearing the desired choice.

Use:

Female Voice:	*Command? <beep>*

---

[18] Note that [Baber97] prefers the term "out-task."
[19] See Guideline 4.2.2.4.

User:	"What are my choices?"
Female Voice:	*You may say ...*
Male Voice:	*Call ... Add a Name ... Delete ...*
User:	"Delete."
Female Voice:	*Name to delete? <beep>*

This dialogue can be deployed in two ways:

- Full duplex with barge-in;
- Half duplex with recognition windowing.

In the full-duplex solution, barge-in is activated while the machine presents the menu list. When the user speaks the word "Delete," the rest of the list is aborted and the application proceeds based on recognition of the command.

In the half-duplex solution, each menu item is a separate audio recording. Items are separated by a short recognition window in which the entire set of menu choices is active. This second solution requires more care in managing the timing and pacing of the menu—as well as in handling spoke-too-soon and spurious responses, which occur more frequently—but is significantly less expensive to implement. See [Balentine99] for a complete description of this method for list interaction.

6.2.1.4   + Present the List as Verbatim Choices

Avoid extraneous words when presenting the user's options. Additional material is distracting rather than helpful in the context of lists. Instead, the list of menu options should be presented in sequence as verbatim choices—thereby encouraging users to repeat a desired item as soon as they hear it. Since the spoken vocabulary words have built-in meaning, it is not necessary to expand upon them with additional information.

Avoid:	*Say "Record," then say "Stop" when you're done.*
	For playback, use the words "Play," "Step," or "Scan"

Use:	*You may choose one of these ...*
	Record ... Stop ... Play ...
	You may also say ...
	Step ... Scan ...

6.2.1.5   + Consider Using a Different Voice for List Presentation

The user may be able to recognize and mimic vocabulary words more easily if they are presented in a unique voice. See Guideline 2.1.2.3.4 for an example.

6.2.2   Number of Selections per Menu

Decisions about menus and other lists must take into account human memory. Recited lists are difficult to remember, even when they contain very few elements, and there is a great deal of information in the psychological literature that can help with retention.[20] In addition to the number of elements in a list, human memory varies in performance according to how the elements relate to each other semantically, which ones appear first and last in the list, and how each element is spoken.

6.2.2.1   √ Absolute Maximum of Nine Items for Interruptible Lists

If the menu can be interrupted, then the user will often make his selection immediately after hearing it. This allows menus to be somewhat longer.

6.2.2.2   √ Absolute Maximum of Five Items for Non-Interruptible Lists

If the menu cannot be interrupted, then the user must remember the entire list, speaking only at the end. This means that the menu should consist of three to five items. The lower number is preferred; the higher number is the maximum.

6.2.2.3   + Use Scanning or Other Methods Rather than Menus for Long Lists

When spoken lists become unmanageably long, they take on different dynamics. Rather than a single object that is made up of list elements, the stream of audio begins to take on the flavor of unstructured data. This data should be navigated using methods that differ from those of the simple menu. See Guideline 6.2.3.6 for an example of a list-scanning device.

6.2.3   List Interruption

6.2.3.1   √ Allow and Encourage User Repetition During List Presentation

One of the easiest actions for a user is repetition. Users should be able to repeat any single list element they hear. The design, in turn, should rely on extra-speech information to recover inter-word rejections and to act upon OOG rejections.

---

[20] See the George Miller work on "The Magical Number Seven" [Miller56]. See Section 6.5.1 for the special case of two-element menus.

6.2.3.2   + Support "Touch to Select" Feature

App: *When you hear your destination city, touch any key.*

   Austin ... Dallas ... Oklahoma City ...

User: <keypress>

App: *Travel to Oklahoma City is ...*

The feature allows the user to interrupt an arbitrary list and make a selection with the same action.

6.2.3.3   + Support "Speak to Select" Feature

A similar scheme for list interruption replaces DTMF with speech for selection.

App: *When you hear your destination city, please repeat it ...*

   Austin ... Dallas ... Oklahoma City ...

User: "Yes, Oklahoma ..."

App: *Travel to Oklahoma City is ...*

See Guideline 4.2.2.4 for a more detailed description of this so-called "point and speak" method. The approach is also called "speak to select," as the user produces any utterance to choose one in a running sequence of elements. The device is handy for browsing lists including *n*-best lists (see Guideline 7.2.3.3).

It is probably not necessary to tell the user exactly what to say to select an item in a long list. In one study, first-time/only-time users produced a bounded range of utterances to select a target within a running list of twenty items (security names). The subjects said predictable phrases, such as "OK," "stop," or "yes," as well as simply repeating the target security name after hearing it. In fact, the seven most-common responses accounted for 78% of all utterances [Hersh98b].

6.2.3.4   √ Respond to Selection with Goal-Oriented Query

If the design supports "touch to select" or "speak to select" features, then it is important that the query be phrased correctly. Many applications use yes-no queries to confirm what the user **said**:

Avoid: *Did you say "Play Messages?"*

This phrasing is usually inappropriate. The reason is that the user may have spoken some "pointing" phrase such as, "Give me that," selecting the option with OOG speech. In such a case, asking the user literally about what he **said** is not helpful. Instead, the application should focus on what the user **wants**, as demonstrated by the timing of the speak to select action.

Use: *Do you want to play your messages?*

Replacing the question, "*Did you say ...*" with the more universal, "*Do you want ...*" is called a **goal-oriented query**.

6.2.3.5   √ Allow for Time-Lags on Selection

Bear in mind that it takes time for a user to hear and recognize the desired element in a list of elements and slightly longer to form the decision to speak. By the time the "touch to select" utterance begins, the list may have moved on to its next element. Considering time lags in such selection behaviors is therefore important.[21]

In one study, subjects were asked to select a specific element in a 20-element spoken list. One out of three responses were delayed past the start of the following element. Most of these selection lags occurred when list items were separated by a short silence (250 milliseconds), but there was a delay in 7% of utterances even when the window was increased to a full half second [Hersh98b]. Since increasing the window is inefficient—500 milliseconds between each element increases the playback time of a 20-element list by 10 seconds—accounting for these time lags is important if the user is to pick a target consistently.

6.2.3.6   + Consider Bi-Directional Navigation

It is possible to design scanners that traverse lists forward and backward. A scanning device is applicable for long lists—for example, the names in a user's phonebook.

User: "List the Phonebook."

App: *Your phonebook has twenty names ...*
         Jonathon Whiting ... Alexander James ... Don Billingsley ... Mom ...
         Susan at work ... My publisher ... Doug ...

User: "Backup."

App: *<backup tone>*
         Doug ... My publisher ... Susan at work ... Mom ... Don Billingsley ...

User: "Forward."

---

[21] See Guideline 4.2.2.4 for an illustration of time lags and list selection.

App: *<forward tone>*
        Don Billingsley ... Mom ... Susan ...

User: "Number."

App: *Number for ... Mom ...*
        555-1212

User: "Previous."

App: *Number for ... Don Billingsley ...*
        444-1212

User: "Call."

App: *Calling ... Don Billingsley ...*

The example is somewhat drawn out to show the many features that such a device might exhibit. Initially, the user activates the scanner—which begins by declaring the size of the list. It then presents each element as quickly as possible.

When desired, the word "Backup" reverses the direction of the scan. The word "Forward" reverses it again. When the user interrupts with a request—in this case for the associated number—the scanner performs the operation on the name just selected. The words "Previous" and "Next" allow the user to choose adjacent entries. Other actions include automated calling, as shown at the end of the example.

A scanning device may be useful for traversing lists including *n*-best lists, holdings in a financial portfolio, appointments in a crowded calendar, or similar information.

6.2.4   Two-Way Branching and Quasi-Menus

There are many points within the dialogue structure that represent two-way branching points. Such points are often treated as though they are menus, resulting in awkward and unnecessarily long prompts. Such **quasi-menus** should be avoided:

Avoid: *To reenter your fund code, say "Continue," or to hear a list of your plan's fund codes, say "Help."*

The prompt is a quasi-menu because its presentation style uses the *"To ... Say"* construct, creating a user expectation that a list of choices will follow. However, the list consists of only two elements. Although there is nothing inherently wrong with a two-element menu, it should be presented exactly like any other menu.

6.2.4.1   + Replace Quasi-Menus with Either/Or Constructs

Two-way branches can sometimes be reformulated with a short either/or construct:

Avoid: *To reenter your fund code, say "Continue," or to hear a list of your plan's fund codes, say "Help."*

Use: *Continue or help?*

Say either "Continue" or "Help."

In the first corrected example, there are only two choices. By asking *"either/or"* the prompt is shorter and clearer. In the second example, the same principle applies but the prompt is cast in the imperative form.[22]

6.2.4.2   + Replace Quasi-Menus with Yes-No Queries

Yes-no queries can be excellent two-way branching devices:

Avoid: *To reenter your fund code, say "Continue," or to hear a list of your plan's fund codes, say "Help."*

Use: *Do you want help?*

In the example, a "yes" answer routes the user to help. A "no" answer routes the user back to the "Continue" branch, allowing reentry of the fund code. The user never needs to use the awkward "Continue" word for reentry.

6.2.5   Hidden Menus

A hidden menu is a recognition window that gives the user an optional opportunity to speak. The menu is "hidden" in the sense that the list of options is never presented. It is often not even announced.[23] Hidden menus provide opportunities for menu flattening by supporting branches that skip past the standard menu hierarchy.

6.2.5.1   ≈ Place Hidden Menus at Strategic Locations in the Dialogue

Hidden menus are opportunities for expert users to "tunnel" through a hierarchy, providing shortcuts that are immune to accidental discovery by novices. Hidden menus should be placed at locations in the dialogue that benefit from shortcuts.

---

[22] Note the similarity of this either/or construct with the newer techniques of two-way and three-way branching [Guideline 8.5.1.2.1]. Although such branching is normally used to enter the major states of a natural language (NL) application, the device is also handy in directed dialogues.

[23] See Section 5.3.3 for a discussion of when to use tones to indicate hidden menus.

6.2.5.1.1   + Immediately After Answering Call

Immediately after answering, a hidden menu can allow repeat callers to skip past opening instructions or help routines.

Use:

App: *Thank you for calling ...*

User: "Scores."

App: *Today's sports scores ...*

6.2.5.1.2   + At Major Menus

Hidden menus can be useful at major menus—activated for a short (two-second) window following a landmark.

6.2.5.2   ≈ Consider Using Hidden Menus to Profile Users

Hidden menus are for experts—those users who already know what to say and when to say it. Novices can be expected to miss the window of opportunity presented by a hidden menu, either not speaking at all or talking conversationally to themselves or others around them.

The approach seems straightforward, but has only been corroborated anecdotally in product demonstrations and informal usability tests. The following two sub-guidelines are therefore marked only as ≈ (Good Practice) because to the authors' knowledge no fielded applications have yet made use of this profiling technique.

6.2.5.2.1   ≈ Use Hidden Menu Success to Identify Expert Users

A hidden menu appears and disappears with no evidence of its presence unless a vocabulary word is recognized with very high confidence. This means that successful selection of a function from within a hidden menu is evidence that the user is an expert. This knowledge can be useful in determining prompts and in suppressing help routines.

6.2.5.2.2   ≈ Use Hidden Menu Failure to Identify Novice Users

The failure to choose an item from within a hidden menu indicates that a user is less than expert. Hidden menus that follow landmarks lead to menu-list presentations if the user does not select properly. This fact allows the application to consider alternate behaviors aimed at novice users.

6.2.5.3   √ Keep Hidden Menus Short

The most likely cause of failure for a hidden menu is a false acceptance—the incorrect recognition of OOG as one of the menu selections. The chances of such a false positive increase when hidden menus have long duration. Bear in mind that a hidden menu is for experts—they already know when to speak. It is not necessary to wait for more than two seconds or so.

6.2.5.4   √ Terminate Hidden Menus on Low-Confidence Speech

Guidelines in this chapter encourage designers to exploit input that might otherwise be regarded as an error. This input—useful in many cases—includes OOG, spoke-too-soon conditions, and silence timeouts. The principle is an important one, but does not apply to hidden menus. Rather, the hidden menu must be extremely tolerant of error conditions, interpreting such conditions as novice user behaviors or background noise and ignoring them.

One user in a usability test, for example, responded to the opening greeting on her very first call. The machine thanked her for calling, and she in turn replied to the welcome message. The system ignored the input, which was recognized as OOG.

App: *Thank you for calling …*

User: "You're welcome."

App: *This is an automated banking system.*

        <continue with opening instructions>

Similarly, an inter-word rejection is too risky to recover at the moment of a hidden menu. Although the speech may have come from an expert, it is also possible that the response is a "near miss"—false acceptance that, luckily, has been rejected via the nearness of the top two recognized results. Rather than risk the latter to recover the former, it is better to ignore such input.

Avoid:

App: *Acme Tele-Message.*

User: <clears throat>

App: *Do you want sports statistics?*

In the example, the sound of the user clearing his throat has been recognized as "statistics" within the hidden menu. The second *n*-best choice is "scores." The two words have similar recognition statistics, resulting in the low confidence[24] associated with an inter-word rejection. Following other guidelines in this book, the designer has chosen to use a yes-no query to recover inter-word rejections—a decision that in this case leads to false acceptance error.

Use:

App: *Acme Tele-Message.*

User: <clears throat>

App: *Thank you for calling our automated system.*

        <continue with opening instructions>

In the improved version, even inter-word rejections are ignored—leading to termination of the hidden menu and presentation of the first opening application instruction. This solution biases the system in favor of robustness for novices over efficiency for experts. The occasional expert will miss the window, having to choose from a standard menu, but a novice will almost never trigger a hidden menu item inadvertently.

6.3   Yes-No Queries

Queries that solicit simple "yes" and "no" responses are singularly important. Not only do they move the dialogue forward at junctures where transactions must be corroborated; they are also the most important procedure for recovering errors. This section discusses details of the yes-no **dialogue component**.

6.3.1   Yes-No Dialogue Design

Yes-no queries must be stable and highly reliable. This means that simple and predictable behavior takes design precedence over "variety" and entertaining dialogues.

6.3.1.1   + Ask a Direct Question

The easiest way to evoke a spontaneous "yes" or "no" from the user is to ask a direct question. This means avoiding convoluted imperative sentence constructions.

Avoid: *If that is correct, please say "yes." Otherwise, say "no."*

---

[24] Remember that low confidence can be interpreted in two ways. The condition may indicate OOG input. It may also indicate that the user has spoken a legal utterance that has matched two different vocabulary entries with very similar recognition scores. Distinguishing between the two is never perfectly reliable.

Do you want me to play that message? ... answer "yes" or "no."

To place another order, say "yes" now.

Use: *Is that correct?*

        Play message?

        Do you want to place another order?

6.3.1.2   ≈ Avoid Yes-No Synonyms

This is a controversial guideline and contradicts many published recommendations or observations by speech industry practitioners [Meisel98]. It also seems to fly in the face of common sense. For these reasons, consider the following:

- This guideline is tagged as only ≈ (Good Practice), indicating that there may be alternate views on the subject of yes-no synonyms.

- The line of reasoning that leads to this guideline is discussed in some detail, allowing the designer to distinguish between those circumstances in which the guideline may apply from those in which some other logic is more suitable.

Arguments **in favor of** yes-no synonyms include:

1. The user may speak in any way that he wishes.

2. Users that say yes-no synonyms are more likely to be recognized the first time without the need for recovery.

3. A responsive yes-no dialogue component will leave the user with a better impression of the intelligence and naturalness of the application.

4. If a user says a yes-no synonym not present in the vocabulary, there is an increased chance that it will be recognized as in-vocabulary (false acceptance).

Arguments **against** yes-no synonyms include:

1. The presence of additional words in the vocabulary is likely to increase inter-word rejection rates.

2. A large yes-no vocabulary is more vulnerable to false acceptance, making the vocabulary less capable of OOG rejection.

3. Users that say a yes-no synonym—provided it is detected as OOG—will be corrected the first time, leading to a narrowing of user behaviors (convergence) as the dialogue proceeds.

All else being equal, it seems as though yes-no synonyms should be viewed, at the very least, as a "tolerant" machine behavior. But the arguments against this are compelling. Since adding synonyms to such a simple vocabulary will almost certainly drive up the rejection rate, the overall performance of yes and no is likely to produce a net decrease in throughput. Similarly, if the application relies on yes-no as a "barrier," (see Guideline 6.3.4.2) as shown in Figure 6.1, then there is no room for even a slight increase in false acceptance).

The designer is cautioned to measure yes-no rejection performance in the fielded application before risking degradation due to synonyms.

6.3.1.3 √ Allow Two Tries Before Backup

A single problem associated with yes-no is easy and reliable to recover. The yes-no subroutine should include a quick turnaround and a second opportunity to capture "yes" or "no" before the dialogue embarks on more time-consuming help.

6.3.2 Yes-No Error Recovery

Yes-no questions are themselves vulnerable to error—primarily inter-word rejection, but occasionally substitutions. Because the vocabulary is a symmetrical (two-word) vocabulary, recovery of yes-no errors requires special considerations.

6.3.2.1 √ Wait for Error Before Presenting Yes-No Instructions

Yes-no—once stable—can be used frequently throughout the dialogue. It is important to resist the temptation to add instructions that are embedded within the prompt.

Avoid: *Please answer "yes" or "no"—is the number correct?*
     Do you want another transaction? ... say "yes" or "no."

Use:

App: *Do you want another transaction?*

User: "I'd like a balance, now."

App: *Please answer "yes" or "no" ...*
     Do you want another transaction?

User: "Yes."

In the example, the user has answered the question with a statement.[25] The recognizer has returned OOG. Now is the time to present the vocabulary—as an error recovery

---

[25] This is an example of mixed-initiative user speech within a machine-initiated dialogue style. Rather than answering "yes" or "no" the caller initiates the next turn without prompting.

prompt rather than an *a priori* embedded instruction. The recovery will work well, and the user has also been negatively reinforced—he is less likely to fall back on yes-no synonyms or mixed-initiative responses in the future. Experts, on the other hand, have been positively reinforced—they do not have to endure the *"Please answer 'yes' or 'no'"* instruction.

6.3.2.2   √ Recover Only the Error Committed

Avoid:

App: *1234 ... Is the number correct? <beep>*

User: <interrupting the beep> "Yes."

App: *Sorry, I didn't understand you.*
         Please wait for the tone, and then say "yes" or "no."
         Now once again ...
         1234 ... Is the number correct? <beep>

User: "Yes."

The dialogue wastes time by using one error-recovery sequence for all errors. The instruction explains both tone and vocabulary, requiring that the entire question be repeated. The error was simply a spoke-too-soon condition—usually a sign of a quick and responsive user. The correction is therefore unnecessarily punishing.

Better:

App: *1234 ... Is the number correct? <beep>*

User: <interrupting the beep> "Yes."

App: *Remember to wait for the tone ...*
         Is the number correct? <beep>

User: "Yes."

Best:

App: *1234 ... Is the number correct? <beep>*

User: <interrupting the beep> "Yes."

App: *Remember to wait for the tone. <beep>*

User: "Yes."

Users repeat what they just said quite easily. Anything that allows that to happen quickly is likely to recover a turn-taking error.

6.3.2.3   √ Use Caution with Inter-Word Yes-No Rejection

An inter-word rejection occurs when two vocabulary words have similar scores. A yes-no question can query the first choice in the *n*-best list. If the user refuses the choice with "no," then the dialogue can query on the second *n*-best choice.

This recovery scheme does not work with the special case of a yes-no vocabulary. The reason is that yes and no will always appear in the *n*-best list—it's a two-word vocabulary. In addition, it is not easy to use the words "yes" and "no" to recover errors in the recognition of "yes" and "no." The goal is to extract a repetition from the user. A good recovery prompt is:

"Was that a yes?"

This solution—apparently silly at first glance—is discussed in Guideline 4.4.2.2 as a recovery method for spoke-too-soon conditions. The solution works equally well for inter-word yes-no rejections. Study the examples to understand why the prompt always causes a repetition of the user's initial answer—regardless of whether it's a "yes" or a "no."

6.3.3   Implicit Yes-No Windows

Sometimes called a **confirmation window** (see Guideline 10.2.2.2), implicit yes-no adopts the "no news is good news" methodology for speedy interactions. The methodology is based on the observation that users often speak when hearing an error—even if they were not prompted. Implicit yes-no is similar to a hidden menu except that it only allows backing up on errors.

6.3.3.1   + Do Not Prompt Implicit Yes-No Confirmation Windows

An implicit yes-no is optional. It is not necessary to call attention to it. Instead, the machine declares its intention and then waits just long enough to allow the user to respond if there is a reason to prevent the incipient machine action.

Avoid:

User: "Call Bob Johnson."

App: *Bob Johnson ...*

Is that correct?

User: "Yes."

App: *Calling ...*

The dialogue as shown is too long. Recognition is usually correct. Even when it's not, the problem is not fatal—the user can always abort the call. So interrupting every time with a yes-no question is unnecessary; it slows the dialogue and makes the interaction seem tentative.

Use:

User: "Call Bob Johnson."

App: *Calling Bob Johnson ...*

User: <no response>

In the improved example, the machine simply announces what it is about to do. The short (2 second) window gives the user the option of speaking, but speech is not required. The active vocabulary is the yes-no sub-vocabulary.

6.3.3.2   √ Close the Window on Confident "Yes" or Timeout

The user may present a "yes" if she wants to. Impatient users can thus move slightly more quickly by closing the window as soon as a confident "yes" is recognized.

Use:

User: "Call Bob Johnson."

App: *Calling Bob Johnson ...*

User: "Yes."

The "yes" is not required, and is not likely to help. But it does not hurt, so there's no reason to punish users for presenting it.

6.3.3.3   √ Treat All Other Conditions as Implicit "No"

The user does not necessarily know about the implicit confirmation window. But the user does recognize a recognition error when it occurs. Such conditions often trigger spontaneous exclamations.

Use:

User: "Call Bob Johnson."

App: *Calling John Wilson ...*

171

User: "Hold it!"

App: *Is that correct?*

In the example, the user has spoken spontaneously. The recognizer has returned OOG. This spurious input is treated as a "no." The same is true of all responses that are neither confident "yes" nor timeout, such as:

- Inter-word rejections, including rejected "yes,"
- OVW rejections, and
- Spoke too soon conditions.

6.3.3.4   + Backup to Explicit Yes-No on Implicit "No"

User interruption should lead to a specific and explicit yes-no question, re-synchronizing the user with the application.

User: "Call Bob Johnson."

App: *Calling John Wilson ...*

User: "Hold it!"

App: *Is that correct?*

User: "No."

App: *Name to call?*

The question, *"Is that correct?"* is a standard yes-no query. This means that the user must speak twice to undo the function. This is slightly more time-consuming than attempts at immediate recovery that may offer greater natural variety. But it is more stable than attempting to move backward to some previous input state—a state that the user may not correctly infer—and therefore less likely to lead to state errors and subsequent error amplification.

6.3.4   Stabilizing Dialogues with Yes-No

As the dialogue component with the smallest vocabulary and therefore the greatest capability to reject OOG input, yes-no is ideally suited to perform the extra task of distinguishing background problems from the foreground inputs that constitute sentient user interaction. Simply put, yes-no queries offer the greatest chance of stabilizing dialogues when they get into trouble. In this discussion, "stability" refers specifically to resistance against false interruptions, false acceptance, and spoke-too-soon problems caused by noise or conversational speech.

6.3.4.1   ≈ Use Yes-No Module to Detect Noise

"Yes" and "no" are both short words that can appear predictably within a specific time, allowing a very short window for "ideal" input. Less-than-ideal conditions may not be legitimate user responses. This simple fact means that the best hope for detecting and filtering out intermittent noises lies in both the timing and the recognition confidence of yes-no responses.

The key to detecting noise with yes-no is to consider the timing of the utterance as it appears at the input. Early or delayed speech, utterances that are too long, inter-word rejections that follow spoke-too-soon events, and repeated OOG responses to yes-no questions are all likely to be extraneous input that should be noted by the application and applied to decisions about the stability of the dialogue.

App: *Do you want to hear your saved messages?*

User: <over background announcement> ... "Yes." ... <more noise>

App: *Please answer "yes" or "no" ...*

    Do you want to hear your saved messages?

User: <more noise> ... "Yes." ... <noise>

App: *Too much background noise.*

    Please remain silent for just a moment.

    <pause>

App: *Now, once again...*

    Do you want to hear your saved messages?

User: <more noise> ... "Yes." ... <noise>

App: *First saved message ...*

It is not obvious from the scripted example what the recognizer "heard," so this discussion steps through each interaction. Imagine that the user is calling from a noisy club with frequent public address announcements for various patrons' tables. After the first prompt, the application receives OOG from the recognizer. This is because background noise surrounding the user's "yes" has been captured as speech. The application hypothesizes that the user has given a conversational reply—a reasonable first assumption—and prompts for a discrete yes-no answer.

The second input also returns OOG. The application now changes its hypothesis, assuming that the user is in a high noise environment. After declaring the condition, the application tells the ASR to check the background and adjust speech-detection thresholds. This occurs during the pause. After adjustment, the application re-invokes the yes-no question. This time the noise—which has not changed—is below the speech detection threshold, allowing the ASR to capture and recognize user speech.

Failure to capture a "yes" on the third try due to OOG implies that the background is too loud to filter out. Conversely, a timeout on the third attempt indicates that thresholds are too high and the user cannot be heard above the noise. Either condition leads to a decision to announce DTMF (keypress) alternatives to the user.

6.3.4.2 + Consider Using Yes-No as a "Barrier"

The previous example shows a mechanism for relying on two OOG responses in a row to detect extensive noise problems. Such a simple algorithm is effective but is not enough to ensure robustness. The following conditions may be additional indicators that the background is "too noisy:"

- Spoke-too-soon followed by OOG,

- Spoke-too-soon followed by inter-word rejection in the same window,

- Two inter-word (yes-no) rejections in a row, and

- Silence timeout followed by OOG or inter-word rejection.

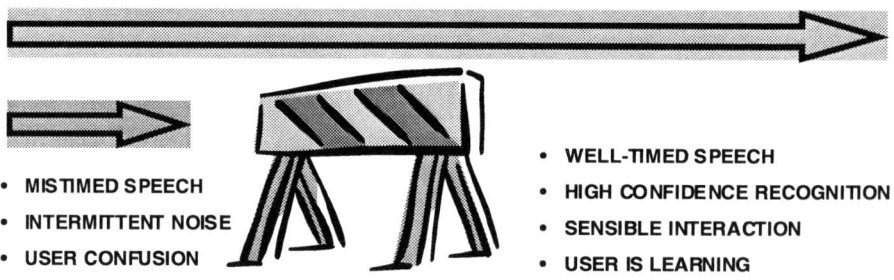

- MISTIMED SPEECH
- INTERMITTENT NOISE
- USER CONFUSION

- WELL-TIMED SPEECH
- HIGH CONFIDENCE RECOGNITION
- SENSIBLE INTERACTION
- USER IS LEARNING

Figure 6.1—**YES-NO BARRIER** stops input that is not reliable. Anything that gets past the barrier is likely to represent sentient user interaction. The yes-no dialogue component thus stabilizes the dialogue by allowing periodic tests of overall input sensibility.

There are other detectors that the designer may wish to construct—detectors aimed at distinguishing **users**, whose behavior changes (adapts) when the machine interacts with them, from **random non-user input**. The detectors illustrate an important use of yes-no, shown in Figure 6.1.

174

6.3.4.2.1   + Consider Switching to Half-Duplex Yes-No in Noise

Algorithms for detecting noise and distinguishing it from user speech can be developed for barge-in systems as well as for half-duplex systems. But barge-in algorithms are much more complex. One of the advantages of a half-duplex system is its ability to ignore background noise whenever the application presents spoken machine output. This makes the juncture at which recognition is first activated a well-known window. Making assumptions at that moment about the background—and then testing the assumptions with subsequent interaction—exerts a stabilizing influence on the dialogue.

In full-duplex systems, frequent interruptions before the prompt is completed may indicate excessive background noise conditions. In such cases, it may be appropriate to switch to half-duplex windowing for yes-no questions.

6.3.4.2.2   + Determine Point of Failure and Give Up Quickly

If the yes-no dialogue component is unable to elicit changes in the input, the problem is probably noise. Users invariably change their behaviors as the machine interacts with them. Persistent conditions that lead to failure should cause the application to abandon speech recognition sooner rather than later.

6.3.4.2.3   + Test Under Worst Case Conditions

When relying on yes-no as a barrier, this dialogue component becomes the cornerstone around which the entire dialogue is built. This means that yes-no should be developed and tested in isolation as early as possible.

Since the yes-no dialogue component will be reused throughout the application, careful testing requires both user input and non-user background experiments. The goal is for the yes-no barrier to give up as quickly as possible when user input cannot be captured and recognized, but to exhibit patience and helpfulness when the problems are user confusion or novice user behaviors. Some useful tests include the following:

1. With no user present, turn on the radio and allow the yes-no dialogue component to interact with it. The software subroutine should give up within 15–30 seconds—after attempting to make sense of the input and after trying various error-recovery alternatives. This stability should be exhibited for radio stations carrying music as well as for talk shows.

2. With no user present, let the yes-no dialogue component interact with re-

cordings of various noise environments. These may include airports, traffic sounds, restaurants, and night clubs. If the subroutine is designed to adjust automatically when it detects noise, test to ensure that it does so. Then ensure that failures in the form of timeouts after such adjustments lead to graceful exits.

6.3.5   One-Shot Yes-No[26]

Users sometimes present mixed-initiative replies to yes-no questions. As a directed dialogue, unfortunately, yes-no is not equipped to handle the "change of topic" that is symptomatic of the mixed-initiative reply. For example, suppose a caller has just specified all information required to complete a travel reservation. The dialogue closes with a yes-no question:

App: *Would you like to book this ticket?*

User: "Do you have anything later … say, closer to noon?"

Instead of answering the yes-no question directly, the user has continued with the dialogue, inquiring about changes that might be possible. The interaction is mixed-initiative because the user **implies** a "no" answer but does not explicitly say "no," preferring instead to initiate a new interaction in response to the yes-no question. The result is a classic state error[27] because the machine—now stuck in a yes-no question—is in one state while the user has moved forward to a new state unbeknownst to the machine. User speech is unrecognizable in the current state and can lead to inappropriate error recovery and error amplification.

A technique known as "one-shot yes-no" can be helpful in managing state errors on yes-no questions with minimum impact on the dialogue flow. The technique recognizes the return of OVW in response to yes-no as an indication of a mixed-initiative reply. Although the recognizer does not know what the user said, a subsequent interaction can suppress yes-no error recovery and stabilize the dialogue quickly.

6.3.5.1   √ Use One-Shot When Mixed Initiative Replies Are Likely

Mixed-initiative replies tend to occur more frequently on certain types of yes-no questions—in particular those questions that revolve around accumulating lists and involving personal names and dates.

---

[26] Section 6.3.5 is new to the second edition. Note that the remainder of the section numbering is the same as the first edition.
[27] See Section 1.2.2.1 for a discussion of state errors.

6.3.5.1.1   √ Terminate Accumulating Lists

In the following example, the user is forwarding an e-mail message. The application must extract one or more personal names to complete the task. Finding a mechanism for terminating the accumulation of names is the design problem. The solution usually relies on yes-no, with the risk of extracting mixed-initiative replies.

Avoid:

App: *Say the name.*

User: "Jason Monroe."

App: *Jason Monroe. Correct?*

User: "Yes."

App: *Add another name?*

User: "Melanie Engleman."

App: *Please answer "yes" or "no." Do you want to add another name?*

User: "Yes."

App: *Say the name.*

User: "Melanie Engleman."

App: *Melanie Engleman. Correct?*

User: "Yes."

The dialogue stumbles at the yes-no question. Because the user has generated a mixed-initiative response to the question, the recognizer detects and rejects the OVW as "garbage." The conventional solution—re-prompting for a "yes" or "no" solves the problem, but at the expense of the natural momentum of the dialogue. A better solution follows:

Use:

App: *Say the name.*

User: "Jason Monroe."

App: *Jason Monroe. Correct?*

User: "Yes."

App: *Add another name?*

User: "Melanie Engleman."

App: *Say the name.*

User: "Melanie Engleman."

App: *Melanie Engleman. Correct?*

User: "Yes."

The "one-shot" yes-no response accepts the OVW and returns immediately, allowing the application to use a more graceful solution, *Say the name.* The user then repeats the name with little impact on momentum.

6.3.5.1.2   √ Streamline Date Queries

A similar use of the one-shot technique resolves mixed-initiative replies to date queries. In the following electronic bill payment application an awkward two-way branching prompt asks the user for a date.

App: *Please say the date that you want the bill paid, or say "today."*

User: "Well either today or in the next couple of days."

This query was observed to produce lots of unpredictable speech from users. After analysis, it became clear that most users by far were choosing today—easily three quarters of users calling the bank assumed that the bill would be paid as soon as the transaction was completed. This observation made a yes-no question a simpler and more reliable interaction technique:

App: *Do you want to pay today?*

User: "No, I want to pay on November 16."

App: *Say the date.*

User: "November 16."

Most users answer "yes" to the question and there is no need to resolve the date. Any reply other than "yes" triggers the more specific prompt, *Say the date.* This prompt captures dates more reliably and the dialogue moves forward quickly and predictably.

6.4   Reusable Dialogue Components

In order to create an aesthetically gratifying and coherent application, we must look closely at each interactive element—ensuring that it exhibits crisp and logical entry and exit points. This is accomplished by isolating common interactions to software subroutines that are then reused throughout the dialogue. If users get bogged down inside one of these elements, then high-level relationships become obscure and unimportant. Once each subroutine is independently stabilized, however, then interactions between the elements begin to dominate the interface.

Rather than striving for discourse models based on programmed machine intelligence, designers may adopt a **behavioral** design. In this distinctly non-human model, interactions between user and machine can be thought of as a nexus of individual automata or dialogue components. A dialogue component is a software subroutine[28] that manages user behaviors for the purpose of advancing the task. The yes-no module, for example, causes the user to utter a spontaneous "yes" or "no." The menu dialogue component triggers a user-selection or -inquiry behavior. User-inquiry behaviors in turn activate the menu-list dialogue component, which compels the user to hear, understand, and then choose one of the list elements. Dialogue components thus reinforce productive user behaviors, thereby injecting negative feedback into the user interface system.[29]

6.4.1   Designing Dialogue Components

Every dialogue component is designed to accomplish a specific task. The task is aimed at extracting a "chunk" of information from the user, and each task relies on its own unique error-recovery and interaction rules to accomplish that. The rules are goal-oriented: a dialogue component attempts to capture reliable information as quickly as possible. All machine behaviors pursue their one goal as individual automata. This means that dialogue components operate independently and without a "big

---

[28] A library of these software objects is often called middleware because it resides between the upper (application) and lower (API) layers of software. The old term subroutine is used here because it is easily understood by laymen.

[29] Charged words such as "cause," "trigger," and "compel" are used deliberately here to convey the behavioral flavor of this paradigm. Unlike linguistic or social approaches, a speech automaton does not attempt to understand users and does not care what they "feel" or "think." Rather, the subroutine is exclusively interested in what the user **does**. If user behavior advances the task, it is rewarded with success. If user behavior diverges from the task, it is negatively reinforced with the appearance of new automata that gravitate inexorably back toward the goals of the task.

picture" of the application as a whole. To the degree that the overall dialogue exhibits any order or intelligence, it is an emergent property of the dialogue components and their relationship with each other.

Several dialogue components have already been coded by various developers:

- Yes-no questions,
- List selection modules (e.g., menus),
- Numeric strings—capture and corroboration (e.g., PIN. or telephone numbers),
- Dates and/or times capture (e.g., scheduling),
- Flag-toggling (e.g., setting urgent or confidential flags on or off), and
- Personal name capture (e.g., voice-activated dialing or automated attendant).

Many speech vendors also have libraries of common interactions.[30] Many of these dialogue components are designed around natural language technologies. As such, they are sometimes based on the (false) assumptions that grammar is the primary attribute of a natural language dialogue, that accurately recognizing user input is the primary (or only) goal of these modules, and that speech recognition technology is the defining influence on options and goals. In fact, **timing** is a much more important attribute of speech-input subroutines, and interactive effects that either amplify or dampen error amplification must be included in dialogue component subroutines. The following guidelines identify both design considerations and software development issues associated with dialogue components.

6.4.1.1   + Design "Closed System" Dialogue Components

The fundamental problem with speech interfaces is the "combinatorial explosion" of possible user input as the interaction unfolds. Spoken exchanges between humans rely on **context**—which implies that the history of both the current and previous interactions carry significant weight when interpreting the current input.

In order to avoid this combinatorial explosion of user input, it is important to process ambiguities locally—within the dialogue component. This means that quick recovery of inter-word rejections must rely only on immediately preceding events, and not on complex and long-lived histories. The same is true of OVW rejections and similar speech-related problems.

---

[30] These middleware modules are referred to variously as DialogModules, Speech Objects, Dialogue Tasks, and Conversational Speech Blocks. This book uses the generic term "dialogue component" as it has been incorporated into the Voice XML (VoXML) standard.

A good example of what is meant by this "closed system" design is the yes-no dialogue component. A formal interaction might present a question to the user, expecting a "yes" or "no" response. However, recognition results include (among others):

- Marginal "yes" or "no" confidence (inter-word rejection),
- OOG ("What was the question again?"),
- Spoke-too-soon (in half-duplex systems), and
- Timeout (all silence).

Each of these errors may have its likely causes within the context of the yes-no query. Therefore, each error must be handled quickly and in a way that is specific and internal to yes-no recognition [Balentine92b]. It is a mistake to ignore these errors, but it is also a mistake to pass them back to the application where they must be recovered independently and repeatedly.

6.4.1.2   √ Unit-Test Dialogue Components in Isolation

One of the major attributes of a dialogue component is **testability**. Each unit accomplishes a specific task that can be uncoupled from other tasks within the application, allowing isolated testing of each unit. A yes-no query, for example, can be expected to behave the same way in a wide variety of contexts. Each unit should be exercised thoroughly in usability labs and in software testing. Testing is straightforward and can be isolated from the rest of the application. Once the timing, prompting, grammar, and rejection-recovery methods are validated, the yes-no dialogue component is reusable throughout the application.

The same principle applies to updates. As problems with yes-no dialogue components appear after deployment, corrections can be made once—in the dialogue component subroutine—which then immediately reflects the change in all yes-no interactions throughout the application.

6.4.1.3   + Use Parameters to Modulate Dialogue Components

Many seemingly different dialogue components differ only slightly. A list-selection unit, for example, may suppress the presentation of the list if it is known to the user, but exhibit other properties that are similar to menus and list browsers. Rather than create several dialogue components with similar common elements, it is better to develop a single unit that can be modulated by the application. Flags that suppress repetitions, variables that control the number of retries, and other standard software arguments that are passed by the calling routine can allow a single dialogue component to exhibit a rich variety of behaviors.

6.4.1.4   ≈ Avoid Unnecessary Variation in Dialogue Components

It is often argued that individual elements within a dialogue deserve special-case treatment. Indeed, the designer is often confronted with the need to choose between consistency and a more natural or otherwise desirable flow of events in a given inter-action. When confronting such cases, it is good to remember that predictability from one element to another is an important attribute of an interface—perhaps more impor-tant than some perceived "variety" or "seamlessness" of dialogue components.

Although only the designer can decide, it is generally best to err on the side of consis-tent and predictable speech behaviors. If a special-case does exist, it may be reason-able to add it to the dialogue component, specifying the behavior via some sort of variable that is passed to the dialogue component.

6.4.1.5   ≈ Minimize the Need for Dialogue Components to Share Data

It is important to resist the urge to make the application too smart. By and large, one dialogue component should not need to know anything about the internal states or data of another dialogue component.

Chapter 7
Mixed Modalities: Speech and DTMF

Mixed-mode applications require more human factors research efforts before firm recommendations can be made. Guidelines in this chapter should therefore be viewed as suggestions for consideration only. Guidelines aimed at avoiding mixed modalities are tagged as required (√). Only if avoiding the subject becomes impractical should the following guidelines be considered.

7.1 Switching Between Speech and DTMF

Speech and DTMF applications are very different in terms of look and feel, structure, and dialogue. As a typical DTMF application migrates to speech, it is often desirable to create intermediate solutions—leading to the problem of compatibility.

On the one hand, speech-driven and DTMF dialogues are best served by their own unique interface designs. On the other hand, practical problems with having two interface designs can become severe, and include:

- Maintaining two versions of the same application,

- Recording both speech and DTMF prompts,

- Designing procedures that allow either the machine or the user to switch from one mode to the other, and

- Minimizing user interface problems, including user habits, prior learning, mode ambiguities, and the like.

This section discusses these problems and proposes effective solutions that represent the proper tradeoff between human factors and practical development and support concerns.

7.1.1 Coupling the Two Modalities

The first issue revolves around "coupling" the two modalities. This addresses the question, "How similar must the DTMF and speech versions of the application be?" Four different approaches are described below.

7.1.1.1 Separate Speech and DTMF Applications

In the first model, the speech and DTMF applications are completely separated. Either the user calls a different phone number , or a "switch" appears at the beginning of the dialogue, allowing the user to select one mode or the other.

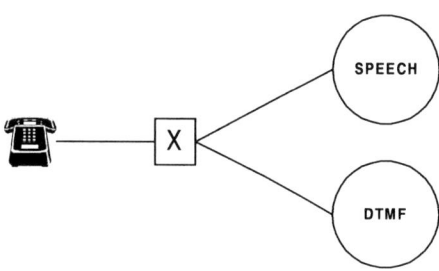

Figure 7.1—**SEPARATE DIALOGUE SOLUTION** is the simplest way to uncouple speech and DTMF. Once the user has connected with the application, an initial interaction selects one modality or the other. The application avoids switching from one mode to the other during a session.

App: *If you want to use the keypad, press 1 now.*
        Otherwise, please hold.
        <wait three to five seconds>
        Do you want to use voice recognition?

User: "Yes."

App: *Command, please.*

The problems with this solution:

1. It requires that two separate applications be maintained.

2. It requires full functionality for both media: New features cannot be developed first for DTMF and then migrated to speech. This impacts development schedules.

3. It requires that the user learn two different interfaces.

4. There is no transfer of learning from one interface to the other.

184

7.1.1.2   Modal Solution

An alternative approach provides a "DTMF Mode" and a "Speech Mode." The user would presumably switch freely from one mode to the other. Perhaps a DTMF "hot key" would allow the user to switch from speech to DTMF and back—as shown by the arrow connecting the two modes.

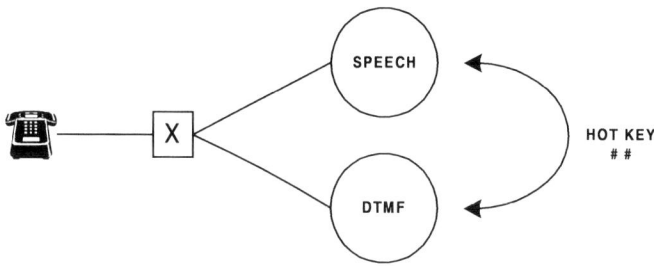

Figure 7.2—**MODAL SOLUTION** allows the user to switch between DTMF and speech modes at will. An example hot key ## is shown.

The problems with this solution:

1.   It requires that the user learn two different interfaces, although they could be made somewhat more similar.

2.   There is little transfer of learning from one interface to the other.

3.   Error-recovery must be designed for user actions that are based on "being in a different mode" than the one expected by the user. Mode errors often cause state errors, which in turn will occasionally amplify spontaneously.

7.1.1.3   DTMF-Constrained Speech

In this model, the speech mode is constrained within the existing DTMF hierarchy. That is, the user maintains only one mental model—that of the menus—but may either speak or use DTMF depending on various factors. This means that speech technology is not used to its full advantage, but instead becomes a "shortcut" to jump through the menu structure or to simplify complicated DTMF sequences.

The problems with this solution:

1.   It constrains the speech technology to mimicking DTMF capabilities.

2.   It is clumsy for the user, as neither medium is used to full advantage.

3.   It does not address users with rotary phones.

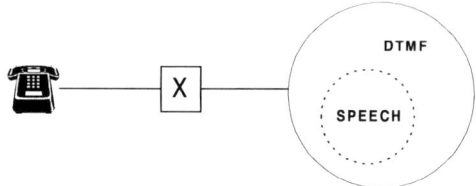

Figure 7.3—**DTMF CONSTRAINED SOLUTION** forces speech into the DTMF mode. Although easiest to develop for a keypress-centric interface, it limits both speech and DTMF modalities.

7.1.1.4   Seamless DTMF-Supported Speech Interface

This solution is the long-term goal where the speech-centric interface replaces the DTMF paradigm. This in turn frees the DTMF medium to be used in support of the speech interface, providing a seamless multimodal user interface that makes best use of both modalities. The problem is that when migrating users from a DTMF application, one of the alternatives described above is thought to be less disruptive to the users—at least as a temporary transition solution.

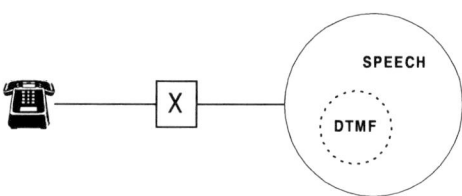

Figure 7.4—**SEAMLESS SPEECH-CENTRIC SOLUTION** uses DTMF as a secondary input, allowing parallel functions and other features that enhance speech recognition.

The problems with this solution:

1. It is the most expensive and time-consuming to design and develop.
2. With no user experience base, all users will be "novices." Prior DTMF "expert users" do not like being demoted to novices. Rebellion is possible.

Note that users who experience a certain number of speech errors (typically three) may be switched automatically to DTMF. This "three strikes and you're out" design means that extremely uncooperative users can be detected and switched to DTMF. This solution, however, points back to the modal design of Figure 7.2. What's more, counting the speech errors is non-trivial, as discussed in Guideline 10.1.1.3, and may not lead to effective error recovery or prevention.

7.1.1.5   + Use a Phased Solution

1. Pursue the "seamless speech interface" approach as a long-term goal, but break it into stages.

2. Create a speech-driven "branch" of the DTMF menu structure. For example, speech-enable only airline departure and arrival times.

3. Test and field this hybrid solution, allowing users to become comfortable with the simplest, most common, and least destructive aspects of speech interaction.

4. Monitor the hybrid system and learn from user behavior.

5. Speech-enable new branches of the tree in subsequent phased rollouts.

The developer should be aware that rolling out new speech recognition functionality will likely increase hardware and system requirements. See Appendix A for a discussion of system provisioning and platform-planning issues.

7.1.2 Switching Modalities

7.1.2.1   √ Understand the Reasons for Switching Modalities

There are at least five possible reasons that a user may need to switch from speech to DTMF or vice versa. Some reasons are based on user interface concerns. Others are related to platform and channel-density limitations.

1. Speech recognition is experiencing errors, so either the user or the machine decides to switch to DTMF mode.

2. Speech recognition is not available for every function, or DTMF input is required for certain operations (legal confirmations).

3. During a high call volume period all speech channels are in use, requiring the next caller to use DTMF by default. This means that the same user may encounter a different interface for different calls, making the opening greeting especially important.

4. The speech system is working fine, but the user simply wants to revert to DTMF for reasons of personal preference.

5. For legal reasons, the developer has chosen to require confirmation of certain transactions with DTMF, for example, *"Press 1 to confirm your order."*

Note that three of the reasons for switching from speech to DTMF are based on conditions beyond the control of the user. For this reason, it is the machine that will typically make the decision to switch to DTMF.

7.1.2.2 √ Switch to DTMF Automatically on Fatal Speech Errors

If speech recognition is experiencing errors, then it may be necessary to switch to DTMF without user intervention. Note that the key to this guideline is the word fatal. All speech applications will experience occasional anomalous errors—either due to speech errors, or due to correct rejection of illegal user behaviors. The application should not be too quick to give up under such circumstances. On the other hand, there are cases[1]—including extremely noisy conditions, goats[2] (perhaps non-native speakers), hopeless confusion, and equipment malfunction—in which the speech recognizer is not working and is not likely to work. In such cases, the application should announce that it is switching to DTMF for the duration of the call.

7.1.2.3 √ Use DTMF, Not Speech, to Allow the User to Switch to DTMF

Some users prefer DTMF. Other users become frustrated when known problems—such as noise—are interfering with productive use of speech. Since it is difficult for the application to tell the difference, the interface that allows the user to select the DTMF modality should rely on DTMF for that selection.

Avoid: *To turn off speech and switch to the telephone keypad, say "touch tone."*

Use: *To switch from speech to the telephone keypad, press the star key twice.*

The converse is true, as well. If the user wants to use the speech mode, then using speech to make the switch helps ensure that recognition will work. The yes-no query is an effective way to do this, as it represents a "barrier" that protects against switching to a modality that will not work within the current noise or user context.

Avoid: *To use the speech recognition system, press "Star S."*

Use: *Do you want to use speech recognition?*

---

[1] See Section 10.1.2.

[2] Goats are users for whom speech recognition consistently performs poorly. See the glossary for a more detailed description.

7.1.2.4   √ Consider Using Yes-No Questions to Remain in Speech

The above guidelines notwithstanding, it is possible to use a yes-no question as an easy way to determine whether to switch between speech and DTMF. In such cases, ensure that the question is about speech rather than about DTMF.

Avoid: *Do you want to switch to keypad operation?*

Use: *Do you want to keep using speech recognition?*

7.1.2.5   √ Avoid Viewing All DTMF Input as Errorful

When the user chooses to use DTMF it does not always indicate problems with the speech subsystem. The following are examples of what the user may do with DTMF and why it may be the preferred modality.

Table 7.1—**REASONS FOR USING DTMF** are not always speech-related. The design should not switch over to speech so readily that these actions are not allowed.

DTMF Action	Possible Reasons
Enter a PIN or passcode	Ensure privacy and security. Enter number faster. Avoid corroboration dialogue (playback).
Select an element in a list	Easier. Less chance of false rejection and inter-word rejection.
Navigate through menus	Take advantage of key ahead.[3] Easier to do mechanically. Less risk of errors.

In the first example, users often want to enter numeric data at the keypad. The main reason is security—so that they cannot be overheard. In the second example, the user is listening to a list—for example a list of destination cities for a given flight. Simply pressing a single key as soon as the city is heard may be preferred by some users. In

---

[3] "Key ahead" is sometimes referred to as "dial ahead" and "dial through." Dial through implies that the user can enter a key during spoken machine output. Strictly speaking, dial ahead is the dial through function, plus the ability of the machine to store user-entered DTMF for subsequent states (i.e., the user can get ahead of the machine).

the third example, many users find that navigating menus is easier with DTMF because of key ahead and other features to which they have grown accustomed.[4]

In each of these three examples these users may switch willingly back to speech when it is the more effective modality—for example when selecting from large lists such as stocks and mutual funds, or when entering information that would otherwise have to be spelled alphabetically.

7.2 Mixing Speech and DTMF

7.2.1 The "Press or Say" Construct

Prompts are sometimes structured according to a *"press or say"* construct:

For Mutual Funds, press "1" or say "Mutual Funds."

The construct also extends to yes-no responses. This section addresses the issues associated with this particular approach to mixed modalities. In general, the solution is not a very good one and should be avoided.

7.2.1.1 ≈ Avoid *"Press or Say"* if Possible

Asking the user to speak a digit for menu selections or other non-numeric data—simply to emulate the DTMF keypad—is extremely awkward. Although speech recognition technologies of several years ago were limited to such vocabularies, this is no longer the case.

7.2.1.2 ≈ Consider Dual-Voice Solution

If mixed modality is desired, it is best to use meaningful words for spoken input while retaining the numeric keypad input for DTMF. This can be accomplished by using a new male voice to recite spoken choices while retaining the application's original female voice for numeric keypad entry. Users that want to speak "tune out" the female voice and mimic the male voice. Users that want keypad entry do the opposite.

Avoid: *For Mutual Fund Prices, press "1" or say "Mutual Funds"*
         For Account Balances, press "2" or say "Balances"

Use: Male & Female: *Main Menu*

---

[4] There are difficulties with the speech equivalent of key ahead, known as "talk ahead." See Guideline 4.1.3.6 to understand why "talk ahead" should be avoided.

Male Voice:	*Mutual Funds*
Female Voice:	*One*
Male Voice:	*Balances*
Female Voice:	*Two*

The application developer should be cautioned that this is an experimental solution that has not been tested in usability labs. It is presented here as an idea, and needs further research.

7.2.1.3   + Use *"Press or Say"* if Speech Is Digits

If spoken digits must be allowed for menu selection, then use *"Press or say."*

Avoid: *Press "1" or say "One"*
            Say or press "One"
Use: *Press or say "One"*

7.2.1.4   √ Precede Non-Digit Speech with DTMF

Since DTMF can be used at any time, while speech sometimes requires waiting for the beep, the prompt for DTMF should precede that for speech if both must be used.

Avoid: *Say "yes" or press "1" <beep>*
Use: *Press "1" or say "yes" <beep>*

7.2.2   Prompt and Feedback Interruption

There are situations in which the user must be given the opportunity to terminate an especially long or frequently repeated instruction or prompt. In these cases, the novice user listens to the instructions, while an expert user "skips straight to the beep" and begins speaking. This feature is common in voicemail systems, wherein the caller skips past the subscriber's greeting and immediately leaves a message.

In a complementary scenario, users that experience speech recognition errors or who simply change their mind about a word that was just spoken may wish to backup—returning to the immediately preceding prompt or beep—and speak again.

These complementary features are referred to as follows:

Interrupting a **prompt**[5] is skipping **forward** to the next opportunity to speak.

---

[5]Note the significance of distinguishing between prompts and feedback. If the user has just spoken, then the ensuing spoken machine output is most likely feedback.

Interrupting **feedback** is skipping **backward** to the previous opportunity to speak.

The ability to interrupt a prompt is needed when a user is listening to instructions, application data, or a long prompt, and would like to stop the audio to skip ahead to the beep. The ability to interrupt feedback is needed when a user is listening to feedback, help, or application data, and would like to stop the audio and return to the preceding input state. The reason may be that the recognized response is incorrect. It may also be that the user has changed his mind and wants to re-renter the information or command.

If these features are supported by DTMF, the user should be told which key skips forward and which key skips back. These issues complicate the problem of mixing DTMF with speech, as ideal keys are almost certainly usurped for other application functions. No industry standards exist for these features.

7.2.2.1   √ Use Speech Rather than DTMF to Interrupt

It is best to avoid the DTMF problem altogether by using menu designs that effectively elicit speech at valid times. For prompt interruption, this includes extremely short prompts, the use of barge-in, or frequent opportunities to speak via recognition "windows."[6] For feedback interruption, this includes yes-no queries and similar machine corroboration, the use of barge-in coupled with "Backup" or "Cancel" commands, or frequent opportunities (windows) for the user to speak.[7]

7.2.2.2   ≈ If DTMF Is the Chosen Method for Backup, Use Any Key

If a user is concentrating on speech and hears an error, it is distracting to hunt for a specific key. An alternative is to press **any** key to backup one state.

The argument against this solution applies to DTMF interfaces that are fully functional (Figure 7.3). If all DTMF keys are available for direct control of the interface, then the key ahead feature will still be enabled and the "any key" solution will not work. One solution is to employ a different approach to DTMF and speech. The modal solution in Figure 7.2, for example, will free all keys for "any key" interruption unless the user explicitly switches to DTMF.

---

[6] Prompts are discussed in Section 2.3. Recognition windowing methods are discussed in Guideline 4.2.2.2.

[7] Backing up with barge-in and user initiated error-recovery methods are discussed in Section 10.2. Machine-corroboration methods are discussed in Section 10.3.

7.2.2.3   ≈ After DTMF Backup, Avoid Repeated Recognition of the Same Word

A DTMF backup to a previous input state is likely to be due to a speech error. If the user backs up to the preceding prompt and speaks again, then ensure that the same word is not recognized a second time.[8] If the recognizer supports *n*-best, this means selecting the second choice if the first is the same as the preceding recognition event. If the recognizer does not support *n*-best, then use grammars, masking, or other supported methods to eliminate the word from the active vocabulary.

The rationale for this guideline is that the user does not want this word. Either it was misrecognized (with an elevated chance that it will appear again), or the user has changed her mind.

7.2.2.4   ≈ Follow the Lead of Existing Solutions

Several deployed solutions use the "#" key for feedback interruption,[9] although at least one solution uses the "1" key. Note the possibility of a two-state backup shortcut using "##" as shown in the table below.

Table 7.2—**BACKUP FUNCTIONS WITH DTMF**. Each press of the # key backs up one input state. In this way, the user may repeatedly move backward some number of states.

User Presses	User Hears
#	*Stock name?*
# #	*Main Menu*

7.2.3   Navigation Through *n*-Best

The *n*-best list presents options to the application in the case of inter-word rejections or if, for any other reason, the application is doubtful of the best recognition result. There are two issues with *n*-best:

• How to trigger the presentation of *n*-best options, and

• How to choose an item in the *n*-best list.

---

[8]This is the same as Guideline 10.1.3.2 except applied to DTMF backup.

[9] "#" is used by Fidelity in *TTX*™, Schwab in *VoiceBroker*™, and in Nortel's *Stock-Talk*™demonstration system.

7.2.3.1 √ Use Machine-Initiated List Presentation When Possible

It is difficult to convey to users what the *n*-best list is and why they may want to browse it. For this reason, *n*-best management is better handled in a machine-driven approach. This means that the machine intervenes automatically whenever a rejection occurs—eliminating the need for the user to trigger the list.

App: *Do you want a quote on Texaco?*

User: "No."

App: *... on PepsiCo?*

User: "Yes."

In this example, an inter-word rejection indicated to the application that the first and second choices in the *n*-best list had similar scores. The condition automatically triggered list presentation—in this case in the form of a yes-no query. The behavior turns out to be justified, as the user refuses the selection. The application then presents the second choice in the *n*-best list, offering a shortened version of the yes-no question. This time the user says "yes" and the rejection is recovered.

7.2.3.2 + Presenting *n*-Best for Homonyms

When there are homonyms in the active vocabulary, the user must disambiguate. The *n*-Best list contains the homonyms, because they experience inter-word rejections:

User: "Cisco"

App: *There are two companies with that name. Do you want ...*

   "Cisco Systems" ... or ... "SysCo Foods?"

User: "Cisco Systems"

7.2.3.3 + Use "1" or "*1" Key to Trigger *n*-Best List Presentation

There may sometimes be reasons for allowing the user to trigger the *n*-best list. For example, a tester may be interested in hearing a recitation of the recognizer's *n*-best list. It may also be that the trigger is based on a backup action as discussed earlier in this chapter. If the user is allowed to request playback of the list, then the question becomes which key to use?

In many DTMF applications, the alphabet on the keypad is used for spelling and entering symbols, such as stock symbols. Mnemonics are also mapped to the keypad, for example 6 (H) for help. The only keys without letters are "1" and "0." The "0" is typically reserved for "transfer to operator." This leaves the "1" key without a universal role (although it is often used to indicate a "yes" response when queried). Therefore, the "1" key should be considered for accessing the n-best list. The "*1" combination may also be considered.[10]

7.2.3.4   + Use Speech or DTMF to Choose an Item in the n-Best List

Once the n-best list is triggered, then the challenge is to provide a method for selecting one of the list elements. In Guideline 7.2.3.1 the simplest solution—a yes-no question—illustrates the ease with which inter-word rejections can be recovered when the confusion is only between a pair of words. The problem is compounded, however, when the size of the n-best list grows.

When there are three or more elements in the n-best list, it is better treated as a list proper—allowing menus or browsing dialogues to recite the choices and give the user opportunities to select. As the list is recited, either speech (point and speak)[11] or DTMF (touch to select)[12] can used to make a selection.

7.2.4   Legal Obligations

7.2.4.1   + Use DTMF to Confirm Legally Significant Transactions

Final confirmation of a transaction must not only be error-free but must be perceived to be error-free by the user. In the example below, the user has entered and validated all transaction data. Machine instructions must now ensure that the user:

- Hears the details of the impending transaction,
- Hears and understands that the transaction must be explicitly confirmed, and
- Understands that the confirmation requires DTMF rather than speech.

App: *You are about to buy 200 shares of IBM from your cash account.*
        For legal reasons you must confirm this transaction using your keypad.
        To confirm the transaction, press 1.
        To cancel, press 2.

Note that there are problems with this approach. First, a mobile user—or any other user with keys in the handset (e.g., portable telephone)—must pull the telephone away from the ear to select a key. These users may not hear the details of the transac-

---

[10] See ISO 13714 for the exact meaning and usage of the "*" key.
[11] See Guideline 4.2.2.4
[12] See Guidelines 6.2.3.2 and 6.2.3.3.

tion. Expert users are the most likely to anticipate the prompt—novices must hear the DTMF prompt before knowing which key to select. If concern that experts may approve a wrong transaction becomes legally important, then timing can be used to discourage the premature removal of the handset. This means disallowing DTMF until after the confirmation prompt ends.

In addition, callers without DTMF (rotary phones) cannot perform these transactions. This is a greater concern, as until this point, they have been using speech and are now powerless to act. Care should be taken to service such users—rare though they may be—by responding appropriately on timeouts.

7.2.4.1.1 √ Use Imperative Prompts for DTMF Confirmation

This sub-guideline is aimed at clearly distinguishing legally-obligated DTMF confirmation from other binary decisions. Users should not confuse this interaction with a speech-centric yes-no. The prompt should therefore be phrased with the DTMF-style imperative prompt, *"To <do function>, press <key>."*

Avoid: *Do you want to transfer?*

  For yes press 1; For no press 2.

Use: *To transfer …., press 1.*

  To cancel, press 2.

Note that this guideline reduces the problem of telephones with keypads in the handsets. These users hear their data first—before they know to pull the telephone away—and then are prompted to choose with DTMF "1" or "2."

7.2.4.1.2 + Use Interrogative Prompts for All Other Yes-No Queries

This is the converse of the previous sub-guideline. Spoken interactions are more flexible and natural when questions remain simple, aimed at evoking a spontaneous "yes" or "no" from the user. DTMF-like imperative forms, on the other hand, are strained and awkward.

Avoid: *You are about to transfer ….*

  To confirm, say "yes," to abandon, say "no."

Use: *Do you want to transfer?*

Chapter 8
Natural Language Interfaces

This chapter is devoted to the unique attributes of natural language (NL) technology and the design of user interfaces that exploit them. An NL application "resembles a command-line interface in that it hides the application's functionality" [Martin96]. The implication is that NL technology allows systems to accept more complex and varied user input than can be conveyed through simple prompting or casual explanation. The sophistication of these interfaces lead to the conclusion that prompting schemes and dialogue structure may—indeed often must—be designed according to an entirely different set of assumptions than those for directed dialogues.

8.1   What Is Natural Language?

Now that NL dialogues are feasible, the term itself has taken on a variety of different meanings by industry professionals and laymen. What's more, it can be a reckless and dangerous term in much the same way that "user-friendly" and "intelligent" are dangerous—that is, the term itself excites a rash of assumptions that lead both the designer and the user directly away from rather than toward a useful and practical understanding of the technology.

To some people, NL speech technology is simply that—a technology—one that allows continuous spoken input, multiple-token[1] sentences, and rejection of disfluencies,[2] among other specific capabilities. To others, the term has more far-reaching implications—conjuring images of intelligence and social awareness, machine personality, and a number of other subjective and anthropomorphic concepts that are contrary to the abilities or utility of the technology.

---

[1] A "token" is the smallest unit of meaningful linguistic input. The term will be discussed in detail later in this chapter.
[2] See the glossary to compare and contrast the terms "disfluency" and "back channel."

This chapter treats natural language for what it is—a technology that expands the range of possible dialogues that designers can create. It is up to the designer to create a compelling interface that serves the user's goals. The NL technology itself cannot accomplish this by itself, because "naturalness" is a by-product of the application design, not an attribute of technology.

8.1.1 NL Technology Components

Application developers should note that NL technology is relatively new, and there is little historical data on the effectiveness of interface design methods or on user acceptance. This chapter presents some of the more common practices, but the developer is cautioned that new techniques for applying NL technology are evolving rapidly—a process that can be expected to produce more definitive observations.

NL technologies typically consist of the following components:[3]

- Barge-In,
- Speech Detector/Endpointer,
- Acoustic Models,
- Dictionary of Phonetic Transcriptions,
- Continuous Recognition Engine,
- Grammars,
- Natural Language Parser or Classifier, and
- Natural Language Dialogue Engine.

All of these components interact to produce the resulting natural language interface, and each is quite complex and sophisticated in its own right. For this reason, providing a detailed definition and description of natural language technologies is beyond the scope of this style guide. Key concepts are discussed later in simple terms—but only as they are needed to understand the proposed guidelines. Developers are encouraged to acquire additional information from published books [Markowitz96], [Schmandt94], journal articles [Comerford97], [Brems95], [Yankelovich95] and technical market studies [Hames97].

---

[3] See the glossary for a brief definition of each component.

8.2   Reaching Terminals in the Hierarchy

To understand the user interface tradeoffs in a natural language VRU application, it is informative to revisit the subject of DTMF interfaces. Standard practices for such interfaces have become well established, making it possible to compare the advantages and drawbacks of DTMF with more sophisticated NL technologies.

8.2.1   DTMF Menu Navigation

A DTMF interface uses keypresses both for user selection and for navigation through the application's hierarchical organization. Only terminals[4] within the hierarchy perform user-specified work. A typical system, represented schematically in Figure 8.1, starts with a Main Menu. This menu may offer immediate access to a terminal—shown at A—accomplishing work with a single keypress. More often, however, the user must pass through an additional menu—shown at B—before arriving at a terminal. Each menu is announced with DTMF prompting as discussed in Section 2.3. Keypresses that navigate to menus rather than terminals represent user interface overhead, reducing the work density achievable by the application. This hierarchical overhead can become quite complex as implied in path C.

A DTMF interface has the following attributes:

- It is machine-driven,
- User actions are selection oriented,
- User actions (i.e., press) require little mental effort, and
- Keeping track of hierarchy and menu relationships requires some mental effort.

As the capability of the application grows, customers often complain about "the number of menus and keypresses" required to complete tasks. This results directly from the growing complexity of hierarchical overhead. Collapsing the menu structure becomes increasingly important, but requires an alternate and more powerful input medium—NL speech. This need to collapse the menu structure is often called "menu flattening"[5] and is a major advantage of NL speech input.

---

[4] The endpoint of a path through any branching structure, such as a tree or network.

[5] Reducing the vertical depth of a menu hierarchy or other tree structure by allowing more elements at each level—in effect making the structure more horizontal. See the glossary for a detailed description of "menu flattening."

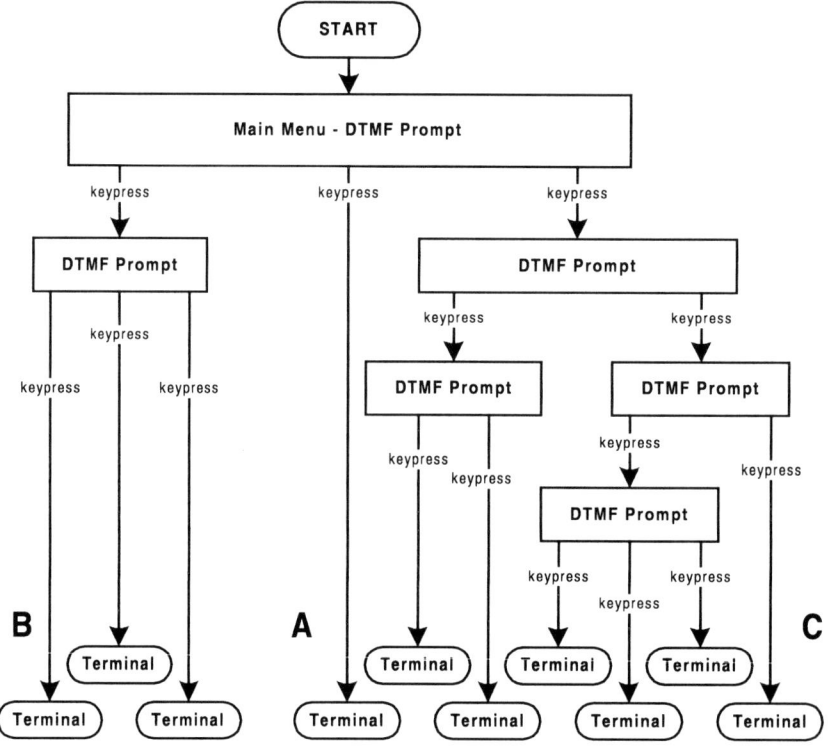

Figure 8.1—**DTMF MENU HIERARCHY** uses keypresses both for user selection and for navigation. The goal is to reach a terminal in the hierarchy. This may require only a single keypress, as shown at A. More often, however, the user must pass through one (B) or more (C) additional menus before reaching a terminal. Keypresses that navigate to menus rather than terminals represent user interface overhead that reduces productivity.

8.2.2   NL Speech Recognition

A natural language interface, represented schematically in Figure 8.2, can be conceptualized hierarchically as a structure that is somewhat similar to DTMF menus or directed speech dialogues. The structure implies that a given interaction requires multiple pieces of information (tokens) before it is complete. Spoken user input may contain all required information—shown at A—thus entering all tokens with a single utterance. More often, however, the user must pass through an additional prompted interaction (B) to allow the machine to corroborate input or to extract additional data.

Each interaction is announced with so-called "feed-forward" prompting as discussed later in this chapter. These multiple interactions represent user interface overhead, thereby reducing the value of the NL interface. This sequential overhead can become quite complex as implied at C.

To understand the concepts and terminology of Figure 8.2, consider the example of a typical stock trade. A productive utterance may include the following:

User: "I'd like to buy 50 shares of AT&T at the market."

In this example, the single utterance contains four **tokens**—specific chunks of information that are required to reach a terminal in which work (in the form of a transaction) can be accomplished. Tokens are underlined in the example. Words in the sentence that are not tokens represent natural language constructions that allow the user to request the transaction intuitively without having to conform to an arbitrary linguistic structure. Such constructions are supported by the application's grammar, which determines the range and variety of word selection and ordering which the user may choose when speaking.

The first token is the action "buy," which designates the type of transaction. Other types may include "sell," "quote," or other functionalities offered by the application. The remaining three tokens—"number of shares," "security name," and "purchase price"—represent the complete set of data required by the VRU to accomplish this transaction. This single utterance therefore provides all user input required to reach a **terminal**—the point in the application where user input is complete and the machine can do work. Such productive input is represented in Figure 8.2 point A.

On the other hand, the user may generate an utterance that contains partial data:

User: "Buy 50 shares of AT&T."

In this example, user input contains only three of the four required tokens. The "purchase price" is missing and so the application has not reached a terminal. The application must present a prompt aimed at capturing this token:

App: ... at what price?

This prompt is called a **feed-forward** prompt because it is aimed at capturing new information to move the dialogue forward. This distinguishes it from **feedback**, which is aimed at corroborating information already spoken by the user. The dialogue might be similar to one represented at point B of Figure 8.2.

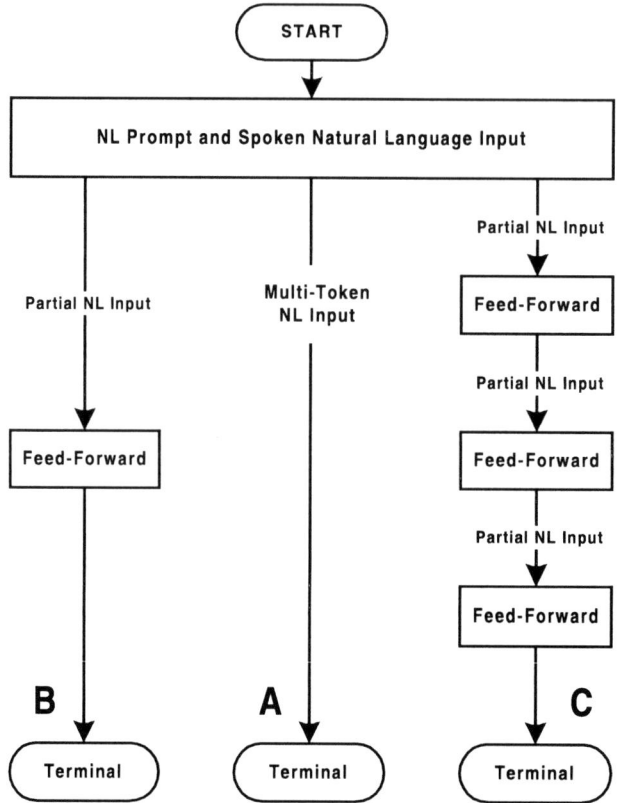

Figure 8.2—**NATURAL LANGUAGE INTERFACE** can be conceptualized as a hierarchy similar to DTMF menus. Spoken input may contain all information required to reach a terminal—shown at A. More commonly, user input contains only partial data, requiring one (B) or more (C) interactions before reaching a terminal. Prompts aimed at capturing additional required data rather than corroborating data already spoken are referred to as *feed-forward* prompts.

Note that it is possible to capture each token separately:

User: "I'd like to buy some stock."

App: *Security name?*

User: "AT&T."

App: *How many shares?*

User: "Fifty shares, please."

App: *At what price?*

User: "At the market."

In this example, each user input contains only one token, requiring multiple interactions to reach the terminal. This is primarily the choice of the user, who makes assumptions about how and why the dialogue might expect certain forms of input. This dialogue represents a more interactive approach to reaching a terminal and therefore resembles path C of Figure 8.2.

Note the similarity to directed dialogues, and in particular to the form-filling dialogues described in Chapter 6. Indeed, one way to think of an NL application is as a form-filling dialogue that allows the user to fill the form as efficiently as desired—by speaking one or more natural sentences that contain the information (tokens) required to accomplish a task. In this model, a token-by-token sequence of feed-forward prompts constitutes the default or "core" behavior of the dialogue. More intelligent entry—in the form of multiple-token utterances—then has the effect of "suppressing" feed-forward prompts, moving the user more quickly to terminals. The suppression of form filling interactions produces the "menu flattening" effect desired by designers as discussed in Section 8.2.1.

An NL interface has the following attributes:

- It supports user-driven or mixed-initiative dialogues,

- User actions are transaction-oriented,

- Immediate user actions—producing a coherent and meaningful statement, query, or command—require more mental effort than performing DTMF selections, and

- Keeping track of hierarchy and menu relationships requires less mental effort than with DTMF applications, provided the structural relationships are "flattened" and well-formulated.

Contrast these attributes with those of DTMF applications described in Section 8.2.1 to understand the concepts and terminology of natural language technology. Note that specific terms such as "token" and "feed-forward" prompts are not currently used by vendors who provide natural language speech recognition. Rather, they are used here to provide generic terms for these important concepts.

8.3   NL Prompt Design

As with all speech applications, prompt design has the biggest impact on the effectiveness of a natural language application. The user's interpretation of the expectations of the application—and his mental model of the technology's capabilities—are formulated in large part by spoken machine output. The design of spoken machine output is more difficult for natural language applications. This is because the user must infer from the prompt how to construct an input utterance that is both meaningful and productive.

8.3.1   NL Prompting

8.3.1.1   + Design Prompts to Encourage Multiple-Token Natural Language

Prompting for a natural language application should itself sound natural. It should be aimed at encouraging the user to construct multiple-token sentences. For these reasons, loosely structured "open-ended" prompts can often work well, provided the user has a clear context for understanding the prompt.

App: *What would you like to do?*
           How may I help you?
           Go ahead.
           What else?

Note that such open-ended prompts may elicit speech that is too unpredictable if the context has not yet been clearly established. Tradeoffs between this and the following guideline on excessive structure are therefore quite subjective.

In the first example—perhaps appropriate for a "Main Menu"—the user is given the greatest number of implied options. Note that the value of this prompt depends on entry instructions and prior experience. For example, a novice may have two interpretations depending on the initial instructions:

Avoid:

App: Thank you for calling. What would you like to do?

User: "umh ... gosh ... how do I make a reservation?"

App: *Sorry, I didn't understand.*

Use:

App: *Thank you for calling the acme automated reservation system.*
           You may speak at any time.
           If you're not sure what to do, just ask for an example.

204

What would you like to do?

User: "Give me an example, please."

App: *To make a reservation, you may say ...*

In the first example, "*What would you like to do?*" is too open-ended—the novice user has no context. In the second example, the same prompt is more logical, as the "lead-in" material gives the user a context with which to begin constructing a reasonable command. Note that the lead-in is suppressed later when the application returns to this state. In other words, "*What would you like to do?*" becomes a generic prompt to which users become rapidly accustomed.

8.3.1.2   √ Avoid Excessively-Structured Prompts

In general, less structured all-purpose prompts are more appropriate for user-driven directed dialogues. This is because the machine takes a short turn and then immediately passes control over to the user. Highly structured prompts, on the other hand, are appropriate only for machine-driven dialogues—in which the machine must keep taking back the turn due to user inability to navigate the application.

Avoid: *Please say the action that you want now.*
          Please say buy or sell followed by a security name and number of shares.
          Please speak in natural language, including the action and specifics now.

Use: *At any time you may say a command or say "Help."*
        When would you like to schedule the meeting?

In the first example, "*Please say the action that you want now*" is too reminiscent of DTMF prompts to be effective. The second example attempts to describe the tokens that are expected, perhaps in the hope that the user will repeat them—substituting real data for the token names and gluing them together into a real sentence. The third example simply declares explicitly that it wants "*natural language,*" with no obvious cues about what that may mean. All three are weak constructions, more likely to evoke unintelligible user speech than clear and purposeful user input.

8.3.1.3   + Coach the User a Little at a Time

It is not necessary to explain everything to the user all at once. Instead, get the user started and then tolerate variant user behavior.

Use: *To get a quote, simply state the company name.*
        Say "Help" for more instructions.

In the first example, the goal is to get the user to say—at the least—a company name. Many users go beyond that, constructing what to them are "logical" queries or commands that contain an embedded company name. It is up to the application developer using Wizard of Oz tests[6] and other user information, as well as careful usability testing prior to application release—to ensure that such logical constructions are predicted and legal.

Once successful, a dialogue design can then encourage additional interaction. Note that well-behaved users tend to learn quickly while awkward novices are still likely to get something accomplished.

In the example, the prompt simply names the single keyword—company name—that the caller is most likely to know. Recognition successfully strips away the extraneous material—both the disfluency at the front and the courtesy filler at the end—to properly recognize this keyword. Note, however, that the input is still just a single token. After the quote, the user utters a two-token phrase and the dialogue moves forward. In this way the user becomes comfortable with productive utterances and gradually begins to drive the dialogue.

In the following example, the fact that the "Help" command has clarifying arguments is withheld until the user indicates a need to know:

App: *Say "Help" for more instructions.*

User: "Help."

App: *For help, say the word "Help" followed by the topic for which you want help—for example, "Help trading ... Help quotes, ... "*

8.3.1.4   √ Consider Embedding Examples Within NL Prompts[7]

Users learn well by example. Short examples embedded directly within the NL prompt will often clarify the machine's requirements.

App: *To trade a stock, say for example, "Buy Apple"... or "Sell Microsoft."*

Note that the embedded example could be recorded with the same voice as all other prompts, or could be recorded with a different voice (see Guideline 2.1.2.3.4).

---

[6] WoZ testing enables a developer to test potential applications with users before building the application. See the glossary and Section 11.3 for a detailed description.

[7] This Guideline has been updated in the second edition as prompting by example has been demonstrated in usability tests to be an especially effective style of NL prompting. Our recommendation level has consequently been upgraded from "Recommended" to "Required."

206

Although not all users respond to the examples with predictable multi-token utter-ances, a significant majority do so quickly—that is, most users formulate their replies by hearing examples and not through explicit machine directives.

Section 8.5 addresses more detailed uses and implications of NL prompting. In addi-tion, the following sub-guidelines clarify some specifics of example prompting.

8.3.1.4.1   √ Present Multi-Token Examples

Users that copy examples do so almost exactly. It is nearly as easy to mimic multi-token example as it is to copy a single-token example. The single-token example above can be modified to form a multiple-token prompt as follows:

App: For trades, you might say, for example, "Buy 50 shares of Apple at the market."

A multi-token example is preferred over two single-token examples in rapid-fire succession. Callers have little difficulty replicating logical correlates of the example (for example replacing "buy" with "sell" and inserting user-specific data into the example).

8.3.1.4.2   √ Don't Use Variables in the Example

Some application designers construct example prompts that replace the items unique to the caller's data with variables—with the goal of emphasizing what the user is expected to provide.

Avoid: Say, for example, "I'd like to go from departure city to destination city on travel date."

Say, for example, "I'd like to buy x number of shares of y."

The prompts are confusing and ineffective.

8.3.1.4.3   ≈ Consider Invented but Credible Example Names

A problem with example prompting is choosing examples. One approach em-ploys common or popular examples ("IBM" as an example security name). Another approach goes the opposite direction, selecting exotic or rare names under the assumption that the user will not accidentally mimic the example.

To prevent situations where the user is confused by the examples in the prompt, some designers are experimenting with the use of invented names:

App: *You might say, for example, "Exchange 50 units of Blue Mountain Fund for Sweetwater Growth."*

8.3.1.5 ≈ Combine Instructions with Prompt to Craft a Single NL Prompt

App: *A trading action might include the words Buy or Sell along with a company name and number of shares.*
      Trading action?

In the example, a long sentence describes an object—in this case something called a "trading action." It is immediately followed by a prompt. The prompt is for the object that has just been defined. The defining instruction and prompt together now constitute a full NL prompt. The technique is based on the following three sub-guidelines.

8.3.1.5.1   + Make the Instruction Define an Object

Invent a useful concept, term, or other meaningful object. In the example above, the object is the term "trading action."

8.3.1.5.2   + Put the Object at the Beginning of the Instruction

Ensure that the object being defined appears at the beginning of the instruction that represents the definition.

8.3.1.5.3   + Use the Object as a Prompt

With the object now defined and still present in the user's short-term memory, use the object as a prompt. The prompt may be constructed as a question, *"What trading action do you want?"* It may also take the imperative form, *"Say the trading action."* More typically, it can be used as a standalone prompt, *"Trading action?"*—a form known as implied interrogative. See Section 2.3.4 for details on crafting implied interrogative prompts.

8.3.2   NL Feed-Forward Prompts

This style guide introduces the term "feed-forward prompts" to refer to NL prompts that are aimed at coaching the user forward through states by prompting for additional tokens needed to reach a terminal. The goal of feed-forward prompts is exclusively to capture additional information for a partially-completed transaction without reverting to "recovery" methods. This feed-forward paradigm is reminiscent of form-filling dialogues. Think of each token that is required to reach a terminal in the dialogue as one of several entries on a form. The user may speak a natural language sentence that fills the form completely with a single utterance. Any missing entries, however, must then be prompted sequentially until the form is filled.

8.3.2.1   √ Use Feed-Forward Prompts to Capture Partial Data

Whenever the user introduces partial data, use feed-forward prompts to extract additional data. Do this before querying any ambiguous items. This allows the user to supply input that may assist in corroborating the old input.

App: *What would you like to do?*

User: "I need a quote on IBM options."

App: *Month and strike price?*

User: "July calls at one-twenty."

App: *Confirming ... IBM one-twenty calls for July. Is that correct?*

User: "Yes."

In the example, the IBM name may have been moderately confident. However, the tokens "quote" and "options" allow a reasonable feed-forward assumption. The feed-forward prompt in turn captures not only the month and strike price but also the additional "calls"—corroborating the assumption that the user wants to purchase future options. The rules engine in turn concludes that IBM was the best security given the strike price. No recovery action was required and the dialogue moved forward with only a single intervening machine prompt.

The principle of skipping past single rejected tokens (which have low confidence) to capture additional data is an important advantage of feed-forward prompts. Such prompts extract data from the user without revealing the previous recognition result. This allows rules based on information outside of speech recognition to corroborate the overall validity of data before announcing it in feedback form to the user.

Note, however, that at least one token must have high confidence, allowing an anchor around which the feed-forward prompts can proceed. Otherwise, incorrect assumptions about previous recognitions lead to extremely illogical feed-forward prompts. Subsequent guidelines provide examples of when not to use feed-forward methods.

8.3.2.2   + Do Not Use Feed-Forward Prompts for Error-Recovery

The assumption of the feed-forward prompt is that the user has already entered some valid data—presumably by speaking an NL sentence that contains at least one token with high confidence. The goal of the feed-forward prompt is to capture the remainder of the data. The user has done nothing wrong and no error condition exists. Feed-forward prompts should therefore not be confused with error recovery dialogues.

Avoid:

User: "I need to sell my Texaco stock."

App: *I think you said "PepsiCo."*
        If that's correct, please say the number of shares you want to sell.
        Otherwise, repeat the company name.

User: "50 … nnoo… it's not Pepsi … hold on a minute."

App: *Confirming … fifteen shares of PepsiCo at market price. Is that correct?*

User: "No, it's all wrong."

There are several problems with the dialogue. First and foremost, it is trying to do too many things at once, thereby encouraging the user to produce free-form speech that amplifies rather than damps the error.

The initial error is a rejection condition from the speech recognizer.[8] Although such conditions are intrinsic to human speech and not an "error" in the technical sense, they must nevertheless be recovered by the application. By attempting to combine rejection recovery with feed-forward prompting the application pulls the user in two directions. An alternate dialogue might be:

Use:

User: "I need to sell my Texaco stock."

App: *How many shares?*

User: "50 shares."

App: *At what price?*

User: "Thirty-eight and a half."

App: *Please repeat the company name …*

User: "Texaco."

App: *Confirming … fifty shares of Texaco at 38 ½. Is that correct?*

User: "Yes."

In this dialogue, the application defers recovery of the rejected company name until later. The feed-forward prompts, *"How many shares?"* and *"At what price?"* capture

---

[8] Rejection is an important concept. See the glossary and Section 1.3.1 for a discussion.

the numeric information from a user that is not yet "contaminated" by assumptions about machine performance. A recovery prompt then evokes an isolated repetition of the company name, thus recovering the previous rejection with little effect on user **set** [Kreitler72] and [Balentine92a].[9]

Note that this strategy only works when the input is in-grammar but includes at least one rejected token. If the entire input is rejected as out-of-grammar,[10] then there is no "sell" or similar keyword to trigger subsequent feed-forward prompts.

The important point here is that the application should capture all information that is possible before engaging in re-prompts or queries aimed at recovering rejections. This is because these behaviors give away the fact the recognizer may have erred. Exposing error conditions causes users to think about—and subsequently to change—their speaking habits. This reaction to recovery prompts often leads to error-amplification effects. By deferring rejection recovery until the very end, such amplification is either reduced or completely eliminated.

8.3.2.3   + Avoid Presenting DTMF-Style Options

Avoid prompts that simply list user options. This DTMF-centric prompting is likely to be very confusing to callers, as it reminds them of DTMF methods rather than encouraging a shift to the NL paradigm. The lists are also hard to remember.

Avoid: *Would you like fund exchanges, balances, quotes, or prior activity?*

You may say "Buy" or "Sell," along with whether you want stock, options, or Mutual Funds. You may also change or cancel an open order ... or you might want to practice making a trade.

Instead, use interrogative or imperative prompts:

Use: *From which account?*

Please state the account number.

---

[9] The concept of psychological set encompasses the user's expectations, interpretation of events, and context within which behaviors are chosen. Machine queries or errors affect this set, leading to user assumptions that change the resulting speech signal. The effect of machine behavior on user set is therefore a major cause of error amplification.

[10] Out-of-grammar is the preferred term for illegal input when using natural language speech recognition. See the glossary for the distinction between OOG and OVW.

8.3.2.4 + Fall Back on Form-Filling Directed Dialogues

When natural-language feed-forward prompting methods fail, then a simple directed dialogue strategy tends to be robust and is often preferred by the user [Walker98]. In this form-filling model, the machine extracts one token at a time from the user, who is thus led by the hand through the completion of the form. The following dialogue is from an application called *Freedom*.[11]

Use:

App: *How may I help you?*

User: "Can I have a reminder call on Tuesday please?"

App: *Set reminder call, thank you. You currently have a single reminder call booked at five thirty on Thursday morning. Would you like to replace it?*

User: "Yes, please."

App: *What time on Tuesday[12] would you like the reminder call?*

User: "Three thirty."

App: *Is that in the morning or the afternoon?*

User: "The morning."

App: *A single reminder call will be booked at three thirty on Tuesday morning. Is this OK?*

User: "Yes."

App: *Confirmed. Reminder call booked.*

The entry prompt is a fully open NL prompt, and it successfully extracts a two-token utterance from the caller. The remainder of the dialogue is a conventional form-filling directed dialogue.

This "user-launched, machine-driven" query scheme is effective but slow. For this reason, it might be desirable to re-acquaint users with example natural language sentences after succeeding with a form-filling dialogue as described in Guideline 8.4.3.2.

---

[11] a prototype spoken language system developed for BT Select Services™ [Attwater97].

[12] Note the use of embedded confirmation. See Section 2.4.2 to understand the importance of applying confidence to this method. Compare also with Guidelines 8.3.2.5 and 8.4.1.2.

8.3.2.5   + Avoid Feed-Forward Methods on Low-Confidence Transactions

Users get confused whenever speech errors—or other errors associated with the machine's state—lead to spoken machine output that is inappropriate. This is especially true for feed-forward prompting. The application should not rely on feed-forward if there is low confidence in the overall transaction that is about to be initiated.

App: *What would you like to do?*

User: "Send me a prospectus on the Aggressive Growth and Income Fund."

App: *Month and strike price?*

User: "What?"

In this example, the recognizer has gotten it completely wrong. Presumably the recognizer's confidence is low, but the application proceeded on the wrong assumption, leading to a feed-forward prompt that is completely illogical. In this example, a better strategy would be to immediately re-prompt.

Note that avoiding these instances of illogical behavior requires a clear understanding of the speech technology—in particular, the reliability and ranges for interpreting scores, confidence, and *n*-best results. The developer is encouraged to work closely with the speech vendor to make best use of these rejection conditions.

8.4   NL Error Prevention and Recovery

8.4.1   NL Feedback

Remember that there are five classes of spoken machine output, reprinted from Chapter 2 into Table 8.1 for convenience.

The basic principles of feedback design discussed in Section 2.4 apply equally to NL and other speech technologies. The following guidelines—although also applicable to VRU applications in a general sense—are restated or clarified versions of those general guidelines as they relate to NL applications.

8.4.1.1   √ Present Feedback as Transaction Goals, Not as Speech

When it is time to present feedback to the user, it is better to announce the actions that are underway, not what the machine recognized.

Avoid: *I heard, "Buy 100 shares of Microsoft."*

You said, "Buy 100 shares of Microsoft."

Use: *Buy 100 shares of Microsoft ... Is that correct?*

Compare this with Guideline 2.4.1.1.

Table 8.1—TYPES OF SPOKEN MACHINE OUTPUT are reprinted from Chapter 2.

Type	Function
Prompts	A prompt indicates it is time for user input. The prompt thus serves as a turn-taking cue.
Feedback	Feedback presents the application state that results from user input, allowing the user to compare original intent with final result.
Instructions	Instructions give information to the user about operating the user interface or understanding the task.
Help	Help instructions often adopt a separate mode or state aimed at coaching the user.
Application Data	Application data represents information—for example, weather, stock information, or travel arrangements—that the machine presents to the user as part of the application task itself.

8.4.1.2   + Combine Feedback/Feed-Forward Only if Previous Entry Is Certain

The result of the previous recognition can be incorporated as feedback—embedded within the next prompt—for maximum message efficiency. This works for recognition with high confidence levels.

App: *How many shares of IBM?*

[handwritten: ※ Best in my opinion. deal w/ negative]

In the example, the initial entry "IBM" was recognized with high confidence. As a result, the keyword "IBM" can appear in the feed-forward prompt as corroborating feedback. This is known as embedded confirmation. If, on the other hand, recognition confidence were marginal, a better feed-forward prompt would be:

App: *How many shares?*

In this example, the feed-forward prompt contains no feedback. That is, it prompts for an amount without revealing which security was recognized.[13] This permits separate recovery dialogues for those tokens that are uncertain. After capturing the number of shares, the application can then recover the rejection:

App: *Please repeat the company name.*

8.4.2   Yes-No and Ambiguity Recovery

8.4.2.1   √ Use Yes-No for Recovery of Ambiguity Whenever Possible

Yes-no queries—including appropriate error-recovery on the yes-no response itself—are among the most robust speech recognition interactions. Yes-no queries are therefore more appropriate than feed-forward or other prompting schemes when attempting to recover ambiguities or user errors.

8.4.2.2   + Discourage Chatty Yes-No User Behaviors

Although the recognizer may be able to recognize without ambiguity most cases of colloquial yes-no synonyms, sloppy and unprofessional behavior on the part of the user are inappropriate for difficult and complex interactions. Sooner or later, colloquial and casual user speech causes problems. Such behaviors should therefore be negatively reinforced.

Avoid allowing the following to stand without comment:

App: *Is that correct?*

User: "You bet it is."

App: *Thanks. Here's the info you wanted.*

Instead politely correct such behavior:

App: *Is that correct?*

User: "You bet it is."

App: *For clarity, please reply with a simple "yes" or "no."*

        For legal reasons, a clear "yes" or "no" is required.

---

[13] Compare this with Guidelines 2.4.2.1 and 2.4.2.2 for more discussion.

8.4.2.3   + Encourage Businesslike Professional Speech

It is tempting to confuse "natural language" in the sense that it is used by speech scientists, with casual, colloquial, or even "friendly" human-like interactions. Such "social" interfaces are complex, and to this day not well studied. It is likely that such dialogues will backfire on designers. Callers are not generally interested in being entertained or in having "fun." The role of the machine, instead, is to be reliable, convenient, and fast.

All spoken machine output should establish and maintain a professional and businesslike demeanor. Prompts should have the effect of discouraging frivolous speech on the user's part. Note that there are alternate views based on studies of human users and their subjective views of media and technology [Reeves96]. The implications of such studies are neither well understood nor easy to apply. Application developers are cautioned to be aware of the controversy.

8.4.3   New User and Transition Tutoring

8.4.3.1   √ Keep Opening Remarks Short

When introducing natural language to callers, it is tempting to give instructions or long-winded descriptions. This temptation should be resisted. Instead, offer an example—at most—and then let users explore on their own. It is always better to let users learn by doing than to lecture or explain.[14]

8.4.3.2   + Offer Post-Acceptance Examples of Shortcuts

After successfully completing a transaction that was acquired in a less-than-optimal manner, the machine might offer examples that convey the most efficient natural language input that the user should have used.

App: *Would you like to hear an example?*

User: "Yes."

App: *You could have said ...*

Male: *"Buy 400 shares of IBM at market from my cash account."*

App: *Would you like to try this for another transaction?*

---

[14] Note the similarity with Guideline 6.2.1.3, "Let the user go first." In addition to being good prompting practice in the interest of managing time, the principle is also important for turn taking [Guideline 4.2.2.1].

User: "Yes."

App: *Go ahead ...*

8.5 Challenges in Implementing NL Systems[15]

Since the first edition of this book was released in 1999, a number of NL applications have been deployed. What's more, a considerable amount of usability research has focused on the performance of these applications. This research has identified several challenges associated with NL designs. This section presents these challenges and their most successful solutions. These new guidelines, isolated here for easy reference, do not replace earlier guidelines but instead complement them—providing clarity on special cases and specificity on design techniques.

8.5.1 User Skill and User Learning

"Natural language" is an unfortunate moniker for the specific mix of technology that currently supports NL dialogues. The term sets very high expectations that encourage "natural" behaviors in the lay sense. In fact, NL dialogues are at their best when users speak predictable multi-token sentences—a user skill that must be learned.

Indeed, almost all NL design challenges involve user learning. This is because NL applications represent a class of dialogues that are complex enough to tolerate a very wide range of user behaviors, but are not so sophisticated that they can respond to any style and variety of user speech. Instead, users are expected to adopt reasonable and predictable speech behaviors and must therefore learn how to interact efficiently with the interface.

It is true that callers usually learn quickly, because valid NL utterances tend to be easy to produce. However, users have trouble with three pitfalls:

• NL grammars—though quite large—are finite,

• Grammars change from state to state, and

• Speaking style requirements vary from state to state.

The first pitfall requires that users learn what they can say indirectly, without being explicitly told. The second and third pitfalls have no corollary in human interactions, and are often confusing to users attempting to learn the rules of the dialogue. For all

---

[15] Section 8.5 is new to the second edition.

of these reasons, the application must present consistent cues that lead to effective learning without slowing the dialogue. Some of the solutions to this user-learning challenge are counterintuitive.[16]

As shown in Figure 8.3, user skills required to succeed with a telephony interface are a function of dialogue complexity. Directed dialogues along the left side of the x-axis require simple speech behaviors—for example, answering yes-no questions, parroting choices in a menu, hearing a choice and speaking a synonym, or verbalizing a known phrase such as a city, state, or company name.

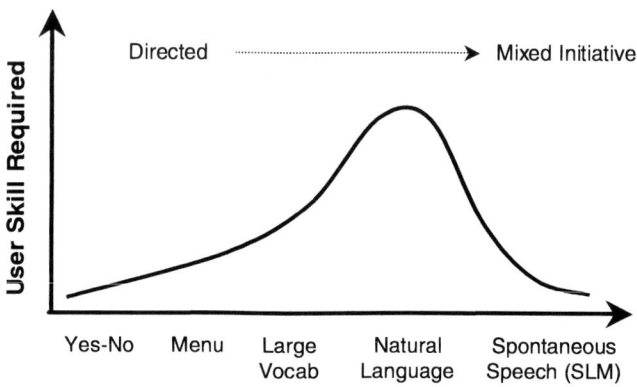

Figure 8.3—USER SKILL REQUIRED TO USE NL SPEECH RECOGNITION EFFECTIVELY increases with the complexity of the technology and dialogue style. Simple directed dialogues—even those that require large vocabularies—are somewhat easy for users to master. This is because the machine is in charge and users produce predictable responses to well-crafted prompts. As dialogues move toward mixed-initiative styles, however, users have more freedom and responses become correspondingly less predictable. Statistical language models (SLM)[17] ease the learning burden by supporting fully spontaneous speech, a solution with its own unique challenges.

As the dialogue style moves to the right along the x-axis, the increase in user freedom leads to a corresponding increase in required user skill. Some users acquire this skill outside of the application—for example, through pocket references, brochures, or other collateral. This is called "priming," and enjoys limited utility. In most cases,

---

[16] Counterintuitive in the sense that they violate assumptions implied by the word "natural." As understood by laymen, a natural interface should not require learning. But since NL dialogues cannot support fully spontaneous speech, teaching users may become onerous. The principle is subtle but important. See Table 6.1 for more on initiative.

[17] See the glossary, index, and Section 8.5.4 for more on SLM technology.

users learn "on the fly" by using the application—responding to prompts, engaging in error-recovery dialogues, and subsequently inferring which speech behaviors are the most fruitful.

Whether acquired through priming or through multiple machine interactions, user skills are inherently more involved for the productive use of NL applications. The best balance—a structured dialogue that encourages productive user behaviors—has the drawback of seeming "unnatural" at first glance. Care must be taken to understand which tradeoffs are most effective, and how to set expectations appropriately by managing the application consistency that leads to reliable user learning.

8.5.1.1   + Divide the Application into a Small Number of States

NL applications benefit from a logical division into two or three broad states. This allows users to develop a clear mental image of the application's organization, making it easy to master the grammar changes between NL states. With large numbers of states, the application becomes dominated by state errors. With only two or three states, simple entry and easy lateral movement between states makes error prevention and recovery more manageable.

A typical approach might be to divide a financial services application into an "information state" and a "transactions" state. The former allows the user to acquire information about stock prices, personal portfolios, 401(k) plans, and other data. The latter allows money transfers, stock trades, fund exchanges, and other activities. The differences are apparent to the user. One state is passive, with no changes to the host database, while the other is interactive, with transactions that leave the database in a different condition. The former is "safe" while the latter is "volatile." The former is easier for the user to understand—and more tolerant of user experimentation—while the latter is reserved for callers with more skill. These distinctions make it easy for users to conceptualize the reasons for the division and the functions of the states.

As will be seen in the following guidelines, these differences can be exploited to reduce errors and to encourage user exploration and learning.

8.5.1.2   + Consider Simple Entry to States

Many studies[18] find that the probability of continued interaction rises dramatically once the user experiences a successful turn—wherein the machine does what the user expected upon speaking. This phenomenon is especially true on the first turn (the

---

[18] For example, [Damhuis97]

user's initial opportunity to speak). According to these studies, the caller behaves in more predictable ways after each successful interaction, and is also more committed to attempting the next turn when the previous turn was successful. Two-way and three-way branches make such initial successes likely, and are discussed in detail in the following sub-guidelines.

8.5.1.2.1   √ Use Two-Way or Three-Way Branches for Simple Entry

One of the simplest entry prompts is the two-way branch. The prompt is not a yes-no question, but is similar in structure and simplicity.

Use:

App: *Would you like to get some information or make a transaction?*

User: "I'd like information, please."

App: *Information.*[19] *Please say, for example, "What's the balance of my checking account?" or "Tell me about my last five transactions."*[20]

The two-way branch as shown produces highly predictable user responses. The grammar is therefore simple and highly reliable, making the prompt a good entry into the application.

A three-way branch is only slightly less effective, shown below:

Use:

App: *Would you like to make a reservation, change an existing reservation, or cancel a ticket?*

User: "Make a reservation."

App: *To make a reservation, you might say—for example—"I'd like to fly from New York to Boston on July 26th."*[21]

---

[19] This lead-in phrase is an example of a landmark, giving feedback to the user by announcing the name of the newly-entered state. See Guideline 6.2.1.2 for more on landmarks.

[20] Notice that the first prompt in the information state happens to be an example prompt—one of only a few NL prompts capable of causing multi-token input. The design might as easily launch a directed dialogue with lists or menus that offer various types of information. Such a design decision does not affect the recommendation to enter the state with a two-way branch.

[21] Here a different type of landmark is followed by a multi-token example prompt. The sequence shows the principle of entering the state and immediately establishing productive NL expectations aimed at cueing the user to know where he is and what he might say.

Users have slightly greater difficulty with three-way branches, as there are more things to remember and the prompt is longer.[22] Nevertheless, the prompt constrains the user to a small universe of options, and responses tend to be highly predictable.

Table 8.2—TYPICAL RESPONSES TO TWO- AND THREE-WAY BRANCHES are easy to predict and codify with simple grammars. Prompts in the left column evoke user responses shown on the right. Infinitive forms produce the most reliable user-sentence constructions (top two prompts). Two-way branches with nouns acting as direct objects are also effective (third prompt). All forms occasionally trigger either ambiguous or task-oriented sentences such as the last response in each row. Because the grammar is highly constrained, this input is reliably detected as OOG and can lead to default transitions [Guideline 8.5.1.2.2].

Machine Prompt	Typical Responses
"Do you want to get some information or make a transaction?"	"I want to get some information."
	"Get some information."
	"Make a transaction."
	"I want a transaction."
	"Information."
	"Well, I want to do both ..."
"Would you like to hear a quote, get account information, or make a trade?"	"I'd like to make a trade."
	"Quotes, please."
	"I want account information."
	"First give me a quote and then maybe I'll make a trade."
"Do you want flight information or reservations?"	"I want to make a reservation."
	"Flight information."
	"Reservations."
	"I want to know the arrival gate for flight one-twenty-three."

---

[22] An extended study [EIG00] demonstrated a small but measurable increase in OOG when going from two- to three-way entry prompts.

Typical responses to two- and three-way branches from one study [EIG00] are shown in Table 8.2. The left column shows machine prompts; the right column gives several spontaneous user responses. Some callers gave discrete replies—"information" or "reservations" for example—but most produced a quasi-conversational reply based on the construction of the prompt itself. For example, users added "I'd like …" or "… please" to create responsive sentences. All of these constructs are easily predicted and grammars can be built that exhibit highly accurate processing of these utterances.

This sub-guideline applies only to the branches shown—the construction does not extend beyond three. A four-way or higher branching sequence should use menus or other methods for prompting.[23]

8.5.1.2.2   + Use Default Transitions at Entry Branch

Two- and three-way branches can often be designed such that one of the branches is a logical default. The chosen default is based on the most frequent, the safest, and/or the most benign state selected by users. If a default can be identified, then callers who fail to negotiate the two-way branch are moved directly to the default—often a better solution than attempting to recover an ambiguous response.

When ambiguous user responses to an opening prompt are treated as errors, the subsequent recovery slows the dialogue—running the risk of amplifying errors as shown in the following example:

Avoid:

App: *Thank you for calling. Would you like to get some information or make a trade?*

User: "What? … Oh, umh, I was just calling about some stock quotes."

App: *Your response was not recognized.*

Please say "information" or "trade."

In this example, the user has been taken by surprise. The recognizer has detected OOG, but the application has been designed to recognize exactly what the user has said at each juncture rather than focusing on the task at hand.

---

[23] See 8.3.2.3 for an example of a four-way branch to see why it is awkward and difficult to remember. Such branches should be avoided.

Sometimes—especially at the beginning of the call—an OOG response implies a novice user. A better solution is simply to move forward.

Use:

App: *Thank you for calling. Would you like to get some information or make a trade?*

User: "What? … Oh, umh, I was just calling about some stock prices."

App: *For information, you may say— for example—"I want a quote on Disney."*

The user's response is rejected as OOG. Rather than correcting the error, the application has made a transition to the default state—in this case the information state. To the user, there has been no error—the application is giving help on what to say and the prompt makes sense. As a result, users have a better chance of moving forward with minimum impact on the dialogue.

Note the correctness of the machine's behavior as perceived by the user when speech from Table 8.2 results in this default transition:

Use:

App: *Thank you for calling. Would you like to get some information or make a trade?*

User: "Well, I want to do both."

App: *For information, you may say— for example—"I want a quote on Disney."*

Responses such as the one shown are rare, and should not be represented in the grammar. Instead, a concise grammar with excellent rejection capabilities fares well with the given response. The recognizer has returned OOG, the application has made a transition to the default state, and the user perceives a correct machine behavior (accurate recognition).

A similar dynamic is at work when users present mixed-initiative replies to the two-way branch, as in the following example:

Use:

App: *"Do you want flight information or reservations?"*

User: "I want to know the arrival gate for flight one-twenty-three."

App: *For information, you can say—for example—"Tell me about the flight from San Francisco to Dallas."*

In this example, the user does not respond to the two-way branch directly. Instead, he **implies** an answer by initiating the next turn without prompting. The result is a state error—a sentence that is legal in the information state but is disallowed in the two-way branching state.

Although it is tempting to include these responses in the entry grammar [so-called "coverage" as discussed in Section 8.5.3.1], the solution causes more problems than it solves. Supporting a broad range of responses on entry represents an attempt to create a single-state modeless application—a solution that virtually guarantees a large number of stumbles at the first prompt. The goal instead must be to make the entry prompt certain to succeed, thereby getting the dialogue off to a good start.

With a default transition, the recognizer simply rejects the user speech as OOG—it is not represented in this entry-state grammar—and the default transition handles the rest of the problem. The user perceives that machine behavior is sensible, and the application avoids detrimental error recovery dialogues at this critical first interaction.

It must be noted here that many designers find this guideline troubling. They fear that accidents, including background noises and user mumbles, may land the caller in the wrong state with disastrous results. The rejoinder is that similar "disasters" result from substitution[24] errors, and yet few designers corroborate every interaction with the goal of detecting all substitutions. Instead, designers accept the fact that there will be occasional misperceptions of user speech by even the best ASR technologies. Their reasoning correctly argues that—on average—it is better to allow a few utterances (one or two percent) to be wrong than it is to slow all dialogues with excessive confirmation.

Why is it alright for occasional substitutions to "slip through," while a similar percentage of incorrect default transitions must be handled by applying error recovery to every occurrence of OOG? The answer is deeply rooted in the sensibilities and culture of the ASR community. "We have devoted immense re-

---

[24] A substitution error is a high-confidence recognition of the wrong word or token after the user has spoken a legal word or phrase. Recognizers cannot detect substitution errors, which can exceed 2% statistical occurrence rates on non-trivial grammars. See Section 1.3 for a discussion of substitutions and other recognition results.

sources to the problem of getting the recognition right," the argument goes, "and OOG is an error. Errors must be corrected."

By adjusting our thinking to a more reasonable user interface philosophy—one that endorses occasional guesses, "getting the gist," and taking a calculated risk to infer user intent when the odds are in our favor—we can apply methods that will work well for most users under most conditions. This means that we need not view every ambiguous result (e.g., rejections, OOG, and timeouts) as errors. Instead, they may be treated at certain dialogue junctures as indirect indicators of user intent. Default transitions at two- or three-way branches fall into this category, as they are rarely wrong.

This principle of well-placed default transitions is beginning to be embraced by designers as a practical solution to many design problems. Compare this guideline with less-controversial recommendations associated with triggering menu lists,[25] responding to failed yes-no questions,[26] and selecting list elements[27] to understand the many conditions that benefit from default machine behaviors. See also the design philosophy discussion in Section 1.1.1.2.

8.5.1.3   √ Retain Consistency with Simple Entry Interactions

Two- and three-way branches have a high likelihood of success. They also teach good speaking habits to users who succeed with them. To take advantage of this user learning, these simple prompting methods may be used liberally at other locations within the dialogue.[28]

Use:

Checking or savings?

Do you want to pay another bill, or go back to the Main Menu?

Would you like to know about flight status, schedules, or airfares?

Do you want news, sports, or weather?

Would you like to get some information, make a trade, or end this call?

The last example offers a good solution to the problem of telling a user how to end the session. Many callers are uncomfortable with simply hanging up. They will some-

---

[25] Guideline 6.2.1.3 and its associated sub-guidelines.

[26] See the discussion in Section 6.3.5 on one-shot yes-no and mixed-initiative responses.

[27] Guideline 4.2.2.4 describes "point and speak" list selection features.

[28] Contrast this NL guideline with two-way branching as applied to directed dialogues discussed in Section 6.2.4.

times bend over backwards to locate a key or command that closes the session and ends the call. The application should not clutter prompts by constantly reminding the user to "press 9" or to "say goodbye." Instead, a two-way branch—especially one that is used as the entry into a main routine—can become a three-way branch after the application has completed a task for the caller.

8.5.1.4 + Remain in Chosen State After Success

Users that call an application to perform multiple tasks are best served when they can repeat successful operations quickly. For this reason, the main states should be "sticky," meaning that the application should remain in the current state until otherwise indicated.

Avoid:

App: *Thank you for calling. Would you like to get some information or make a trade?*

User: "I'd like to make a trade."

App: *Stock trades. You can say, for example, "Sell 300 shares of Cisco at the market."*

User: "Buy 150 shares of Intel."

App: *Intel Corporation ... buy ... 150 shares ... at market price. Is that correct?*

User: "Yes."

App: *(Announces the details of the transaction, a process that could take a number of seconds. The application then completes the transaction.)*

App: *Done. Would you like to make another trade?*

User: "Yes."

App: *You can say, for example, "Sell 300 shares of Cisco at the market."*

User: "I'd like to buy 1000 shares of LittleCo."

In this example, the user has been successful with a transaction. The application then uses a yes-no question to determine that the user wants to perform another transaction that is virtually identical to the just-completed trade. After a "yes" response, the application repeats the example prompt. The sequence is both time-consuming and unnecessary. A better solution is to assume that user wants to repeat a transaction that may be similar to the task just completed. This is what is meant by "stickiness."

The following sub-guidelines describe some techniques for making a sticky state reliable and effective.

8.5.1.4.1   + Reward User with Quick Re-Prompt

If the caller responds to an example prompt and succeeds with a transaction, it is not necessary to repeat the example. Instead a quick turnaround prompt triggers a repetition of the success.

Use:

User: "Buy 150 shares of Intel."

App: *Intel Corporation ... buy ... 150 shares ... at market price. Is that correct?*

User: "Yes."

App: *(Announces the details of the transaction, a process that could take a number of seconds. The application then completes the transaction.)*

App: *What else?*

User: "Now I'd like to buy 1000 shares of LittleCo."

In this example, the user has successfully used a natural language utterance to make a trade. The task completion may take quite a long time, but—once successful—the application prompts with a short, "*What else?*" The prompt represents closure of the previous task, and conveys that the application remains in the same state awaiting another trade.

Users get a lot of work accomplished efficiently within the same state. This prompt has been tested extensively in a number of contexts and is quite effective at extracting repetitive tasks from callers.[29]

8.5.1.4.2   ≈ Maintain Consistency in Example Prompts

The goal of an example prompt is to equip users with a model or template which they can reuse for many different application functions. This learning is fast and tends to be easily retained. Effectiveness is enhanced when all func-

---

[29] The reader is encouraged to try the prompt in meetings with colleagues. After all comments have been delivered on a specific agenda item, pause for a moment and then say, "What else?" Note that it leaves the floor open for additional interaction if there is unfinished business, but—if the current subject is exhausted—it also does a good job of closing discussion and introducing the next agenda item. The prompt becomes a "task separator."

tions exhibit a grammatical consistency—that is, examples are similar in every way possible.

8.5.1.5   + Return to Application Entry to Test for State Errors

When the user has completed one or more tasks within a given state, then we can be relatively sure that the example prompting has been effective and that the user is not confused. Once errors begin to accumulate in that state, it is reasonable to assume that the user is attempting to perform tasks that are not supported by the current state. This implies that the user is speaking phrases that are represented by the grammar of some other state—in other words, a state error exists.

One way to test this assumption is to return to the entry prompt—the two- or three-way branch that routed the caller to the current state. If the caller in fact wants another state, then the transition is quick and prevents error amplification. If the caller wants to stay in the current state, then the test can lead to new example prompts that gradually expose the user to additional functions within the state.

8.5.2   The Convergence Problem

It seems logical for an application to respond to partial input by capturing individual tokens from the user—filling the form as quickly as possible.[30] The problem however, is that this often "teaches" users to degrade their speech from NL to a single-token speaking style. The application then converges[31] with the users to a directed dialogue, leading to the loss of productive NL utterances. The following is a transcription of one such an event that occurred during live usability testing [EIG00].

User: "I'd like to transfer … umh … three th …"

App: *(interrupting user) From whi …*

User: (continuing) "… thousand dollars …"

App: *(pause) From which fund would you like to transfer three thousand dollars?*

User: "Magellan."

App: *Transfer to which fund?*

User: "Evergreen … Growth and Income … Class A."

---

[30] Guideline 8.3.4.2 discusses this solution, which is usually successful.
[31] Convergence is observed in a number of contexts in speech applications [Baber97a]. See Guidelines 3.2.2.2 and 6.3.1.2 for other examples.

The user started a natural language utterance and then paused with "… umh."[32] The pause led to a timeout, and the machine concluded that the user was finished. The machine then began a directed-dialogue error recovery. The user, however, continued speaking—he believed that he still had the turn.[33] This new speech barges in, and the machine stops. Its prompt.

However, the user has heard the machine begin to speak, and therefore yields the turn. After a pause, the machine again speaks its recovery prompt. The prompt, *From which fund …*, contains very strong cues for directed dialogue. The user answers the question and awaits the next prompt. The final user response is spoken tentatively with pauses, indicating that the user has formed a new understanding of what the machine expects, adopting a discrete word speaking strategy. This style of speaking is rewarded. Caller and machine have now **converged to a directed dialogue**.

The four quadrants in Figure 8.4 show the underlying reason for this convergence. The culprit is the error recovery dialogues, which are invariably single-token directed dialogues. Users—even those that are generating productive NL sentences—will sooner or later fail with NL. Whatever the cause, the failure moves the user from quadrant 1 through quadrant 2 to quadrant 3, where directed dialogues recover the error. The user has unintentionally been "punished" for using NL behaviors in quadrant 1, and "rewarded" for directed dialogue behaviors in quadrant 3. The result of this conditioning is a strong tendency to remain in quadrant 3, which can thought of as the easiest and most successful state of the system.

Note that quadrant 4, although it does occur, does not play a part in convergence. The convergence problem is severe in all NL applications, because it prevents sustained exploitation of the very behaviors claimed as the advantage of NL dialogues. Since quadrant 3 is the most stable state of the system, users will eventually converge to that quadrant. Indeed there is every incentive to arrive at quadrant 3, and little incentive to return to quadrant 1.

It should be clear from the foregoing discussion that the key to effective NL dialogue design is to make quadrant 1 the most stable and attractive speaking style for the application. This means rewarding NL behaviors, and "punishing" directed dialogue.

There are only a few known solutions to the convergence problem. All have to do with making NL more stable and directed dialogue less stable.

---

[32] This paralinguistic utterance often occurs when the user is thinking but wants to keep the turn—a behavior known as "floor-holding" in the turn-taking literature.
[33] See Chapter 4—specifically Section 4.2—for more on turn taking.

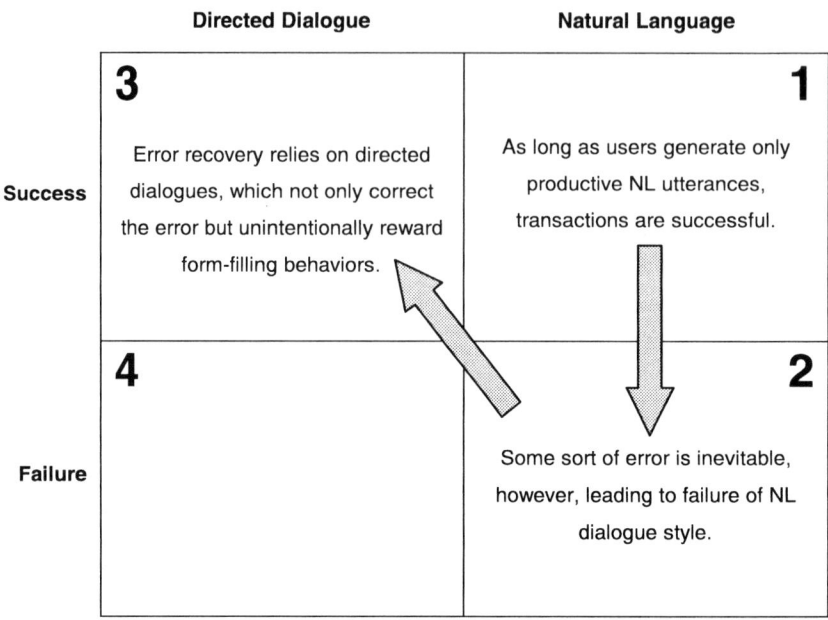

Figure 8.4—**NATURAL GRAVITATION OF NL DIALOGUE** exposes the underlying explanation for convergence. Applications that begin with users speaking NL utterances will sooner or later experience an error—causing a transition from quadrant 1 to quadrant 2. Either the user speaks OOG, or a false acceptance or substitution error triggers recovery dialogues. Such dialogues tend to be directed (quadrant 3). Success then rewards the user for directed dialogue behaviors, which become entrenched.

8.5.2.1   √ Avoid Degradation from NL

Users need clear cues that convey the rules of the dialogue. If the preferred style of speaking is natural language, then these cues—in the form of example prompts, longer user turns, and multi-token feedback—should reinforce this NL preference. The design strategy must be to reward NL behaviors and to resist directed dialogues every time the machine speaks. Some applications present NL examples in opening instructions or help sequences, but then switch arbitrarily to directed-dialogue cues as they interact with the user. The following example is transcribed from a test call[34] to a demonstration system fielded in the Boston area.

---

[34] The example is from a multi-phase study [EIG00] of several NL applications in 1999-2000.

Avoid:

App: *Thank you for calling the electronic restaurant guide.*

This guide allows you to ask for a restaurant using conversational speech. You will be asked for the type of food, the restaurant location, and how much you would like to spend.

Here is an example of what you might say. "I'm looking for a Chinese restaurant in Chinatown for around ten dollars a person."

Are you ready to begin?

User: "Yes."

App: *At what type of restaurant would you like to eat?*

User: "Seafood."

App: *Where would you like to go out for seafood?*

User: "In the Kendall Square area."

App: *How much do you want to pay per person for a seafood restaurant in Kendall Square?*

User: "No more than thirty dollars."

App: *Are you looking for a seafood restaurant in Kendall Square at no more than thirty dollars per person?*

User: "Yes."

The dialogue is inherently inconsistent. On one hand, the opening tutorial—and indeed the design of the grammar—encourage NL speech. The tutorial specifically refers to "conversational" speech and provides a three-token example to underscore the application's NL preference.

On the other hand, the yes-no question stands between the example and the user's first opportunity to speak, reducing the immediacy of the example. When it is the user's turn, the prompt—*At what type of restaurant would you like to eat?*—contains strong cues for the user to present a single token. The user is unable to resist the cues, and provides a reply, which in turn leads to a classic form-filling dialogue. The advantage of NL is completely lost.

In one series of tests, not a single caller used NL sentences when speaking to this application! The conclusion is that directed dialogue cues overwhelm the preferred NL speaking style.

8.5.2.2 √ Defer Form-Filling Error Recovery

Some applications do a better job of starting out with strong cues for NL speech, but then give up too quickly and revert to form-filling directed speaking styles. It is best to defer such degradation when encountering errors, focusing instead on achieving and then stabilizing on multi-token NL speech.

Avoid:

App: *Thank you for calling the automated railroad reservation system.*

What can I do for you?

User: "Umh …help."

App: *You might say, for example, "I'd like to travel from New York to Phoenix on August sixteenth."*

User: "No, that's not what I want to do."

App: *Please say the departure city.*

User: "Hartford."

App: *Destination city?*

User: "Philadelphia."

App: *On what date?*

User: "August thirty-first."

The user replies to the initial prompt with a request for help. The machine responds with an example prompt. But the user's first attempt is unproductive, and the machine either recognizes the "refusal" or rejects it outright as OOG. The utterance is not necessarily a major problem, and the user should be given a chance to re-craft a response that is more appropriate. This initial response is, after all, a typical behavior among novice users, who need to learn to mimic the NL example, replacing cities and dates with their own data in a multi-token utterance.

The machine, however, "panics" too quickly—immediately degrading to a directed dialogue. The user has now learned two things:

- "If I just talk to the machine like I would to a person, it doesn't work."
- "When it asks a question and I reply, it works well."

Users tend to learn these "rules" of the dialogue quickly, and continue using behaviors which are successful. By moving to a form-filling directed dialogue too quickly, the application designer has unintentionally rewarded the user for speaking single tokens—and has punished him for attempting NL speech. This is the essence of the convergence problem.

8.5.2.3   √ Enforce and Reward NL Behaviors

The previous two guidelines describe the tendency toward convergence, suggesting what **not** to do. The question is what can be done? The answer is to generate consistent cues that point toward NL as the preferred and reliable way to interact with the application. Consistency of speaking style is the primary issue—it is very difficult to establish consistency and to enforce it, due to the strong gravitation represented by convergence. Internal consistency—a natural and innate preference for NL sentences—provides a strong cue to callers and conditions their behaviors accordingly.

Consider the degraded example of Guideline 8.5.2.1. That dialogue was dominated by cues that led the caller to a directed dialogue. In the alternative dialogue that follows, the application eliminates the opening tutorial and moves straight to the dialogue—giving the turn quickly to the caller. The opening prompt relies on an example rather than a single-token query.

Use:

App: *Thank you for calling the electronic restaurant guide.*

        Please speak your request, for example. "I'm looking for a Chinese restaurant in Chinatown for around ten dollars a person."

User: "No, I want seafood."

App: *For seafood, you might say, for example, "I want a seafood restaurant at Fisherman's Wharf for less than twenty dollars a person."*

User: "I want a seafood restaurant in the Kendall Square area for less than thirty dollars a person."

App: *The Legal Seafood is located near ... Kendall Square ... would you like more information on that?*

User: "Yes."

The recognizer properly captured the single-token reply "seafood" from the user. The application, however, **did not reward** the user for generating this single token. Instead, the recognized token was used to construct a new example prompt—one that sends strong cues for multi-token NL. The user is learning. As the dialogue proceeds, the application resists token-by-token interactions, emphasizing instead comfortable and easy-to-say NL sentences. Note that the user is expected to repeat the word "seafood," a level of redundancy that helps with error prevention and recovery.

Now refer to the degraded example of 8.5.2.2. The dialogue presented a good example, but—when the first response was rejected as OOG—the machine failed to stick to its NL commitment. A better solution would be:

Use:

App: *Thank you for calling the automated railroad reservation system.*

       What can I do for you?

User: "Umh …help."

App: *You might say, for example, "I'd like to travel from New York to Phoenix on August sixteenth."*

User: "No, that's not what I want to do,"

App: *You might also try, just as an example, "I'd like to go from Providence to Baltimore on September the first."*

User: "I'd like to go from Hartford to Philadelphia on August thirty-first?"

App: *Morning or afternoon?*

User: "I'd like to leave at 10:00 AM."

Here the learning is more appropriate—and often occurs as quickly as the transcribed dialogue shows. The initial conversational speech is replaced by a productive, multi-token utterance. Note the question mark at the end. Users often are unsure as they experiment, and so tend to construct tentative utterances—almost as though they are looking for "approval" from the machine. Responses to the example prompt are also often slower, with disfluencies or pauses. The design of the grammar and the timing values for the endpointer[35] must take this predictable user behavior into account.

Notice that the example prompt is simply a repetition of the initial example with a different date and city names. This variety helps convey that it is the structure that the machine is after, not the example data. In this example, the user has learned that NL sentences work, that the machine prefers sentences that mimic the model, and that

---

[35] See the glossary for a detailed description of the endpointer.

success leads to shorter and quicker dialogues. This user is therefore more likely to repeat this behavior in the future.

This is the counterintuitive "unnaturalness" of successful NL applications. By enforcing a preference for NL input, the application at first seems intolerant—perhaps even unforgiving. It certainly is not conversational in any human way. If the solution successfully teaches users the preferred style of speaking, however, then it is well worth the effort, because users will stabilize on NL more often than they will converge to directed dialogue. This behavior benefits of both the user and the application.

8.5.2.4   √ Avoid Reserving NL for Experts

NL prompting is difficult and sometimes unnatural. For this reason, many designers construct a simple directed dialogue with an underlying hidden NL grammar. That is, the user "may" speak NL sentences, but all prompting is directed.[36]

The argument for concealing NL grammars beneath a directed dialogue interface is that the directed prompting is for "novices" while NL is for "experts." The problem, of course, is figuring out a way to make novices into experts. Figure 8.4 demonstrates that repeat users are almost certain to adopt directed dialogue behaviors because of convergence: we must remember that the cues of a directed dialogue prompt are very strong. The only alternative, therefore, is to find a way that users can be "primed" for NL through collateral information—for example, pocket reference, mailing, or web page instructions.

Unfortunately, knowledge gained from external collateral has a low retention, whereas dialogue experience conditioned by convergence is powerfully retained. The end result is that "expert" users rely almost exclusively on directed dialogues as the interaction style of choice—experts don't use NL.[37]

---

[36] The approach of supporting multi-token NL within a directed dialogue can be viewed as an attempt to create a "talk-ahead" feature [Section 4.1.3.6]. The goal is to flatten menus without reconstructing the dialogue according to NL principles. Were users to take advantage of the design, confusion regarding grammar changes and timing would likely lead to major turn-taking and state error conditions.

[37] Note the subtle distinction between hidden NL and "hidden menus" as discussed in Section 6.2.5. The difference is that hidden menus are about when to speak and not about how to speak. Users that fail to take advantage of hidden menus are not working at odds with the preferred speaking style of the application, making hidden menus truly optional.

8.5.3   Designing Well-Balanced Grammars

A good grammar is difficult to design. Grammars that are too small and restricted tend to confine the user to unnecessarily limited speech behaviors. The symptom of a grammar that is too restricted is an excessive number of OOG rejections[38] when user speech is reasonable. Conversely, a grammar that is bloated has the effect of encouraging the user to engage in unbounded speech behaviors that eventually prove detrimental to the stability of the dialogue. The symptom of a bloated grammar is excessive false acceptance.[39] The following guidelines help with balancing NL grammars.

8.5.3.1   + Avoid Excessive Coverage

Design and deployment of speech applications includes post-deployment tuning. One of the tuning steps is the collection of sample calls. To improve accuracy, speech specialists record and transcribe caller utterances, using them to update the grammar—a process referred to as "grammar coverage." The goal is to increase the ability of the grammar to recognize caller responses to the application's prompts. Many designers go overboard, however, covering every user utterance that occurs during field trials or tests. The process eventually becomes self-defeating.

Increasing coverage is important, and helps with first-time recognition accuracy by accounting for grammatical structures that were not originally conceived by the grammar designers. The effect is to make quadrant 1 of Figure 8.4 as robust as possible by recognizing a wider array of legitimate user responses. In other words, coverage reduces the failure rate of quadrant 1, and is therefore an error-prevention rather than and error-recovery solution.

However, attempts to improve coverage do not eliminate the convergence problem. There will eventually be an error, and once it occurs, quadrant 1 becomes immediately unstable. What's more, grammar updates based on captured user responses tend to focus on single-token responses—increasing first-time recognition at the expense of teaching users about NL productivity. As coverage increases, more users begin in quadrant 3 and stay there. Regardless of grammar coverage, users eventually explore the interface, discover that directed dialogues are the most reliable and predictable style of interaction, and become conditioned to them.

---

[38] See Section 1.3.1.3 to distinguish correct rejection from false rejection.
[39] False acceptance is also known as an insertion error. See Section 1.3.2 for a discussion.

The best grammars cover all appropriate utterances that are supported by the rules of the dialogue—that is the preferred speaking style that defines the application's look and feel.[40]

8.5.3.2   ≈ Avoid Single-Token Grammars

This guideline is an especially tough one.[41] The problem with large vocabularies that allow single-token responses in the grammar is the loss of OOG rejection. Users of such applications tend to get stuck due to state errors because whatever they say is recognized as a word in the large vocabulary rather than being rejected as OOG.

In one example, a stock application might include a collection of security names. The list of stock names is very large—numbering in the thousands. Users that present multi-token sentences for trades are likely to get good results on legal speech. Conversely, when users present illegal speech, the recognizer is likely to respond with detectable rejection of OOG.

This rejection ability is diminished when there is only one token in the grammar. This leads to problems such as those in the following composite:

User: "IBM."

App: *International Business Machines.*

        One-hundred five and one-quarter. Up three-quarters.

        What else?

User: "Microsoft."

App: *Microsoft Corporation.*

        Eighty-three point seven. Down two point four.

        What else?

User: "<throat clear>"

App: *Sisco Foods.*

        Nineteen point three. Down ...

User: "No, hold it ..."

---

[40] For example, a good grammar for NL applications includes the idealized sentences represented by all example prompts plus reasonable variants. The variants may include courtesy fillers and disfluencies, as well as word-order alternatives that are genuinely likely to occur.

[41] Note the conflict with Guideline 8.3.1.3 to understand the drawbacks to this guideline.

App: *Nolan Al ...*

User: "Now I need to buy some ... umh ..."

App: *Texas Instruments. Thirty ...* [42]

In this example, everything seems to be going quite well as long as the user and the application are synchronized. Once there is an unexpected event—represented here by a throat clearing—the inability of the large vocabulary to reject OOG is exposed.[43] Improving rejection is technically difficult, because speaker independent vocabularies are specifically designed to tolerate variation.[44] As a result, false acceptance begins to dominate the interaction in an error-amplification cascade.

The final user utterance exemplifies the core problem with false acceptance—state errors. In this case, the caller wants to perform a transaction rather than get quotes. To illustrate the problem, the example assumes that such transactions are supported in a different state and are not represented in the grammar for this state. The inability to detect OOG makes it difficult to detect the state error, leading instead to conditions that are frustrating and unproductive.

Where possible, grammars should not support single tokens.

8.5.3.3   √ Test for OOG Robustness

False acceptance errors are potentially devastating to NL applications because they can cause persistent state errors. Grammars should be tested extensively both in noise and with example OOG utterances to ensure robustness of rejection. If the grammar fails even a few percent on OOG tests, the performance will be much worse in the field. Bloated grammars should be carefully studied in conjunction with prompt design to find the best balance between coverage and OOG rejection.

---

[42] Note that false acceptance is a statistical anomaly, and that recognized words do not always "sound like" the spoken OOG [Section 3.1.2.2].

[43] The example is only intended to convey an understanding of the problem. In fact, throat clearings and lip smacks are well-rejected because they are modeled and therefore represented in the vocabulary. But the point—that unexpected acoustical events are likely to occur, and that such events have a high false acceptance rate—remains valid.

[44] Caller speech exhibits a wide variety of acoustical features, including dialects and foreign accents. The hallmark of speaker independence—its ability to recognize user speech despite such variability—becomes a limitation when it comes to distinguishing between OOG and a highly distorted version of a legal word.

8.5.3.4   √ Consider "Tunneling Grammars" for Lateral Transitions

Users often say phrases relevant to one state when they are in other unrelated states. So-called lateral moves from state to state complicate grammars, but must be considered in the light of these common user behaviors.

Moving laterally from one state to another without returning to an entry point or passing through a Main Menu is called **tunneling**. Support for tunneling is always problematic, because it easily leads to excessively large grammars.

One useful strategy is to support multi-token sentences for tunneling phrases. This means that the utterances must be formulated in the exact grammatical form as the example prompts for the target state. For example, if the user is in the information state and says, "I'd like to travel from Toronto to Montreal on September the seventh," then the utterance is an exemplary model for the reservations state. Support for such models does not add a huge burden to the information grammar, and could be included in the information-state grammar to support tunneling. On the other hand, single-token and disfluent speech relevant to the reservation state should be rejected as OOG in the information state—requiring that the user return to an entry point or otherwise move formally from one state to the other to initiate reservations.

By supporting tunneling on exemplary speech, the user is rewarded for productive NL behaviors while the application retains stability in terms of coverage and robust rejection of OOG.

8.5.4   Statistical Language Models

Speech recognition technologies known as statistical language models (SLM) have progressed well over the past few years and are touched upon briefly here. Although related to NL technology—at least in terms of the ultimate goals of NL applications—the technology today is a specialized approach to ASR that performs well in certain bounded tasks. However, the technology is easily misapplied, and so the following guidelines are aimed at helping designers understand SLM capabilities and the human factors that affect their utility.

A detailed discussion of SLM is beyond the scope of this style guide, and the reader is encouraged to obtain detailed information from the speech technology vendors that currently offer SLM products. [45]

---

[45] See [Markowitz96] for a good overview of N-grams. See [Larson02] for more on SLM technology and the voice web. Most speech vendors offer an SLM product.

Unlike grammar-driven recognition technologies used for NL telephony applications, SLM is based on a very large vocabulary of words—similar to a dictation system—with speech recognition guided by a method called N-gram processing. An N-gram uses statistical probabilities to determine which words within a given context tend to follow other words. SLM systems use word pairs (bigrams) or triplets (trigrams) as the recognition grammar.

Conventional NL applications are based on hand coded finite state grammars. In contrast, an SLM is trained from an example corpus[46] of transcribed utterances. These corpora are extremely expensive and time-consuming to collect and annotate. SLM technology is therefore most suitable in situations where there is already a source of example requests to train the system.

The goal of an application using SLM is to allow users to speak spontaneously—with no priming—aiming to recognize caller intentions by considering the statistical probabilities that have been computed from the corpus of speech samples. As such, an SLM is useful for systems where the topic of the call is not easy to elicit in directed or natural language dialogue. One example of such a situation is in call routing tasks where potential users have a wide range of topics to discuss but little or no time to learn the characteristics of the user interface.

Although per-word recognition accuracy in these situations may be quite low, allowing the caller to speak freely often results in longer, more redundant inputs. This redundancy is exploited by a natural language parser or classifier—which observes how different words or phrases contribute towards different topics. The sum of these contributions may then be used to decide the topic a caller is discussing—allowing the SLM technology to get the "gist" of the spoken user input. In certain well-bounded applications, performance of SLM technology on this gisting task is quite accurate. The natural language parser may also catch more specific items of information in the input, such as a customer account number or pin.

As shown in Table 8.3, the user generates spontaneous speech. The speech is constrained only by the context of the caller and by whatever effect the prompt has on the

---

[46] A corpus is literally a "body" of recorded voice samples. The plural is "corpora." Think of the corpus as a very large database which contains individual audio files of authentic user speech, plus associated text files that annotate (transcribe) the pronunciation and meaning of each audio file. Speech specialists collect such corpora by deploying a trial system and then recording the spontaneous responses that users produce when they call and interact with it. The resulting quality depends sensitively on the prompts and the context of the caller.

user. Speech is often disfluent, and sometimes quite lengthy and chatty.[47] This pro-vides ample material for the recognizer, which in turn comes back with the most probable sequence of words in the utterance. A classifier trained on examples of typical utterances for each destination then returns the probability that the caller wants one of a handful of options—in this case, one of four different help desks for a telephone company.

Table 8.3—**STATISTICAL LANGUAGE MODEL** gets the gist of user speech (first row) by searching word pairs (bigrams) or triplets (trigrams) according to statistical occurrences within the context. Although per-word accuracy is low (second row), statistical trends are reliably extracted. Notice that although apparently illogical, each word pair makes sense. A classifier—trained on examples from the corpus—then outputs the probability that the caller wants one of a limited set of options (third row).

Source	Data	
Spoken by user	"I... I've been trying for the past three quarters of an hour to get through customer services of e... East Pickford Electricity and all I'm getting is a buzzing sound"	
Literally recognized	I'm getting trying to pest recall to the now to get through to customer services it he's picking it and still it was a tape hello um could to the book in sound"	
Call type probability from classifier	line test	41%
	other	35%
	customer service	17%
	nuisance calls	7%

8.5.4.1   + Use SLM for Routing and Other "One-Shot" Interactions

The primary use of SLM technology today is call routing—using freeform speech to route the caller to one of several different help desks, VRU applications, or company

---

[47] Al Gorin has presented clear evidence that U.S. callers use either natural speech or sponta-neously-invented discrete commands (menu-speak) at the SLM prompt [Gorin97] and [Ric-cardi00]. Investigators in the U.K. have seen the same effect but in much lower proportions—only a few percent of callers [Attwater01b]. The difference may be due to prior exposure, con-vergence effects, or a mix of other reasons.

departments.[48] As a "gisting" technology, SLM along with language classifiers are good at capturing a general idea of what the caller wants and then routing the call. This is a "one-shot" application, meaning that the caller takes a single turn and the transaction is completed—correctly or incorrectly.

8.5.4.2   ≈ Use Caution When Mixing SLM, NL, and Directed Dialogues

SLM and other dialogue styles generally don't mix well. There are two related reasons. First, SLM prefers chatty and lengthy speech.[49] The technology is at its best when the caller is voluble, providing ample material to the recognizer to find "hot words" and word groupings. Second, SLM prompts are open-ended, expecting the caller to present a spontaneous description of her problem. The dialogue is inherently unstructured, and the role of the machine in SLM applications is passive—attempting to recognize speech with minimal intervention—rather than interactive.[50] Directed dialogues and their NL counterparts are, on the other hand, inherently structured and intensely interactive—requiring that users collaborate with the machine according to specific rules that move the user toward a goal.

Because SLM operates uniquely well on unstructured spontaneous speech while other dialogue types prefer structured speech, there is an in-built dissonance that results from this inconsistency of speaking styles. Mixed applications often use SLM as the initial entry—replacing menus or similar devices—following up the resulting gist with a more structured dialogue. The problem is that the caller has just been rewarded for freeform speech, a behavior that does not serve him well during the subsequent dialogue. It is as though the rules change from one point of the dialogue to the next, leading users to complain of confusion and lack of consistency.

It should be noted that inconsistencies in dialogue style are not always unnatural, and can sometimes be managed by the designer. For example, David Attwater of BTexact Technologies,[51] makes the case that customer service representatives (agents) often converse with callers such that the interaction becomes increasingly structured:

---

[48] Call routing is sometimes called "steering." This style guide treats the terms synonymously.

[49] to achieve the redundancy and rich statistical content required by the classifier.

[50] Interactivity—as discussed throughout this style guide—is essential in both NL and directed dialogues for preventing and recovering errors, teaching users, influencing their behaviors, and guiding them to success. All non-trivial applications (that is, those that require more than one turn), must become increasingly interactive as complexity increases.

[51] Attwater is Head of Research, Advanced Speech Technology Unit. BTexact Technologies is the research division of British Telecom.

A normal human-human dialogue in call-center situations often becomes closed and directed by the agent very soon after the task is identified—so there is a precedent in ordinary conversation [for changing the dialogue style]. The inherent risk lies not in closing down the prompting style but in leaving callers with the impression that they can spontaneously open it up whenever they wish. This is the dissonance [between SLM and other styles] issue. The problem could be dealt with partially, however, by the techniques of reinforcing a center of gravity[52] towards closed dialogue after the initial encounter [Attwater01a] and [Attwater01b].

Attwater concludes with the observation, "I believe that you can move from open to closed prompting styles with careful design—but you probably can't go the other way. As long as there are few repeat callers and the direction of convergence is maintained, a trajectory through the dialogue space is credible."

The following dialogue hints at how this converged SLM solution might work. The first user speech is presented to an SLM and classifier. Subsequent narrowing of the dialogue then conforms to the stages of negotiation typical for these kinds of calls. This is an example only, and not a recommendation:

Consider:

App: *How may I help you?*

User: "Hi, my name is <name> and we have a problem here … there's someone who's trying to … er … call … er … who is calling us the whole time trying to fax us something, we haven't got a fax machine so must, must have the wrong number, it's been going on the whole day."

App: *Are you having trouble with a wrong number?*

User: "Yes, but it's not us calling. It's the fax …"

App: *The fax is calling you?*

User: "Yes."

App: *Let me connect you with someone who can trace that number. Please hold.*

It must be emphasized that this example is not a real transcription of a dialogue event, although the opening user speech is paraphrased from [Attwater01a]. The sequence is

---

[52] Attwater is referring here to Figure 8.4 and associated discussion of the natural gravitation of NL dialogues. The implication is that the innate tendency toward convergence might be exploited, based on the fact that different styles of dialogue actually match different stages of a human-to-human transaction.

credible, however, and might be a mechanism for allowing completely open speech to trigger increasingly specific queries that eventually settle the user and achieve a terminal in the task hierarchy.

In cases where the natural language parser captures more specific items—for example telephone numbers that are embedded within the caller's spontaneous speech—then it becomes possible to extend the dialogue with less risk. In other words, once the application is into information gathering—and as long as all questions are appropriate (i.e. the application has definitely ascertained the correct dialogue state)—then information gathering can continue provided it is increasingly structured. It is not necessary to hand callers off to a steered destination immediately.

8.5.4.3   ≈ Consider NL Prompting Techniques for SLM

Although SLM is designed for spontaneous speech, it is possible that it may benefit from example prompting and other methods useful to NL. The prompt for SLM technologies is critically important, and considerable experimentation is required before the expense of data collection is applied to the capture of sufficient data to train the SLM. The reader is cautioned that NL prompting for SLM technologies is not supported by field data, and should be approached cautiously.

8.5.4.4   √ Test Prompts and Context Before Collecting Corpus

The speech generated by users can vary dramatically depending on the context of the call and the specific attributes of the prompt. This is true of both NL and SLM. However, SLM N-grams are built from corpora that are expensive and time-consuming to collect. Accuracy sensitively on the authenticity of utterances captured from callers who have specific needs and who are responding to a specific prompt. This includes not only the wording, but the subtle prosodic attributes of the prompt.[53] Prompt wording and style should therefore be modeled in context as accurately as possible.

In the worst cases, substantive changes to prompt wording can require recollection of the corpus. It is best to exercise all prompts for a proposed SLM application carefully—before data collection begins—to avoid data authenticity problems. Using wizard tests to collect initial samples and to get close to the right prompt will produce a better match between models and reality.

---

[53] Edgington, et al. have hard data on HMIHY ("How may I help you?") prompting. Their study shows that tone of voice is more important than wording for the initial prompt.

Chapter 9
Personified Interfaces

This chapter addresses the social and technical issues that are inherent in the design of interfaces that have lifelike "personalities." Developers who are not creating a personified interface, however, may still find these guidelines helpful when considering attention words (gatekeeper states), mixed-initiative dialogues, and professionalism as a "look and feel" goal.

An interface is personified when the designer has imbued it with specific personality traits. That is, it appears to have an internal self-awareness (consciousness) as well as some kind of willful decision-making ability. Personified interfaces amplify social responses that are already lurking under the surface [Reeves96]. Specifically, users tend to anthropomorphize[1] personified interfaces.

The reasons for designing a personified interface may be marketing, design, or aesthetic in origin.[2] They are not likely to be based on productivity arguments or ergonomic principles. For this reason, social issues must be well understood and managed. In effect, choosing a personified design represents a philosophical statement about the role of machines in human society. Designers that choose to make such statements should have informed opinions.

9.1 Issues with Personification

Some considerations that revolve around social and intelligent machine behavior are applicable to non-personified interfaces as well as to personified ones. Certainly different users form different mental images of the technologies with which they interact, and certainly these images are influenced by assumptions about the "thinking" of

---

[1] To attribute human qualities to non-human beings or things—in this case, expecting the application to interact verbally like humans in a social context.
[2] See Guideline 1.2.4.1

the machine—even when the interaction devices are deterministic and mechanical. Understanding anthropomorphism and similar phenomena will help the designer sort through the common personality attributes shared by all dialogues, allowing a clearer separation of deliberately personified designs and of the characteristics that amplify the user's social responses to such designs.

9.1.1   Anthropomorphism

Anthropomorphism is the attribution of human characteristics to non-human beings or things. What this means is that all humans exhibit a natural tendency to interpret the outside world in human terms. This tendency is well-known among pet owners, who tend to ascribe human traits to their animals. Pet owners describe their dog's love of attention as "smiling," or refer to their cat's "stubborn aloofness." Baby talk and affectionate cooing are easy to present to animals and even to plants—even though the human-like behavior is almost certainly not interpreted in as personal a way as the speaker might wish.

Similarly, people report seeing "faces" in inanimate objects. The headlights of a car become its "eyes," and the grill its "mouth." This is just one example of anthropomorphism, which means literally "taking the form of a human."

The difference between anthropomorphism and personification is one of reference. The user is free to anthropomorphize applications—there is nothing the designer can do about it. But a personified interface is deliberately designed to encourage and to exploit anthropomorphism.

9.1.2   Personalization

Note the difference between personified and **personalized** interfaces. Personalized interfaces employ unique knowledge of a specific user. Such personalization may be as simple as alternate ordering for presented information—changes in machine behavior such as "user customized" features in desktop interfaces. In some cases, personalization attempts to profile a user's wants and needs—for example, to control "filtering" on search engines [Maes97]—in a more sophisticated way. Personalization has its features and drawbacks, but will not be discussed here.

9.1.3   Personification

Very little is known about effective design techniques for personified interfaces. Although there are some services available, they are used primarily by early adopters and common practices are difficult to infer. Note that early adopters have different motivations than mainstream users [Moore91]. In addition, personified interfaces often strive toward unique characterizations aimed at product differentiation and look-and-feel concepts. Finally, there are well-researched arguments against the design of personified interfaces and the anthropomorphism that they encourage— arguments with which the designer should become familiar [Balentine92b], [Maes97], and [Shneiderman97].

This style guide does not take a stand on whether to personify or not. Although the subject is certainly important and relevant, there is simply not enough page space to give the controversy a proper treatment. Instead, the goal here is to provide design tips and dialogue ideas, as well as to raise ethical questions and other design issues that are aimed at maximizing benefit and reducing risk.

Because there are so many difficulties with the look and feel of personified interfaces, and because the risk of user backlash increases when anthropomorphism is amplified, it is important to look even more closely at the consistency of the interface and the goals of the design. The following guidelines apply to all dialogues, but are especially critical in personified interfaces.

9.1.3.1   √ Specify Design Objectives Explicitly

Some applications pursue productivity as a primary design objective. These applications must, above all, be effective and efficient in assisting the user as she engages in her work. Other applications have "high-touch" factors that aim to appeal to the user's aesthetic sensibilities—what some people refer to as the "cool" factor. Still others are concerned with entertaining or engaging users that are primarily novices, and therefore presumed—rightly or wrongly—to possess both short attention spans and little patience. None of these design objectives is intrinsically right or wrong. But they can often be competitive, and are sometimes mutually exclusive.

It is essential that the designer specify precisely what the measure of success will be for the application, service, or product. In this way, design tradeoffs are made early in the development cycle. Note the following:

- In cases where the end user is not the buyer, it is probably a good idea to specify design objectives that favor the buyer rather than the user. This is true, for example, in cases where the employer acquires productivity tools for employees. "User happiness" is probably a secondary concern. Ergonomic issues like "easy to learn" and "fast (inexpensive) to use" are more important objectives.[3]

- In cases where the end user may "try out" a service before subscribing, aesthetic issues such as the initial experience and both "fun and easy to learn" are much more important than productivity. This is especially true in cases where the user— once subscribed—is "locked in" to the service and will find it difficult to change to a different service provider later.

- In cases where a service provider benefits from longer user interactions (e.g., longer airtime), designers may or may not hold user productivity as a major objective. Such a decision, of course, depends on the service provider's end users and their compelling reason to subscribe to the service.

Regardless of the application's end users, an explicit mission statement regarding design objectives is an important first step in specifying dialogue structure, making look and feel decisions, and defining test procedures. These decisions are sometimes brutally cynical.[4]

9.1.3.2   √ Prioritize Conflicting Design Objectives

All of the objectives in Guideline 9.1.3.1 above are legitimate design objectives. However, it should be apparent to the designer that they are in conflict. "Friendly" applications are often slow for experts to use. "Efficient" applications are often intimidating to novice users as they learn the details of the interface. Applications that intelligently profile users—changing their behavior as novices become experts—are often complex and expensive to design, develop, and test. Design objectives should always be prioritized, allowing informed tradeoffs when conflicts between design objectives inevitably appear.

9.1.4   Social and Professional Issues

All users respond unconsciously to certain social aspects of interactive media [Reeves96]. These social attributes are implicit in the interaction whether placed there deliberately by the designer or not. This means that it is the designer's responsibility to take a stance on the social role of the machine and its impact on the goals of the application.

---

[3] This principle of giving primary service to the buyer rather than the user also applies to cost-saving applications, as discussed in Section 1.2.4.3.

[4] The term cynical is deliberately emotive here. A common motivation for personification is to make the user "like" and to "trust" the system. To the designer, such a goal is unquestioned and self-explanatory, but may not be shared by business stakeholders.

There are a number of studies that demonstrate—and in some cases attempt to quantify—the social response to various media. Such studies should be treated cautiously, however, when it comes to applying this information to specific designs. The reason is that some applications aim to **exploit** the effects of social responses—encouraging casual and unconscious social behaviors to the advantage of the user, the application, or both. Conversely, other applications focus specifically on design methods that **minimize** social effects—discouraging such user behaviors on the grounds that they are difficult to detect, expensive and complex to handle, distracting to the user, and likely to cause error amplification.

In other words, the social relationship between the application and the user is one of several style decisions that are dependent on five closely related but distinctly different issues, summarized in Table 1.1 (see Section 1.2.4.1).

9.1.4.1   √ Ensure that Professional Applications Use Professional Protocols

A professional protocol includes certain specific social attitudes, behaviors, and personality traits. Whether the application is personified or not, an understanding of professional behavioral protocols is helpful—not only when phrasing prompts and feedback, but also when composing the overall look and feel of the interaction. Those of us who work with and respect professional leaders may note that they consistently exhibit the following traits when interacting with others [Balentine92b].

A professional:

- Always sticks to the point,
- Does not let herself be distracted by irrelevant issues,
- Remains unperturbed at confusion, annoyance, or anger,
- Is understanding and helpful when progress is slow,
- Is quick and direct when communication is good,
- Calls off the interaction if communication is clearly failing,
- Focuses on the goal,
- Is courteous and polite, but never overly solicitous or obsequious,
- Does not apologize or blame,
- Never calls attention to himself by being cute, intimidating, talkative, overly animated, or repetitive,
- Always says just the right thing—no more, no less,

- Listens attentively—never appears to be rushed, and
- Controls the interaction without being overbearing or inflexible.

Note the degree to which these behaviors are at odds with the unstated goals of some personified interfaces. This list of protocols may be more easily stated than implemented. But by establishing such "personality traits" from the start, designers of personified interfaces may avoid the danger of imbuing their designs with too many social and not enough professional characteristics. Note that this is not an argument against personification. It is only an argument against unprofessional behavior.

9.1.4.2 √ Balance Social and Productivity Behaviors

Many applications have both professional and social goals. This may be true, for example, of telephone-based personal assistants. Such applications often use chatty or personable social traits as key features for product differentiation. In such cases, social interactions—sometimes even including humor—are adopted as methods for entertaining the user or engaging his interest.

It is important to remember that applications have productivity goals. The user may, for example, wish to schedule events for the future, specify alternate telephone numbers, or deposit and review memoranda. Such tasks are complex and, presumably, important to the user.

In the following example, a personal assistant application is attempting to exploit the known social effects of users and new media.[5]

Avoid:

User: "Schedule a one hour appointment with Jim at 11:00 Saturday morning."

App: *You really are dedicated to be working on the weekend!*

All successful people have to work weekends sometimes.

You really do work hard!

User: "Gee, thanks."

---

[5] This example is based on the observation that users respond positively to flattery—even when it is insincere [Reeves96]. The problem is that, although true, the principle is overgeneralized. People do not <u>always</u> enjoy insincere flattery. Otherwise we would not have words in the English language such as sycophant, "suck-up," yes-man, toady, or "brownnose." Even social devices that sometimes work are often inappropriate for applications.

The assistant, noting that the scheduled date is on a weekend, applies this information socially rather than professionally—apparently with the goal of helping the user enjoy the interaction. There are two problems with the dialogue.

- It places social considerations above productivity. This is fine if design objectives explicitly state that social amenities are a top priority. If, however, the application is primarily aimed at enhancing productivity, then such unctuousness calls the user's attention to the machine as a social partner. Users often perceive this as frivolous and patronizing—and therefore insulting to the user and self-defeating to the machine's goal.

- By engaging in banter on its own part, the application encourages similar deviation from the application's recognition vocabulary. When the user leaves the machine's core competence and engages in unbounded social interaction, the behavior invariably amplifies OOG false acceptance errors,[6] leading to an eventual breakdown in the interface illusion.

It is better to stay focused on the task, reserving social discourse for humans.

9.1.5   Persona Versus Personality[7]

A recent trend in the speech recognition community emphasizes what is called the **persona** as an essential part of a telephony application. A persona is distinguished from a personality in its emphasis on the fictional nature of the character.[8] Promoters of this trend specify the persona thoroughly and painstakingly before approaching other details of the application—implying a belief that the persona is the foundation for every other design element. In many cases, considerable time and expense are devoted to the persona, including focus groups, psychological profiles, and voice talent audition and selection.[9]

A persona need not be a full-fledged personality in the sense of having a name and character. However, most efforts adopt personification design methods. Interest in personae has grown due to advances in speech recognition technologies and the somewhat new voice browser applications. These applications attempt to attract more

---

[6] See the glossary and Section 1.3.1 for a discussion of speech recognition error types.

[7] Section 9.1.5 is new to the second edition.

[8] The distinctions between personality, persona, personalization, and personification are subtle and the reader is encouraged to use these terms in consistent ways. Detailed definitions derived from [Merriam-Webster93] appear in the glossary to assist with this consistency.

[9] See Appendix C for more on voice talent and recording.

consumers to both cost-saving and value-add applications—calling for product differentiation and enhanced user experience.

Persona design takes the form of storyboarding and characterization—following long-established traditions in screenwriting.[10] The history, background, and other personal attributes of a character are developed and committed to written description. The goal is not to convey all of these characteristics to the listener, but to provide an underlying model that guides and motivates spoken material.

There are three reasons for specifying the persona at an early design stage:

- Consistency,
- Branding, and
- User satisfaction, liking, and trust.

The reasons are not always valid. The following guidelines introduce the reader to persona specification issues, playing the role of devil's advocate to counterbalance current opinion. Note that little rigorous testing has been applied to persona-driven designs, and the reader is cautioned to form opinions with care.

9.1.5.1 ≈ Be Cautious of Consistency as a Guideline

Most usability challenges regarding telephony dialogues must be resolved by applying the fundamentals of information management, human memory, effective organization, and related ergonomic principles. To the degree that these fundamentals conflict with the persona, they must take precedence. The consistency issue therefore leads to circular reasoning: do we bend the design to maintain consistency with the persona, or do we adjust the persona to fit the best design solution? Or, for that matter, do we just ignore any inconsistency?

There is little evidence that persona inconsistencies in otherwise effective dialogues have any detrimental effect on the user.[11] For this reason, the effectiveness and usability of the dialogue is a better place to apply resource. However, if consistency is viewed as an important criterion worthy of persona development, then it is important to identify design elements that will be changed in the name of consistency. These elements are presumably the wording of spoken machine output, but may also include the order in which questions are asked, the manner and style of error

[10] Voice actors familiar with persona design can help with this process. It is a good idea to include them in planning, as described in Appendix C.

[11] See [Grudin89] for a lucid discussion of the problem. In the ACM article, Grudin argues persuasively that consistency is not a good criterion for deign decisions. Setting it as a goal usually leads designers away from rather than toward effective user interfaces.

the order in which questions are asked, the manner and style of error recovery, and other issues that affect usability. Cohen suggests that:

> Even if there is no desire for branding or the creation of some specific corporate image, there is an advantage to an explicit persona definition step prior to work on prompt wording in order to achieve a more consistent and appropriate underlying characterization for an application [Cohen01].

9.1.5.2   ≈ Work with Marketing on Branding Efforts

Businesses benefit from customer loyalty over long periods of time. Visual and audio logos, slogans, jingles, and celebrity testimonials have a positive influence on buyer preference, brand recognition, and customer habits. Certainly it is credible that the persona of a frequently-called telephone application might similarly influence users— including their relationship with the business and their opinion of its products and services.

There are cases in which the persona of a telephony application is reproduced at the related web site through the use of an **avatar**—an animated character that speaks and moves. The telephony and web manifestations of this persona presumably reinforce each other.

The problem, of course, is that branding is a marketing, not a usability issue. What's more, to the degree that there are conflicts or inconsistencies, the telephony design and development team must defend usability against all interference.[12] For this reason, branding efforts should be overseen—and financially sponsored by—marketing stakeholders.[13] Branding decisions must be tested for usability impact and rejected in cases of negative impact.

9.1.5.3   ≈ Consider Moving Persona Decisions to the End of Development

Those features of a telephony dialogue that are associated with personae are **surface features**—presented through the dialect[14] and the quality of the voice. The features are easily managed by professionals in parallel with design and development, and final persona decisions can be made quite late in the program. Any association with other aspects of the application that contribute to branding, including character

---

[12] Certainly marketing stakeholders would agree—no one wants an unusable application.

[13] This is true not only because of fairness, but because of quality of final result. Technical people are rarely skilled at marketing and tend to underestimate its subtleties.

[14] Dialect here means both word choice and sentence structure, as well as pronunciation. See the glossary to understand more about dialect and accent.

names, avatars, and underlying characterization, however, can and should fall within marketing sponsorship and may therefore have different schedules.

Once the application is well-tested and robust, the surface features can be turned over to the voice talent as described in Appendix C. The coach and talent together will do two things. First, they will take the somewhat formal wording that may have emerged from design and translate it into more idiomatic structures appropriate to speech—changing "cannot" into "can't," and adjusting awkward tongue-twisters into mellifluous and undemanding articulations. Second, they will ensure that a clean and acceptable persona emerges from the spoken messages—controlling pace, inflection, and other production qualities to deliver a professional result.

There is little evidence that persona work at the beginning of the design contributes to additional application quality or user acceptance.

9.1.5.4   ≈ Devote Design Resources to the User, Not the Persona

The design goal is for the user to succeed with tasks—a goal that depends on clear and unambiguous prompts, coherent organization, quick error recovery, damped error amplification, and effective use of default machine behaviors. Since speech is an inherently uncertain input, these design principles are difficult and time-consuming to implement. They deserve the majority of the design and development resource.

The key to making good design decisions is to remain **user-centered**. That is, to understand the user, the task, and the context of use. These are the fundamentals that pose interaction challenges and therefore should be the elements of focus. The persona, by its very nature, is **machine-centered**—more interested in amusing the user with its own characteristics than in serving the user's needs. When in doubt, it is best to devote design resources to the user, not the persona.[15]

9.2   Choosing Personality Traits

9.2.1   Personae, Names, and Gatekeepers

A personified interface features a character—very much like characters in movies, short stories, comic books, television, and radio. This character has specific motivations, personality traits, and styles of interaction—all based presumably on an internal

---

[15] This principle is especially true when we consider that those subtle human characteristics most likely to make truly likable personae cannot be achieved with current or incipient speech recognition technologies.

mental makeup that constitutes "how it thinks" and "what makes it tick." As with all fictional characters, there is no actual thinking, so this mental makeup must be thought through by the designer and incorporated into a well-rounded, believable, and interesting persona.

9.2.1.1   + Give the Persona a Name

Adopting a personified design encourages users to conceptualize the application as an entity that is imbued with certain traits—personalized and social attributes that the user has already encountered in everyday life. Such traits presumably cause the user to interpret machine behavior in terms of intentional and willful internal states. It also can be argued that these traits lead users to unconsciously adopt certain speech constructs that the application can predict and therefore recognize.

Regardless of the reasons for adopting this design model, personification is enhanced when the application is given a personal name. Table 9.1 shows some naming conventions that can be adopted when considering character names.

Table 9.1— **NAMES OF APPLICATION PERSONAE** can be based on human, invented abbreviation, product, or fictional character naming conventions.

Convention	Examples	Pro	Con
Standard Proper Names	*Bob* *Albert* *Charlie*	• easy to learn • easy to remember • human-like	• user acquaintance may have same name • human-like[16]
Acronyms	*C.H.I.P.* *HANC* *I.N.D.A.*	• easy to pronounce • easy to learn and to remember • different from human	• no obvious sense
Product Names or Nicknames	*Wildfire*™ *R2*	• easy to pronounce • easy to learn and to remember • different from human • brand recognition and product differentiation	• machine-like (no spontaneous user model for interaction)
Fictional Characters	*Zå* *'Borg* π	• smart but non-human • different from human • brand recognition and product differentiation	• not obvious how to pronounce • an odd name without context

---

[16] "Human-like" may be a feature or a drawback depending on the position adopted by the designer on such issues.

9.2.1.2   + Use the Persona's Name as an Attention Word

An attention word is a specific word that is spoken to "get the attention" of the machine. The machine is in a **gatekeeper** state [Balentine92b], where it attempts to distinguish between background noise and the attention word. The goal is to be sure that the user is addressing the machine before allowing the machine to risk generating its own overt response. By minimizing false acceptance,[17] the attention word makes the application responsive without being pushy.

When the underlying speech technology is discrete-word recognition, such words are spoken in isolation during a discrete gatekeeper state. The state is designed to reject all input other than the single attention word. When the user speaks this attention word, then (and only then) the "gate is opened." Table 9.2 shows one example based on a voice-activated dialing (VAD) application. The system is initially in a gatekeeper state. Although actively recognizing, the application does not exhibit externally observable behavior when out-of-vocabulary word (OVW) or inter-word rejections[18] appear. At each silence, the recognition restarts in search of the attention word—in effect resynchronizing with the user.

Table 9.2—DISCRETE GATEKEEPER STATE requires silence followed by a properly recognized attention word to "open the gate" (perform a transition to an active state).

User Speech/Background	Application Response
(talking to friend at airport) " … was going to be delayed. Let's check." (silence)	*(rejected as OVW)* *(restart recognition)*
(loud background noise)	*(rejected as OVW)*
(silence)	*(restart recognition)*
"Computer?"	*Ready …*
"Call …"	*Name to call?*

---

[17] False acceptance is used here to mean, specifically, an insertion error. See Section 4.3.2 to understand false acceptance in the context of barge-in as opposed to recognition. See the glossary and Section 1.3.2 for a discussion of insertion errors.

[18] Note that a gatekeeper state typically activates a relatively large vocabulary to minimize false acceptance errors. This means that certain words may fall close to the attention word, resulting in inter-word rejection. Such "near misses" are ignored, as are all OVW rejections.

The first input in Table 9.2 is user speech that is not directed at the machine. This speech is a very poor match against the attention word and is therefore rejected. At the next silence, the application restarts recognition. The next input is background noise, which the recognizer again rejects. At the following silence, the application restarts recognition. When the attention word, "Computer?" appears, it is confidently recognized and the gate is opened. The application prompts with some starting word, such as, *Ready*, or *<beep>*. From this point on, the dialogue proceeds state-by-state through some simple task—in this case, placing a phone call. At the conclusion of the task, or when instructed by the user, the system returns to its gatekeeper state.

When the application uses a natural language dialogue model, attention words are used to synchronize the start of user-driven input sentences. **Error! Not a valid bookmark self-reference.** shows an NL version of the same example discussed in Table 9.2. Similar to the discrete recognition gatekeeper state, the "start" word disallows all spurious input with the additional advantage of allowing the attention word and the command or request to appear as a single continuous utterance. Note that—as with discrete gatekeepers—the attention word must be preceded by silence.

Table 9.3—**NL GATEKEEPER** requires silence followed by a legal sentence that starts with the attention word. The silence plus the required attention word are unlikely to be recognized accidentally as a result of the background, thus keeping the gate locked until needed.

User Speech/Background	Application Response
(talking to friend at airport) " … was going to be delayed. Let's check." (silence)	*(rejected as OOG)* *(restart recognition)*
(loud background noise)	*(rejected as OOG)*
(silence)	*(restart recognition)*
"Albert, please call the reservations desk."	*Calling …*

9.2.1.3   + Consider Machine Versus Human Personae

The designer who is determined to create a personified interface is presumably doing so to acquire the assumed benefits of a machine persona: a high-tech, high-touch, natural interaction that fulfills user expectations. The designer should still be concerned with avoiding the drawbacks of personae: unconstrained user behaviors, social assumptions, and the evocation of human emotions. It may be that a well-crafted personality that is distinctly machine-like rather than human-like is one way to achieve both of these conflicting goals.

9.2.2   Machine/User Relationship

9.2.2.1   √ Understand and Address Power Issues in the Relationship

It is important to understand that human/human interactions have undercurrents based on the **power** relationship between the interlocutors. This makes spoken communication, including apparently benign social interactions, extremely complex and multi-leveled. Human interactions include indirect meaning, sarcasm, and even outright deception as a normal part of conversation.

Although it is impractical to implement and exploit these subtle human attributes, the application nevertheless gives the user the impression that it can. This means that users may engage in misleading behaviors that the machine can ill-afford to interpret.

Speech applications should avoid encouraging power-related speech behaviors. However, the designer must be aware that such behaviors are likely to occur. The look and feel of the application must therefore consider power issues that are ingrained in user associations with spoken language. Consider the following:

- The personified character should have no power over the user.[19]
- The user must know explicitly that the character has no power.
- The user does have power over the machine.
- But the power possessed by the user is unlike that in normal human discourse, and therefore may be discomforting—at least at first.
- User anger must be avoided, but user amusement is also problematic. Designers should avoid replacing socially ignorant machine behaviors with humor. This is because socially ignorant comedy is no less offensive and no more intelligent.

This last comment requires some expansion. We have all observed the awkward social experience of a "joke that falls flat." Sometimes, a colleague tells a joke that is inappropriate for the context—perhaps his partners are having trouble with some aspect of work, and do not appreciate the humor given the gravity of the circumstances.

---

[19] This is not always true. There are cases in which a VRU application might refuse to give a caller an extension on a payment, for example, or might charge a fee for sending a fax. Although these are "business rules," and cannot be blamed on the machine, it is the machine that delivers the bad news and therefore the machine that apparently has the power. These circumstances exacerbate issues associated with power.

At other times, special conditions exist—a light-hearted rib about relationships becomes insensitive when one of the group is recently divorced. Sometimes the attempt at humor undercuts power assumptions—a junior partner with a little too much alcohol "teases" the boss in a way that is a little too personal.

The fact is that humor is among the most complex of all human dealings—a minefield that a machine dialogue is ill equipped to navigate. And yet, designers of personified interfaces often use humor in an attempt to engage the user—hoping, perhaps, that a positive response to the humor will be confused with personal well-being, and that a little of that positive emotion will rub off on the machine in terms of user satisfaction or product loyalty.

More often than not, the joke falls flat. The pre-paid phone card runs out in the European telephone booth before the chatty virtual assistant has completed her tasks. The "sleepy voice" that greets a call after midnight is met with irritation when the user calls from a different time zone. The flirtatious voice takes on a grating edge when the traveler finally locates a payphone after a delayed flight. All of these "best laid plans" become insulting when the spoken machine output is received under conditions about which the machine has no knowledge and over which it has no control.

9.2.2.2   + Guidelines for Business Applications

The following suggestions apply to personified interfaces that are aimed at business users for productivity, information management, or other business goals.

9.2.2.2.1   + Avoid Cute Personae

Business users are busy. Cute personality tics and conversational banter work well on the trade show exhibit floor and in television ads for a product. The novelty wears off quickly.

9.2.2.2.2   + Minimize Colloquial Interactions

Certain speech constructs are more appropriate for non-business interactions:

Avoid:

Got it!

You betcha!

Well all-righty, then

Why not?

Rock on.

Hmmm ...

Well, let's just take a look ...

Such phrases convey a lack of seriousness to the user. Although possibly useful in playing games or applications targeting certain user groups, colloquial speech is inappropriate in business applications.

9.2.2.2.3   + Focus on the User's Work

The best behavior for a mechanical assistant is the same as the appropriate behavior for any junior employee in a company.

9.2.2.2.4   + Assume the User Is Busy

Most personified telephone-based applications are productivity-centered in their marketing claims. They should be so in reality.

9.2.2.3   ≈ Consider Separate Characters for Functional Areas (Multiple Agents)

Once the design is committed to a personified dialogue model, there is no reason to limit it to just one personality. It is possible to design a "team" of personal agents—one, for example, to handle faxes, while another manages telephone calls. In this approach, each functional area of the application relies on a different personality, routing the dialogue between agents. The model is similar to the traveling salesman who—calling home to the office—first asks one "character" if there are messages. After interacting with this secretary character, the salesman then asks to speak to an account manager—a different character who knows about a specific client. After that interaction, the salesman may be returned to the secretary, who then routes the call to yet another character for inquiries about accounting, to leave a voicemail message, or to ask a technical question about his laptop computer.

The vocal quality, style of speech, and context of the subject matter bound the dialogue for each agent, making it (presumably) easier for the caller to keep track of the task at hand. In a sense, the changes in "personality" represent multi-leveled cues that serve as landmarks—providing parallel context information through a separate, non-semantic audio channel. This can be thought of as a type of "personality menu," allowing the user to choose the task domain by choosing the character.

See [Balentine94] for an example of a desktop multimedia application that takes advantage of this multiple-agent notion. Daryle Gardner-Bonneau, in her IVR guidelines [Gardner-Bonneau99], suggests that applications of the future will require such multi-leveled cues.

> If one envisions calls in which there are multiple participants, and in which one or more of these participants is a machine, it may well be the case that anthropomorphism becomes an *essential* element of the user interface. For example, anthropomorphism may need to serve as the means by which machine participants are uniquely identified by the human participants throughout the course of a dialogue. In teleconferences, humans identify each other by voice characteristics, personality characteristics, and communication styles. How will humans identify machines in such a situation, if not by similar characteristics?[20]

9.3   The HANC Application Persona

The following discussion is based on an early concept prototype for a robot named HANC.[21] The robot dispenses medication, tracks vital signs—including blood pressure, temperature, weight, and EKG—and maintains adherence to a scheduled medical regimen, communicating via modem with a "Central Station."

The HANC interface was conceived as a personified interface. "He" interacts with the user from a distance, relying on speech recognition as well as buttons for user input, and presenting data via a combination of text-based and speech output. The unit is basically a **scheduler**—managing the patient's medical regimen by tracking the schedule and then summoning the patient when it is time for some sort of medical activity. The user also may inquire of HANC—asking about and even changing the schedule within specified constraints—and launching certain additional personal activities as allowed.

The HANC examples are presented here for four reasons:

1.   The machine is a mixed-initiative design, supporting both user-initiated and machine-driven dialogues.

---

[20] In the quotation, Gardner-Bonneau is using "anthropomorphism" to mean "machine personality." The user, able to perceive vocal characteristics quite sensitively, relies on those characteristics to distinguish between multiple machine and human participants.

[21] The product is a home-based medical robot that is leased from a home nursing or hospital supply company and communicates with the leasing organization via modem. The acronym stands for Home-Assisted Nursing Care [HANC89]. The prototype was built in 1989, and used speaker independent ASR and custom-designed buttons for input with a color display and audio for output. The prototype was coded in a UNIX environment.

2. The machine is a scheduler, and therefore engages in behaviors that are relevant to many of today's Personal Assistant or Virtual Assistant telephony applications.

3. The machine was built some years ago, allowing designers to understand dialogue methods that are not based on current state-of-the-art speech recognition technologies.

4. As a concept prototype, the machine was exposed to various types of users, providing useful information on the effects of anthropomorphism and personified interfaces in a real implementation.

Note that HANC is a local, physical entity rather than a remote, telephone-based agent. Nevertheless, the principles derived from this design translate well to telephony applications.

9.3.1   Initiative and User Knowledge

The appropriate design for a dialogue depends greatly on the amount of knowledge possessed by the user. This knowledge affects both the design of vocabulary in terms of "commands" available to the user, as well as the degree of dialogue initiative that should be given to the user.

9.3.1.1   + Consider User-Initiated, Machine-Driven Models

The following is a typical example of a PCA[22] dialogue with HANC.

User: "HANC, what time is it?"

App: *It's around a quarter till.*

User: "I don't feel well."

App: *It's been more than two hours since your last pain medication.*
        Would you like more?

User: "Yes, please."

App: *Do you have water?*

User: "Yes."

App: *Fine. I'm dispensing your medicine now.*
        (after a pause) Have you taken your medication?

---

[22] Patient-controlled analgesia, an important aspect of post-surgery home healthcare.

User: "Yes, HANC."

App: *Good. I'll note it in your log.*

The dialogue is **user-initiated**—in this case, the user inquires about the time.[23] Knowing that another pill may be allowed, the patient continues by announcing his state of being ("I don't feel well."). The machine, under the control of its schedule, determines that the current time is within the allowed window for PCA, and dispenses a pain pill.[24] The rest of the dialogue is **machine-driven**. HANC directs the patient through each step, requiring only yes-no responses to each state.

This user-initiated, machine-driven strategy has the following advantages:

- The user does not need to know anything about the capabilities of the machine or about the changing conditions of the schedule.

- The user is given limited power in a concise and structured form, making learning and use easy.

The strategy has the following disadvantages:

- It is slow, as the machine must do a lot of talking.

- It does not allow for precision schedule changes.

9.3.1.2   ≈ Consider Referring to Times and Dates in Human Terms

Personified interfaces might benefit from the use of human scales of precision for handling complex information such as times and dates, avoiding unnecessarily precise representations.

Avoid: *It is now five twenty-five. You have an appointment at 5:30 PM.*

Use: *It's just about half past. You have an appointment coming up.*

See Figure 9.1 for an example of U.S. English vernacular for clock time. Machine speech that announces times—for scheduling and similar personal assistant functions—may help the user comfortably grasp the attributes of a personified interface. Bear in mind that such a claim assumes that being human-like is one of the objectives of a personified model—an assumption that may be invalid. See [Maes97] and [Schneiderman97].

---

[23] A heightened interest in keeping track of time is a common preoccupation among the elderly as well as those recovering from surgery—typical HANC patients.

[24] The mechanical design resembles a vending machine, and is quite secure.

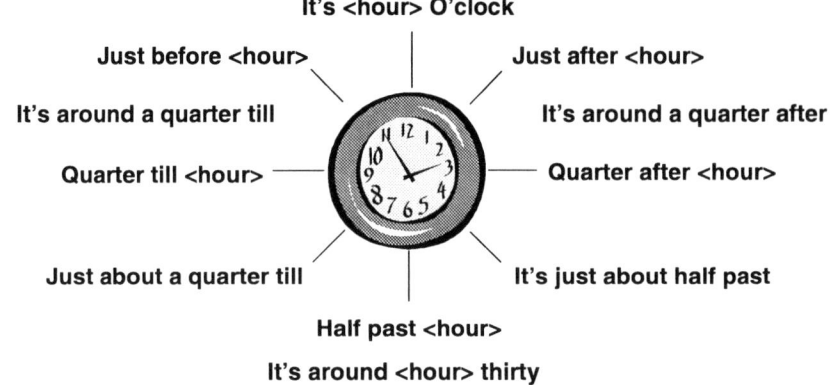

Figure 9.1—**ROUGH-PRECISION TIME** as might be used by humans. This spoken machine output may be presented in response to user questions such as, "What time is it?" or perhaps, "When is my next appointment?" Such responses could arguably convey a more natural or human-like model of time than high-precision declarations associated with computers.[25]

9.3.1.3   ≈ Avoid Requiring that the User Give Direct Commands

Personal assistants and other agents that use a personified look and feel often approach scheduling behaviors by providing "commands" that the user may issue to direct the agent explicitly. To expose the problem with this approach, here are two dialogues between a business executive and her human secretary—dialogues that compare brute-force commanding behaviors with more subtle negotiations.

Human Example of Commanding:

Boss: "Frank?"

Sec: "Yes, Ma'am?"

Boss: "Move my two o'clock appointment to three."

"Cancel the four o'clock."

"Then schedule a new two o'clock."

"I'll be at the Green Room anyway, so just book it for three more people."

"It's the Gross Systems account—I think we're gonna close today."

---

[25] This argument is based on the assumption that users think of high-precision information as indicative of machine "coldness." Such an assumption can only be supported anecdotally. However, there are good reasons to assume that "rough time" is more effective than precise time for cognitive reasons.

Sec: "Got it … will do."

This kind of interaction rarely works well with humans, because the "commander" doesn't knows this much about her schedule. In fact, the appropriateness of a commanded schedule goes straight to the heart of the "what the user knows" issue.[26]

If the user knows the following, then "commanding" is an appropriate behavior:

• When all other appointments are scheduled;

• The relative importance and priority of all other appointments;

• The likelihood that all existing appointments will occur as scheduled.

If the user possesses this information and analyzes it correctly, then and only then does she possess the information required to form a command—that is, when the new appointment is to be scheduled.[27] If the user does not possess this information, then a command-oriented interface gives too much power to the user. Power without knowledge is the flaw of command-oriented interfaces. See Table 6.1 for a refresher on the appropriate dialogue models for various degrees of user knowledge.

At its core, the command model misses the character of human scheduling, which more often takes the form of a **negotiation**. The user, not knowing her schedule, gives a set of criteria to her secretary—criteria about urgency, priority, and contingencies. The assistant, in turn, offers options for scheduling. The two then home in on the best compromise. The prior dialogue example is more likely to resemble the following.

Human Example of Negotiation:

Boss: "Frank?"

Sec: "Yes, Ma'am?"

Boss: "What have I got this afternoon?"

Sec: "Two o'clock you're with Mr. Benson."
         "Then at four is the weekly staff meeting."

Boss: "Cancel the four o'clock."
         "Then schedule a new two o'clock."

---

[26] See Section 6.1 for a discussion of the pros and cons of command-and-control dialogue models.

[27] Users who are able to mentally manage this knowledge generally do not need schedulers or personal assistants.

Sec: "Where?"

Boss: "The Green Room."

Sec: "That's right, you're there for lunch. How many people?"

Boss: "Three more."

Sec: "That's a total of four at the Green Room— two o'clock."
         "What about Benson?"

Boss: "Move him to later. He'll understand. ..."

Sec: "Good. I'll schedule him for three."

Boss: "No, make it three thirty."
         "I think we're gonna close Gross Systems today."

Sec: "Got it ... will do."

The "give and take" of this second example is a more realistic view of information extraction and schedule manipulation as negotiated between humans.

9.3.1.4   + Support "Negotiation" Over "Commanding" for Scheduling

The HANC personified interface manages medical schedules. Just as in the human examples above, "commanding" is not always an effective model for interactions.

HANC Examples of "Commanding" (originally considered):

Avoid: "HANC, reschedule my medications for later."
         "Move my two o'clock appointment back to three o'clock."
         "Turn on call screening."
         "Give me a pill at five."

The HANC designers originally considered these apparently natural phrases. After further consideration, however, they decided to avoid these commanding behaviors— considering them too taxing for the user. Instead of requiring that the user give direct commands, HANC instead relies on inquiry, collaboration, or negotiation as preferred user behaviors—basing its vocabulary on this user-initiated, machine-driven paradigm. All schedule manipulations, for example, are initiated with a simple user query:

Use: "HANC, what's on the schedule?"

This inquiry then triggers a negotiated interaction between HANC and the user—a negotiation that is driven by HANC and that relies primarily on yes-no responses by the user. This is what is meant by a user-initiated, machine-driven dialogue.

By asking the machine a question, the user sets a context. It is then up to the machine to ask appropriate questions or to offer relevant operations as it negotiates with the user toward a goal. Precision is sacrificed in favor of simplicity.

HANC Example of "Negotiating" (actually implemented):

User: "HANC, what's on the schedule?"

App: *Our next activity is medication.*
        It's coming up pretty soon.
        Would you like to proceed now?

User: "Yes."

App: *Fine. Please get a glass of water ...*
        ... and then let me know when you're ready.

User: (after a delay going to get water) "HANC?"[28]

App: *Do you have water?*

User: "Yes."

App: *Fine. I'm dispensing your medicine now.*

In this example the user asks about the medical schedule. The machine answers with a specific reply that is based on the schedule. It then continues with additional information, based on the fact that the scheduled event falls within an allowable time window. Because the medication may be dispensed now, this option is offered to the user through a yes-no query. In this way, the user exerts limited control over the schedule without having to know anything about it. In the example, the user moves the event forward—accepting the medication slightly ahead of schedule.

Note that the current time compared against the scheduled time is what the machine references when choosing its behavior. If, for example, a scheduled event were somewhat further out, the dialogue would be different:

---

[28] The HANC robot uses his name as a gatekeeper (attention word). Whenever there is a pause in the dialogue—as when HANC awaits a user who is gone, for example to get water—he enters this gatekeeper state, which is highly resistant to insertions caused by environmental speech or sounds. The user is instructed to "get HANC's attention" whenever approaching the machine to start an interaction.

User: "HANC, what's on the schedule?"

App: *Our next activity is vital signs measurement.*
        It's scheduled for around five o'clock.
        But we can do it sooner.
        Would you like to start at ... say ... three thirty?

User: "No."

App: *That's alright. We can delay for nearly two hours.*
        Would you like to wait until ... oh ... half-past six?

User: "Yes."

App: *Fine. I'll wait until then.*

The dialogue appears to be natural and conversational. This is because the machine is in control. The user has limited power—in this case, moving the event window forward or back by an hour or two. Note that HANC does not know or care why the user asked about the schedule. Rather, he announces his current "plan" (the schedule), offers the closest allowable time for change, and then uses a yes-no question to allow the user to choose this option. Given a "no" response, the only alternative is to delay the event to its latest possible time. Although limited in scope, it is adequate for those reasons that the user may typically have for schedule changes—the desire to take a walk or to watch a TV program.

9.3.2   Vocabulary Selection

9.3.2.1   ≈ Consider Inquiry-Oriented Vocabularies

It is sometimes effective to provide a simple rule to the user—a rule that constrains the input that he is likely to construct. One such rule is, "Ask the machine a question." The user will tend to construct questions that revolve around tasks or data in which he is interested. Grammars then anticipate the various constructions that may be generated—inquiries that are likely to be more predictable than task-oriented commands.

"What's on the schedule?"

"What time is it?"

"Are there any messages?"

As described in the HANC example, once the recognizer processes a query the application may proceed with inferred options, based on the reasons that a user may have asked such questions.

9.3.2.2   ≈ Consider User-Announced Intentions or Conditions

One thing that users always know is what they want and what they are going to do. User-centered vocabularies can take advantage of this by encouraging the user to simply announce her intentions.

"I'm leaving."

"I'm going to sleep, now."

"I don't feel well."

In the examples, the user is notifying HANC of her intentions. The machine, in turn, responds to the declaration by checking its schedule and making a decision about upcoming events. In certain cases, for example, an action can be moved forward:

Your medication is coming up pretty soon.

Would you like to go ahead now?

The solution allows the machine to provide a scheduled action—in this case, the automatic dispensing of medication—within an allowable window of time. The offer is based on the relationship between the user's declared intent, the current time, and the constraints of the schedule. The user need not understand the details of the schedule, nor remember how to ask for certain machine actions.

Similar actions that are more distant can be pushed farther out:

User: "HANC, I'm going to sleep."

App: *I have to take your blood pressure in about two hours ...*
         But it can wait.
         Would you like me to wake you at five o'clock?

Use: "Yes."

App: *Fine. Sleep well.*

In other words, the machine automatically adjusts a scheduled item based on the fact that the user wants to sleep. There is no danger that any medical activity will go undone—only the convenience of slight adjustments forward or backward is allowed.

Because the scheduling activity is complex, the user is not given direct control over it. Rather, the user is encouraged simply to talk about herself using a few simple descriptive and self-explanatory commands[29]

9.3.2.3   ≈ Consider "Collaborative" Commands

Sometimes it is effective to select vocabulary that gives the user a feeling of collaboration with the machine. Phrases built around first person plural (e.g., let's, we, we're, us) accomplish this collaborative perception.

User: "HANC, let's change your settings."

App: *What would you like me to do?*

User: "Change your volume."

App: *Tell me when it's loud enough.*

User: "Louder."

App: *Tell me when it's loud enough.*

User: (after several adjustments) "OK, HANC."

App: *Thank you.*

The phrase "Let's change your settings" allows the user to perform HANC system functions—much like the "options" menus in many voicemail systems. The functions include raising and lowering the volume of HANC's voice (loudspeaker), turning clock chimes on and off, and similar housekeeping functions. The collaborative phrase activates a separate menu for these functions.

Once the user has selected the operation—in this case, turning up the volume—the dialogue is again machine-driven. HANC repeats the phrase, *"Tell me when it's loud enough"* at the current volume as long as the user experiments. The user may say "Louder," or "Softer," causing HANC to repeat the phrase at the new volume. When the user is satisfied, the "OK, HANC" acknowledgement exits the menu and returns HANC to his quiescent state automatically.

---

[29] The phrases that the user can say are printed on HANC's display. In a telephony version of a similar scheduler, the phrase list could be easily memorized or stored on a quick reference pocket card.

Chapter 10
Error Recovery and Prevention

When designers are first exposed to speech recognition technology, error recovery is often the first thing that comes to mind. This is because the word "error" implies flaws in the technology, becomes linked in the designer's mind with recognition accuracy, and imposes the greatest burden in terms of imagined design constraints. Fear of error then leads to excessively verbose instructions or prompting, constant "yes" or "no" after-the-fact corroboration, and a generally slow or even cautious look and feel. The resulting interface tends to "get in the way" of the user, causing many of the problems that the designer had hoped to prevent.

In fact, errors in speech recognition are not as common as errors of intent, errors of behavior, or errors of interpretation (on the part of either the machine or the user). Even when the recognizer itself does commit errors, the origin often lies elsewhere—perhaps in user confusion, timing or turn taking errors, or in the background acoustical environment in which the user is speaking.

This chapter approaches error prevention by suggesting methods whereby the designer can discover their underlying origin. This means devising algorithms that separate errors into a broad set of classes rather than agonizing over errors as things that need to be counted, reported, explained, and corrected. The core philosophy is to damp error amplification by preventing errors whenever possible and by correcting them interactively and gracefully when they occur.

10.1 Detecting and Handling Errors

This section addresses classifying errors into categories that fit the cause. It also focuses on avoiding the common pitfall of allowing error recovery to cause new, harder to detect errors.

10.1.1 Distinguishing Error Types

Speech applications exhibit a great deal of complexity. But at its core, a spoken interface has two basic objectives when it comes to managing its user:

1. Ensure that the user knows **what** to say from state to state.

2. Ensure that the user knows **when** to speak.

Considered from this viewpoint, the art of designing a speech interface is quite simple. The goal of all spoken machine output—from simple menus to sophisticated natural language prompts—is to cause the user to construct legal spoken utterances. The job of the prompt and its associated turn-taking protocol is to cause the user to produce legal utterances at the appropriate time. The job of the active vocabulary[1] is to recognize the utterance correctly.

In an attempt to simplify the combinatorial explosion of states and user inputs, designers often approach error recovery as a "lists of things that can go wrong." Hence, designs that have "correct path" machine behaviors based on confident recognition, and "error path" designs that return to previous states when "errors," such as the following, occur:[2]

• Out-of-grammar (OOG),

• Inter-word rejection,

• Timeout,

• Spoke-too-soon, and

• Other spurious or rejection errors.

The function of the error path is to report the condition to the user, who is then expected to present new speech to the application—presumably "better" speech that somehow "fixes" the problem. This approach to error recovery tends to be ineffective in temporal-based interfaces such as speech. The reason is that the above errors are often not errors per se. They are better thought of as "conditions" that may occur for a number reasons—and should not punish the user by default.

Indeed, the objective of all interactions should be to avoid error conditions altogether, replacing them with appropriate goal-oriented dialogues that are designed to

---

[1] The active vocabulary includes the sub-vocabulary or grammar. See the glossary for a detailed description of "active vocabulary."

[2] See Section 1.3 to understand these error conditions.

272

satisfy what the user intends and wants—regardless of the recognized utterance. Failure to achieve this goal often leads to a breakdown in the dialogue flow.

For these reasons, it is important that errors be well understood and properly classified. In general, errors derive from three distinct sources:

1. Recognition (classification) errors,

2. Behavioral (user interaction) errors, and

3. Environmental (noise and echo) errors.

All three sources may be recoverable in some instances and not in others.

10.1.1.1   √ Differentiate Fatal from Non-Fatal Errors

Fatal errors include:

*   Inability to acquire a recognition resource;

*   A user who is a goat;[3]

*   Background noise so high that recognition failure is likely;

*   Frequent intermittent background noises.

When the application detects these conditions—and they are not at all easy to detect—then it is better to give up earlier than later. Such problems are not likely to be fixed by any user or machine action, so any error-recovery messages presented to the user are pointless.

Non-fatal errors include:

*   Turn-taking errors (even frequent ones);

*   Occasional recognition errors (even substitutions);

*   OOG provided it is caused by illegal user speech and not the environment.

These conditions are the normal result of user behaviors and can be corrected through helpful interaction provided they are properly detected. Care in distinguishing between fatal and non-fatal errors thus becomes an important first step in successful error-recovery designs.

There are a number of methods for distinguishing between these conditions, usually involving machine assumptions. The idea is to make a "safe" assumption, engage in an additional interaction, and then use the results of the new interaction to prove or

---

[3] A user for whom the speech recognizer performs poorly for no apparent reason. See the glossary for a detailed description of "goat."

disprove the prior assumption. Although details of these methods are beyond the scope of this style guide, the examples that follow are a good starting point.

10.1.1.2 + Detect and Track Behavioral Errors

A behavioral error occurs when the user does something that the machine cannot handle. Although such user behavior may cause a recognition problem, the core challenge is managing user behavior rather than fixing the recognizer. Such behavioral errors include:

- Turn-taking errors (speaking at the wrong time),
- Speaking OOG, and
- Failing to speak at all.

To the degree possible, the application should classify these errors separately. Because these errors are usually recoverable—users rarely repeat the same behaviors over and over—the application should be more tolerant with them. Note that "lecturing" the user rarely accomplishes much, but effective adjustment of machine behavior will almost always cause adaptations on the part of users. The challenge of error recovery is to make the user adapt in a direction that is useful to the application rather than in the direction of error amplification.

10.1.1.3 √ Avoid Simply Counting Errors

Many applications increment counters every time an error occurs. After exceeding some threshold, the user is penalized in some way. Some designs use "three strikes and you're out" approaches, passing the user to a help desk or switching to DTMF. Other designs use these error traps to trigger tutorials or help routines.

Such solutions miss the point of user learning. Users learn from mistakes as well as (or even more effectively than) through formal lectures or tutoring sessions. Counting also place all errors into the same class. The result is usually an increase in user confusion, as the application moves from one context to another, rather than improving user learning. For example, consider this simple half-duplex[4] example with the recognizer output indicated by automatic speech recognition (ASR):

App: *Do you want to delete this message? <beep>*

User: (speaking during beep) "Next Message."

ASR: <returns spoke-too-soon>

---

[4] See Section 4.4 for a description of half-duplex interactions.

App: *Sorry, I didn't understand you.*

        Please wait for the tone and then say "yes," "no," …

User: (speaking during prompt) "Yes."

App: (continuing with prompt) *… or "Cancel." <beep>*

User: "Oh, I forgot to wait ..."

ASR: <returns OVW>

App: *Sorry, I didn't understand you …*

User: (speaking during prompt) "Yes."

App: *To go back, say "Cancel." <beep>*

User: "Delete."

ASR: <returns OVW>

App: *You have one more chance.*

        Do you want to delete this message? <beep>

User: (speaking during beep) "Yes."

ASR: <returns spoke-too-soon>

App: *Sorry for the confusion. Let's switch to keypad entry.*

These types of dialogues are not uncommon in speech recognition applications of all kinds. The dialogue becomes so confused that the individual states are blurred and misunderstood. Indeed, both user and developer would probably make comments about how "inaccurate" the recognizer's performance was—despite the fact the there were no recognition errors at all. There were in fact seven behavioral problems: four turn-taking errors, and three out-of-vocabulary words (OVWs). The application, however, sees only four "errors:" two spoke-too-soon and two OVW responses. Most of these errors are actually caused by the dialogue, and there is quite a bit of user behavior that is appropriate—albeit undetected.

The first error is the failure of the user to produce a "yes" in response to the question. Rather, the user jumps ahead and commands, "Next Message." This is logical, although wrong for the yes-no state. If the user had spoken this phrase within the allowed window, the situation may have been better, since the application would probably present a retry on yes-no due to an OVW detected.

Instead, the spoke-too-soon error triggered a lengthy message. Since the application is half duplex, the user's self-correction—"yes"—is missed. This correct but embedded response is a turn-taking error that happens twice in the example. On the next opportunity to speak, the user realizes that he forgot to wait—unconsciously expressing this observation by muttering. The resulting OVW is the second "error."

By the time it is the user's turn to speak again, he has forgotten the yes-no context in which the machine is stuck. He therefore provides a concise command, "Delete" to tell the machine what he thinks it wants to hear. The resulting OVW is strike three. But the application—in a last-ditch attempt to "teach" the user what he already knows, presents a threatening last chance. The user behaves correctly and responds, but—unfortunately—speaks slightly too soon.

It may be difficult for the designer, at first glance, to see how two spoke-too-soon and two OVW errors could possibly be interpreted in any other way than fatal. But the fact is that the design has failed to construct an effective turn-taking protocol, and therefore cannot derive any meaning from the input. Simply counting errors when turn taking is not addressed means that turn-taking errors go undetected.

10.1.1.4   √ Exhibit Special Consideration for Environmental Noise

It is very difficult to distinguish between environmental noise and recognition or behavior problems. See Section 6.3.4 on the value of yes-no queries in detecting noise.

10.1.2 Giving Up and Disconnecting

10.1.2.1   √ Allow Multiple User Errors Before Disconnecting

Except for possible security procedures, a single user error must not cause the system to disconnect.[5]

10.1.2.2   √ Exhibit Special Consideration for Yes-No Errors

Yes-no is a critical dialogue component, as it is used to recover many other commonly occurring errors. But what if there are recognition problems associated with the words "yes" and "no" themselves? It happens occasionally that a goat appears who has problems with this vocabulary. Such occurrences are unfortunate, as they are extremely difficult to detect—particularly if they manifest themselves as substitution rather than rejection errors.

---

[5] This guideline is based on Ameritech Standard 4.1.1.a. (which in turn references ASI GUI Standards).

Because of the difficulty of detection, it is important to be alert for yes-no problems. Typically, the application notes that the user is backing up to correct an "error." The user then selects the same item as before. A yes-no query asks for corroboration, but the user answers with a clear and confident "yes." After proceeding, a similar correction behavior occurs. The behavior clearly casts doubt on the recognized "yes."

Algorithms to detect this behavior must be explicitly designed and put into the dialogue, as yes-no problems can not be detected in any other way. Although "yes" and "no" are extremely robust vocabularies in most languages, failures can cause major problems. Note that the occasional yes-no error may be recoverable, but "yes-no goats" experience fatal problems, and the application should detect and give up on them quickly.

10.1.3 Avoiding Repeated Mistakes

10.1.3.1   + Use *n*-Best Query Rather than Simple User Repetition

The user that experiences a recognition error on a given word has an increased chance of a subsequent error when asked to repeat the word. For this reason, a query based on *n*-best is more likely to recover a problem than is a request for the user to repeat.

Note that presenting *n*-best is not appropriate if it appears that the user did not say a legal word. In this case, the user must be prompted to speak, but the application must be cautious and avoid referring to this as a request to "repeat" the input. Such prompts often cause the user to repeat the same illegal input.

Unless there is reason to suspect illegal input, it is generally better to query the *n*-best list, using "yes" or "no" to corroborate input. The likelihood of failure is diminished, as the user must now introduce error on two rather than one of the vocabulary words.

10.1.3.2   + Reject a First Choice that Has Just Been Refused

If error-recovery interaction determines that a given recognition result has been refused by the user, and if the immediately following input results in the same refused choice, then assume a recognition error and proceed with the second choice in the *n*-best list of recognition candidates.

10.2 User-Initiated Error Recovery

It is important to understand that certain errors can occur without the knowledge of the application. In these cases, the user must initiate error recovery. Examples of conditions unknown to the application include:

- Speech recognition substitution and false acceptance,
- Application state error, and
- User change of mind.

10.2.1 Approaches for Barge-In

When the system supports barge-in (see Chapter 4), user-initiated error recovery can be based on detecting and optionally recognizing user speech during the moments following the machine's response to user input.

10.2.1.1 ≈ Treat Barge-In After Input as a "Back-Up" Command

When the system supports barge-in, treat any detected user speech immediately after a user-input juncture as a request to return to the previous input state. This can recover both machine errors and a change in the user's mind without prejudice.

Example 1 (substitution error)

App: *Stock name?*

User: "Electronic Data Systems."

App: *Electronic Medicines up one and ...*

User: "No, stop!"

App: *Backing up.*

Stock name?

Example 2 (user changes or clarifies goal)

App: *Stock name?*

User: "General Motors."

App: *General Motors Class A up three ...*

User: "Oh, no, I meant ..."

App: *Backing up.*

Stock name?

User: "General Motors Class E."

10.2.1.1.1   ≈ Cue the User that Backup Is Occurring

If relying on barge-in to support user-initiated error recovery, ensure that the machine conveys that it is returning to a previous state.

10.2.1.1.2   ≈ Use Short Purposeful Cues for Backup

When backing up as a result of barge-in, use sounds or phrases that do not assume an error on the part of either machine or user.

Avoid: *Sorry.*

   <error tone>

Instead, it is better to simply announce the machine action, or to present a prompt that encourages the user to speak again.

Use: *Backing up.*

   Again?

   Please re-enter.

   <backup tone>

10.2.1.1.3   ≈ Leave Backup State After Three to Five Seconds

If no user speech appears within the first few seconds, then subsequent barge-in should not be interpreted as error recovery. Instead, the machine should assume that the user has heard what was desired, and proceed forward to the end of the message-playing sequence as though the message had played out.

10.2.1.2   + Empower the User with Barge-In Commands

When the system supports barge-in, the application should provide user-initiated error recovery words as a standard part of the spoken user interface. Such words may include: "Cancel," "Backup," "Correction," "Start Over," and "Start Again."

10.2.1.2.1   + Use Concise Verbs for Barge-In Error Recovery

When the user is empowered with barge-in, the command recognized should differentiate between a changed user goal, a recognition error, or other reasons for interrupting.

Avoid: "No."

Use: "Backup."

        "Cancel."

        "Start Over."

10.2.1.2.2   + Make a Safe Guess When Barge-In Words Are Rejected

Command words spoken by the user to interrupt spoken machine output can experience substitution and rejection errors as can any other user input. Such errors should not lead to an infinite regress of error recovery. Rather, the system should interpret the input cautiously, inferring error and returning the user to the safest known point.

The definition of "safe" here is deliberately left open according to the particular circumstances. In general, the safest return point is the most recent input. In the following example, the barge-in commands are interpreted as:

"Backup."   Backup to immediately-preceding prompt.

"Cancel."   Cancel this interaction and return to the current menu.

"Start Over."   Stop this interaction and return to the Main Menu.

For example, the user has selected stock quotes from a personal portfolio branch off the Main Menu. When prompted, the user has spoken a stock name. Three seconds into the spoken machine output, the user suddenly interrupts. Recognition confidence is low, but the following *n-best* list appears:

"Start Over."   1st choice, poor score

"Backup."   2nd choice

"Cancel."   3rd choice

Rather than query the user to confirm the command, the best action is to assume that the user said "Backup" and initiate backup logic as though the user has decided to correct the previous input.

10.2.2 Approaches for Half-Duplex Systems

In half-duplex designs, user-initiated error recovery is more difficult. The key to supporting error recovery is to provide ample opportunity for the user to take back the turn using both explicit and implicit recognition windowing.[6] It also means effective support for DTMF input. Note that—despite the inherent disadvantages—there are also some advantages to half-duplex designs, including more reliable control over timing, a more structured and therefore comprehensible turn-taking protocol, and improved performance in noise.

10.2.2.1   √ Allow DTMF Interruption

Many speech-driven VRU applications evolved from pre-existing DTMF applications. One advantage of DTMF applications is the unambiguous interruption afforded by keypress actions. In half-duplex spoken interfaces, the keypress is the only way that the user can willfully interrupt spoken machine output.

There are three approaches to offering DTMF interruption:

1.   Support the legacy DTMF interface in its entirety along with speech.

2.   Support an alternative, parallel DTMF interface along with speech.

3.   Support a simple "press any key" interruption scheme.

Section 7.2.2 discusses these options in somewhat more detail. In the context of this guideline, any of the three methods satisfies the guideline to empower the user with an interruption capability.

10.2.2.2   ≈ Use Confirmation Windows

Spoken machine output that serves as feedback can also be inflected such that it implies a prompt to speak:

App: *Fund name?*

User: "Growth and Income Fund."

App: *Growth and Income Fund?*

        <two-second recognition window>

        As of November 14, the Growth and Income fund … <continue with data>

With or without the inflection, however, the momentary window provides an opportunity for the user to correct the machine:

App: *Fund name?*

User: "European Growth."

---

[6] See Guideline 4.2.2.2 and the glossary for a more detailed description of "windowing."

App: *Japanese Growth ...*

         <two-second recognition window>

User: "No."

App: *Again. Fund name?*

User: "European Growth."

App: *European Growth ...*

         <two-second recognition window>

         As of June 18, the European Growth fund ... <continue with data>

In this example, the inflection implies both a question and a decision to search for information. If the user does not speak (the typical scenario), the machine simply proceeds and the "pause" is interpreted as natural and benign by the user. Note that the key is to make the inflection neutral, dropping in pitch from high to low and then rising again. Although it is difficult to describe pitch inflections, the reader is encouraged to repeat the words "Growth and Income Fund" with different inflections. After some experimentation, an inflection will appear that makes sense both as an announced action for feedback, and as a query that evokes yes-no responses.

10.3 Machine-Initiated Corroboration or Recovery

Some error conditions are detected and therefore known to the application. In these instances, error recovery can be initiated by the application. In addition, certain destructive functions are not tolerant of even rare errors, and therefore must be confirmed through direct interaction with the user—just in case there's an error or user misunderstanding. In both cases, the machine initiates a corroboration dialogue.

Examples of conditions that call for machine-corroboration dialogues include:

- Speech recognition rejection,
- Spurious error (spoke-too-soon, no-speech timeout, etc.), and
- Destructive action.

10.3.1 Yes-No Queries

One of the most common machine-corroboration methods is the yes-no query. The structure of the dialogue is discussed in Section 6.3. See that section for details of yes-no as applied to error recovery.

10.3.2 Digit Strings

The recognition and corroboration of digit strings is an important interaction for many if not most VRU applications. Surprisingly, however, effective error recovery for these interactions has not been well researched at the user interface level. Instead, emphasis is placed on exceedingly high standards for raw recognition accuracy—a position that increases risk and cost. While the results have been quite impressive—today's telephone-based digit recognizers exhibit exceptionally high performance, even in the harshest wireless environments—there will always be false acceptance and false rejection problems, as well as predictable substitutions on numeric vocabularies. This means that dialogues that are well thought out and well-behaved about corroboration and querying are essential.

10.3.2.1 √ Avoid Requiring String Repetition if Possible

Even highly-accurate recognizers exhibit "point errors" within a string—perhaps the substitution of a nine for a one with very similar scores—some small percentage of the time. The problem is that as strings increase in length, the likelihood of an error rises rapidly. Even a 97% digit-level accuracy can result in string-level accuracies of 60% or less when the strings are long; especially when the number of digits is unknown.

For this reason, it is important to search for ways that allow the user to enter numbers, detect errors, and repair incorrect substitutions without having to repeat the entire number. Not only does repetition take a long time, it also changes the user's speech—which may become elongated or exaggerated to be "clear" to the machine. Error amplification is the inevitable result.

10.3.2.2 + Devise Methods for Acquiring Per-Digit Rejection Information

The key to robust performance on digit-string interactions lies in obtaining effective confidence levels. There is an aphorism, popular in speech interface design circles, "If you can detect an error, you can correct the error." Unfortunately, the opposite phrase holds true as well, "If you can't detect an error, you can't correct the error." Speech recognizers that report limited or unreliable confidence information require that the designer adopt one of three strategies:

1. Leave it up to the user to determine that the string is in error.
2. Introduce yes-no questions and other interactions at every dialogue juncture under the assumption that undetected errors could occur at any time.

3.   Simply ignore the problem and "leave it up to the recognizer."

The following sub-guidelines describe methods for acquiring rejection information on digit strings.

10.3.2.2.1   + Get Rejection Information Directly from Recognizer

Some recognizers, such as discrete digit, are able to present per-digit recognition confidence directly. One of the sacrifices of moving from discrete to continuous recognition, however, is the loss of known digit boundaries. The designer should communicate with the speech vendor to ensure that all features of a given technology are exploited. If the digit recognizer in use is able to report confidence levels or scores for each digit in the digit string, then this is the most reliable way to acquire rejection information. If it is not, then the vendor may be able to assist in ways to infer this information.

10.3.2.2.2   + Use *n*-Best to Infer Rejection

Even if the recognition technology cannot report per-digit recognition scores, there are very simple algorithms that allow the application to infer which digit(s) may be in question. Although details are beyond the scope of this text, the developer may wish to experiment with some simple solutions of his own, and so the problem is discussed briefly here.

Many recognizers—especially those based on HMM[7] technology—return *n*-best* digit strings after the user's input utterance is completed. These strings represent the first few hypothetical candidates for the digit string.

10.3.2.2.3   + Use Repeated String to Infer Rejection

Another method to identify digits in the digit string that may be questionable is to retain the results from previous utterances spoken by the user. These strings—previously rejected by the user at a yes-no query—may be thought of as the refused choices in an *n-best* list.

10.3.2.3   + Interrupt String Playback with Queries

The key to recovering errors with digit strings lies in the playback phase—that portion of the dialogue that reads the recognized string back to the user. If (and this is a

---

[7] Hidden Markov Model. Most speech recognition engines use HMMs to match the unit of speech against the word using *a priori* probability estimates of those units for that word.

big if) there is real or inferred per-digit rejection as described above, then one option is for the machine to interrupt itself as it repeats the recognized digits:

App: *One, two,*

           Is the next digit three?

User: "Yes."

App: *Three, four, five, six, seven.*

           Is that correct?

User: "Yes."

Since more than half of inter-word rejections are correct, the answer to the question is usually, "yes," resulting in only a short detour. If the answer is "no," then the second n-best choice for that digit is offered, thus recovering the most common entry errors. In addition, the effect of the interruption can be enhanced if the machine voices change:

Male Voice: *One, two, three ...*

                   Four, five ..

Female Voice: *Is the next digit two?*

User: "No."

Female Voice: *Is it six?*

User: "Yes."

Male Voice: *Six, seven. eight, nine.*

Female Voice: *Is that correct?*

User: "Yes."

The single rejection turns out to be a substitution—the user would have had to repeat the entire string if not for the interruption. Single inter-word rejections that are recovered when the correct digit is in second place—and two such rejections when the first choice is correct—result in faster overall entry and corroboration than repetition of the entire string.[8]

---

[8] Tests by one author (Balentine) on a small number of subjects with both discrete-digit and continuous-digit entry demonstrated that playback interruption was faster unless the yes-no query itself experienced problems. The informal tests occurred in 1989-1990 and again in 1993-1994.

10.3.2.4   + Rely on Inflected Playback to Imply Queries

A somewhat more graceful alternative to the string interruption methods of Guideline 10.3.2.3 relies on different inflections for the playback of each digit. This strategy requires four different recordings for each digit, as illustrated in Figure 10.1. The first recording (A) is made in a monotone—that is, little or no variation in pitch-and is applied to confident digits embedded in a group. The second (B) is a downward inflection, and is used to end confident groups of digits. The third inflection (C) has a rising pitch, and represents a query—the user is expected to hear this inflection as if it were a question. Users often respond to such queries by repeating the group. The final inflection (D) is a stressed downward inflection, used to emphasize digits during playback that have changed.

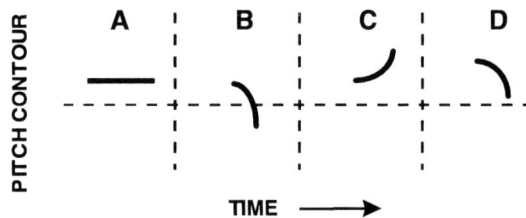

Figure 10.1 —**FOUR DIGIT INFLECTIONS** allow natural playback of digit strings with implied queries. They are monotone (A), downward inflection (B), upward inflection (C), and a stressed downward inflection (D).

Note the similarity to the digit inflection strategy discussed in Guideline 2.7.2.3. In that discussion, the inflections are used to pace and present the digit string to the user. The goal is to allow the user to hear a rapidly announced string clearly and to integrate each chunk without error.[9] In this discussion, there is a new goal: to identify digits within the string that the recognizer finds questionable, and to inflect the playback of those digits in such a way as to encourage immediate user speech.

In particular, the upward inflection in Figure 10.1 (C) is intended to sound like a query. The inflection itself serves to cue the user that the digit is in question. For the recovery of single-point digit rejections using the brute-force method of Guideline 10.3.2.3 this can be illustrated as follows.

---

[9] See Section 2.7.1 and the glossary entry for "chunking" to understand this principle.

App: *One, two,*

            Is the next digit eight?

User: "No."

App: *Is it three?*

User: "Yes."

App: *Three, four, five, six, seven.*

            Correct?

User: "Yes."

A similar but subtler method can work within the corroborative phase of digit entry:

Male Voice: *One, two,*

Female Voice: *Eight?*

User: "No, one two <u>three</u>."

Male Voice: *One, two, three,*

                  four, five, six, seven.

Female Voice: *Correct?*

User: "Yes."

Figure 10.2 shows an example of these inflections as applied to a typical digit-string. In the example, the nine-digit Social Security number is known to consist of specific groupings. Thus, as discussed in Section 2.7.1, the number is played back in natural groups. In this case, however, the inflections are slightly different, accommodating the querying scheme just discussed.

The first triplet in Figure 10.2 (A), "nine-two-seven," is confident, and requires no special inflection. Note that this confidence may be returned directly by the recognizer or may be inferred according to Guideline 10.3.3.2. Therefore, the first two digits are played with a monotone, and the third digit uses a downward inflection—indicating that it is the end of a group. An added silence at (B) after the end of the triplet, lasts exactly one beat[10]—allowing the user to integrate this group as a chunk.

The second group contains a rejected digit (C). Since the second "seven" is in doubt, it is expressed with upward-inflected playback (C). The user hears, "Three-<u>seven</u>?"

---

[10] See Section 2.1.2 for a description of "beat" timings in spoken machine output.

Because the user is expected to respond to this implied question, the post-group pause (D) is two beats long. Any user input during window (E) is probably user correction of the second group. The final group relies on normal inflections (F). The absence of user input implicitly corroborates the output at (C).

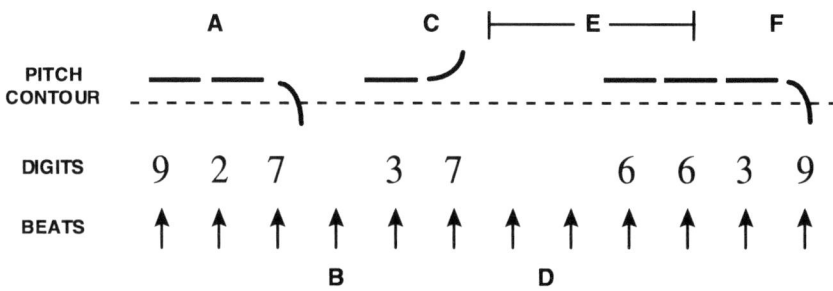

Figure 10.2—**INFLECTED DIGIT PLAYBACK** encourages the user to interpret a rejected digit as if queried and to interrupt if the digit is in error. In this example, the machine is playing back a recognized Social Security number. The arrows along the bottom of the figure show metrical presentation in terms of beats (See Section 2.7.2.3).

The inflection at (C) and the pause at (D) are compelling if the user has just heard the wrong digit. The likely user response is easily predictable, allowing grammars to recognize the utterance. Some responses may include:

User: "No."

"No, three six."

"Three six."

"No, <unintelligible>."

"<unintelligible>."

Note that the user is most likely to present meaningful correction at the group level during the recognition window represented by (E) in the figure. Since this design requires barge-in, the user may begin speaking the correction after the machine has begun speaking the final group. Careful attention to timing thus allows a graceful and highly interactive way to correct subsets of the entire digit string.

10.3.3 Resolving Ambiguities

10.3.3.1   ≈ Consider Recovering Spelling Ambiguities with the Military Alphabet

This solution is usually dismissed out-of-hand by saying "users don't know the military alphabet." While that is true, users do in fact recognize and understand military alphabet words when they hear them. The following example shows a method for presenting the *n-best* recognition choices to the user in military alphabet form. The user is not expected to remember the military alphabet, but merely to parrot back the one that represents a correct letter after hearing a list of two or three possible choices:

App: *Please spell the company name.*

User: "IBM."

App: *Is the second letter "Delta," "Bravo," or "Victor?"*

User: "Bravo."

App: *Third letter "Mike" or "November?"*

User: "Mike."

 App: *IBM. Correct?*

User: "Yes."

The solution should work with up to three *n*-best letters. Note that this is an experimental solution and requires considerable testing. The solution is presented here not as a true guideline but as an "idea trigger" for this very difficult speech recognition error-recovery problem. The point is this: users will select and repeat one element from a short list, even if they do not have prior knowledge of the elements. This means that useful associations such as the military alphabet may be applicable even though users do not know the association.

10.3.3.2   + Prompt for Alternative Words Where Possible

Some users experience repeated recognition errors. Goats, of course, are notorious for stumbling into "stubborn" words that the recognizer refuses to classify correctly. Other users, however, will occasionally experience repeated errors on a given input for other reasons. The phenomenon where one error leads to another is called error amplification.[11]

---

[11] A condition in which one application error causes subsequent errors. See the glossary for a more detailed description of "error amplification."

A very effective technique for minimizing error amplification is to prompt the user to say a different word rather than to repeat the same word.

App: *Scheduled for what day?*

User: "The sixteenth."

App: *Monday or Tuesday?*

User: "Tuesday."

App: *Confirmed for three o'clock, Tuesday, November 16th.*

In this example—a snippet of a virtual assistant application—the user has scheduled an event for the 16th of the month. Possibly the words 15th and 16th have experienced an inter-word rejection—the two are fairly confusable, especially over the telephone. Simply asking, *"Please repeat the date,"* is not going to be effective. The strategy of asking, *"Did you say the 15th?"* with a yes-no question is a plausible solution. However, there may be other options if the application has access to calendar information. By prompting for the day of the week, the application is able to recover the previous rejection with an alternate word. Error amplification is much less likely, and the interaction focuses the user on information that she is almost certain to know.

10.4 Error Prevention

Prevention is always better than detection and correction. This section describes several methods for preventing user speech errors.

10.4.1 Expecting, Preventing, and Detecting Rejections

10.4.1.1   ≈ Consider Detecting Handset[12] Keypads

Many users have telephones that they must pull away from their ears to find and press keys (cellular phones, portables, etc.). These users often make bumping noises as they handle the phone. They also introduce pauses before pressing keys. Applications that require DTMF input can detect that the user probably has such a telephone. The detection is based on the time delay after the prompt but before DTMF is received.

---

[12] Handsets are the part of the telephone held by the user and containing the speaker and microphone. Most mobile phones are a single unit with a keypad integrated into the handset.

10.4.1.1.1   ≈ Use Stringent Confidence Criteria with Handset Keypads

If handset keypad detection is positive, it is likely that a recognition event immediately after a prompt is actually the noise of the user handling the phone. Careful attention to OOG is required for concurrent DTMF/speech.

Figure 10.3—**HANDHELD TELEPHONES** such as mobile phones must be pulled from the ear to manipulate keys. Such fumbling actions cause noises that may interfere with recognition.

10.4.1.1.2   ≈ Delay Prompt Timing with In-Handset Keypads

If handset keypad detection is positive, it is possible that the user missed a prompt that appeared too quickly after a key selection. Such missed prompts often lead to muttering and other spurious speech input which in turn leads to recognition errors. To prevent such errors, delay the prompt for two seconds after DTMF entry when handset detection is positive.

10.4.1.2   + Expect Problems with Initial Input Application Start Up

It is often the case that the first thing the user says is errorful. This is especially true for novices. It may be reasonable to require very high confidence criteria on the first input, and to discard results that do not meet these criteria.

Chapter 11
Usability Tests and Performance Reports

Once the first pass of a design is completed, there remain many obstacles to a successful product release. These obstacles represent risks that must be confronted as early in the development cycle as possible. The first risk-management task is to conduct a usability test with a small population of potential users. Such tests identify problems with the voice user interface early—before the product is committed to code—allowing iterative refinements to the design while they are still inexpensive.

Several phases of usability testing may occur during the design and development process. If performed properly, such tests reduce the risk that even small design flaws will find their way into the final product.

After the application is launched, continued testing is aimed at validating design quality and tracking product or population drift. This is done in two ways. The first is based on monitoring of real user events. Monitoring is sometimes live, real-time listening. More often, practical monitoring exploits logging and performance reporting capabilities of contemporary speech software tools.

Log files contain recognition results along with digital recordings of the callers' individual utterances. Speech experts at the vendor site review these logs, using them to make decisions on accuracy, grammar coverage, and parameter tuning. Developers at the client site may also monitor live calls, review digital recordings, and/or study performance reports to infer overall effectiveness.

Although monitoring may be sufficient to measure and tune recognition performance, however, it is generally not sufficient to understand how efficiently callers are interacting with the system. To do that, the application developer should insert diagnostic reporting into the application, as discussed in Section 11.2.

The second type of testing uses more controlled laboratory techniques. In addition to monitoring and diagnostic reporting described above, ongoing usability tests are important to ensure that the design is performing as expected.

11.1 Introduction to Usability Testing[1]

Usability testing[2] is just as important for simple DTMF applications as it is for complex NL applications. In general, the more control the user has over the application (user-driven) the more testing will be required and the more valuable this testing will be. Although the science of testing software designs is well established, details are beyond the scope of this Style Guide. Several aspects of usability testing relevant to speech recognition are touched on briefly here. The subject is a complex one, and both designers and developers are encouraged to develop formal, documented test plans early in the product life cycle.

Usability testing is best conducted in an environment in which the user's behavior can be observed while interacting with the system. A dedicated environment for usability testing is called a **usability lab**. The lab is equipped with one or more cameras to record the user's face, gestures, hands, and the telephone keypad. Audio recording equipment is configured to record both the user's speech and the application's spoken machine output. This recording is extremely important, as many speech "errors" are caused by preceding events that transpire very quickly. Only analysis of recorded interactions can expose their underlying causes.

11.1.1 Types of Usability Tests

There are several types of usability tests, each with its own unique requirements. Each type of test only measures certain characteristics of the overall design. Mismeasurement of the user interface often results from the application of one type of test to a problem that it is not intended to uncover. Table 11.1 shows several of the most common types of usability tests with their associated objectives.

As shown in the table, objectives are often competitive. Focus groups, for example, tend to extract user opinions but have little predictive validity regarding task completion, confusion during use, or the impact of error-recovery routines. Wizard tests, on

---

[1] Section 11.1 and 11.2 is new to the second edition. Original sections are moved to later sections in this chapter.

[2] Live tests conducted with potential users in a controlled environment or laboratory. See the glossary for a more detailed description of "Usability Testing."

the other hand, provide coarse measurements of behavior after prompts, memory problems with lists, and the behavior of lost users (to name just a few), but have little to say about recognition accuracy, barge-in errors, or subtle timing effects.

Table 11.1—**USABILITY TESTING IS CONFOUNDED** by competing objectives that are similar but not identical. A clear distinction between these closely related issues can reduce conflict among members of the development team and improve the quality of test results.

Type of Test	Objectives
Focus Groups	user opinions, likes, and dislikes; likely user buying behaviors; product value
Wizard Tests	coarse design measurements; information ordering; jargon detection; prompt effects
Prototypes	same as wizard tests plus timing data, more refined OOG and accuracy data, barge-in behaviors; some coding insights
Isolated Modules	robustness under extreme circumstances, error recovery, reusability; reliability
Integration Tests	interactions between modules; application complexity;

In fact, each type of test is useful only at particular stages of development, and a suite of tests in an overall plan should take into account those stages at which various types of usability tests are most useful.

11.1.1.1   √ Define Test Objectives

Usability testing, like all psychological or sociological measurements, entails a great deal of subjectivity and can easily produce misleading results. In particular, human factors tests say as much about the investigators as they do about human subjects, and can easily become self-fulfilling "proof" of design philosophies.

One way to avoid wasting money and time on a false test—one that only demonstrates what the investigator already knows or believes—is to honestly state those beliefs in advance and to employ rigorous methods for achieving test objectives. The following two sub-guidelines can help with this process.

11.1.1.1.1   √ Don't Run Tests Without Knowing What You Want to Learn

Complex applications are assembled from many subcomponents, each one of which affects the overall usability of the system. The look and feel of the final application is an emergent property of these interacting components. Objectives should state explicitly what outcome is expected from testing.

In one anecdotal example from a real testing event, subjects were observed interacting with a speech recognition application that was faring somewhat poorly. Stakeholders in the speech technology noted that subjects spoke more slowly—with exaggerated pronunciation—whenever error-recovery dialogues were triggered. Such user behaviors, commonly observed and well-known to speech designers, led to subsequent errors in a cascade of error-amplification events. The stakeholders concluded that users should be told to "stop slowing down," and subsequently added dialogue instructions to that effect.

The instructions had no effect on users, of course, who were in fact engaging in a perfectly reasonable and natural approach to spoken communication. On review of the tapes by dialogue experts who had less stake in the technology itself, it became clear that the design of error-recovery interactions was at the core of the problem. By removing certain social assumptions and delaying exposure of the underlying error that triggered the recovery routine, runaway error amplification was damped by the improved error-recovery design.

In the former solution, observers wanted to learn how to tell callers what to do in the hopes that users would consciously adjust their behaviors to fit the needs of the technology. In the latter solution, the designers accepted caller behavior, and focused instead on how machine behaviors might be improved to encourage users to rely on their natural instincts, unconsciously adapting their behaviors to the needs of the task.

The lesson of the anecdote is that you tend to learn what you want to learn from usability tests. Careful statements at the front of the test design can prevent such biases, leading instead to a deeper understanding of what is happening when users interact with spoken dialogues.

11.1.1.1.2   √ Don't Run Tests If You Can't Act on Negative Results

Human factors specialists are often asked to "validate" a design. The implication is that the purpose of tests is merely to reassure product managers that everything is alright. In fact, properly-designed tests will almost always uncover design flaws, and the discovery of such flaws begs the question of what to do about them.

Usability tests should occur early in the development cycle, in support of the design phase of product management. When results are analyzed, changes to the design are invariably called for. Such changes should be easy, as the goal of the test is prevent expensive discovery of design flaws later in the program

On the other hand, usability test results that appear late in development are almost always ignored on the grounds that the schedule is inviolable. If this is the response to the test results, then the usability tests should not have been run in the first place.

It wastes time and money to perform usability tests after a design is frozen

11.1.1.2   √ Apply Laboratory Testing at Appropriate Stages of Development

Laboratory tests are controlled tests that use recruited subjects, and include focus groups, wizard tests, prototype tests, and observed call-in integration tests. Each type of test has its own objectives, and should be applied only at the stages that are likely to benefit from test outputs.

11.1.1.2.1   + Market Testing in Product Concept Stage

Focus groups and similar testing techniques have lost favor in recent years. One of the reasons is that they are difficult to facilitate. Another is that they are primarily designed for marketing and not for design.

Focus groups suffer from the following problems:

- Certain subjects dominate the interaction,
- Subjects easily infer what the facilitator wants to hear,
- The test shows what subjects think and believe, not what they'll do,
- Group interaction generates faulty data, and
- Group interaction says nothing about true dialogue design.

Although these problems can be overcome by a skilled facilitator—both by improving traditional focus groups and by applying newer and more rigorous research methods—the major flaw in using them for design is that they are marketing- rather than interface-relevant. For this reason, such tests should usually be performed only at the earliest stages of product planning, and should not be confused with usability testing.

An exception is that market testing might be useful at prototype stages later in the development cycle—when subjects are shown mockups of dialogues and asked to comment. Even then, the information derived from focus groups tends to be limited in value. It is better to apply one-on-one usability tests even at the prototype stage.

11.1.1.2.2 √ Wizard Testing Early in Design Stage

Wizard of Oz testing is a low-fidelity simulation of a dialogue, and can therefore provide only coarse measurements of A design. These tests should be performed in the earliest stages of design—before writing code—if they are to be useful. See Section 11.3 for a detailed discussion of wizard testing.

Wizard tests are good at uncovering:

- Jargon in audio messages that is confusing or meaningless to callers,
- Phrasing of prompts and their ability to elicit meaningful and predictable utterances from the user,
- What happens when substitution or false acceptance errors deposit users into wrong states,
- What callers do when they are presented with specific questions, asked to select from lists, or confronted with specific options, and
- What kinds of (and how many) lateral jumps from one application function to another are easily handled before users are overloaded and begin committing errors.

Wizard tests are bad at discovering:

- Turn-taking errors that depend on time precisions within 100ms or so,
- The effects of tiny delays in stopping audio after barge-in,
- The effects of voice quality or persona design on user behaviors, and
- Recognition accuracy or other technology statistics.

11.1.1.2.3 √ Prototype Testing Early in Coding Stage

Prototypes are often viewed as a detour around development. This is especially true when the prototype is on a different platform and therefore has limited reusability in the final product. Prototypes should therefore be used cautiously when development risks are high.

Prototypes are <u>good</u> at:

- Test-coding of experimental algorithms, thereby defining more fully any implementation problems with a proposed design,

- Testing especially complex designs that are too difficult for a human wizard to control,

- Supporting long-term tests of callers over multiple days from multiple locations,

- Exhaustive testing of isolated modules,

- Higher fidelity simulations that include barge-in, and

- Holding the user interface constant across many test subjects.

Prototypes are <u>bad</u> at:

- Measuring the effects of host transactions, including latencies, wrong data, and user decisions based on changing information,

- Stress testing, response-time measurements, or other parameters that depend completely on the final product implementation, and

- Exposing the effects of voice quality or persona design on user behaviors.

11.1.1.2.4   √ System Usability Testing in Late Stages

It is only in the final stages of development that all subcomponents—dialogue components, error-recovery routines, persona details, high-quality voice recordings—come together into a single integrated whole. System usability testing should therefore be aimed only at those aspects of the design that are truly dependent on the interaction between all of these components.

11.1.2 Reductionist Testing Strategies

The complexity of a spoken user interface is such that usability tests should focus on individual components first, followed by an increasingly integrated overall dialogue. By reducing the design to separate components, each of which can be exercised in isolation, it is easier to locate design flaws that are likely to dominate the VRU application. Note that this reductionist test philosophy assumes a very modular design.

11.1.2.1 √ Test Modules in Isolation Whenever Possible

It is a bad idea to wait until the very end of development to perform usability tests, because it is impossible to pull apart the many attributes of the interface that may be contributing to a particular usability problem. Instead, it is best to reduce the application design to a series of individual modules, testing each in isolation.

11.1.2.2 √ Exhaustively Test Yes-No Modules

Robust yes-no dialogue components are critical to the success of any speech-enabled application. Observations should quantify the following.

1. Percentage of authentic yes-no inputs versus colloquial "synonyms,"

2. Absolute accuracy of truly discrete "yes" and "no" inputs, as well as the colloquial synonyms,

3. Rejection rates and percentage of rejections recovered,

4. Average, maximum, and minimum times elapsed from the start of a yes-no query to the success or failure of the interaction, and

5. Recovery of timeouts, out-of-grammar (OOG), and other conditions.

Note that yes-no queries are invariably used to recover recognition rejections and user-identified substitutions. This means that the standard for performance must be much higher than for other application states. Many applications strive to complicate yes-no questions in the name of naturalness. The price paid, however, is often an increase in rejection rates for legitimate "yes" or "no" responses, or—perhaps worse— an increase in false acceptance of illegal conversational speech as though it were legitimate user input of a yes-no synonym.

Only testing can quantify these errors. If "yes" or "no" responses from users are ever rejected due to the presence in the grammar of colloquial synonyms, then it may be appropriate to consider reducing the complexity of the yes-no dialogue in preference for maximum performance on legal "yes" or "no" responses. In this case, the yes-no prompting and rejection/recovery instructions must be tested to ensure that they extract legal responses across the population as a whole.

11.1.2.3 √ Thoroughly Test Frequently-Used Modules

Modules that are more complex than yes-no probably cannot be exhaustively tested. The term "thoroughly" is used here to emphasize that frequently used modules warrant extensive usability testing because they will appear within many contexts within the application.

Such frequently-used dialogue components may include such interactions as:

- Lists Managers and Browsers
- Menus
- Message Players and Readers

11.1.2.4   √ Functionally Test NL States

Natural language states can be extremely complex, and cannot be thoroughly tested for usability. Instead, the grammar must be thoroughly exercised outside of the application, allowing usability tests to measure functional behavior only.

11.2 Laboratory Tests

Initial usability tests often uncover several serious problems. So it is important to schedule more than one session with test subjects. There should be enough time between usability tests to make changes to the application, and it is important to track changes in usability over time.

11.2.1 Physical Laboratory Setup

There are a number of ways to set up a lab. Figure 11.1 shows one configuration that is typical. A subject test room and an observation room are adjoining, allowing video and audio cables to connect the two. Sometimes the test "room" is in a moving vehicle, a public place, or any other location that creates a realistic environment from which the subject places telephone calls. In the latter case, observation is either delayed (tape reviews only) or requires a wireless transmission system.

The setup shown in Figure 11.1 is only one of many. For early-stage wizard tests, note that the wizard may be remote, as a telephone connection all that's required.

11.2.1.1   √ Videotape Sessions if Possible

Video is superior to audio monitoring. Observers frequently make note of the body movements and facial expressions of subjects. Cases where users prepare to speak— only to be interrupted by the machine before they emit a sound—allow adjustments to timeout values. Users that are simply reading from their task sheets can be noted. Boredom is seen before it can be heard, and lengthy announcements truncated or eliminated. Finally, video clips are helpful tools for internal selling, as managers are often more responsive to visual information than they are to simple audio clips.

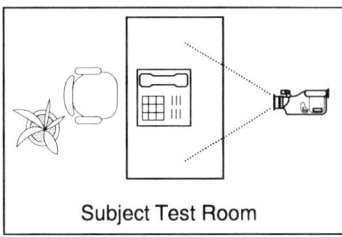
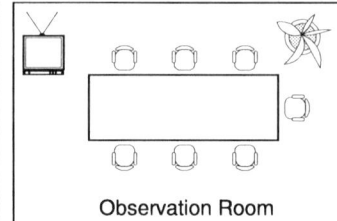

| Subject Test Room | Observation Room | Wizard Room |

Figure 11.1— USABILITY LABORATORY allows investigators to make controlled observations of designs at various stages of development. The subject test room (left) is arranged like a comfortable office. The subject makes telephone calls to a live application, to a prototype, or to a wizard who is simulating the dialogue. A camera captures the interaction and feeds audio and video to the observation room (middle), where stakeholders watch on television. The wizard (right) operates a special wizard tool to simulate the machine's role in the interaction.

11.2.1.2 √ Control Sound Leakage Between Rooms

Subjects must not hear any sound from the observation room. This includes both the amplified sound of their own interactions, as well as talking or laughter by observers. Such leakage makes subjects self-conscious, calls attention to the artificiality of the test context, and diminishes the quality of the data.

11.2.1.3 √ Encourage Observation by Stakeholders

Observing controlled laboratory usability tests is extremely informative for stakeholders, including product designers, developers, managers, and business analysts. The observation room should be large enough to accommodate several attendees, with a conference table or other writing surface to allow copious note taking.

11.2.2 General Test Design Principles

11.2.2.1 + Recruit Appropriate Test Subjects

When recruiting subjects, ensure that they represent a cross-section of first time, casual, and power users. Select a sufficient number of test subjects, at least five for a simple DTMF application and 16 for a complex NL application [Virzi92]. If test subjects will be used frequently, it is important to build a database of personal information, including, for example, the following:

• Gender and age,

- Social/economic status,

- Current and previous residence, as well as place of birth—conditions which may have affected regional accents,

- Computer literacy, and

- Previous experience with VRUs, especially any that use speech recognition.

Test subjects that frequently use VRUs or even voicemail will often transfer skills learned in a previous application to this application. Even if using standard conventions, designers should be aware of the mnemonics and vocabulary introduced by industry leaders or early adopters of this technology.

11.2.2.2   √ Provide Subjects with Specific Tasks

Usability tests should exercise all application functionality. Designers must use caution when providing literal instructions for testing speech recognition applications, as the user can be expected to parrot them back to the system—especially if they get into trouble with the interface. Such literal instructions will not provide the spontaneous responses to prompts that are insightful for the developer. Instead, provide the test subject with a list of tasks to perform. The subject will listen to the prompts more carefully and not be predisposed to the "command verbs" contained in the instructions.

Avoid: Task 1—Open your mailbox and find out how many voicemails you have.
Task 2—Create a voicemail for Bill and copy it to Annmarie and Rick.
Task 3—Tell them you can't make tomorrow's meeting.

Use: Task 1—You should have 16 voicemails. Check to see if this is correct.
Task 2—Let Bill know that you can't make tomorrow's meeting.
Task 3—Tell Annmarie and Rick as well.

11.2.2.3   √ Uncouple Prompt Testing from Recognition Accuracy

Users sometimes produce legal speech despite bad prompts. Conversely, well-designed grammars with a good recognizer often recognize user speech—even when it is sloppy and unproductive. Tests that measure recognition accuracy do a good job of testing the speech technology itself, but say nothing about the prompts or the dialogue. It is important to devise tests that measure each independently—an excellent recognizer is of little use if the prompts solicit OOG utterances, while a poorly-performing recognizer can obscure effective dialogues.

The job of a recognizer is to recognize what users say. The job of a prompt is to cause users to say useful and productive—as well as legal—utterances that achieve application goals reliably and quickly. Tests for prompts should therefore focus on effective user speech regardless of recognition accuracy. High recognition rates should not be allowed to obscure less-than-optimal prompts, as finding and fixing such problems can correct other aspects of the interface including reliability, throughput, and user satisfaction.

11.2.2.4 √ Test Prompt Effectiveness by Measuring Token-Density

Since natural language speech recognition is somewhat new, there are few clearly established guidelines for prompting strategies. For this reason, usability testing must be aimed at uncovering those prompting methods that tend to work well across the population as a whole.

The key to this testing is to have a clear goal for success, allowing a comparative analysis of competing prompting schemes. Casual monitoring of dialogues is often misleading, as many observers become impressed with the technology's ability to properly recognize complex sentences—including sentences that contain extraneous user-speech. Although this is an important capability for the technology, the prompt may have failed to capture enough data from the user to achieve the menu flattening and throughput advantages that make the interface powerful.

For this reason, one approach is to design tests that focus on the token-density of the input rather than the "naturalness" or casual character of the user's speech. Stated as a goal, this means that—all else being equal—the better prompt is the one that gets the most users to a terminal in the hierarchy with the fewest intervening feed-forward prompts (see Section 8.2). With a specific goal in hand, these tests can root out prompts that are "adequate" but not ideal.

Fix prompts that consistently generate the following kind of user input:

"Yes, I'd like some information about my account, please."

"Account balances."

"Ummh, account balances menu, please."

"Who am I speaking with?"

Use and build on prompts that generate the following kind of user input:

"Give me a balance on account number <number>, please."

"Buy 500 shares of Microsoft at the market."

"Umh … Give me a quote on IBM March one-twenty calls."

In the first set of examples, the user is engaged in "natural" but unproductive speech. The first example contains only a single token—the keyword "account"—requiring subsequent feed-forward prompts to capture additional tokens. In the next two examples the user is falling back on old DTMF habits—using speech to select a menu rather than to describe a desired transaction. The fourth example is social telephone behavior that is predictable (i.e. it can be recognized) but completely unproductive.

The second set of examples show more effective use of natural language. The token "balance" followed by an account number jumps the user straight to a terminal. In the second example, four tokens appear in a single sentence. In the third and final example, a five-token sentence happens to include a disfluency—easily recovered by the technology and not detrimental to the transaction.

Improved token density leads to shorter call duration and lower demand on the speech recognition resource. Conversely, if users are consistently providing single-token input, then the application is not benefiting from the primary value of NL technology—menu flattening through multiple-token input. This means that feed-forward prompts are appearing too frequently, resulting in token-by-token form filling dialogues—possibly due to convergence.

11.2.2.5   √ Observe Speech After the NL Prompt

A specific focus of usability tests should be to observe the user speech that occurs immediately after an NL prompt. Data should be acquired on:

1.   Token density of utterances,

2.   Percentage of utterances that are grammatically illegal, and

3.   Percentage of utterances that contain back channels and disfluencies.[3]

If these elements can be quantified—even roughly—then alternate prompts can be devised and measured.

11.2.2.6   √ Observe Speech After Feed-Forward Prompts

User behavior after feed-forward prompts should be quantified according to the same criteria described for NL prompts in general.

11.2.3 OOG Post-Test Interviews and Questionnaires

In some cases, questionnaires may be sufficient to acquire user feedback. However, interviews can also uncover useful information regarding user assumptions about the application.

11.2.3.1 + Use Interviews to Acquire Subjective Opinions

Even though the test subjects know that they are conversing with a machine, they often bring an expectation of human-like "normal" conversational behavior to the interaction. Test subjects are usually willing to discuss these expectations, pointing out the protocols of typical human conversation. The test subjects will also evaluate the professional voice with regard to the look and feel of the application. This may result in comments like "She was rude, she kept interrupting me." or "He seemed condescending, always giving me help when I didn't need it." Although such observations are not to be taken literally as though they were measured empirically, they are often able to point toward dialogues that are awkward or ineffective.

Opinions to look for in the interview include:

- Did the test subject feel rushed? When no speech was detected did the machine come back too soon and say, *"I'm waiting for your next command."*

- Ask the subject about the "person" at the other end. Were they professional? Did they provide help when help was needed?

- Were there any features that the subject did not use (or example, barge-in or multi-token input)? Why?

- Ask detailed questions about tasks that the subjects failed to complete. These must be fixed before the application can be fielded, and the information the subject provides may indicate the root cause of the problem.

Don't expect users to know where they went wrong when they failed to accomplish a task. Instead, review the recordings for problems discussed throughout this Style Guide—for example, turn taking, stuttering, false rejection, and error amplification.

11.2.3.2 √ Use Well-Designed and Well-Tested Scientific Questionnaires

Measuring user satisfaction empirically is a scientific endeavor in its own right. Usability studies sometimes generate opinions with little or no rigorous method for un-

---

[3] See the glossary for the distinction between "back channels" and "disfluencies."

derstanding and applying the result. For this reason, it is often helpful to use questionnaires that have been developed by professionals.[4]

11.3 Wizard of Oz and Prototype Testing

An especially effective type of usability testing during the earliest stages of design is so-called Wizard of Oz[5] testing, or more simply, **wizard tests**. These tests provide valuable insights into usability at a stage of product development when the design is the most flexible. Wizard tests are handy for refining both architectural (call flow) and machine speech (scripting) design elements.

11.3.1 What Is Wizard Testing?

Wizard testing is one of a class of tests known as simulations. In a simulation, an application or product is unavailable for testing and so cannot be directly operated by a user. The product may be non-existent or only partially developed (as in software applications), or the product may be unavailable for other reasons, including expense or physical danger. Aircraft simulators, for example, have been used for years to train pilots. Such simulators allow student pilots to practice maneuvers safely—without risk either to expensive aircraft or to life.

For VRU designs, a trained tester serves as the Wizard of Oz. This "man behind the curtain" operates a software program running on a desktop or laptop computer. The program plays audio (.wav) files into a telephone line. A test subject then calls the test line from a remote location. The caller believes that she is calling a VRU.

After answering the telephone, the wizard plays introductory greeting prompts by clicking on the appropriate .wav file. When it is the user's turn to interact, she presents data to the "VRU." She might press a key on the telephone keypad, or she might speak. The wizard in turn detects user input—viewing keypad data on a DTMF detector, or listening to and recognizing user speech.

After evaluating the input and making a decision based on the VRU design, the wizard plays voice responses to the user by selecting from the library of .wav files and

---

[4] For example, see the *Questionnaire for User Interaction Satisfaction* (QUIS), Version 7.0, May, 1998, developed by Shneiderman, et al. The instrument is licensed by the Office of Technology Liaison, University of Maryland, http://www.cs.umd.edu/hcil/pubs/quis.html.
[5] After the famous novel by Frank L. Baum.

clicking the appropriate one. The result is a simulation of the VRU in which the wizard substitutes for the recognizer and the as-yet-undeveloped application software.

11.3.2 Wizard Methodologies

11.3.2.1 √ Avoid Exhaustive Testing

Wizard tests are low-fidelity simulations. As such, they are not effective at uncovering complex interactions between various areas of a dialogue. Compounding this problem, wizard tests are errorful, as the wizard makes mistakes when dialogues are arduous. The purpose of wizard testing is therefore to expose major, coarse design flaws early in the product development cycle, and not to exhaustively exercise every nook and cranny.

Wizard testing should be focused on specific sub-dialogues and not on complex details of the application as a whole.

11.3.2.2 √ Test High-Risk Design Elements First

Certain devices—for example yes-no questions—are well-known and are therefore predictable in terms of user behavior and acceptance. This is especially true of reusable components that have been shaken down in previous trials or products. Such devices need not be tested in early wizard testing, which should be aimed instead at new design techniques or other unknown and therefore risky parts of the VRU application design.

Some wizard methodologies incorporate a mix of automated devices and human wizard sequences. Such techniques allow the human wizard to execute macro-level dialogue components that interact with the user automatically. After such modules are finished, the wizard takes back control. The technique is harder to set up, but reduces wizard fatigue and wizard mistakes, allowing focus on the high-risk un-coded dialogues that are more important to exercise early.

11.3.2.3 + Re-Test Problem Areas

Wizard tests are quick and inexpensive. As problem areas are discovered, changes to the design should be re-tested. The iterative refinement of design through wizard testing is the least expensive method for arriving at a stable and effective interface.

Changes include minor changes in wording, or fundamental structural modifications. Follow-on tests can occur quickly—on the same day in many cases—so frequent re-testing of elements that have changed can generally be included in wizard plans.

Note that regression testing of successful design elements is prudent in the case of major changes to the organization of the application. A run-through of the improved design with a handful of callers—taking care to avoid any changes—will turn up any negative effects associated with design changes.

11.3.2.4   + Set High Success Standards

Wizard tests represent "best-case" usability tests for the following reasons:

- The wizard is a human, and therefore a much better recognizer than the targeted speech recognition technology.

- Subjects in a laboratory setting often want to please the investigators.

- Task scenarios sometimes convey more helpful information to test subjects than they would arrive at on their own in a natural setting.

- Wizards can unconsciously guide subjects with slightly longer pauses, altered prosody, or other speech cues that give away the correct solution to a task.

For these reasons, applications that successfully pass wizard tests may still exhibit major usability problems in the field. Conversely, wizard tests that produce poor results in the lab are likely to predict even poorer performance in the field.

Wizard test standards should therefore be quite high. In general, any part of the dialogue that causes several users to stumble should be redesigned. Only failures that can be dismissed as anomalous or subject-specific idiosyncrasies should be viewed without concern.

11.4 Logging and Reporting

Once the application is launched, everyone who has a stake in its success wants to know how it is performing. Responses such as "There haven't been any problems reported on the machines," and "We haven't received any complaints from our customers," are not what stakeholders are looking for. Similarly, the fact that the application took twice as many calls yesterday as the old DTMF system does not provide insight into the application's acceptance. For speech recognition applications, new metrics must be described to characterize application performance.

11.4.1 What to Log and Measure

Well before application launch, both the developer and the client for whom the application is being developed (marketing, sales, support, and other stakeholders) must state the goals and objectives of the application. For each objective they must also characterize success or failure. Too often success is measured solely in terms of recognition accuracy. This is perhaps the worst metric. Is an application that obtains 90% accuracy and automates 85% of calls for a business better or worse than one that achieves 97% recognition and automates 40% of calls? On the other hand, poor recognition performance will be obvious right away. Superior recognition performance will become even more evident over time. Logging becomes critical for the middle ground, which is where your new application will start out.

The following is a list of some data that should be logged and measured. Reports on these values should be made available and reviewed on a daily basis. At a minimum, this list will guide designers and developers to a clearer definition of those data that are most important for a specific application.

11.4.1.1 √ Check All Provisioning Estimates

Hardware provisioning is an especially important component to understand and measure early. See Appendix A for a methodical approach to such provisioning in at least one architectural context. Nonetheless, the developer should ensue there is sufficient CPU for the speech recognition engine.

11.4.1.2 + Measure Call Abandons

When the application is first deployed, many people may hang up, thinking they dialed the wrong number. Hence the importance of opening greetings (see Section 2.2.3). When they call back, they realize it's the right number and attempt to use the new application. On the first day you might see your calls double, and your call abandon rate at 50%. Over time your rate should decline to the industry average abandonment rate for automated systems [TARP97].

11.4.1.3 √ Measure Transfers to the Operator or Agent

Measure transfers out of the application to the operator. Are transfers lower relative to a legacy DTMF system or industry averages [TARP97]? Where are the transfers occurring? Is it always at the same point in the application? If so, then consider making modifications to the application.

11.4.1.4 √ Monitor Barge-in Performance

If barge-in has been enabled it is critical to obtain feedback on its performance as soon as the application is deployed. Is it too easy or too hard to trigger barge-in? Should the energy detection levels be raised or lowered a few dB? Do some calls have an unusually large number of instances in which barge-in was used? Should barge-in be turned off for some parts of the application? Are the assumptions that were made regarding turn taking valid (see Section 4.2)?

11.4.1.5   √ Measure Completion Rate

It is important to get a good idea of how many customers actually complete their transactions on the automated system. This rate indicates overall success without regard to efficiency (throughput). In other words, users that complete transactions have overcome all errors regardless of cause or severity. This rate gives direct evidence for basic business computations such as return on investment, and it also allows inferences about the overall effectiveness of user interface design. This is especially important as changes are made during the life of an application, because such changes should be focused on producing a net increase in this rate.

The application should track:

• Graceful conclusions (hang-up after completing transaction),

• Transaction count (number of transactions completed),

• Calls transferred to an agent, operator, or help desk by user request, and

• Average call duration.

These values allow the application developer to calculate successful completion. Be sure to measure information-inquiry tasks as transactions—asking for and receiving information is a valid user interaction. The average call duration should correlate with the successful-completion measure. For example, callers who explore an interface but choose not to perform tasks may not be experiencing difficulties. Similarly, calls that are very short may represent wrong numbers or may be aborted for reasons other than user interface obstacles. On the other hand, calls of medium duration—particularly those that are dominated by task reversals or spurious errors—may point toward design flaws. Similarly, calls that result in transfers to an agent are more problematic when they have been lengthy—implying that the user attempted but failed to navigate the application. Agent transfers that occur soon after the start of a call generally identify callers that want a human representative in the first place.

In addition, the application should track and distinguish between:

• Calls abandoned (both before and after transaction attempts),

• Calls transferred to an agent, operator, or help desk due to fatal errors, and

• Tasks interrupted before they were complete.

311

These measures may point toward interface problems.

11.4.1.6 + Multi-Token Input and Short Cuts

If the application makes use of multi-token natural language (see Section 8.2.2), it is important to ensure that users are taking full advantage of it. If users are reaching non-terminal states and consistently require feed-forward prompting to achieve their goals, then both the call duration and the number of recognition requests per call are inflated. If most users do not make use of multi-token input shortly after the application is deployed, try rewording the prompts or recommending a short cut to the user once the terminal is reached.[6]

App: *In the future, you may obtain the same information by saying "Buy 200 shares of IBM at the market."*

11.4.1.7 + Monitor the Migration Rate from DTMF to Speech Recognition

If equivalent functionality is offered for speech recognition and DTMF, what percentage of callers are migrating to the speech system? Is the migration slow and steady? Has there been a retreat in the migration percentage, with customers reverting to DTMF? Is the percentage higher on weekends?

11.4.2 Analyzing Logged Data

11.4.2.1 + Locate Per-Prompt Error Clustering

Every prompt is presumably followed by some user action. If each prompt represents an opportunity for the user to accomplish something productive, then prompts or application states that have problems will tend to exhibit high error rates across many users. This means that errors will cluster around user interface obstacles. A quick scan of the log files will usually identify the two or three places where most users are having problems.

The application should be set up to track:

• Rejections from the recognizer, usually due to OVW/OOG utterances,

• No speech, in which the user was silent,

• Spoke too soon conditions, and

• Cancel and abort actions initiated by the user.

---

[6] This tip technique is popular in many applications, and has both advantages and drawbacks.

If certain prompts are consistently followed by rejections or silence timeouts, then the prompt itself may be at fault. Go back to the prompt and analyze it for possible explanations. In instances where spoke too soon errors are high, trim the prompts aggressively, as described in Guideline 2.1.4.2. If the prompts are already trimmed, then re-word the prompt to deposit key information later. If the user is canceling or aborting more often at certain states than at others, then the prompt or a specific sequence of immediately preceding prompts may be the culprit.

11.4.2.2   + Consider Time-Lags When Inferring Problems

Often a cluster of problems at a specific juncture does not indicate a problem with that state. Due to time lags, the cause can be somewhat sooner in the dialogue than the point where the problem actually manifests itself, as shown in Figure 11.2.

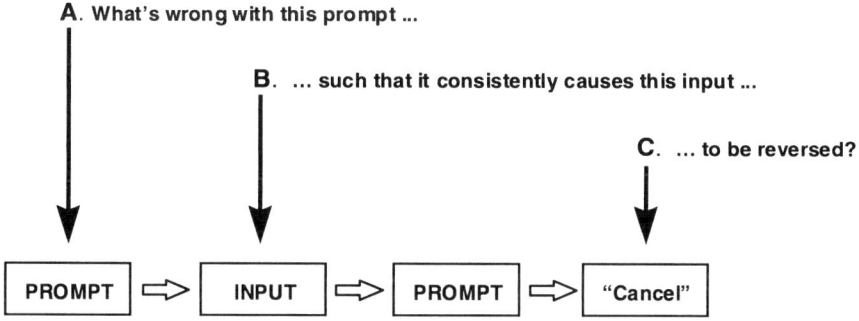

Figure 11.2—**ANALYSIS BASED ON TIME LAGS** is important when tracing dialogue problems. If the word "cancel" appears frequently at point C, it would be tempting to blame the immediately preceding prompt. The actual problem is more likely to be at A, since it is the input recognized at B that the user is canceling. Log files will identify the error clusters—points in the dialogue with anomalous problems—but time lags should be considered when analyzing these files.

11.4.3 Voice Logging

The only accurate way to determine speech recognition performance is by logging each individual utterance and then transcribing it off line. Logging the utterances requires provisioning the hardware with a significant amount of disk space. The speech files should be saved in raw 64 kbps[7] format, the same data rate presented to the

---

[7] Kilobits per second. Telephony systems digitize speech by capturing 8,000 samples per second (8Hz sampling rate), using μ-Law (North America and Japan) or A-Law (Europe) 8-bit encoding. This means that there are 64,000 bits for each second of speech. See [Kientzle98] for a detailed discussion of encoding formats.

speech recognizer. The logged files should be removed from the system on a regular basis, to avoid running out of disk space. The system should be set up to disable logging when the disk space fills up to a predetermined level (for example 80%).

If several machines are running the same application, it may not be necessary to enable voice logging on every machine. Furthermore, you may choose not to log utterances in certain parts of the application, for example, responses to yes-no inquires. However, it is necessary to obtain a statistically significant amount of data in order to adequately estimate recognition accuracy. However, when the application is first launched, the speech recognition vendor may want to obtain as much live speech data as possible to tune their recognizer. Logging all utterances should be encouraged for this purpose.

Transcription is a very time consuming process. Transcription not only helps determine recognition accuracy, but it helps uncover synonyms and unpredicted but common user behaviors, which in turn can be used to modify the grammar. Transcription should be performed on an ongoing basis, perhaps at increasing intervals over time.

One item to look for in transcriptions is consecutive repetitions of an utterance by a user. This may be indicative of repeated failure or frustration. It may also indicate that the user is having trouble formulating "in-grammar" utterances. In this instance, the application might interject with help. Repetitions are also indicative of an unexpected response from the application. If the user is expecting a quote on GM Class C and the recognizer repeatedly returns GM Class A, then perhaps the recognizer is mapped to the wrong equity.

11.5 Summary

The goal of this Style Guide has been to provide the application designer and developer with the guidance that will help ensure the successful launch of automated telephony applications employing speech recognition. This industry is still in its infancy, and the authors hope that by collecting their experience, reviewing the literature, and distilling design principles from the current art, that these guidelines will prove useful.

The reader is encouraged to contact the authors with information and experiences that can serve to improve this Style Guide. We will try to incorporate this information into future editions. Feel free to send us your comments regarding this Style Guide to the following e-mail address:

styleguide@eiginc.com

We close with the following quote by Shneiderman, who concisely summarizes the ultimate goal of interface design. In this section of his textbook, he is discussing human-centered design:

> Concentrate attention on the users and on the tasks that they must accomplish. Make users the center of attention and build feelings of competence, mastery, clarity, and predictability. Construct well-organized menu trees, provide meaningful structure in command languages, present specific and constructive instructions and messages, develop uncluttered displays, offer informative feedback, enable easy error handling, ensure appropriate display rates and response time, and produce comprehensible learning materials [Shneiderman97].

Good Luck!

Appendix A
NL Hardware Provisioning

Hardware provisioning is a key factor in deploying NL applications, but is not directly related to the user interface. For this reason it is in a separate appendix. The goal is to help application developers determine the hardware necessary to host the speech recognizer. Provisioning speech recognition systems is a process that must be undertaken to ensure that the deployed system delivers quick responses to the end user. If it doesn't, users may question whether they were heard, and repeat themselves. This not only disrupts the turn taking protocol that the application developer worked hard to establish, but leads to error amplification and other side effects.

Speech recognition is a computationally intense task and the application requires that the recognizer respond promptly to the user's input. An industry goal is to provide 95% of recognition responses in under two seconds. In other words, system latency from the end of user speech until the system begins its response should be less than two seconds. Two-second response time must be assured under peak load, during busy hour. Table A.1 illustrates the output of the provisioning process.

A.1 Wizard Tests Estimate Hardware Requirements

As described in Section 11.3, wizard testing involves a user—call her Dorothy—who interacts with a VRU application. In actuality, there is no automated application. Instead, a wizard "behind a curtain" knows the application intimately and observes Dorothy's actions. To conduct this Wizard of Oz test, the application developer needs to script a call flow for the wizard. Dorothy then must be briefed on the tasks she is being asked to accomplish—for example, getting a stock quote, checking her cash balance, and then purchasing a stock.[1]

---

[1] See Guideline 11.2.2.2 for suggestions on providing instructions to complete tasks without predisposing the user to the application hierarchy.

The application developer will then time the interaction, making note of the amount of time both Dorothy and the wizard speak and the average call duration. If the application has barge-in, the wizard has to stop speaking when Dorothy speaks, and move to the next state of the application. This experiment should be repeated several times with different tasks presented to Dorothy until the application developer is comfortable that the wizard and Dorothy are behaving as experienced customers would with a speech-enabled VRU application.

The application developer then computes a "duty cycle[2]" which is the percentage of time the user is speaking given the total length of the application. For example, if Dorothy speaks on average for 14 seconds in a 100-second application, the duty cycle is 14%. The application developer should select a duty cycle that is aggressive (high), but that he feels comfortable with. Examples of duty cycles might be 5-10% for half-duplex applications, and 12-25% for full-duplex applications employing barge-in. Finally, the application developer needs to calculate the average number of recognition requests per call, and the average utterance length (in seconds).

A.2 Computing the Required Number of Licenses

The number of speech recognition licenses required for an application is dependent on the number of ports configured for each VRU. VRU call capacity is then computed using a blocking rate (1% is typical). The VRU configuration and blocking rate are then used to determine the effective number of ports that should be provisioned. An Erlang table is used to derive this number. For example, a 96-port VRU at 1% blocking has a capacity of 80 Erlangs [IEEE84]. That means that on average the VRU can provision 80 simultaneous calls while keeping the probability of blocking a new call under 1%.

The application developer must understand the VRU deployment to determine whether blocking is determined on the VRU level, the site level, or the enterprise level. If several VRUs are deployed at a single site—and if the phone provider accesses all VRUs using a hunt group[3]—then the 1% blocking should be applied to the number of ports at the site. For example, a site with 192 ports would have a capacity of 172 Erlangs.

---

[2] A metric to determine the percentage of time that the user is speaking relative to the call duration. See the glossary for a detailed description of "duty cycle."

[3] A series of telephone lines organized in such a way that if the first line is busy the next line is hunted and so on until a free line is found.

Table A.1—**EXAMPLE OF PROVISIONING PROCESS** for a half-duplex Equity Quotes application and full-duplex Equity Trading applications.

System Provisioning Estimates in Busy Hour Recognition Requests (BHRR)[4]

Application	Equity Quotes half-duplex	Equity Trading full duplex	Notes
A. average call duration	140	155	seconds
B. requests/call	3.5	5.2	3.5 quotes, .5 trades, 1.2 maintenance
C. avg. utterance length	2.8	3.9	seconds
D. duty cycle	0.07	0.13	C * B/A
E. ports/ Erlangs	80	80	at 1% blocking 96 ports is 80 Erlangs
F. sec. per hour	3600	3600	
G. busy hour calls	2058	1859	F/A * E
H. BHRR needed	7203	9666.8	G * B
J. machine	IBM AIX server	IBM AIX server	machine capacity rating of 50
K. busy hour latency (sec)	.38 avg. 95% < .52 38% CPU	.52 avg. 95% < 1.2 63% CPU	95% of responses under 2 sec acceptable
L. vendor grammar rating	0.1	0.093	composite complexity rating
M. application complexity	28	38.688	L * E * B
N. BHRR est. for machine	14000	11000	

---

[4] The number of speech recognition requests that can be supported by a specific machine in a busy hour. A busy hour can be defined by either observing the call volume, or by empirically calculating the maximum number of calls given the call duration and the number of ports.

Similarly, if the enterprise uses load balancing at the network level and calls are distributed to each site based on VRU availability, then the 1% blocking should be applied to the number of ports in the enterprise. For example, if the organization has 144 ports at two sites, this configuration would have a capacity of approximately 272 Erlangs.

One way to compute the number of licenses needed is to determine how many simultaneous recognition requests need to be processed. If the speech recognition vendor requires one dedicated license for each port, then this is academic. However, if the vendor licenses technology by the number of active ports, it is important to calculate the simultaneous recognition requests. Either way, this number will be needed later for speech recognition hardware provisioning.

The arrival of speech recognition requests from the VRU application can be approximated using a **Poisson distribution** [Stein77]. The Poisson formula is given by the expression:

$$f_n(x) = (mx)^n \, e^{-mx} / \, n!$$

where n is the number of licenses needed, m is the mean number of recognition requests, and x is the observation period (1 second). We want the sum of $f_n(x)$, $F_n(x)$ to be 95%. Table A.2 shows an example of the license calculation for a 96-port system at 1% blocking (80 Erlangs) with a 7% duty cycle. Nine licenses are needed to ensure that 94.1% of the time there is a licensed recognizer available at that given second. Obviously, it would be prohibitively expensive to have a license available 100% of the time, especially since the Poisson distribution is an asymptotic function.

To determine if a license will become available the remaining 5.9% of the time, start with the fact that we were evaluating a Poisson distribution in a one second window. Assume a 2.8 second average utterance duration. At any given second, how many 2.8 second utterances will be completing? Once again the Poisson distribution can be evaluated for m=2.8, which is shown in Table A.3. This table shows that 23.1% of the utterances will be completing, hence those licenses will be freeing up to service new spoken input. If recognition requests are queued, they will easily be serviced within one second. If peak capacity is sustained for an extended period then the new recognition requests will become backlogged and it is possible that the application will not meet the service level of 95% of responses under 2 seconds. Now it becomes apparent how important the Wizard of Oz test is, and its estimate of the duty cycle.

Table A.2—**NUMBER OF SPEECH RECOGNITION LICENSES NEEDED** for a 7% duty cycle.

n	f(x=1)	F(x=1)
m = 5.6 (80*.07)		
0	0.004	0.004
1	0.021	0.024
2	0.058	0.082
3	0.108	0.191
4	0.152	0.342
5	0.170	0.512
6	0.158	0.670
7	0.127	0.797
8	0.089	0.886
9	0.055	0.941
10	0.031	0.972

Table A.3—**NUMBER OF SPEECH RECOGNITION LICENSES FREEING UP** in any given second.

n	f(x=1)	F(x=1)
m = 2.8 second utterance		
0	0.061	0.061
1	0.170	0.231
2	0.238	0.469
3	0.222	0.692
4	0.156	0.848

A.3 Hardware Provisioning

Determining the amount of hardware needed is a function of the complexity of the application. If the application uses just one grammar then the application developer can benchmark the hardware based on the number of BHRRs. In an equity quotation application, for example, if the end user were always accessing the same list of equities then the BHRR would be computed by taking the number of busy hour calls and multiplying it by the average number of recognition requests per call.

The next step is to rate the speech recognition server for a given BHRR. This can be accomplished in two ways. Unfortunately, the first is brute force. To do this, set up a testing configuration that will model the call flow and generate the appropriate number of recognition requests. Then measure the average and peak latency, and CPU load on the machine. Have the testing configuration cycle through different call profiles. For example, for a 96-port loading, test the machine with 150 calls with different call duration, number of recognition requests, and timing of those requests within the call.

It will soon become obvious that latency is not a linear function of CPU loading. There will probably be a minimum latency for the grammar that will be observed for CPU loadings of 0-50% (for example, a half second). Then there will be a linear region in which the latency will increase as the CPU loading increases. Finally, there will be a saturation point at which the latency is increasing exponentially for small increases in the CPU utilization. This will probably occur around 80% average CPU loading, depending on the machine's RAM and internal architecture.

Table A.1 shows example results obtained for busy hour latency testing. For the "Equity Quotes" grammar, the average latency was .38 seconds. 95% of responses were obtained in less than .52 seconds. Average CPU loading was 38%. This machine is more than capable of servicing a 96-port VRU running this application. In this case, the VRU could probably run the 96-port application with the speech recognition server "co-resident."

The second way to obtain a BHRR rating for a grammar relies on information provided by the vendor. The vendor should be able to derive a complexity rating for each grammar they develop. They should also be willing to rate grammars created by the application developer. The vendor should also be able to benchmark machines and determine a capacity rating. If the grammar complexity is .10, then an 80 Erlang loading with 3.5 requests per call would require a server rated for at least 28. In Table A.1, we see that the vendor has assigned the machine a rating of 50, sufficient for this task.

When the VRU application requires that several grammars be invoked at different times in the call flow, provisioning becomes more difficult. Typically the grammars range in complexity and are invoked different numbers of times for each caller. For example, Dorothy was instructed to get a quote, check her cash balance, and execute a trade. Other callers might trade more or less frequently.

If the application developer has prior information about the content of calls or desired actions of the callers, the developer can make some assumptions about which grammar is more important to measure. Or this information could be obtained from previous caller interactions with operators, agents, or a pre-existing DTMF based VRU application. For example, if the average caller makes 3.5 quotes, .5 trades, and 1.2 account maintenance inquiries using an existing DTMF system, then the average call would have 5.2 average requests per call (see Table A.1).

The application grammar complexity would then be a function of each grammar complexity and the number of requests per grammar. In the example in Table A.1 the trading grammar is more complex than quotes, and account maintenance is far less complex. As a result, the overall composite grammar complexity is .093. At 5.2 requests per call, the application complexity is 38.69, still within spec for the machine rating.

A.4 Other Issues to Consider

Deploying speech recognition will often impact other aspects of VRU performance. Typically there is a speech recognition client associated with each VRU port. This client is responsible for streaming speech to the recognition process. It may also be performing echo cancellation and speech endpointing. In either case, it will require additional CPU cycles beyond those budgeted above.

Another aspect to consider is whether the VRU architecture can support streaming 64 kbps speech data (or speech features at a lower data rate) to either the host processor or an external speech recognition server. PCI bus machines will probably have the bandwidth to support speech streaming, but it is unlikely that ISA bus machines will. In this instance, the bus should be able to support the peak number of simultaneously active channels, not the average, or some percentile. If the bus cannot support the peak traffic users will experience discontinuities (silence or stuttering) in the playback of machine output. Be aware that speech recording does not necessarily replace bandwidth that was otherwise allocated for spoken machine output. Prompts can be cached and are often compressed when retrieved from disk. VRU architectures have been optimized for manipulating prompts.

Finally, a resource manager may be needed if the speech recognition resources are available on more than one machine. This will help smooth out machine utilization and provide optimal latency. Overall, less hardware will be needed to support the same number of channels if a resource manager is available. In addition, the resource manager should be robust enough to recognize machine outages and remove them from the resource pool.

A.5 The Consequences of Insufficient Provisioning

Did you provision the application with enough recognition hardware? How do you know for sure? You don't want to find out on the busiest day of the year when the recognition requests queue up to such a degree that they bring down the speech recognition engine and shut down the automated application along with it. Now all your customers will be routed to the operator or agent!

Be sure to measure the application's duty cycle and latency, comparing them with your original estimates. If you have a little headroom, good—if not, repeat the provisioning exercises using the most recent statistics. To determine duty cycle, you must measure call duration, average utterance length, and the number of recognition requests per call. For applications with multiple grammars, the number of recognition requests per grammar needs to be tracked.

Note that several of these parameters will almost certainly change over time. Call duration and average utterance length should decrease as users become more experienced with the application. The number of rejections due to out-of-grammar (OOG) utterances should also drop. Most recognizers incur a higher latency for illegal utterances than for in-grammar utterances.[5] It may be worthwhile to compute OOG latency separately.

---

[5] Out-of-vocabulary and out-of grammar speech (OOG) tends to be longer and thus places a heavier computational burden on the recognizer.

Appendix B
Voice Portals

Since the first edition of this style guide was written, a new breed of ASR applications called voice portals has matured. Although voice portals can extend beyond the telephone medium, this appendix focuses only on the human factors and design issues that are relevant to the telephony user interface.[1] Understanding these issues requires an overview of voice portals—what they are, how developers implement them, and how they can be classified in terms of the look and feel that they present to users. It is also important to contrast voice portal interfaces with traditional VRU applications.

B.1 What Is a Voice Portal?

In its broadest definition, a voice portal is an entry point into a specific information domain in which the primary communication method is through spoken language. This broad definition includes VoIP[2] in conjunction with traditional web browsing at a desktop multimedia computer, as well as voice access to corporate information through a number of channels and media. However, voice portals have become popularized as systems that provide telephone access to the Internet, and the discussion here centers around this more limited definition.

Users call Internet voice portals with the goal of accomplishing tasks that are usually performed with a web browser.[3] Internet voice portals are among the most ambitious and complex of all telephone-based speech applications. However, the Internet voice

---

[1] Most voice portals have adopted the use of VoiceXML to exchange information between the user interface and a web server. The reader is encouraged to refer to the many books on the subject, for example [Edgar01] and [Larson01].

[2] Voice over IP, the transmission of digitized voice—for example from a microphone connected to the computer's sound card—across the Internet using Internet Protocol (IP).

[3] For example, Microsoft® Internet Explorer, browsers from service providers such as AOL or Prodigy™, and portable wireless devices such as palm computers or mobile telephones.

portal has just recently achieved technical feasibility, and so tends to trigger effusive, and often unfounded, excitement. Most existing voice portals are in fact quite modest in their capabilities. This is due to the nature of spoken human language, user memory, social and environmental issues, user attention, and similar human factors that define the fundamental limits of the voice user interface. Consequently, voice portal capabilities are not likely to change appreciably—even as improvements to speech recognition technologies occur.

A block diagram of a voice portal is shown in Figure B.1. The voice portal user interface is called a **voice browser**. The voice browser runs on a **speech server**. A user dials a telephone number to reach the portal.

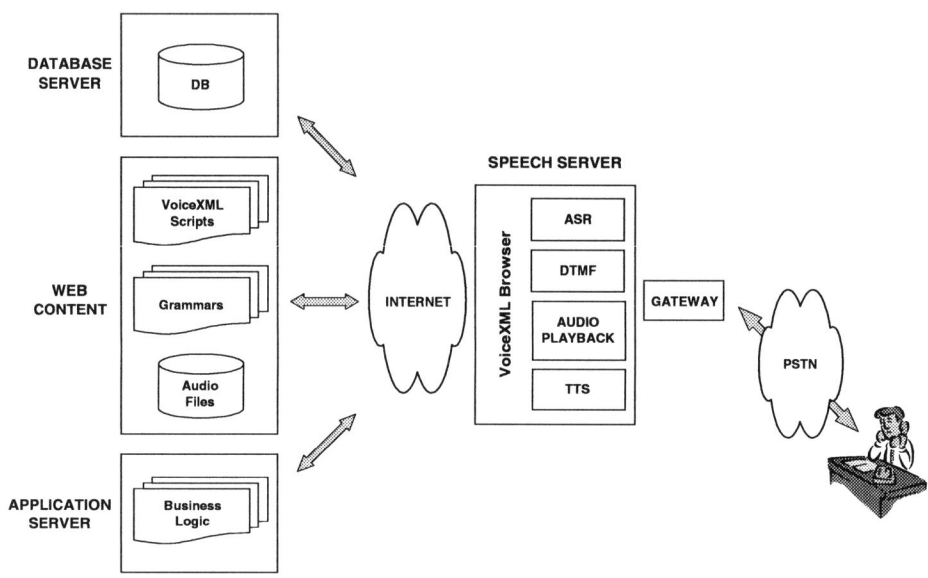

Figure B.1—**AN INTERNET VOICE PORTAL** offers the voice equivalent of web browsing. It supports a rich body of local content and services. In addition, it may provide access to other web sites via hyperlinks and search engines. To the user, the Internet can be an overwhelmingly large and unstructured system. Because voice is the only navigation mechanism, care must be taken to constrain and manage the dialogue.

A device known as a **gateway** answers the telephone, performs switching functions, and connects the telephone signal to the speech server. The speech server invokes an instance of the browser, which then delivers content to the user via a spoken user interface. The browser plays a welcome message, typically followed by a list of user options—in effect, a Main Menu. The user then selects one of the options and is routed to the appropriate web content.

B.1.1   Voice Portal Utility

Portals with a bounded domain[4] usually use digitized voice prompts, making them sound very much like conventional VRU applications. It is not unusual for the caller to encounter different voices while navigating the site.[5] For example, the portal's navigation voice may be a professional female talent, while news clips or sports announcements may be pre-recorded by a male speaker. When the portal domain is unbounded, or when information is unknown or rapidly changing, TTS technology[6] is often employed due to the quantity of content that must be read to the user.

As with a web browser, the voice browser represents a "content window" that supports four generic tasks. Users can:

- Acquire information passively,
- Navigate from page to page or site to site,
- Engage in transactions interactively, and
- Perform intelligent search and negotiation.

Acquiring information is often the simplest task. Typical inquiries are about flight arrivals and departures, restaurants, and stocks—as well as the ubiquitous news, sports, and weather. Speech recognition is used to specify the desired information. The portal then delivers the information through spoken machine output.

Navigation tasks typically include choosing from lists of options, calling out names or keywords, and similar methods for specifying user intent. Speech recognition is used to indicate the desired location, and the browser then navigates to the location. Most navigation is user interface overhead—a sort of necessary evil required to get the user to a location—and does not accomplish work directly. But the portal must present all navigation options (both meaningful and undesirable) to the user, thereby devoting a great deal of time to this presentation overhead. It is therefore important to manage navigation tasks carefully.

---

[4] A bounded domain contains a finite set of operations. An unbounded domain extends across multiple domains, without any control over their subsequent operations.
[5] Guideline 2.1.2.3 describes how the voice interface can make use of mixed male and female voices and voices representing specialized personal agents.
[6] Speech that has been synthesized directly from text. Refer to Section 2.1.3 for guidelines on using TTS versus recorded machine output.

Transactions are more complex. Typical transactions include e-commerce activities such as travel ticketing and financial transactions. Users calling a portal must first identify themselves to gain access or get permission to make transactions. Users must then interact with the portal to provide transaction information, such as account names, dollar amounts, shipping information, and similar transaction-specific data. The portal must deliver the information verbally, move state-by-state through the interaction, confirm, and then process the transaction to completion.

Search and negotiation tasks are the most complex of all, described well by Attwater:

> The goal is to use the real power of language to specify a problem—negotiating a settlement and reaching an ultimate solution without referring to anything in the immediate audioscape of the caller.[7] Instead, we want to use language for what it is good at—pointing to things in abstract and complex ways [Attwater01b].

Search and negotiation can be viewed as the "web surfing" problem and, to some extent, the call routing problem. The technology challenge is that the task requires the full capabilities of mixed initiative spoken dialogue using large vocabulary recognition—along with the application of background knowledge. This is referred to in natural language literature as the "AI complete" problem—and it remains a technology barrier today and for the foreseeable future.

B.1.2 Portal Architecture

Voice portals access the domain via a speech server that runs multiple instances (channels) of the voice browser. The voice browser is an exact corollary of web browsers except that it is remote from the user, a fact necessitated by the reality that the user's telephone is a dumb terminal. As shown in Figure B.1, the telephone line is connected to the server via a gateway.

The speech server communicates with web servers, which serve up content. The content may be in traditional HTML format, or can be optimized to communicate with the voice browser using the VoiceXML[8] standard as shown in Figure B.1. These web content servers send pages of information—for example, grammars, audio files, and other user interface objects to the speech server—to instruct the voice browser as it interacts with the user.

---

[7] That is, not parroting something just heard (like a menu item or example phrase).
[8] VoiceXML is a markup language, emerging as a de facto standard for voice portal development. See the glossary, [Edgar01] and [Larson01] to learn more about VoiceXML.

Standard HTML content does not include provisions for voice browsers. The voice browser, however, can sometimes pre-process the interactions with these web pages. Text is converted to speech and presented via TTS, pictures are deleted (although their captions may be spoken), and hyperlinks are dynamically captured to generate speech grammars. Thus, although it is somewhat clumsy, voice browsing of standard HTML sites remains possible.

Finally, application servers provide control logic that manages the flow of data between the speech server and the back-end servers providing access to business information for inquiries and transactions. Figure B.1 demonstrates that application servers can give callers access to corporate databases.

B.1.3   Comparing Voice Portals and VRU Systems

A voice portal differs from a VRU in architecture, implementation, and sometimes in its business goals. However, the user interface is generally identical in look and feel to a traditional speech-enabled VRU application. This fact is somewhat comforting, because a voice browser can be successfully designed using many of the guidelines presented in this style guide. Having said that, voice browsers present additional user interface challenges due to:

- The conversion of visually complex pages to a voice interface,
- The breadth and variety of content that is available, and
- The visual metaphor brought by users from their previous browsing experiences.

It is likely that callers who have previously visited a web site will "see" (visualize) the site a little more effectively as a result of their web browsing experience. It is possible that the mix of voices and the order in which content is presented can complement this visual memory. As a result, the user experience with even a relatively simple voice portal can seem quite different from a stand alone speech-enabled VRU application that has no analogous web page.

B.1.4   Enterprise Portals

The primary difference between "enterprise" and "consumer" portals is not the user interface but the business model. Enterprise portals typically adopt a cost-saving business model, and are growing somewhat rapidly as a result of the strong business case associated with that model. Consumer portals, on the other hand, tend to rely on the value-add model—deriving revenue from one or a mix of advertising, subscription, or pay-per-use.[9]

Another difference is that enterprise portals offer a bounded set of tasks that are domain-specific, for example banking, as shown in Figure B.2. Likewise, a VRU for a shipping company presents tasks relevant to shipping only; a utility company presents information appropriate for the knowledge domain of the utility. Contrast this with consumer portals that typically offer a mix of popular content: news, sports, weather, stock quotes, and horoscopes. This seemingly unbounded domain can be perceived by the caller as an almost arbitrary collection of data that are difficult to cluster into categories. The result is that consumer portals tend to have menus that are broad but shallow—long lists of keywords that are not organized into submenus.

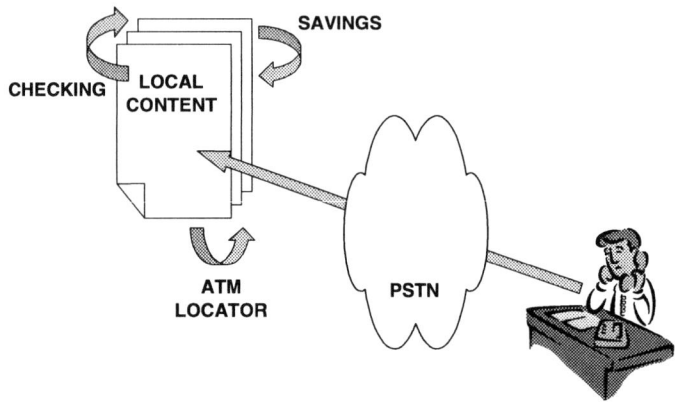

Figure B.2—**ENTERPRISE PORTALS** are growing rapidly in utility, primarily because the business model is compelling. To the user, the application resembles a speech-enabled customer application such as a banking self-service VRU. Some pages may be unrestricted—an ATM locator, for example. Others restrict access and require an account number and PIN.

Enterprise portals may be extensions of a pre-existing corporate web site, or may be built instead on a corporate VRU operating in a call center environment. There are three categories of enterprise portals:

- Business to business (B2B),
- Business to consumer (B2C), and
- Business to employee (B2E).

---

[9] See Section 1.2.4.3 for a discussion of these two business models.

The B2B portal delivers product information, ordering capabilities, and order tracking features between vendors and corporate buyers. The look and feel is quite similar to a VRU system, usually based on menu navigation to application terminals where transactions take place. Because users are often repeat callers, a natural language dialogue style can also be appealing for B2B voice portals.[10]

Most B2C applications today evolved from of call center infrastructure rather than web infrastructure. This is because most customer service functions to date are dominated by telephone contact. As a result, the distinction between VRU and voice portal is mainly a marketing difference.

B2C voice portals that evolve from web infrastructure are often referred to as "Web-Lite." That is, the enterprise provides a feature- and information-rich web site for customer self-service, but deploys only a subset of this functionality in a voice portal (often aimed at servicing mobile customers). An airline, for example, may limit the voice portal to gate arrival and departure information, frequent flyer status, and seat upgrades because these functions are frequently requested by mobile users and easy to complete with a voice browser.

Another popular enterprise portal application is the automated attendant used for call routing within the enterprise. This application may prompt for a specific name, but in its more powerful form extracts a general description of the user's problem or question. To acquire input, a statistical language model (SLM[11]) is employed to get the gist of the user's request. The portal then routes the call to its destination.[12]

B2E portals are similar to B2C portals except they provide information and transaction processing to employees. Typical B2E portals are Human Resources sites—designed to assist employees with sick leave and vacation time, access to data about retirement funds, stock options, and similar information.

B.1.5   Consumer Portals

In addition to accessing popular content and voice browsing the Internet, consumer portals can offer enhanced services that are typically provided for a monthly fee. This

---

[10] See Figures 9.1 and 9.2 to understand application terminals and to distinguish between directed and NL methods for reaching them.

[11] See the glossary and Section 8.5.4 for a discussion of statistical language models. Note that some call routing portals can capture account numbers and other information, calling for certain follow-on dialogues in addition to the initial interaction.

[12] See Guideline 3.2.4.2 for a discussion of call routing.

value-add model applies to existing web-based service providers and a number of telecommunications providers (especially wireless service providers). They include:

- Voicemail,
- Call forwarding and follow me features,
- Speech-enabled e-mail,
- Speech-enabled calendar management, and
- Voice dialing.

In addition, enhanced services are growing to include a number of more sophisticated personal virtual assistant and productivity applications. In many cases, these applications are converging with corporate contact management systems as the portals provide a productivity infrastructure for their employees.

The business model for enhanced services tends to be mixed. In the early "dot.com" era, voice portals provided enhanced services such as e-mail readers to attract customers. The services were free, and advertisements accounted for the financial income. Others began with free services, switching to a pay-per-use or subscription model after a trial period. Neither model has fared well as the transition from free to paid services has occurred—users tend to drop the services after experimentation, implying that they (the customers) perceive low value.

Enhanced services can resemble enterprise B2C voice portals because a common user interface can be created to both the telephone and the web. The user sets up personal addresses, alternate phone numbers, e-mail addresses, and other personalized data using a web browser, because this is difficult and time consuming to accomplish with a voice browser.[13] The user then takes advantage of the voice browser to perform time-critical and location-insensitive tasks such as listening to and replying to e-mail, and sending and receiving voice messages.

B.2 Voice Web Guidelines

From a user interface design perspective, voice portals fall into a number of different categories, based on several factors:

- Business model,

---

[13] See Section 9.1.2 for a discussion of personalization. The proper distribution of user tasks between a web page and its associated voice portal is critical for usability.

- Size and scope of topic domain,
- Complexity and number of typical interactions per session, and
- Psychological set and setting brought by the user to the session.

These factors affect the level of user commitment and therefore the manner in which information can be presented. They also can affect the duty cycle[14] of the application, because different types of portals tend to emphasize different mixes of information: inquiry, navigation, transaction, and search dialogues.

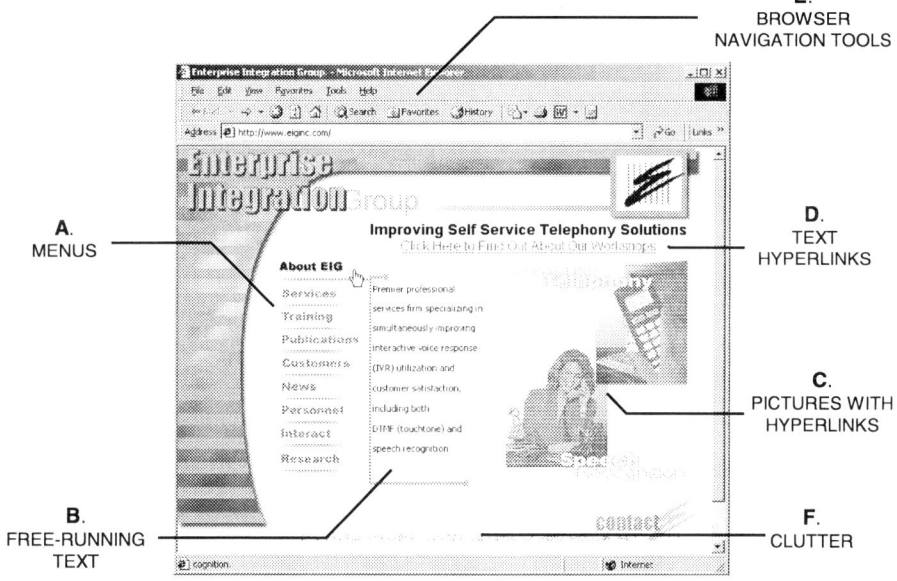

Figure B.3—**TYPICAL WEB PAGE** organizes and presents information through the use of various visual devices (A, B) and makes tools available to the user for selecting (C, D), navigating and searching (E), and performing operations. A voice browser must convert these standard devices and tools into reliable audio form, translating spatial and mechanical metaphors into appropriate speech recognition dialogue components.

When a user browses a web site, he is confronted with a rich set of visual choices that represent both local web content and access to the entire Internet. The user may navigate via hyperlinks from page to page or from site to site—with no prior expectation or assumption regarding "where" things are. In addition, the user may invoke one of several search engines, hunting for keywords and using Boolean operations to man-

---

[14] See the glossary and Appendix A for a definition and discussion of duty cycle.

age the search. As shown in Figure B.3, the tools available to the user are presented visually, and remain persistent and conveniently available in a parallel medium.[15] In a voice portal, identical user tasks are assumed. But the caller will be required to formulate his actions verbally, selecting from audio information that is not persistent, and that must be presented through a medium that is serial.

Figure B.3 shows a nine-element menu running down the left-hand column (A). The user is pointing at the top item (highlighted), which has opened a small free-running text window in the center of the display (B). This text may be lengthy, and often contains embedded hyperlinks. Other hyperlinks are associated with pictures (C) or free-standing text (D) which may appear at any location on the screen. In addition, the browser itself (E) provides tools for navigating, searching, and managing data.

B.2.1 Relationship Between the Voice Browser and Web Browser

Telephony application designers have the option of providing voice access to an existing web site or developing a comparable service that is independent of the web site. The following guidelines assist with the decisions that affect the coupling that exists between these two modalities.

B.2.1.1 √ Maintain Focus on Business Model

This is the most important voice portal guideline and is the only one that is tagged √ (Required). Voice portals and voice browsers are not yet established in terms of value and user acceptance. This will likely remain true for the next few years, as various designs and products adjust to the changing business and consumer landscape. It is easy under these circumstances to become distracted by new design philosophies and user interface trends.

When formulating your application design, it is best to return to the business model at hand and to create dialogues that serve that business model. Value-add applications must add value, as users will be asked to pay for the service. Cost-saving applications must benefit the enterprise with minimum impact on the caller—benefits that include reduced call duration, better self-service automation, and fewer transfers to agents.

Applications that deliver on their business promise are likely to succeed, even when mistakes are made in the interface design. Conversely, applications that stray from their core business focus are likely to fail, even when an engaging and natural interface impresses the user.

---

[15] See Section 1.2.1.2 to understand persistence and its importance in user interface media.

B.2.1.2   + Avoid Direct Rendition of Existing Site

Visual and speech modalities are fundamentally different. As discussed in Section B.1.2, HTML web servers can be processed in such a way as to voice-enable them, but results are generally disappointing. Any approach that attempts to render a web page directly into a spoken interface is unlikely to succeed.

Although the content of the page may be appropriate for telephony, the mechanisms for delivering it—including information ordering, terminology, and primary functions—will likely prove very difficult. A better method for approaching the problem of voice-enabling existing web pages is to study the underlying organization of the site, and then redesign the pages using established voice interface principles.

B.2.1.3   ≈ Maintain Rough Organizational Correspondence

Despite the argument in Guideline B.2.1.2 that a voice-enabled site must be a redesign, not just a rendition, it is likely that the two interfaces should maintain some correspondence in terms of their basic organization. To the degree that callers are able to bring some visual memory of the web site to the voice interface, this transfer of learning should be supported. More research is needed in this regard, and repeated interaction with visual and voice instances of the same web site will likely lead to specific and quantifiable design principles. Until then, it is probably wise to maintain at least a rough organizational correspondence between the two modalities. In Figure B.3, for example, the left-hand column at point A might serve as the Main Menu for the voice portal. In this case, menu ordering should be retained, and changes to the web page should always be reflected in the voice portal.

B.2.1.4   + Identify a Subset of Functions Appropriate for Telephony

It's generally not a good idea to cram functionality into a voice portal with the goal of offering an "information-rich" experience. Users often have different goals when they are using a telephone than when they are using a computer. It is best to voice-enable only those functions that are appropriate for a telephone interaction. The following sub-guidelines can help with selecting functions that are most appropriate for a telephony interface.

B.2.1.4.1   + Consider Session Duration

Most callers will not spend as much time interacting with a voice browser as they do with the web browser. The reason they are using the telephone in the first place is that they don't have the time, attention, or need for the kind of web browsing that is supported on the desktop . Unless there is good reason otherwise, it is best to assume that users will call the portal for specific and well-bounded tasks that are short and easily-completed.

B.2.1.4.2   ≈ Consider Intermediate Information

Some interactions expect the user to keep track of intermediate information before making a decision. For example, airplane ticketing includes a complex negotiation phase where the user identifies flight criteria. Once the system presents travel options, the user must consider the degree to which each criterion is weighted. One flight leaves a little too early, but is less expensive. Another flight costs more but is the user's frequent flyer preference. Yet another is non-stop but arrives too late for a business meeting—a meeting that the user may be able to change. The caller must remember all of these flights, taking into account pros and cons of each to make a final decision. This type of interaction is clumsy and time-consuming even in human discourse, and is more tedious with an automated system.

The problem with a telephone interface is that the user cannot see this intermediate information. Although it is manageable if the caller is sitting at a desk and taking notes, the problem is untenable otherwise. Therefore, it is best to avoid these transactions in a voice portal.

If such a transaction must be supported, the caller should be warned in advance about intermediate information:

App: *Please have pencil and paper ready to note the flights.*

B.2.1.4.3   ≈ Profile the User Context and Environment

It is important to understand target users. This includes landline versus mobile phone callers, the nature of the environment from which they are calling, and the attention span and level of commitment that they bring to the interaction.

For example, many designers assume that voice browsing is for mobile users—the reason callers prefer the telephone to the desktop or laptop computer is mobility. So-called "road warriors" are often cited as examples. But these users live and work in a noisy and distracting environment. They are likely to exhibit specific behaviors relevant to that environment—a willingness to interrupt one call to accept another incoming call, a desire to speak with numerous people (and machines) asynchronously, a need to suspend an interaction while performing some task, and many other behaviors commonly observed among these target users.

Taking this into account, tasks to be voice enabled must be chosen carefully. It is not unusual to see designers make decisions without considering usage cases of the target caller. Knowledge of the user and the task must be augmented with knowledge of the social context and physical environment of the caller.

B.2.1.5   + Eliminate Clutter

Web pages include material that few people notice, let alone explore.[16] Copyright and legal notices in very small fonts are prime examples, but there are a number of other cases of visual clutter. Voice browsers cannot afford to present this clutter because it occupies presentation time that could otherwise be devoted to more productive functions. The design should eliminate all non-essential elements on the web page.

B.2.2   Presenting a Web Page

Presentation guidelines for a voice portal will generally resemble those discussed elsewhere in this style guide. Suggestions and cross references that help designers approach the problem of voice enabling a web page are provided in this section.

B.2.2.1   + Order Navigational Elements According to Voice Precedence

Visual web pages present navigation controls in a number of forms, for example:

• Topics organized as elements of one or more menus,

• Hyperlinks embedded within text,

• Hyperlinks associated with pictures and icons, and

• Navigation buttons on the browser itself.

In general, a voice-enabled version of the same page can present these navigational elements in similar ways. However, human factors principles associated with voice take precedence over those associated with web browsers.

B.2.2.1.1   + Ensure that Menus Conform to Voice Guidelines

Spoken menus, for example, cannot be as long as lists displayed on web pages. Guidelines in Section 6.2.2 describe typical menu limits. Some voice portals get around this limitation by supporting hidden or secondary-menu options. One well-known portal, for example, presents the option "popular choices" at

---

[16] See Figure B.4, point F.

the end of the main menu. The option is a secondary list of items—including weather, horoscopes, and lottery results—that are presented as a sub-menu but may in fact be spoken at the main menu. The result is a main menu that supports a much larger number of choices than those presented. This technique is effective to a point—particularly among frequent callers—but care should be taken to avoid exceeding user memory limitations.

Note that naming a list of choices something other than a menu does not change these menu-length limitations. For example, long lists of "hot" words or "key" words are menus in disguise, and very long lists of such words should not be recited verbatim.

Most popular voice portals as of this writing conform to Guidelines 6.2.1.1, 6.2.1.2, and 6.2.1.4, which allow slightly longer menus and provide clear feedback regarding the user's location in the hierarchy. Most are beginning to embrace the turn-taking and error avoidance methods described in the other guidelines of Section 6.2.1. All of today's portals support list interruption (Section 6.2.3), but many are still lacking in alternate selection methods of Guidelines 6.2.3.2 through 6.2.3.6.[17]

B.2.2.1.2   ≈ Consider Auditory Cues for Hyperlinks

Very few designers have experimented with voice versions of hyperlinks embedded within free running text. It is possible that employing mixed voices as discussed in Guideline 2.1.2.3 and its sub-guidelines can apply to this problem. The challenge is how to construct a dynamic grammar that "decays" as the user's memory decays after presenting these hyperlinks. Alternatively, voice browser designs that support hyperlinks may instead group these items into a short menu that appears before or after the text itself.

B.2.2.1.3   ≈ Support Global Commands

Menu-driven voice portals almost universally support the "Main Menu" landmark of Guideline 6.2.1.2 to return to their starting point. Global commands such as "next" and "back" are used to varying degrees. "Go back" appears to be an effective way to return to the immediately preceding state.

---

[17] These guidelines discuss interruption, selection, disambiguation, and confirmation methods for spoken lists.

B.2.2.2   ≈ Draw on Visual Memory Where Possible

Some voice portals exist **in place of** visual web sites. These portals have no visual corollary and cannot benefit from visual memory.

However, if users are likely to have prior visual experience with a web page, then direct reference to that experience might assist with the design of presentation audio and grammars for the voice portal. Caller commands such as "upper left" and audio descriptions such as *moving down the page* represent direct and literal references to the web page layout. If such a page metaphor is selected, then care must be taken to maintain it throughout the voice experience.

Consistency of this visual "page" metaphor may include:

• Presentation of audio "frames"—which, like the web page, may be located at the top of the page, left hand side, or in a main body,

• Navigation between frames with phrases such "main body," or "tabs,"

• Declaring a page name landmark after the user selects a hyperlink, and

• Direct reference to the appearance of the page.

B.2.2.3   ≈ Rely on Directed Dialogue Techniques Where Appropriate

Certain transactions inherently require single-token dialogues. E-mail readers and voicemail services, for example, do not benefit significantly from multi-token NL utterances that are helpful in flattening a vertical menu hierarchy. The reason is that users must listen to mail—one piece at a time—before knowing what subsequent operations to perform.

Dialogues that do not benefit from NL methods should remain directed. Techniques for directed dialogues are well-known and effective. These techniques include menus as discussed earlier, but also include two-way and three-way branching devices (Section 6.2.4 and Guidelines 8.5.1.2.1 and 8.5.1.3), yes-no questions of all types (all of Section 6.3), and various streamlined prompting and feedback mechanisms (Sections 2.3.1 and 2.4.2).

B.2.2.4   ≈ Consider NL Dialogues for Multi-Token Transactions

Some voice portals support tasks that lend themselves to NL techniques—that is, grammars can be specified that accept multi-token utterances. These portals might take advantage of the guidelines in Chapter 8, particularly new methods discussed in Section 8.5 for enforcing and rewarding multi-token speech. As of this writing, voice portals tend to be strongly directed. Some support "hidden" NL grammars—discouraged by Guideline 8.5.2.4. Designers that want to complicate user input with multi-token grammars without embracing NL prompting techniques that reinforce the use of these grammars are strongly encouraged to understand the convergence problem as discussed throughout Section 8.5.2.

B.2.3   Style and Personality Issues

Style and personality issues are primarily look and feel decisions.[18] This means that they are driven as much by aesthetic or marketing considerations as they are by ergonomics. The following guidelines help voice portal designers confront tradeoffs between task-completion goals versus the difficult to quantify satisfaction with look and feel, likes and dislikes, matters of trust, and building customer loyalty.

B.2.3.1   + Make Enterprise Portals Professional

Enterprise portals are paid for by enterprises. The goal is to automate services at lower cost with customer self-service—an overarching principle that drives design decisions including those associated with look and feel. The business is not interested in delivering a "personality" that some callers like at the expense of losing other callers who dislike it unless a case can be made that it serves the self-service goal.

Consequently, businesses tend to be conservative. In the workplace, humans narrow their range of emotional expression—speaking guardedly when interacting with workplace colleagues. This attenuated behavior is considered "professional." Similarly, ensuring that callers have an equally conservative and professional experience requires that the application reduce its emotional range—staying well focused and composed as it interacts with users.

The narrowed range of affect that is characteristic of a professional is perceived by users as cool-headed, purposeful, and goal-oriented. In a professional interaction, users are not likely to notice the personality. Instead they prefer to focus on their tasks. See Guidelines 8.4.2.3, and 9.1.4.1, and 9.1.4.2.

---

[18] "Look and feel" is discussed in the introductory material of Section 1.1.1.1 and 1.1.3, as well as in pertinent sections associated with audio prompting (2.1.2.2), turn taking (5.2.1), and dialogue style (Chapters 6 and 8). VRU applications, of course, exploit the senses of speech and hearing as opposed to sight and touch—making the terms "look and feel" metaphorical rather than literal.

B.2.3.2   + Be Creative with Consumer Portals

Consumer portals are paid for by consumers. Their business cases are more complex and varied than enterprise portals. For this reason, product differentiation and other look and feel issues can dominate product design. The consumer portal is the place to experiment with mixed personae, youthful, exuberant, and "over the top" characters, aggressive weirdoes, oddball contexts, strained metaphors, and other elements normally associated with entertainment or *le haut monde*. Although some users will spontaneously dislike the persona, others will find it endearing and "catchy."[19]

B.2.4   Search and Negotiation Issues

An imaginary example explains the real challenge of the search and negotiation task. Suppose you call a friend over the phone and speak with her as she navigates the Internet. You communicate with her using the full power of human language—not the limited version of speech supported by today's technologies. You ask her to perform increasingly complex searches and information inquiries.

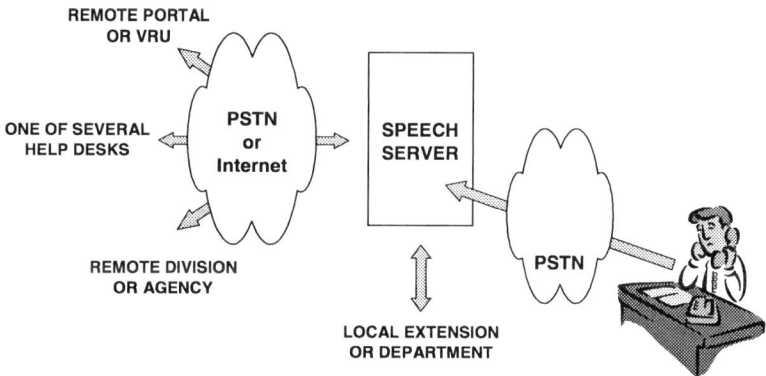

Figure B.4—CALL ROUTING VOICE PORTAL provides no content or transactions on its own, but is used to steer callers to different help desks or to remote corporate divisions. It can even reroute calls to other portals or VRU systems.

Even with speech technology removed from the equation, the interaction is still neither gratifying nor productive. The underlying problem is the need to remember intermediate steps during the negotiation, as well as where to put all of the information

---

[19] Be sure to choose well.

once it is successfully located. Do you write it down? Does your friend keep repeating it? Can these tasks be performed effectively without some sort of text or graphical interface that you can reference as you speak?

B.2.4.1 ≈ Avoid Unconstrained Search and Negotiation Applications

For the above reasons, it is unwise to offer fully unconstrained search capabilities as though the user is going to "surf" in a manner that resembles the use of web browsers.

B.2.4.2 ≈ Limit Call-Routing Portals

Call routing is a specific manifestation of the general search problem.[20] It usually relies on SLM technology to steer the caller to one of a limited number of destinations, as shown in figure B.4. In the figure, a user has called the voice portal, which in turn produces a well-crafted prompt that is aimed at extracting a general description of the caller's problem or question. This type of voice portal may be used in call centers to perform skills-based routing—connecting callers to different help desks (left middle). It may also be used to steer calls to appropriate business divisions or governmental agencies (left bottom) or even to one of several VRU systems (left top).

Although the capabilities of SLM technology will improve over the years, current systems are best when the number of branches is kept quite small. Fifteen is a good number, with up to fifty or so representing the maximum for such applications.

In the case of a names-based automated attendant, in which a system connects the caller to a local extension (lower center), the application is more likely to use a large-vocabulary grammar-driven recognizer. These systems support very large directories of some several million names.

---

[20] Section B.1.1.

Appendix C
Voice Talent and Recording

Spoken machine output can take two forms.[1] A speech synthesizer might be used to convert computer-readable text directly into speech. Alternatively, a human speaker might record voice files that are then played in sequence to present information to the caller. This Appendix discusses best practices for human voice recordings, the most common approach to machine speech.

C.1 Voice Recording

The human speaker that creates digitized recordings is known as the **voice talent**, or more simply, the **talent**. Usually a trained professional, the talent is expert in producing clear, articulate, and properly-inflected speech. Usually skilled in singing, public speaking, broadcasting, speech and language pathology, and/or other areas that make her expert in vocal control and production, the talent works in a recording studio. Large firms have studios on premise, but most organizations outsource recording to a voice services specialist. The talent works closely with a **coach**. The coach is usually a member of the design team, and serves as the guardian of the integrity, persona, look and feel, and other style attributes of the VRU application. The coach is responsible for understanding the application in detail and the talent is responsible for producing the vocal quality that realizes design goals.

C.1.1 Subtleties of Voice Files

Users are quite sensitive to subtleties in the human voice. Even the smallest variations in quality are perceived by users and affect their interpretation of the meaning and intent of machine speech.

---

[1] Chapter 2 provides guidelines on spoken machine output; the focus of this Appendix is on selecting and coaching the voice talent.

C.1.1.1   ≈ Consider Varied Recordings

Audio messages that appear frequently—for example the entry to a main menu—are often noted by users as "mechanical" because of their exact repetition of prosodic[2] information. Some designers have addressed this subtlety by creating multiple recordings of these prompts to create variety and to reduce listening fatigue.

There are two types of variety:

• Slight changes in the wording of voice files, and

• Multiple recordings of the same wording.

In both cases, the goal is to provide a slightly-less repetitive audio message with minimal impact on the caller's understanding of its meaning. In some cases, the variants are presented one after the other, ensuring that the caller hears a different version on each presentation of the message. In other cases, the machine speech is randomized, with variants appearing in unpredictable order.

The effects of this design technique are slight, and should be considered only after other more important aspects of the design are well in hand. There are some indications from field research, however, that—although subtle—the technique has some measurable effect on user performance and satisfaction.

The danger of varied recordings from a user interface perspective is that the same sensitivity that affects callers when machine behavior is mechanical may affect callers when machine behavior is varied. Subtle changes might occur, for example, when users (perhaps unconsciously) perceive that variations in machine speech represent an implicit encouragement to vary their own speech. This danger can only be dismissed by careful observation during usability tests.

In addition to the danger of negatively impacting user performance, there are three drawbacks to varied recordings:

• The practical problem of organizing and managing a larger number of audio files,

• Increased expense and complexity of developing and testing the code, and

• Longer and more expensive recording sessions.

These drawbacks create practical concerns that can dominate design decisions. Note that some application developers—aiming to ameliorate the effect that such drawbacks have on the development process—argue that "mechanical" is exactly the de-

---

[2] See the glossary for a more detailed description of prosody.

sired behavior of a machine, and leads to user assumptions that are helpful to dialogue success. Precise repetition of prompts, for example, makes the interface highly predictable. The reader is therefore cautioned that introducing variety for the sake of variety should be tested carefully to avoid unpredictable user behavior.

C.1.1.2   √ Above All, Do No Harm

Development teams have a tendency to delight in experimenting with the various attributes of voice recording. This is probably because voice is the externally observable part of the dialogue—what is known as a **surface feature** of the interface—and so tends to evoke a lot of excitement and show-business thrall. Though participating in surface-feature design is fun, however, it often happens that uninformed opinions find their way into finished product to the detriment of user and business alike.

A hypothesis about voice recordings is like singing in the shower—it always sounds good until someone else hears it. Well-known and effective practices make voice recording perhaps the lowest-risk aspect of VRU design, but involvement by amateurs can undo good practices. For this reason, avoiding damage to the interface must be the number one criterion for making final decisions.

All contributions to the persona itself, and especially to the voice production aspects of the recordings, should be tested against this guideline. If vocal acrobatics are executed by a professional, then even somewhat extreme persona characteristics will likely be benign. But whenever frivolity, over-pronunciation, or risky over-the-top behaviors mislead users, then discipline must be applied to maintain focus on the task-completion goals of the interface.

C.1.1.3   √ Be Cautious with Digits

Digits are concatenated[3] in complex ways. The talent must understand how numeric recordings will be used, paying close attention to duration, inflection, and articulation of individual digits[4]. The talent should be especially aware of concatenation issues.

C.1.1.4   + Avoid Calling Attention to Voice

A VRU voice is like a basketball referee—if bad it gets in the way of the game; if good it goes unnoticed. Remember that the VRU is about the user, not about the ma-

---

[3] Concatenation is the technique of playing multiple recordings one after the other to create the appearance of complete sentences or data sequences.
[4] See Section 2.7.2 for a more detailed discussion of timing and inflection of digit strings and Guideline 10.3.2.4 on inflected playback to imply queries.

chine. Calling attention to the voice (which **is** the machine as far as the user is concerned) draws user attention away from the task and should be avoided. The following sub-guidelines discuss specific voice errors commonly found in VRU systems that call attention to the voice.

C.1.1.4.1 + Avoid Excessively "Professional" Speaking Styles

Many applications use radio-announcer voices that are excessively polished and that make use of especially exaggerated inflections. The caller comes to feel that she is participating in a game show rather than interacting with the application. It is best to tone down such vocal bravura.

C.1.1.4.2 + Be Careful of Too Much "Grin"

A good technique for professional recording is to smile when speaking—a technique known as "grin." The technique forces the mouth into positions that color the resulting speech, producing a pleasing cheerfulness that carries over the telephone and is perceived by the user.

Good talent and good coaches are both skilled in the appropriate use of grin. The technique should not be exaggerated, however, as it can backfire. Too much grin conveys the impression that the application is not serious about the caller's needs. In extreme cases (for example during error-recovery routines), the machine seems to be mocking the user, as though amused by an error.

C.1.1.4.3 + Reduce Fatiguing Effects

Telephones are narrowband devices with inexpensive loudspeakers. There are resonances associated with the chamber that houses the earpiece, and these resonances can "ping" the ear when the VRU voice hits one of them. A professional talent is well trained in smoothing the voice when inflecting speech. During playback of VRU speech over a mobile telephone, in particular, the talent can note resonant frequencies that fatigue the ear. Untrained talent tends to over-modulate in an attempt to be "friendly," with the unfortunate side effect of tiring the user during long VRU sessions.

Care should be taken to test audio in harsh environments—especially noisy places when the caller is likely to turn up the volume. Any audio that tends to jump out or become irritating when repeated should then be re-recorded with an ear toward reducing the fatigue.

C.1.1.4.4   ≈ Scale Recording Effort to Application

A small and simple VRU is exactly that. Adding unnecessary complexity by making recording into a huge and expensive undertaking should be avoided. The number of recordings should be kept to a minimum, and the use of variants and other complications should be avoided.

That is not to say that small applications can get away with amateur voice recordings. Even the simplest application should use professional talent that is properly coached.

A large and complex VRU is exactly that. When users are offered complex choices—and when the potential for error is great—then the recording effort should be scaled up accordingly. Even small differences can have great effect, and multiple recording sessions with careful management are necessary.

C.1.1.5   √ Plan for Changes and Late Additions

There will be modifications to voice recordings at the eleventh hour. It is best to admit that fact as an unalterable reality, schedule the recording sessions, and secure the talent early for strategic calendar dates during alpha and beta testing.

C.1.1.6   + Review Recordings via Telephone

A VRU application will always be used over the telephone. How voice recordings sound over loudspeakers in a studio is therefore irrelevant (except to the extent that they allow the recording engineer to control quality and consistency). The audio engineering team, the voice talent, and the coach should review the recordings with a telephone to ensure that the voice is optimized for that channel.

The best way to do this is to find a way to play all audio recordings through a dial-up system, allowing team members to call and review from a number of locations.

Reviewers should listen through:

- Different telephones, including mobile phones,
- Speakerphones, headsets, and hands-free kits, and in
- Noisy environments.

Reviewers should listen for:

- Flat frequency response, without "boomy," muffled, or tinny sound quality, and free of resonances that may fatigue the ear,

- Intelligibility,
- Consistency in loudness, and
- Appropriateness of prosody.

C.1.2   Preliminary Test Recordings

C.1.2.1   + Use Easily-Accessed Talent

"Quick and dirty" is the operative phrase for preliminary test recordings. Make sure that the person recording voice files is easily accessible, willing to donate his voice frequently, and likely to be available at the "drop of a hat."

C.1.2.2   √ Avoid Unnecessary Effort

There's no sense in being sloppy, even with test recordings. Files should therefore be reasonably clean, without flubs or noises, and adequately trimmed[5]. But test recordings will probably be redone often, and certainly will be thrown away when the professional talent enters the picture, so excessive emphasis on quality is wasteful.

Efforts to avoid include:

- Recording over and over to get the right inflection,
- Using varied recordings,
- Perfecting concatenation,
- Worrying too much over single versus multiple voices,
- Spending money on studios or other special locations, and
- Fretting over little flaws.

All of these will become important in-studio, when the final voice files are recorded. It's best to reserve budget and time for that effort, minimizing the resources that are required to get "quick and dirty" early results.

C.1.2.3   √ Be Prepared to Record Frequently

A sound-editing program on a laptop makes quick recording easy. It is best to avoid having to go to a special room, get access to a dedicated machine, or locate special recording equipment. Use a small, portable, and inexpensive microphone.

---

[5] See Guideline 2.1.4.2 for a discussion of trimming prompts to remove trailing silence.

C.1.2.4   + Warm Up Before Recording

Like any other set of muscles in the body, the voice performs better when it is exercised methodically. Warm-up regimens produce clear and consistent speech because they exercise the articulators and focus the mind. Warming up is also important for the long-term health of the entire vocal system.

Professionally-trained voice talents have learned to warm up carefully before speaking or singing. Non-professionals have not acquired this discipline—one of several reasons why they fatigue quickly and articulate inconsistently from prompt to prompt. A short and thoughtful warm up is always advisable.

See Table C.1 for a sample warm-up exercise developed by Susan Berkley, a professional voice talent in New York. It is a short version of more thorough warm-up techniques and exercises that she has developed for IVR and other vocal presentations [Berkley01]. Note that these are not tongue twisters, but instead provide coverage of various sounds and sound combinations for English.

It is advisable to drink a warm glass of water before speaking the phrases. Each sentence should be spoken slowly, pronouncing every word carefully and properly. It is important to avoid racing, concentrating instead on the natural flow and easy production of each syllable.

The reader should note that the voice, like any other part of the body, can become strained or injured. Care for the voice is important.

> While doing the warm up, if your throat becomes sore or your voice feels strained, stop immediately. Work up gradually until you can comfortably do the entire exercise. And of course, if you have persistent hoarseness, weakness or any kind of throat or voice problem, please see your doctor [Berkley01].

After warming up for a few minutes, it is a good idea to practice with a few of the VRU prompts, concentrating on clarity and consistency. Then begin the recording session in earnest.

C.1.3   Selecting and Coaching Voice Talent

The voice talent for spoken machine output must be selected and coached in the details of the design. This process is well known and fully mature within organizations that produce a lot of VRU applications. For those organizations that have less experience, the following guidelines can save a lot of money and time.

349

C.1.3.1 √ Use Professional Talent

Non-professional voices are fine for experimenting and for early prototype testing. Later in development, however, and certainly before releasing the product, all spoken machine output should be recorded by a professional voice talent.

Many organizations make the mistake of finding a colleague—perhaps someone with prior voice training, or a staff member who has a "nice voice"—to serve as the voice talent. The problem is that such employees are not devoting their daily career to voice work, and do not have the professional control that is required to produce truly effective recordings. Callers recognize this instantly, with unpredictable (and usually negative) reactions.

C.1.3.2 + Use a Professional Coach

Voice coaching is also a specialized skill. This guideline is more difficult to follow, because the coach—almost by definition—must be an involved member of the design and development team.

The job of the coach is to:

- Know and understand the call flow and scripting throughout the application,
- Be familiar with persona and other subjective aspects of the design,
- Have a good ear for subtle voice differences, and
- Describe desired voice attributes in ways that are helpful to the talent.

This last one is especially important. Voice professionals, of course, are cooperative and eager to please. On the other hand, they have difficulty responding to coaches that wave their hands and ask for a "wispy effect," or make meaningless comments about "helping the caller feel relaxed." Instead, the coach should simply describe user perceptions and reactions that are desired for a given prompt, leaving it to the talent to understand intent and translate it into the desired vocal attributes.

C.1.3.3 √ Ensure that the Talent Understands the Application

The more the talent knows, the better the result will be. Coaches should ensure that the talent understands why she is saying what she is saying. This includes the various ways that an audio message will be used, the intent and purpose of a given prompt, and the call flow events that come before and after a spoken phrase. The following three sub-guidelines provide more detail.

350

Table C.1—**Voice Warm Up** is specifically designed to work many of the vowel and consonant sounds in the English language.

MY FAVORITE TWO-MINUTE VOCAL WARM UP[6]

Green tea ice cream is a treat to eat.

Amy aimed at the gate.

Ed said get into bed.

This itchy sweater comes from Italy.

Old folks row slowly.

Tom was rather calm as he took the bomb from the box.

Go with the flow to stay in the know.

My boss slurped the succulent sauce.

Buffy's tough buddy had fallen in love.

The red head fell at the sound of the bell.

Mean men may cause harm.

Pay the mime a dime, his performance is sublime.

She lost her poise after hearing the noise.

Put the oily oysters on the doily.

Sheila gave Dave a shampoo and a shave.

I knew the crew in the blue canoe.

It's our duty to salute the new recruit.

The breeze made her sneeze as she walked through the trees.

There was a shortage of blood because of the flood.

Tell the truth to the rude recruit.

Veronica put the vivid violets in the Victorian vase.

The odd opera singer had a four octave range.

Todd placed the pot on the rock.

The anchor signed off on the nightly news.

Dirty deeds done dirt cheap.

Throughout the night he thought things through.

Emily's enterprise enjoyed success.

---

[6] Quoted directly from [Berkley01].

351

C.1.3.3.1   √ Practice with Concatenation

The coach should describe to the talent how message sequences will be concatenated. This includes not only numeric information, but also text that describes the transaction itself. The talent should take the time to practice concatenating speech fragments until the desired flow is well understood.

C.1.3.3.2   √ Understand the Persona

Anything that is relevant to the desired sound quality of the voice recording, including underlying personality traits or motivation, must be well-understood if the voice talent is to do her job well.[7]

C.1.3.3.3   √ Discuss the Reasons for Prosodic Variation

Changes in prosody—inflection, stress, "grin," and other vocal attributes—have a big effect on the overall look and feel of the application. Coach and talent together should understand the mechanics of prosodic variations, and should agree on the reasons for a particular sound quality.

C.1.3.4   √ Establish Trust Between Coach and Talent

It takes time for coach and talent to become accustomed to each other's way of working. An initial session aimed at establishing this working style is important.

C.1.3.5   √ Avoid Interrupting

Voice talents seek a natural rhythm when speaking audio phrases. The talent hears flaws but often wants to maintain this rhythm, preferring to correct errors after completing an initial pass. Though different talents have different preferences in this regard, it is best to avoid stopping the talent to correct flaws immediately.

Constant interrupting leads to inconsistencies when audio messages are concatenated. As a general rule, coaches should remain silent during a recording sequence, allowing the talent to decide when to stop and discuss the results.

C.1.3.6   ≈ Test Music with Talent and Engineer

Many applications today include music that is interspersed with or mixed into voice messages. The music can have an impact on intelligibility. The talent should have an opportunity to hear the music, and the recording engineer should be allowed to ex-

---

[7] See Chapter 9 for details on personality and personification. See especially 9.1.5 to understand personae and how dependent a persona design is on the voice recordings.

periment with various mixing techniques. There are cases in which the talent will choose a different vocalization in response to the music, and in which the engineer will change equalization and mixing levels.

If music will be mixed with voice, the talent should have headphones, allowing her to speak while hearing the music. This multi-channel approach to recording will have subtle effects on the rhythm, pacing, and voice qualities of the ultimate recording.

C.2 Recording in Foreign Languages

Most applications are not "multilingual" in the sense that they alternate between two or more languages.[8] Similarly, non-English applications that are developed in full by native speakers of the target language cannot be thought of as "foreign" in any real sense of the word. However, there are cases in which English speakers develop an English application and then "translate" it to another language. Such translations can be considered "foreign language" applications in the sense that the design team has less knowledge of or stake in the target language and the culture in which it is deployed. This leads to a common mistake: the team carefully designs the English version—agonizing over the tiniest attribute of the dialogue—only to give short shrift to the foreign language version, assuming that it is not as subtle as English.[9]

C.2.1 Selecting Foreign Language Voice Talent

C.2.1.1 √ Consider Dialect

Non-English languages are as rich in subtlety and variety as various dialects of English. The voice talent for a Spanish application may speak formal Castilian Spanish, may come from various places in Mexico or Puerto Rico, or may be influenced by many other regions or groups that encompass various dialects of Spanish. The sensitivity of target users to subtleties of dialect is easy for English-speaking designers to forget.[10] To many, "French sounds like French," and subtle differences between dialects are lost. On the other hand, these same designers are likely to notice and have opinions about tiny differences in English as spoken in Boston versus English as spo-

---

[8] There are some exceptions to this claim, *e.g.*, certain applications in Quebec, Canada.

[9] American developers, in particular, tend to underestimate the subtleties of a foreign language due to the geographic and historical realities of American culture.

[10] It is well known in the linguistic community that adult speakers of one language lose the ability to hear subtle details of the phonemes of another language—a phenomenon known as neural commitment and pruning.

ken in Dallas. A native speaker of the language and representatives of the target user population should therefore be consulted when selecting the voice talent. All aspects of the design—from persona to speech rates and inflection—should be rethought, recast, and enforced with the target language in mind.

C.2.1.2 √ Consider Cultural Gender Issues

Every society can be expected to respond differently to cultural associations implied by the gender of the voice talent. Designers should avoid carrying social and political assumptions from their own culture into another. Local experts in the culture and language are essential for foreign-language translations of English VRU applications.

C.2.2 Coaching Foreign Language Voice Talent

C.2.2.1 √ Use Fluent Coach

The coach should be a fluent speaker of the language, and preferably a native of the target country. If this is impossible, then the coach should have an assistant that can help with subtle implications of the voice, allowing the coach to develop a good ear for the language and exhibit good judgment on pace and inflection. Working through a translator is inherently more fatiguing and errorful, so time for recording sessions should be appropriately elongated if this method must be adopted.

Note that many professional voices and voice-recording firms have multilingual talents. The exceptional talents can work in a truly multilingual fashion, solving this problem elegantly. In other cases, the talent does not possess the vernacular production skills for a given person. In these later cases, such talent might still take the role of coach, working in English with the English designers, but coaching in the target language effectively.

C.2.2.2 √ Understand Changes in Concatenation Rules

Concatenation rules may be different in foreign languages. Digits and super-numeric[11] data sequences are especially important, and the talent and coach together must understand the speaking style required to present numeric information to the caller. Dates, times, and proper use of cardinal and ordinal numbers are also culturally variant and must be well understood.

---

[11] See the glossary and Section 2.7.1 for a discussion of super-numerics.

Bibliography

[Attwater01a] D. Attwater, M. Edgington, P. Durston, and S. Whittaker, "Practical Issues in the Application of Speech Technology to Network and Customer Service Applications," in *Speech Communication*, August, 2000.

[Attwater01b] D. Attwater, Personal Communications, October, 2001.

[Allen87] J. Allen, *Natural Language Understanding*. The Benjamin/Cummings Publishing Company, Inc., Menlo Park, CA, 1987.

[Alty98] J. Alty and D. Rigas, "Communicating Graphical Information to Blind Users Using Music: The Role of Context," in *Proceedings of the CHI '98 Conference on Human Factors in Computing Systems*, Los Angeles, CA, April 1998, ACM Press.

[ANSI96] American National Standard for Information Technology—Document Processing and Related Communication—User Interface to Telephone-Based Services—Voice Messaging Applications. ANSI/ISO/IEC 13714–1995. American National Standards Institute, New York, NY, 1996.

[AT&T94] *Application Design Handbook: Intuity*™ *CONVERSANT*® *voice information system, version 5.0*. AT&T Product Documentation Development, Denver, CO, 1994.

[Baber97a] C. Baber, *Beyond the Desktop*. Academic Press, San Diego, CA, 1997.

[Baber97b] C. Baber, G. Johnson, and D. Cleaver, "Factors Affecting Users' Choice of Words in Speech-Based Interaction with Public Technology," in *International Journal of Speech Technology*, Vol. 2 (1), May 1997, pp. 45–59.

[Bailey96] J. Bailey, *After Thought, The Computer Challenge to Human Intelligence*. BasicBooks, New York, 1996.

[Balentine87] B. Balentine, *Multilingua*® *Courseware Authoring Environment Reference Manual, Prototype Version 0.855*, Scott Instruments Corporation, Denton, TX, 1987.

[Balentine89] B. Balentine, S. Kaufman, and M. Preston, *Home Assisted Nursing Companion, Internal Product Design Notes*, HealthTech Services Corporation, Chicago, IL, 1989.

[Balentine92a] B. Balentine and B. Scott, "Goal-Orientation and Adaptivity in a Spoken Human Interface," in *Journal of the American Voice Input/Output Society*, AVIOS, San Jose, CA, February 1992.

[Balentine92b] B. Balentine, *GoodListener Cookbook*. Scott Instruments Corporation, Denton, TX, 1992.

[Balentine94] B. Balentine, "A Multimedia Interface: Speech, Sound, Sight, and Touch," in *Proceedings of AVIOS '94*, American Voice Input/Output Society, San Jose, CA, 1994.

[Balentine97a] B. Balentine, C. Ayer, C. Miller, and B. Scott, "Debouncing the Speech Button: A Sliding Capture Window Device for Synchronizing Turn-Taking," in *International Journal of Speech Technology*, Vol. 2 (1), May 1997, pp. 7–19.

[Balentine97b] B. Balentine, *A Practical Guide to Phonetic Recognition*. Voice Control Systems, Inc., Dallas, TX, 1997.

[Bartholomew98] *Dialogue Engineering Style Guide,* M. Bartholomew, C. Durrant and M. Jack (eds), The University of Edinburgh, 1998.

[Basson96] S. Basson, S. Springer, C. Fong, H. Leung, E. Man, M. Olson, J. Pitrelli, R. Singh, and S. Wong, "User Participation and Compliance in Speech Automated Telecommunications Applications," in *Proceedings of the International Conference on Spoken Language Processing*, Philadelphia, PA, 1996.

[Berkley01] S. Berkley, *Speak to Influence, How to Unlock the Hidden Power of Your Voice*. Campbell Hall Press, Englewood Cliffs, NJ, 1999.

[Blattner89] M. Blattner, D. Sumikawa, and R. Greenberg, "Earcons and Icons: Their Structure and Common Design Principles," in *HCI Journal*, 1989.

[Brems95] D.J. Brems, M.D. Rabin, and J.L. Waggett, "Using Natural Language Conventions in the User Interface Design of Automatic Speech Recognition Systems," in *Human Factors*, Vol. 37 (2), 1995.

[Brewster97] S. Brewster, "Using Non-Speech Sound to Overcome Information Overload," in *Displays*, Vol. 17, Numbers 3–4, May 1997.

[Brewster98] S. Brewster, "Using Earcons to Provide Navigation Cues in Telephone-Based Interfaces," in Transactions on Computer Human Interaction (ToCHI), ACM, Vol. 5, 1998.

[Buie99] E. Buie, "HCI Standards: A Mixed Blessing," in *Interactions*, Vol. vi.2, March–April 1999, pp. 36–42.

[Cadwallader98] A. Cadwallader and D. Gagné, *Analysis of Tonal Music, A Schenkerian Approach*. Oxford University Press, New York, 1998.

[Catford94] J. Catford, *A Practical Introduction to Phonetics*. Oxford University Press, New York, 1994.

[Chicago93] *The Chicago Manual of Style, Fourteenth Edition*. The University of Chicago Press, Chicago, 1993.

[Churchill55] W. Churchill, *Churchill's History of the English-Speaking Peoples—Arranged for One Volume by Henry Steele Commager*. Barnes & Noble, New York, 1995

[Cohen01] M. Cohen, Personal Communications, September, 2001.

[Comerford97] R. Comerford, J. Makhoul, and R. Schwartz, "The Voice of the Computer is Heard in the Land," *IEEE Spectrum,* Vol. 34 (12), December 1997, pp. 39-47.

[Cox99] E. Cox, *The Fuzzy Systems Handbook Second Edition*. Academic Press, San Diego, CA, 1999.

[Crystal85] D. Crystal, *A Dictionary of Linguistics and Phonetics Second Edition*, Basil Blackwell Ltd., Oxford, 1985.

[Damhuis97] M. Damhuis, D. Kadijk, M. Emons, P. van Splunder, and L. Boves, "Field Trial of a Voice Dialing Application for the Dutch Cellular Network," in *Proceedings of AVIOS '97*, American Voice Input/Output Society, San Jose, CA, 1997.

[Deffner92] G. Deffner, "Improvement of Telephone Interface Technology: Why and How," in *Proceedings of AVIOS '92 Voice Input/Output Systems Applications Conference*, pp. 113–119, American Voice Input/Output Society, San Jose, CA, 1992.

[Deller93] J. Deller, J. Proakis, and J. Hansen, *Discrete-Time Processing of Speech Signals*. Macmillan Publishing Company, New York, NY, 1993.

[Digital83] *DECtalk DTC01 Programmer Reference Manual*. Digital Equipment Corporation, December 1983.

[Durston01] P. Durston, M. Farrell, D. Attwater, J. Allen, H-KJ. Kuo, M. Afify, E. Fosler-Lussier, and C-H. Lee, "OASIS Natural Language Call Steering Trial," in *Proceedings of EuroSpeech 2001*, Denmark, 2001.

[Edgar01] B. Edgar, *The VoiceXML Handbook*. CMP Books, New York, NY, 2001.

[Edgington99] M. Edgington, D. Attwater, P. Durston, "OASIS—A Framework for Spoken Language Call Steering," in *Proceedings of EuroSpeech 1999*, Budapest, 1999.

[EIG96] *Improving Interactive Voice Response, A Landmark Study of IVR Implementation in the United States*. Enterprise Integration Group, San Ramon, CA, 1996.

[EIG00] *Speech Recognition 1999 R&D Program, User Interface Design Recommendations, Final Report*. Enterprise Integration Group, San Ramon, CA, 2000.

[Fay94] D. Fay, "User Acceptance of Automatic Speech Recognition in Telephone Services," in *Proceedings of the International Conference on Spoken Language Processing*, Yokohama, Japan, July 1994.

[Foster93] P. Foster and T.J. Schalk, *Speech Recognition—The Complete Practical Reference Guide*. Telecom Library, New York, 1993.

[Gardner-Bonneau99] D. Gardner-Bonneau (editor), *Human Factors and Voice Interactive Systems*. Kluwer Academic Publishers, Norwell, MA, 1999.

[Gellman88] L. Gellman and W. Whitten, "Simulating an Automatic Operator Service to Optimize Customer Success," in *Proceedings of the 12th International Symposium on Human Factors in Telecommunications*, 1988.

[Gorin97] A. Gorin, G. Riccardi, and J. Wright, "How may I help you?" in *Speech Communication*, 23, pp. 113-127, 1997.

[Grudin89] J. Grudin, "The Case Against User Interface Consistency," in *Communications of the ACM*, Vol. 32 (10), October 1989, pp. 1164–1173.

[Hames97] B. Hames, M. Jack, N. Millner, C. Prophet, and F. Stentiford, *Integration—A study of the Impact of Computer Telephony Integration in the US Financial Services Industries*. Dialogues 2000, University of Edinburgh, U.K., July 1997.

[Hasty97] C. Hasty, *Meter as Rhythm*. Oxford University Press, New York, 1997.

[Heins97] R. Heins, M. Franzke, M. Durian, and A. Bayya, "Turn-Taking as a Design Principle for Barge-In in Spoken Language Systems," in *International Journal of Speech Technology*, Vol. 2 (2), 1997, pp. 155–164.

[Hersh98a] H. Hersh and L. Chance, *TickerTalk Demo: Usability Study—Highlights Report*, Confidential Internal Report, Fidelity Investments HID Labs, Boston, MA, 1998.

[Hersh98b] H. Hersh, *Just Say "Stop:" Managing Auditory Lists*, Confidential Internal Report, Fidelity Investments HID Labs, Boston, MA, 1998.

[Hersh99] H. Hersh, Private Communications, 1999.

[IEEE84] *IEEE Standard Dictionary of Electrical and Electronics Terms, Third Edition*. IEEE Inc., New York, NY, 1984.

[Josephs67] J. Josephs, *The Physics of Musical Sound*. D. Van Nostrand Company, Inc., Princeton, NJ, 1967.

[Karis97] D. Karis, "Speech Recognition Systems: Performance, Preference, and Design," in *Proceedings of the 16th International Symposium on Human Factors in Telecommunications*, Oslo, Norway, May 1997.

[Kientzle98] T. Kientzle, *A Programmer's Guide to Sound*. Addison-Wesley, Reading, MA, 1998.

[Kreitler72] H. Kreitler and S. Kreitler, *Psychology of the Arts*. Duke University Press, Durham, NC, 1972.

[Larson01] J. Larson, *VoiceXML: Introduction to Developing Speech Applications*. Pre-publication review copy, Pearson Education, Inc., Upper Saddle River, NJ, 2001.

[Lewis81] H. Lewis and C. Papadimitriou, *Elements of the Theory of Computation*. Prentice-Hall, Inc., Englewood Cliffs, NJ, 1981.

[Lundin67] R. Lundin, *An Objective Psychology of Music*. The Ronald Press Company, New York, 1967.

[Maes97] P. Maes and B. Shneiderman, "Direct Manipulation vs. Interface Agents: Excerpts from Debates at IUI 97 and CHI 97," in *Interactions*, Vol. 6, November–December 1997, pp. 42–61.

[Marics88] M. Marics and B. Williges, "The Intelligibility of Synthesized Speech in Data Inquiry Systems," in *Human Factors*, Vol. 30, pp. 719-732.

[Markowitz96] J.A. Markowitz, *Using Speech Recognition*. Prentice Hall PTR, NJ, 1996.

[Martin96] P. Martin, F. Crabbe, S. Adams, E. Baatz, and N. Yankelovich, "Speech Acts: A Spoken Language Framework," in *Computer*, Vol. 29 (7), July 1996.

[McArthur92] T. McArthur, *The Oxford Companion to the English Language*. Oxford University Press, New York, 1992.

[Meisel98] W. Meisel, *Speech Recognition Update*. No. 59, TMA Associates, Tarzana, CA, May 1998.

[Merriam-Webster91] *Concise Handbook for Writers*. Merriam-Webster, Inc., Springfield, MA, 1991.

[Merriam-Webster93] *Merrium-Webster's Collegiate Dictionary Tenth Edition*. Merriam-Webster, Inc., Springfield, MA, 1993.

[Miller56] G.A. Miller, "The Magical Number Seven, Plus Or Minus Two: Some Limits On Our Capacity For Processing Information," in *Psychological Science*, Vol. 63, 1956, pp. 81-97.

[Miller96] G.A. Miller, *The Science of Words*. Scientific American Library, New York, 1996.

[Moore91] G.A. Moore, *Crossing the Chasm*. HarperBusiness Publishers, New York, 1991.

[Morgan91] D.P. Morgan and C.L. Scofield, *Neural Networks and Speech Processing*. Kluwer Academic Publishers, Norwell, MA, 1990.

[Mynatt98] E. Mynatt, M. Back, R. Want, M Baer, and J. Ellis, "Designing Audio Aura," in *Proceedings of the CHI '98 Conference on Human Factors in Computing Systems*, Los Angeles, CA, April 1998, ACM Press.

[Nuance97] *Nuance Speech Recognition System, Developer's Manual, Version 6*. Nuance Communications, Menlo Park, CA, 1997.

[Oberteuffer98] J. Oberteuffer, *ASRNews*. Voice Information Associates, Lexington, MA, 1998.

[Ottman61] R. Ottman, *Elementary Harmony: Theory and Practice* and *Advanced Harmony: Theory and Practice*. Prentice-Hall, Inc., Englewood Cliffs, NJ, 1961.

[Pierce65] J.R. Pierce, *Symbols, Signals, and Noise*. Harper & Row, New York, 1965.

[Pinker94] S. Pinker, *The Language Instinct*. HarperCollins Publishers, New York, 1994.

[Rabiner93] L. Rabiner and B-H Juang, *Fundamentals of Speech Recognition*. Prentice Hall Inc., Englewood Cliffs, NJ, 1993.

[Reeves96] B. Reeves and C. Nass, *The Media Equation*. CSLI Publications and Cambridge University Press, Cambridge, UK, 1996.

[Riccardi00] G. Riccardi, "Stochastic Language Adaptation over Time and State in Natural Spoken Dialog Systems," in *IEEE Transactions on Speech and Audio Processing*, Vol. 8 No. 1, January, 2000.

[Rosenfeld01] R. Rosenfeld, D. Olsen and A. Rudnicky, "Universal Speech Interfaces," in *interactions*, Vol. viii.6, November + December, 2001, pp. 34-44.

[Rubinstein84] R. Rubinstein and H. Hersh, *The Human Factor*. Digital Press, Bedford, MA, 1984.

[Rudnicky93] A.I. Rudnicky, "Mode Preference in a Simple Data-Retrieval Task," in *INTER-CHI '93 Adjunct Proceedings*, Amsterdam, The Netherlands, ACM/SIGCHI, 1993.

[Schiffman82] H. Schiffman, *Sensation and Perception: An Integrated Approach, 2nd Edition*. Wiley Publishing, New York, 1982.

[Schmandt94] C. Schmandt, *Voice Communication with Computers*. Van Nostrand Reinhold, New York, 1994.

[Schmidt96] M. Schmidt, "Dialogues for Speaker Verification/Operator Hand-over, Apology Strategies, Security Data, Insult Rate and Completion Procedures," Dialogues 2000 Report No. 5, University of Edinburgh, U.K., 1996.

[Schumacher95] R. Schumacher, M. Hardzinski, and A. Schwartz, "Increasing the Usability of Interactive Voice Response Systems: Research and Guidelines for Phone-Based Interfaces," in *Human Factors*, Vol. 37 (2), 1995, pp. 251-264.

[Schwartz93] A. Schwartz and M. Hardzinski, *Ameritech Phone-Based User Interface Standards and Design Guidelines*. Ameritech Services, Inc., Human Factors Group, Hoffman Estates, IL, 1993.
(http://www.ameritech.com/corporate/testtown/library/standard/std-pbix.html)

[Scott90] B. Scott and B. Balentine, "Reducing the Distinction between Speaker Dependence and Speaker Independence," *Proceedings IEEE MidCon '90*, Dallas, TX, September 1990.

[Shneiderman97] B. Shneiderman, *Designing the User Interface, Third Edition*. Addison-Wesley, Reading, MA, 1997.

[Stanton88] B. Stanton, *Robust Recognition of Loud and Lombard Speech in the Fighter Cockpit Environment*. Ph.D. dissertation, Purdue University, 1988.

[Stein77] S. Stein, *Calculus and Analytic Geometry*. McGraw-Hill Book Company, New York, NY, 1977.

[Strunk79] W. Strunk and E. White, *The Elements of Style, Third Edition*. Macmillan Publishing, New York, 1979.

[TARP95] *Key Factors to Successful Implementation and Acceptance of Automated Response Systems. 1995 Benchmarking Results*. Technical Assistance Research Programs, Inc., Arlington, VA, 1995.

[TARP97] *1996 Automated Response System—Benchmark Study—North American Results*. Technical Assistance Research Programs, Inc., Arlington, VA, 1997.

[Tavris98] C. Tavris, "The Paradox of Gender," in *Scientific American*, October 1998, pp. 126–128.

[Tufte83] E. Tufte, *The Visual Display of Quantitative Information*. Graphics Press, Cheshire, CT, 1983.

[Tufte90] E. Tufte, *Envisioning Information*. Graphics Press, Cheshire, CT, 1990.

[Tufte97] E. Tufte, *Visual Explanations*. Graphics Press, Cheshire, CT, 1997.

[VCS91] *Designing Speech Recognition Applications*. Technical reference manual, Voice Processing Corporation [now Philips Speech Processing], Dallas, TX, 1991.

[Virzi92] R. Virzi, "Refining The Test Phase Of Usability Evaluation: How Many Subjects Is Enough?", in *Human Factors*, Vol. 34, 457-468, 1992.

[Weinschenk00] S. Weinschenk, and D. Barker, *Designing Effective Speech Interfaces*. John Wiley and Sons, New York, NY, 1983.

[Yankelovich95] N. Yankelovich, G. Levow, and M. Marx, "Designing Speech Acts: Issues in Speech User Interfaces," in *Proceedings of the CHI '95 Conference on Human Factors in Computing Systems*, Denver, CO, 1995, ACM Press.

[Young96] S. Young, "A Review of Large-Vocabulary Continuous-Speech Recognition," in *IEEE Signal Processing Magazine*, Vol. 13 (5), September, 1996.

Other Standards

The following is a sampling of organizations, standards, and guidelines for further reading and reference. These are derived from [Buie99]. See that article for a discussion of these standards and their relevance to product development, usability testing, and the HCI community.

National and International

International Organization for Standardization (ISO), (http://www.iso.ch/), especially ISO 9241, *Ergonomic Requirements for Office Work with Visual Display Terminals*, (http://www.iso.ch/cate/cat.html [search on ISO 9241]).

American National Standards Institute (ANSI), (http://www.ansi.org/).

British Standards Institution (BSI), (http://www.bsi-global.com/index.html).

Human Factors and Ergonomics Society (HFES), (http://hfes.org/), especially HFES-200, *Ergonomics of Software User Interfaces* (in process).

National Institute of Standards and Technology (NIST) (http://www.nist.gov/speech/tests/index.htm).

Military and Government

MIL-STD-1472D, *Human Engineering Design Criteria for Military Systems, Equipment and Facilities*, (http://tecnet0.jcte.jcs.mil:9000/htdocs/teinfo/directives/soft/humeng.html).

MIL-STK-1472D [a HyperCard stack version of the above standard], (ftp://ftp.cis.ohio-state.edu/pub/hci/1472).

ESD-TR-86-278, *Guidelines for Designing User Interface Software*, [developed in 1986 for the US Air Force by the MITRE Corporation] (ftp://ftp.cis.ohio-state.edu/pub/hci/Guidelines/).

Industry

Apple Computer Corp., *Macintosh Human Interface Guidelines*, (http://developer.apple.com/techpubs/mac/HIGuidelines/HIGuidelines-2.html).

IBM, *Common User Access* (CUA), (http://www.ibm.com/ibm/hci/designer/docs/cua.html).

IBM, *HCI Guidelines*, (http://www.ibm.com/IBM/HCI/guidelines/guidelines.html).

Glossary

Accent The cumulative auditory effects of those features of a person's pronunciation which identify where he is from, regionally or socially. The linguistics literature emphasizes that the term refers to pronunciation only, and is thus distinct from dialect, which refers to grammar and vocabulary as well [Crystal85]. *Contrast with* **Dialect**.

Active Vocabulary The valid utterances allowed by the speech recognition engine at a given point in the application. Utterances represented in the active vocabulary are referred to as legal speech. *See* **Grammar.**

Active Voice A sentence construction in which the subject performs the action represented by the verb, e.g., This store gives refunds." *Contrast with* **Passive Voice**.

Alphanumeric Data represented as an unpronounceable grouping of alphabetic and numeric characters. Although the grouping may exhibit order and structure, it must be spoken as a continuous string of letters and numbers, as opposed to phonetically like a word.

Anthropo-morphism The attribution of human qualities to non-humans or things. In this text, the term refers to applications that are expected to verbally interact like humans in a social context. Note that anthropomorphism is what *users* experience. Personification is what *designers* do to create anthropomorphic interfaces. *Contrast with* **Personification.** *See* **Colloquial Speech.**

Attention Word A vocabulary word that is used to "get the attention" of a speech recognition system—that is, to switch the application from a waiting or standby state to a task-oriented listening state. *Contrast* with **Gatekeeper**.

Avatar Formally defined as "…an incarnation in human form; an embodiment (as of a concept or philosophy) often in a person; a variant phase or version of a continuing basic entity…" [Merrium-Webster93]. In multimedia applications, an avatar is a persona in the form of an animated character, usually displayed on a web page, that moves and talks. In some telephony applications, the voice talent for the voice portal or VRU is also used for the avatar on the corporate web site.

Back Channel A sound such as "mm-hmmm" or "huh" that is uttered spontaneously **by the listener** in conversational speech. The utterance is not a legal "word" in the sense of having a specific meaning. Such sounds often occur in human conversation as a social behavior—aimed at encouraging the other party to continue—and are not intended to indicate a change in turn. But such paralinguistic speech causes problems with ASR, including false acceptance with barge-in systems. *Contrast with* **Disfluency.**

Barge-In The ability to speak to a telephony speech application and be recognized in the presence of spoken machine output. This requires the use of echo cancellation technology to subtract the delayed machine output from the incoming data stream, allowing the VRU to detect and recognize what was spoken. Barge-in changes the turn-taking characteristics of the application. Alternatively referred to as "cut-through," "talk-over," and "talk-through." *See* **Echo Cancellation** *and* **Full Duplex**. *Contrast with* **Speak after Beep**.

Call Abandon A term typically used when the caller hangs up on a ring no answer or when on hold. In VRU applications with speech recognition, this definition is extended to include hang ups when the person is first prompted to speak.

Cardinal Number A number that is used in simple counting to indicate quantity or size (e.g., "one, three, sixteen"). *Contrast with* **Ordinal Number**. *See* **Numeric** *and* **Super-Numeric**.

Chunking Organizing data into appropriately-sized units that fall within the information-processing capabilities of users [Miller56].

Coarticulation The coloration (change in sound) of a phoneme as a result of the influence of its neighbors. Because the vocal tract is in a constant state of motion during speech, the trajectory of the articulators—lips, tongue, and related structures—is different as it moves from one phone to another. The resulting sound may be an allophonic variation—the change in /p/ as in "pin" when preceded by /s/ as in "spin"—or may result in the substitution of an entirely different phoneme—the replacement of the second /d/ in "Did you..." with /j/ as in "Dijou." Coarticulation between words can lead to the insertion of an additional phoneme that does not belong to either word—as in the /y/ in "three eight." Coarticulation is a major contributor to the variability of phones and is one of the attributes of human speech that makes continuous speech recognition difficult.

Colloquial Speech
An informal conversational speaking style, sometimes mimicking friendly or human-like interactions. It also refers to common and everyday usage of a term that does not conform to a rigorous formal definition, but rather is characteristic of familiar and informal conversation.

Concatenation
The technique of joining together two or more objects into a single larger object. In the context of synthesis, prerecorded phones are concatenated and smoothed to create intelligible syllables and words. In the context of audio messages for IVR, multiple phrase recordings are played one after another to create the appearance of complete sentences or data sequences. *See* **Phone, Phoneme,** *and* **Synthesized Speech.**

Confidence Level
A value derived from the scores produced by the speech recognition engine. A good match between the spoken utterance and the recognized words will have a high confidence level. *See **n-Best**, **Rejection**,* *and* **Scores.**

Continuous Recognition
An approach to speech recognition in which spoken words are not required or assumed to be separated by intervening pauses. Recognizing continuous input entails both properly segmenting the spoken input into individual words and properly classifying phonemes that are highly colored by coarticulation. These two challenges make continuous recognition less accurate and more compute intensive than discrete recognition. *Contrast with* **Discrete Recognition.** *See* **Coarticulation** *and* **Segmentation.**

Cut-Through
See **Barge-In.**

Declarative
A statement or declaration. A sentence structure that is typically used to provide instructions in the application. *Contrast with* **Imperative** *and* **Interrogative.**

Deletion
In continuous recognition, an error in which input is improperly segmented—causing two words to be recognized as one (e.g., "283" becomes "23"). *Contrast with* **Deletion and Substitution.** *See* **Rejection** *and* **Segmentation.**

Dialect
A regionally or socially distinctive variety of language, identified by a particular set of words or grammatical structures. Spoken dialects are usually associated with a distinctive pronunciation, or accent [Crystal85]. *Contrast with* **Accent.**

Dialogue Component
A term used in the industry standard VoiceXML specification to describe reusable dialogues that are designed to accomplish a

specific task. A dialogue component (DC) attempts to quickly and reliably extract a specific piece of information from the user. It contains its own error-recovery methods and operates independently of the application. Examples of dialogue components include credit card number entry, navigating an *n*-best list, scheduling a time for an appointment, as well as simpler sub-dialogues such as yes-no questions.

Digit String   A type of numeric data in which digits are spoken individually in sequence. The number 7227, for example, is spoken "seven two two seven." The digits may be spoken as discrete units or may be co-articulated as a single utterance, but there is always the same number of spoken words as there are digits in the string. The term applies both to numbers spoken by the user and to data presented by the machine. *Contrast with* **Natural Numbers** *and* **Super-Numeric**. *See* **Alphanumeric** *and* **Numeric**.

Directed Dialogue   *See* **Machine-Driven**.

Discrete Recognition   An approach to speech recognition in which each legal utterance must begin and end with a short silence. *Contrast with* **Continuous Recognition**.

Disfluency   A grunt, breath noise, or sound such as "umh" or "er" that is uttered spontaneously **by the talker** in conversational speech. The utterance is not a legal "word" in the sense of having a specific meaning. Such sounds often occur in human conversation as a social behavior—aimed at acquiring or keeping a turn to speak—and are not intended to convey meaning. The term also refers to false starts and stutters—speech behaviors that are often associated with turn-taking cues. Such paralinguistic speech causes many problems with ASR applications, including deletion, false rejection, or substitution errors. *Contrast with* **Back Channel**.

DTMF   Dual Tone Multiple Frequency. The so-called "touch tones" of the contemporary telephone keypad. In this text, the term is also used—somewhat incorrectly—to refer to keypresses in general, including wireless networks that do not actually use DTMF for signaling. This is not really misleading, however, as practitioners who develop VRU applications are almost universally experienced with DTMF interface methods. Note that "DTMF" is preferred as the generic term over "touch tone," which was once reserved as an AT&T trademark.

DTMF Prompt   A standard method for prompting the user of a DTMF-only application. The DTMF prompt presents an application function in terms meaningful to the user followed by a corresponding user action in terms meaningful to the machine: *To hear your messages, press one.*"

Duty Cycle   A metric to determine the percentage of time the user is speaking relative to the call duration. For example, if the user were to speak for 10 seconds in a 100-second call, the duty cycle would be 10%. This metric is useful for ensuring sufficient speech recognition resources. Alternatively referred to as the "Speech Density" of the application.

Echo Cancellation   The ability to cancel the near-side and far-side echo of the machine prompt. The echo is removed from the user's speech, and the processed speech signal is passed to the speech recognizer. This enables barge-in to be used in the application. *See* **Far End Echo** *and* **Near End Echo.**

Endpointer   A process responsible for detecting the onset and offset (coda) of user speech. Some recognition engines wait for the endpointer to finish before attempting to recognize the utterance. More often, the recognizer runs concurrently with endpointing. Note that in some architectures, the endpointer runs as a separate thread on the client, while the recognition engine runs on a shared resource that resides on the server. These architectural differences affect latency, duty cycle, and barge-in options.

Enrollment   *See* **Training**.

Erlangs   A unit of traffic density for telephone systems related to the average number of simultaneous connections observed per measurement period.

Error Amplification   A condition in which an application error (typically associated with recognition or barge-in) causes subsequent errors. Sometimes this is due to a state error: user input is illegal for the current state due to errors in some previous state. Other times, a recognition error leads to a change in user speech, resulting in additional errors. Such problems often lead to a "runaway" condition that frustrates the user. To avoid this, the application should detect multiple errors, providing the user with the ability to guide the application back to some previous state. *See* **State Error, Error Recovery,** *and* **Turn Taking.**

Error Recovery   Interactive behavior aimed at correcting a past error rather than moving ahead to the next state. Some errors are detected by the recognizer or application, leading to machine-initiated error recovery. However, errors often occur without the knowledge of the application. The user must initiate the recovery of these errors. Good error recovery strategies are consistent across the application and are not verbose. *See* **Error Amplification.**

False Acceptance
An error in which illegal speech or noise is recognized. In discrete recognition this occurs when out-of-vocabulary input (speech, grunts, breath noises, or background noises) is classified as a legal vocabulary word. In continuous recognition, the problem occurs when input is improperly segmented—causing one word to be recognized as multiple words (e.g., "three" becomes "3 + e"). This latter error is more appropriately called an insertion error. *Contrast with* **Deletion and Substitution**. *See* **Rejection** *and* **Segmentation**.

False Rejection
An error in which a valid utterance has not been recognized. *See* **Rejection**. *Contrast with* **False Acceptance** *and* **Substitution**.

Far End Echo
Echo that occurs at the user's end of the circuit (relative to the VRU). *Contrast with* **Near End Echo.**

Feedback
See **Prompt.**

Feed-Forward Prompting
A term introduced in this text to refer to a prompt that is aimed at coaching the user to present additional tokens. The prompt structure is intended to encourage NL input speech without requiring repetition of tokens already recognized.

First Person
Refers to the sentence structure of spoken machine output. Unless the voice interface uses an anthropomorphic design, spoken machine output should avoid the first person (either in the form "I" or "We"). *See* **Anthropomorphic.**

Forced Prompt
A prompt that the user cannot interrupt and must hear in its entirety. Full duplex systems typically disable barge-in during the period that the prompt is playing. Often used to convey important legal information or messages.

Full Duplex
Applications that allow the machine to speak and listen at the same time. Specifically, the machine is equipped with barge-in. *Contrast with* **Half Duplex.**

Gatekeeper
A quiescent application state that is awaiting a specific attention word. In a gatekeeper state, the application is constantly recognizing, but does not perform any action until the "gate is unlocked" by the attention word. A gatekeeper is useful for ignoring extraneous conversation and background noise during extended waits—for example while the user is getting a credit card number or bill statement. *Contrast with* **Attention Word**.

Goal-Oriented   A model for user interface design in which the interaction focuses on user goals rather than user speech. Sometimes referred to as "task-oriented," this model should be viewed as complementary with and not contradictory to the objectives of a speech-driven application.

Goat   An user for whom the speech recognition system performs poorly for no obvious reason. Goats experience consistent as opposed to anomalous recognition errors. *Contrast with* **Sheep.**

Grammar   The ordered relationship of words within an utterance. Natural language speech recognition uses the grammar—typically specified using Backus-Naur form (BNF) or a similar symbolic notation—to analyze spoken input in terms of legal transitions from one word to the next. Writing the grammar for a sophisticated application is complex, and is usually done by or in close cooperation with the speech vendor.

Half Duplex   Applications that do **not** allow the machine to speak and listen at the same time. Since the user cannot interrupt the machine, half-duplex designs must give the user frequent opportunities to speak. *Contrast with* **Full Duplex.**

Imperative   A sentence structure used to expresses a clear and unambiguous command or request. The imperative form implies that the user is expected to speak in response to the action represented by the verb. *Contrast with* **Declarative** *and* **Interrogative.**

Inflection   An alteration of the pitch or tone of voice, for example an upward inflection on the last word of a sentence. Such an upward inflection often implies a question. *See* **Pitch.**

Insertion   In continuous recognition, an error in which input is improperly segmented—causing one word to be recognized as multiple words (e.g., "three" becomes "3 + e"). *Contrast with* **Deletion and Substitution.** *See* **Rejection** *and* **Segmentation.**

Interrogative   A sentence structure that asks a question. Prompts that elicit a clear and unambiguous response (such as "yes" or "no") are the most common example, but other forms of interrogative spoken machine output can be constructed. Questions which solicit a broad or unpredictable range of responses should be avoided (e.g., *"How old are you?"* "I'll be 65 in July."). *Contrast with* **Imperative** *and* **Declarative.**

Interactive Voice Response (IVR)   IVR has historically referred to a DTMF-based application, making voice response unit (VRU) the preferred term for the host computer. However, an IVR system can be viewed synonymously with a VRU. *See* **VRU.**

Key Ahead   The ability to enter DTMF for the next state before the application has requested it. This feature is appealing to expert users. For DTMF-based applications, it is unlikely that the user can enter information faster than the machine can change states, so input need not be queued. In "key through," the DTMF input is entered while the prompt is playing—stopping spoken machine output. In either case the machine proceeds to the next state based on DTMF input. Sometimes referred to as "dial ahead" and "dial through." *Contrast with* **Talk Ahead.**

Landmark   Feedback given to users to indicate their current menu, mode, or state. A landmark can also serve as a prompt, consisting of the landmark itself—either a tone or short phrase—followed by a list of allowed actions, e.g., *"Main menu <beep>, say one of the following..." See* **Prompt.**

Logging   Storing events during application execution. Logged data may include user actions, application states, and recognized words. Voice logging refers to storing the recorded utterances.

Lombard Speech   The specific distortions of the vocal tract—and hence the resulting acoustical signal—caused by speaking while concurrently hearing speech, noise, or both. The effect is pronounced in extremely noisy environments, but can influence speech recognizers in a subtle way when the user attempts to speak over a machine prompt.

Look and Feel   A characterization of the application's user interface to include the subjective reaction of users and observers as they interact with the application. A consistent look and feel across the enterprises' VRU applications provides branding and allows users to transfer knowledge and skills.

Machine-Driven   A term used to refer to directed dialogues that prompt the user step-by-step through an application. DTMF applications adopt this model by convention. Pick-list applications—although allowing the user to speak a fund name or other large-vocabulary entry—are also machine-driven in structure. *Contrast with* **User-Driven**. *See* **Pick-List** *and* **Mixed Initiative**.

Menu Flattening   Reducing the vertical depth of a menu hierarchy or other tree structure by allowing more elements at each level—in effect making the structure more horizontal. DTMF menus restrict each node of the tree (menu) to at most twelve items—one for each key on the telephone keypad. Although speech interfaces can support more items in a menu, this increases the memory burden on users, who must now remember more items within a given state. True menu flattening usually entails a shift to natural language (NL) dialogues. Typically, NL multiple-token utterances allow a single spoken input to specify many or all of the required elements for a desired user action. This results in direct access to the terminals of the tree—in effect "flattening" the menu hierarchy. *See* **Natural Language, Terminal,** *and* **Token.**

Mixed Initiative

A dialogue in which interactions are sometimes initiated by the user and sometimes by the machine. Mixed-initiative dialogues often introduce complexity in terms of prompt phrasing and turn taking. For example, users may initiate an unexpected turn when the machine is directing the dialogue—a behavior that can lead to state errors. See Guideline 6.3.2.1 and Section 6.3.5 for examples. *Contrast with* **Machine-Driven** *and* **User-Driven.**

Mixed Modality

Systems that simultaneously enable speech and DTMF input.

Mnemonic

Any device that aids memory. In VRU applications, a shortcut designed so that it is easy to remember. For example, "help" has a mnemonic equivalent of *H, or *4 on the keypad. A consistent mnemonic for "repeat" might be *R.

n-Best

The top "n" list of recognition results, sometimes called "hypotheses." The best match ($n=1$) is usually the correct response to the user's spoken input. However, the application may determine that this response is illogical based on context. Perhaps the user has recently refused this choice, or perhaps the input does not correlate well with other task-related information. It is also possible that the user has indicated an error by backing up or canceling. In either case, the application may offer the second or third hypothesis as part of an error-correction dialogue. In some cases, it may even be worthwhile to allow the user to select directly from the n-best list, much like a menu-selection activity. The maximum value of n is set by the application, but recognizers may return fewer than n choices.

Natural Language (NL)

A term used differently by various industry professionals. To many (and in this text), NL speech recognition allows continuous input, multiple-token sentences, and rejection of disfluencies. To others, the term implies intelligence and social awareness, application "personality," and other subjective concepts.

Natural Language Parser

A parser that takes the natural language output of the recognizer and extracts the tokens from this text. The goal is to reduce the effort required for the application to extract relevant work-oriented actions or data from the input utterance.

Natural Language Prompt

A prompt or prompting strategy that elicits spoken input aimed at making the most accurate and efficient use of the recognizer. Speech recognition in general—and natural language in particular—do not benefit from traditional DTMF prompting methods. This means that guidelines for new prompting methods must be devised and tested.

Natural Numbers

A way of referring to numeric data in which digit groupings affect the spoken input. The number 7227, for example, may be spoken as "seven thousand two hundred twenty seven," or may be divided into the doublet, "seventy-two, twenty-seven." Because natural numbers may use a different number of utterances to represent the same number of digits, the possible permutations are greater than with simple digit strings. The term applies both to numbers spoken by the user and to data presented by the machine. *Contrast with* **Digit String** *and* **Super-Numeric**. *See* **Alphanumeric** *and* **Numeric**.

Near End Echo

Echo that occurs at the VRU end of the circuit (closest to the speech recognizer). *Contrast with* **Far End Echo.**

Numeric

Any data exchanged between the user and machine that contains numbers. Numeric data may consist of simple digit or alphanumeric strings, and may also include more complex representations of cardinal and ordinal numbers as with dates, times, dollar amounts, and similar information. Note that numeric vocabularies often contain non-numeric words such as "point," "January," or "o'clock." *See* **Alphanumeric**, **Cardinal**, **Ordinal**, *and* **Super-Numeric**.

Ordinal Number

A number that designates position in an ordered sequence of items (e.g., "first, second, third"). *Contrast with* **Cardinal Number**. *See* **Numeric** *and* **Super-Numeric**.

Out of Grammar (OOG)

An utterance that is not legal as specified by the grammar for a given application state. The utterance may contain an invalid word or invalid word ordering. The input may also be non-speech noise. The term OOG is reserved for grammar-driven recognizers such as those used by natural language technologies. *Contrast with* **Out of Vocabulary Word**. *See* **Rejection of Illegal Input**.

Out of Vocabulary Word (OVW)

A word or non-speech noise that does not belong to the active vocabulary for a given application state. The term OVW is usually reserved for discrete or continuous-digit recognizers. *Contrast with* **Out-of-grammar**. *See* **Rejection of Illegal Input**.

Passive Voice

A sentence structure in which the subject receives the action represented by the verb, e.g., "Refunds are given by this store." *Contrast with* **Active Voice**.

Pattern Matcher   Typically referred to as the speech recognition engine, the pattern matcher compares the unknown input speech against its pre-stored vocabulary (which models the "patterns" that distinguish one word from another).

Peak Clipping   A condition in which the peak amplitude of the speech signal exceeds the dynamic range of the recording device. When this occurs with spoken machine output, it results in audible distortion. When it occurs with the input signal, it results in degraded speech quality, which may impact the performance of speech recognition.

Persona   Formally defined as "… an individual's social façade or front that … reflects the role in life the individual is playing; a character in a fictional presentation (as a novel or play) …" [Merrium-Webster93]. In this context, the personality traits projected by a voice portal or VRU application. A persona is often but not always a fully personified character. *Contrast with* **Avatar**, **Personality**, **Personalization**, *and* **Personification**.

Personal Assistant   *See* **Virtual Assistant**.

Personality   Formally defined as "… the complex of characteristics that distinguishes an individual or a nation or group; *esp*: the totality of an individual's behavioral and emotional characteristics …" [Merrium-Webster93]. In this context, the traits projected by a voice portal or VRU application that lead the user to form opinions on what it is and how it works. *Contrast with* **Avatar**, **Persona**, **Personalization**, *and* **Personification**.

Personalization   The use of data about a user to modify the behavior of an application—in this context, a telephony application. For example, personal preferences entered by a user at a web page may be applied to a voice portal to change the presentation ordering, style, or other application attributes. Personal data may come from a corporate database, a form previously filled by the user, or other sources. *Contrast with* **Personification**.

Personification   The deliberate intention to create a design that exhibits lifelike, human-like traits with the goal of evoking anthropomorphic responses from human observers (users). In the context of VRU applications, personified interfaces exhibit "personalities" with distinct identities and unique behavioral idiosyncrasies. Users, in turn, respond by anthropomorphizing the application, making unconscious assumptions about its emotions, intelligence, and social awareness. Note that anthropomorphism is what *users* do. Personification is what *designers* do to create anthropomorphic interfaces. *Contrast with* **Anthropomorphism**. *See* **Personality**.

Phone
A specific acoustical instance or realization of a phoneme—that is, a speech sound considered without reference to its status as a perceived component of language. Unlike a phoneme, a phone has a physical manifestation. In speech recognition, the term is used not only to refer to the acoustical properties of phonemes being uttered by a user, but also to the mathematical (statistical) models of those sounds that are used to represent and recognize human speech.

Phoneme
The smallest linguistic unit that can convey a distinction in meaning, as the "*m*" in *mat* and the "*b*" *in bat* in English. Unlike phones, phonemes do not exist as a physical entity. Instead, phonemes are idealized abstractions of phones, based on human perception. As physical objects, phones vary considerably from one instance to the next. Thus every occurrence of a phoneme (or its variants—called allophones) has different acoustical properties. *Contrast with* **Phone**.

Phonetic Recognition
A speech recognition technology based on models of phones rather than entire words. Due to acoustical variation between phones, classifying each instance of a given phone into its corresponding phoneme is a challenge for a recognizer. Although vocabularies constructed with phonetic descriptions are inherently more flexible than word-specific vocabularies, they suffer from limitations that make word-specific technologies more practical in certain applications. *Contrast with* **Word-Specific Recognition.**

Pick-List
A colloquial term referring to hybrid DTMF-plus-speech applications. In this approach, the user navigates through menus with DTMF. At a juncture for choosing from a large list of words, the user is prompted with a beep and then speaks the desired word. Typical large vocabulary lists include stock names, cities, or employees in a company. The approach solves a major problem of DTMF interfaces—picking from large-vocabulary lists. These hybrid solutions are useful, but cannot be viewed as speech-driven in the sense used in this text.

Pitch
The subjective perception of frequency. In speech, the pitch of an utterance is caused by the periodic excitation of the vocal tract by the opening and closing of the vocal folds of the larynx. This periodic excitation is called the fundamental pitch or fun-

damental frequency.

Poisson Distribution A probabilistic distribution based on a mean with a known value. The distribution provides a numeric value in a given unit of time. For example, the number of cars passing through an intersection during one light cycle, or the number of recognition requests at any given second on a 96-port VRU.

Prompt Spoken machine output that indicates it is time for user input. Prompts are turn-taking cues that cause the user to speak or enter input. They may also (optionally) convey information about what input is valid in that state. In this text, *prompt* is differentiated from *instructions*—which give information about the application interface, *help*—which is a separate state for coaching the user, *feedback*—which informs the user about the status of an immediately preceding event, and *application data*—which presents application-specific data. The use of "announcement" and "message" in VRU applications are ambiguous and are avoided in this text.

Prosody Those attributes of speech that are not related to meaning but instead convey the intent, expectation, and emotion of the talker. Prosodic characteristics include intonation—sometimes called inflection or pitch contour—as well as stress, phrasing, rate of speech, and meter.

Provisioning Supplying the necessary capacity for a system. In this text, it refers to supplying sufficient hardware and bandwidth to service a given call volume with demanded VRU and speech recognition resources.

Rejection A condition in which the recognizer has detected input but confidence in the result is low. Note that some recognizers reject this input automatically—providing no recognition candidates for the application to evaluate. Most recognizers, appropriately, report the condition and then leave it to the application to decide whether and how to reject the input. In either case, specific speech recognition thresholds can usually be adjusted to modulate the rejection rate.

There are two types of rejection: either the input is considered illegal (OOG) or two or more words are considered similar to each other (inter-word). Distinguishing one from the other is a major challenge. It is important, however, as error recovery methods differ between the two—one case leads to a re-prompt, while the other triggers a yes-no query. Because of the confusion between these two types, they are discussed in individual glossary entries below.

See **Spurious Error**, **Deletion, Rejection,** *and* **Substitution**.

Rejection (Inter-Word)

A condition in which the recognizer has returned two or more candidates with similar scores—suggesting that that they cannot be clearly distinguished. Words with similar scores have a higher probability of being substituted. Although the likelihood is high that the input is legal speech, the recognizer cannot risk choosing between the two. The purpose of inter-word rejection is to detect word-pair confusions that may represent substitution errors, as rejections are easier to recover than substitutions. A common example is the English digit pair *five* and *nine*.

Most recognizers return *n*-best candidate responses for disambiguation. The typical machine response to inter-word rejection is to ask a yes-no question about the first candidate (*n*=1). On a "no" response, a query on the second candidate (*n*=2) is not uncommon. Substitution rates can be reduced by 50% or more when inter-word rejection strategies are implemented. The strategy has a price, however—an increase in false rejection. This type 2 error occurs when there is low confidence in a word that proves later to be the one spoken by the user.

Rejection of (OOG)

A condition in which the recognizer or application determines that input is illegal in the sense that the input does not belong to the active vocabulary or grammar. Some recognizers return a "no response" (null); others return the condition explicitly as OVW or OOG. Still others infer the condition from recognition scores or allow the application to do so. The typical machine response to OOG rejection is to prompt the user to produce new input. Note that incorrectly classifying legal speech as OOG is called false rejection.

Scores

Values computed by the recognizer for all hypothesized spoken input at each processing interval (typically 10–25 ms). As speech processing proceeds, these scores accumulate for each hypothesis. At the conclusion of user speech, recognizers return the score to the application along with (typically) the *n-best* matches (those with the best scores). Some recognition engines also calculate additional scores or confidence levels—numbers which are scaled or normalized—from these raw score values. *See* **Confidence Level.**

Second Person

Refers to the sentence structure of spoken machine output. The second person (you), which is both singular and plural, is often implied—especially in imperative sentence structures. *Contrast with* **First Person.**

Segmentation   The process of analyzing a stream of spoken input to identify the boundaries that separate words. This is easier said than done because continuous human speech includes coarticulation effects that complicate segmentation. In the digit string "two-eight-two," for example, both the beginning and end of the embedded "eight" are strongly transformed by the surrounding words. It is not unusual for the "eight" to be **deleted** especially among fast speakers. Deletion errors are usually caused by the failure of the segmentation process to detect the boundary between the end of "two" and the beginning of "eight," and between the end of "eight" and the beginning of "two." *See* **Deletion** *and* **Insertion**.

Sheep   An individual for whom the speech recognition system consistently performs well. Note that sheep still experience occasional errors, but do not suffer the stubborn and repeated errors that plague "goats." *Contrast with* **Goat.**

Speak After Beep   A colloquial term used in this text in conjunction with a speech recognition interface that is half duplex (no barge-in). Regardless of whether the recognition technology is discrete, continuous, or natural language, the primary turn-taking attribute of waiting for the beep defines the look and feel of the interface. Note that there are half-duplex designs that do not use beeps. Even in such cases, however, the result is a directed dialogue in which the machine explicitly hands each turn over to the user through some kind of formal cue. In response to such cues, the user then speaks. These designs may thus be described as "speak after the virtual beep."

Speaker Dependent   A speech recognition engine that is trained by, and optimized for, a specific speaker. Other speakers who attempt to use the system may incur significantly more recognition errors. It is a common misconception that such a system "won't recognize" other speakers—implying that a speaker dependent engine somehow identifies the speaker who trained it. In reality, some randomly-selected users may achieve performance identical to that of the training speaker, while others will experience high substitution rates. *Contrast with* **Speaker Independent**.

Speaker Independent   A speech recognition engine that is designed to classify spoken input according to features universal to all speakers. Unlike speaker-dependent systems, the speaker does not need to conduct a time-consuming training procedure. However, performance is generally poorer than with speaker-dependent recognizers. This is because examples of a specific user's speech cannot be made available to the engine in advance. Speaker independent systems rely on collected samples of recorded human speech from which statistical models based on the user population are estimated. The amount of deviation of these samples from the actual user population is one primary determiner of recognition accuracy. *Contrast with* **Speaker Dependent.**

Spoke-too-Soon A turn taking error that can occur when the application is not barge-in enabled. After playing a prompt the application engages the recognizer. Speech is detected immediately. Either the user began speaking too soon or background noise was detected as speech. Although often treated as a recognition error, it is in fact a turn-taking anomaly, easily recovered by effective half-duplex designs. *See* **Speak after Beep.**

Spurious Error The general term for the non-interpretable class of errors in which the recognizer does not return any recognized result. Spurious errors include spoke-too-soon, OVW, OOG, null, and non-speech timeouts. This is in contrast to insertion, false rejection, and substitution errors where recognized words are reported (albeit sometimes in error). Recovering spurious errors requires more sophisticated recovery strategies, as yes-no questions are precluded by the absence of a recognition hypothesis.

State A software application is often conceived as a series of execution steps or "states." A state is like a context—within a given state, all conditions remain roughly the same. When the machine moves from one state to another—what is called a "state transition"—conditions then change. In a speech application, one of the major changes from state to state is the set of legal words, as specified by the active vocabulary or grammar. Bear in mind that the machine executes many different actions within a state—for example, retrieving a prompt from memory, playing the prompt, invoking recognition, correcting errors, etc. But the basic conditions—the context for capturing and interpreting input—remain the same until the state changes. From the user's perspective, relevant states are those in which the machine is soliciting and waiting for user input and then using that input to determine when and how to perform a transition to a new state. *See* **State Errors, State Transitions,** *and* **Turn Taking.**

State Errors In a successful interaction, the user and the machine begin in the same initial state, make transitions to new states based on interactions, and terminate the application when the user hangs up. State errors occur when either user input or machine interpretation experience errors. As a consequence, the user (cognitively) and the machine make transitions to different states. Users that are not synchronized with the current machine state tend to produce illegal speech. *See* **Error Amplification**, **State**, **State Transitions**, *and* **Turn Taking**.

State Transition

State transitions usually occur after user input. In some cases, e.g., when background noise is falsely accepted as speech, the user may not be aware that a state transition has occurred. *See* **Error Amplification**, **State, State Errors,** *and* **Turn Taking**.

Statistical Language Model (SLM)

A speech recognition technology based on N-gram grammars— word pairs (bigrams) or triplets (trigrams) that are weighted statistically according to frequency of occurrence in certain application domains. A large corpus of recorded speech is required to train the SLM. In conjunction with a classifier, an SLM system can model utterances that have not been observed in the training corpus, providing a natural broadening of grammar coverage versus closed finite state (NL) technologies. *See* **Natural Language**, **Grammar**.

Substitution

An error in which the recognizer returns a different word than the one spoken. Confidence is high, preventing the error from being detected. One word has *substituted* for another. *See* **Rejection**. *Contrast with* **Deletion** *and* **Insertion**.

Super-Numeric

A spoken representation of data that include numbers of various types in conjunction with additional non-numeric words. Examples include times and dates, in which the user may speak cardinal ("five o'clock") or ordinal ("July the Fourth") numbers that are conjoined with additional words. *Contrast with* **Digit String** *and* **Natural Numbers**. *See* **Alphanumeric** *and* **Numeric**.

Synthesized Speech

Computer synthesized speech is based on letter-to-sound rules as well as phonetic and prosodic information unique to the language. Synthesized speech has much lower quality than human speech, although some techniques that concatenate recorded human speech sound very good for applications with a limited vocabulary. Synonymous with "text-to-speech."

Talk Ahead

The ability to provide spoken input for the next state before the application has requested it. This allows expert users to provide multiple commands to the system. The problem is that combination of speech endpointers, grammars, and recognition latency combine to make this a difficult feature to implement. *Contrast with* **Key Ahead**.

Terminal

The endpoint of a path through any branching structure. In branching structures—such as trees or networks—each branch constitutes a logical decision point. The sequence of decisions required to arrive at a terminal represents a *path* to that terminal. In a speech application, the user interface has accomplished its job when the application arrives at a terminal and can do work—such as placing an order, transferring funds, or booking a reservation for the user.

Token   A term that refers to the smallest unit of input that is meaningful to the application. For example, consider the input sentence, "Yeah, I'd like to buy 300 shares of IBM if you don't mind." The sentence contains 13 words. However, only certain words—*buy*, *300 shares*, *IBM*—represent data required by the application to accomplish a transaction, and so the input is said to contain three tokens. The remaining words constitute user interface overhead. Designing prompts that increase token density and minimize overhead speech is a major goal of these guidelines. Alternatively referred to as a "slot."

Training   Providing examples of speech to a recognizer for the purpose of creating or updating its models. Usually applied to speaker-dependent recognizers, the term is also used with speaker-independent technologies to describe the laboratory process of building vocabularies from pre-recorded examples of speech. Also referred to as "enrollment."

Transitive Prompt   A prompt or prompting strategy in which a transitive verb is used to solicit spoken input. A transitive verb is one that requires a direct object. For example, in the prompt, *Say "Mutual Funds,"* the intent is to elicit a repetition of the direct object from the user, thus minimizing the breadth of user responses.

Turn Taking   The protocol in which the user and machine take turns giving and receiving information. In a successful application, the user provides input, the machine responds, asks the user for additional input, and the user takes the turn back and responds. Turns pass back and forth between user and application. For barge-in enabled systems, users may interrupt the system and take their turn back at any time. *See also* **State** *and* **State Transitions.**

Usability Tests   Live tests conducted with potential users of the system in a controlled environment or laboratory. By recording the user's interaction with the system, the application developer can "shake out" the system and improve the human interface prior to deployment.

User-Driven   A term used in this text to refer to applications that allow the user to determine the pace of the dialogue and the path to terminals. User-driven dialogues require some knowledge on the part

	of the user of the application's capabilities. *Contrast with* **Machine-Driven** *and* **Mixed Initiative**.
Utterance	A single spoken event that may consist of a single word or of several words spoken continuously. Utterances also include paralinguistic sounds such as back channels or disfluencies. A background noise or other non-user sound is not an utterance—but recognizers often incorrectly detect them as such.
Virtual Assistant	A class of application—usually but not always telephone-based—that is designed to assist the user with a variety of personal or work-related information, including scheduling and appointments, screening and/or redirecting of telephone calls, controlled paging, message or memo management, and other features similar to early Personal Information Management (PIM) applications. Many virtual assistant products are becoming speech-enabled. Some but not all adopt a personified look and feel. *See* **Personification** *and* **Anthropomorphism**.
Voice Activated Dialing (VAD)	A telephone-based application that allows the user to place calls by saying the name of the person or company they want to reach. Also referred to as "name dialing." Voice dialers typically support numeric dialing as well—allowing the user to say the telephone number if a name is not available. The goal of VAD applications is hands-free operation of the telephone keypad.
Voice Portal	The portal is an entrance or gateway that allows a user to access information available on the world wide web using speech recognition over the telephone. This information often spans several data sources and can be personalized, e.g., with weather for a given zip code, selected stock quotes, sports, and news. A voice portal implies but does not require that there is an analogous web interface that aggregates the same content.
Voice Response Unit (VRU)	A VRU is a computer that has been modified to interface to telephone channels. In the past, they hosted primarily DTMF applications, although now they are the primary targets of speech recognition applications. A common synonym for VRU applications is Interactive Voice Response (IVR), which refers to an interactive DTMF application, such as call center self-service or help desk systems. *Contrast with* **Interactive Voice Response**.
Voice Talent	The individual(s) that record the spoken machine output and are in effect the "voice of the application." The voice talent is usually a trained professional that is expert in producing clear, articulate and properly-inflected speech.

VoiceXML   A standards-based language for writing applications that allow telephone access to web content. Originally developed by an industry group called the VoiceXML Forum, the language is being refined by the World Wide Web Consortium (W3C) Voice Browser Working Group [Edgar01 and Larson01].

Windowing   A turn-taking design for half-duplex systems in which a window of silence (typically a second or so) is inserted between prompts. During the window, the recognizer is active, providing frequent opportunities for the user to take a turn. For example, a menu landmark might be followed by a 1500 millisecond recognition window. If the user does not speak, the list is presented. Each menu item is separated by short (750 ms) windows, giving the user the opportunity to reclaim the turn. Windowing can give the impression of a full-duplex (barge-in) system.

Wizard of Oz (WoZ) Test   Also called a "Wizard Test." A test that allows early evaluation of a design or dialogue component prior to programming. The approach uses a trained human tester—the "wizard"—to simulate the machine side of the dialogue. WoZ tests allow the developer to make initial estimates of call duration, vocabulary words, average utterance length, prompt clarity, and similar usability attributes of the design.

Index

A

accent, 20, 39, 238, 253, 303, 365, 367
active vocabulary
    and homonyms, 194
    and OVW/OOG, 374, 378
    and state errors, 124
    and state transitions, 380
    definition of, 13, 365
    effect of turn-taking on, 118
    purpose of, 272
    to suppress error repetition, 193
    yes/no questions, 171
active voice. *See* English grammar
adaptation
    by the recognizer, 82
    by users, 274
aesthetics, 16, 295
agents
    and commanding, 264
    for multilinguality, 37
    multiple, 260
alphanumeric, 365, 368, 374, 381
Ameritech guidelines
    identify the system, 44
    let user know this is machine, 44
    machine speech loudness, 34
    machine speech quality, 33
    male voices, 35
    mixed voices, 36
    prompt design, 53
    rate of synthesized speech, 41
anthropomorphism
    argument in favor of, 261
    definition and discussion, 365, 375,
        245–47
    distinction between personification

    and, 246
    HANC introduction, 262
apologizing, 55, 249, 361
application data, 42, 65, 70, 192, 214, 377
application program interface, 179
arpeggiated. *See* musical terms
attention word. *See* gatekeeper
audio
    and sonification of widgets, 131, 357
    as a Gestalt, 131
    as feedback, 54
    as landmarks, 137
    as waiting tone, 142
    attributes of, 130
    caution, 141
    logo, 44, 129
    mixed with speech, 132
    to announce help, 142
    to recover spoke-too-soon, 123
auditory icon, 30, 129, 130, 133
authentic cadence, 138, 140
automated attendant, 180, 331
avatar, 253

B

back channel, 108, 197, 305, 306, 366,
    368, 383
background noise
    and communication theory, 361
    and error recovery, 276
    and false acceptance, 73, 74
    and false prompt cutoff, 102, 103
    and false rejection, 103
    and half-duplex systems, 281
    and Lombard speech, 104, 105
    and prompt cutoff, 107
    and recognition technology, 72

and recorded speech, 33
and rejection, 20, 22, 24, 25, 103
and spoke-too-soon conditions, 25
and vocabulary size, 76
announcements about, 60
as a cause of errors, 83
breath noise, 22
in recorded prompts, 348
obscuring effects, 85
physical properties, 33
statistical, 78–81
using to detect handset keypads, 290, 291
backing up states
and timeout, 279
and tone cues, 161, 279
as a result of barge-in, 278, 279
avoiding repeated errors, 193
by interrupting feedback, 191
by speaking, 192
cuing the user, 279
during list scanning, 162
interpreting *n*-best, 280, 373
prompting for, 44
to correct an error, 277
using DTMF, 192, 193, 194
using implicit yes-no, 170, 172
within yes-no queries, 168
words for, 279, 280
bandwidth, 36, 135, 323, 377
barge-in
stabilizing, 117
stopping prompts, 106
suppressing, 119
synonyms, 26, 366, 367
beat, 68, 69, 70, 287, 288
BHRR. *See* busy hour recognition
requests
bi-directional navigation, 161
bigrams. *See* statistical language model
blaming, 249, 313
breath noise. *See* background noise
browser, 325–42
business model
cost-saving, 17–19, 329
value-add, 17, 18, 17–19, 330
busy hour recognition requests, 317–23

C

call abandon, 310, 366
call flow, 144, 145
call routing, 240, 241, 328, 331
cancel
and endpointing, 85, 87, 88
as a command, 264, 265
disambiguating, 48, 280
for logging and analysis, 312, 313
of echo, 100, 369
prompting for, 44, 48, 122, 195, 275
recognition of, 75
specific meaning of, 280
spoken by user, 125, 264, 265, 280
to interrupt, 192, 279
uses for, 77
cardinal, 154, 366, 374, 381
chord, 140
chunking, 37, 286, 366
client, 32, 100, 323, 369
coarticulation, 366, 367, 379
colloquial speech, 95, 215, 216, 259, 260, 300, 365, 367, 376, 379
command and control, 30, 145, 146, 147, 148
concatenation, 38, 58, 67, 345, 348, 352, 354
confidence. *See* rejection
confirmation
embedded, 55, 56, 212, 214
explicit, 55
implicit, 55
consonants, 74, 80, 81, 85, 86
convergence, 95, 167, 228–33, 243, 340
corpus, 240, 241, 244, 381
cost-saving. *See* business model
coughs and throat clearing, 20, 27, 102, 108, 165, 166

D

data prompt. *See* prompt
date entry, 49
deletion. *See* speech recognition errors
dialect, 20, 72, 238, 253, 353, 365, 367
dialogue
commanding, 264, 266
components, reusable, 6, 30, 31, 138,

144, 166, 172, 174, 175, 179–82, 299, 301, 308, 333, 367
negotiating, 267
yes/no. *See* yes/no
digit string, 25, 31, 65–70, 65, 138, 149, 283–88, 368, 374, 379, 381
groupings, 65, 66, 374
digitized speech, 38, 39, 50, 99, 100
digits
super-numeric, 354
directed dialogue, 144, 147, 203, 212, 368, 372, 379
disconnect. *See* speech recognition
disconnect, when to, 276
disfluencies, 108, 109, 197, 206, 305, 306, 366, 368, 373, 383
dovetail speech, 110, 118
DTMF, 4, 105, 110, 121, 151, 188, 189, 193
and *n*-best list, 194, 195
and state errors, 13, 14
and state transitions, 13
as discussed in this book, 7, 17
backing up, 193
combined with speech, 17, 30, 160, 281, 312, 373
combined with speech, 189–92
definition of, 368
delaying the prompt, 291
distinction with speech, 4, 11, 15, 17, 20, 40, 51, 151, 154, 199, 200, 202, 203, 205, 211, 309
for confirmation, 119, 120, 187, 195, 196
for privacy, 189
help, 62, 64
ignoring noises from the use of, 290, 291
key ahead, 105, 192, 372
keypad, 4, 30, 61, 92, 122, 160, 174, 184, 186, 188, 189, 190, 194, 195, 199, 200, 275, 281, 290, 291, 294, 307, 368, 372, 373, 383
machine-driven, 372
menu navigation, 199, 200, 203, 372, 376
migrating from, 312, 323
mnemonics, 61
prior experience with, 4, 92, 151, 188,

281, 305, 310, 383
prompting, 51, 368, 374
reasons for using, 189, 190
reserved words, 53
switching over to, 174, 186, 187, 188, 274
to interrupt, 121, 122, 192, 281
using any key, 192
duty cycle, 100, 145, 318, 319, 320, 321, 324, 369

E

earcon
abstract, 130
representational, 130, 140
echo cancellation
far end, 98, 99, 116, 369, 370, 374
near end, 99, 101, 116, 369, 370, 374
either/or constructs, 163
endpointer, 26, 73, 75, 76, 78, 83, 84, 85, 86, 87, 102, 103, 105, 107, 109, 198, 199, 323, 369, 381
energy detection, 106, 107, 310
English grammar
declarative, 59, 60, 367, 371
exclamatory, 59, 60
imperative form, 28, 42, 43, 44, 47, 48, 49, 51, 54, 59, 60, 94, 163, 166, 196, 208, 211, 367, 371, 378
implied interrogative, 49, 50, 208
indicative mood, 43, 44, 264, 314
interrogative form, 47, 48, 49, 50, 53, 54, 59, 60, 196, 208, 211, 367, 371
present tense, 43
subjunctive mood, 43, 44
transitive, 52, 53, 382
voice, 42, 365, 374
enrollment. *See* training
envelope, 16, 127, 128
equalization, 35
ergonomic, 9, 16, 245, 247, 295, 363
error amplification, 14, 15, 31, 54, 102, 103, 108, 117, 172, 176, 180, 211, 249, 271, 274, 289, 290, 306, 317, 369, 380, 381
exaggerated user speech, 102, 107, 283

F

false starts. *See* turn taking
far end. *See* echo cancellation
fatal error, 188, 273, 311
feed forward. *See* prompts
feedback, 7, 9, 30, 39, 54, 55, 56, 95, 123,
    127, 128, 137, 146, 150, 152, 153,
    179, 191, 192, 193, 201, 209, 213,
    214, 215, 249, 281, 282, 306, 310,
    315, 377
female voice. *See* voices
field trial, 118, 358
first-time/only-time. *See* one-time callers
flattening. *See* menu flattening
form filling, 30, 49, 145, 146, 147, 148,
    149, 203, 208, 212, 305
found sound, 128
fricative, 74, 80
full duplex, 15, 27, 97, 99, 110, 111, 112,
    113, 114, 115, 116, 120, 132, 158,
    175, 235, 318, 319, 370, 371, 384

G

gatekeeper, 91, 245, 254, 256, 257, 267
goal-oriented query, 12, 44, 161, 179, 272
goat, 273, 276, 371, 379
grammar, 23, 24, 39, 71, 105, 106, 111,
    149, 180, 181, 193, 201, 211, 217–44,
    217

H

half duplex, 15, 27, 46, 77, 97, 110, 111,
    112, 115, 120, 121, 122, 125, 132,
    133, 136, 152, 154, 158, 175, 181,
    274, 276, 280, 281, 318, 319, 370,
    371, 379, 380, 384
HANC prototype, 255, 261, 262, 263,
    266, 267, 268, 269, 270
hands-free, 86, 102, 104, 108, 130, 383
harmonic progression, 137–40
harmony, 139, 140
help
    coach, 36, 62, 63, 142
    mode, 64
    Wizard, 64, 132
hidden menus, 112, 136, 137, 163, 164,
    165
    announcing, 136
    logos to announce, 137
HMIHY. *See* statistical language model
hot key, 185
How May I Help You?. *See* statistical
    language model

I

inflection, 48, 49, 58, 66, 67, 68, 69, 70,
    117, 153, 281, 282, 286, 287, 288,
    371, 377
insertion. *See* speech recognition errors
instructions, 42, 45, 57, 58, 59, 60, 100,
    168, 208, 214
intelligibility, 33, 34, 35, 38, 39
Interactive Voice Response, 3, 17, 35,
    133, 260, 358, 362, 371, 383
inter-word rejection. *See* rejection
intrusion. *See* speech recognition errors

K

key ahead, 105, 189, 190, 192, 372, 381
key information, where to place, 46, 47,
    117, 121, 313
keypress, keypad. *See* DTMF

L

landmarks, 112, 127, 128, 129, 131, 134,
    137, 140, 152, 153, 154, 155, 164,
    260, 372, 384
    data objects, 153
    for navigation, 154
    menu names, 153
latency, 39, 71, 98, 100, 106, 109, 110,
    317, 319, 322, 324, 369, 381
leading tone, 140
list manager, 150
logging, 31, 293, 309, 310, 313, 314, 353,
    372
logo, 64, 129, 136, 137
Lombard speech, 104, 107, 109, 362, 372
look and feel, 5, 6, 9, 10, 16, 28, 29, 31,
    35, 36, 97, 99, 133, 143, 183, 245,
    247, 248, 249, 258, 264, 271, 306,
    372, 379, 383

loudness contour. *See* envelope

M

machine initiated. *See* machine-driven
machine-centered, 254
machine-driven, 146, 147, 148, 155, 194,
    199, 205, 212, 261, 262, 263, 266,
    267, 270, 282, 368, 369, 372, 373, 382
male voice. *See* voices
marketing, 3, 16, 245, 260, 295, 309
masking, 193
mechanical, 11, 151, 153, 246, 260, 263
menu flattening, 106, 163, 199, 203, 304,
    305, 372
meter, 67, 68, 142, 359, 377
military alphabet, 289
mimicking, 52, 63, 149, 289, 303
mixed initiative, 146, 147, 203, 245, 261,
    372, 373, 382
mixed modalities, 30, 183, 190
    DTMF-centric, 185
    separate, 184
    speech-centric, 186
    switching, 185
mnemonic, 61, 92, 131, 373
model user, 37, 63, 114
monotone, 286, 287
multiple voices. *See* voices
musical terms
    arpeggiated, 140
    dominant, 137, 138, 140
    keys and key signatures, 138, 140
    seventh chord, 140
    subdominant, 137, 140
    tonic, 137, 138, 140

N

natural numbers, 65, 66, 368, 374, 381
n-best, 56, 90, 92, 160, 162, 165, 170,
    193, 194, 195, 213, 277, 280, 284,
    285, 289, 367, 373, 378
near end. *See* echo cancellation
noise. *See* background noise
noise detection
    using yes-no, 173
non-fatal errors, 273
numeric, 13, 49, 65, 66, 67, 68, 138, 180,

189, 190, 211, 283, 365, 366, 368,
374, 377, 381, 383

O

one-time callers, 110, 111, 155, 160
opening greeting, 44, 165, 187, 310
ordinal, 154, 366, 374, 381

P

parallel, 11, 17, 88, 94, 186, 260, 281
parametric, 39, 84
parrot. *See* mimicking
passive voice. *See* English grammar
pattern matcher, 375
peak clipping, 375
periodicity, 67, 68
persistence of information, 2, 11, 12
persona, 250, 251–54, 255, 256, 257,
    259, 343, 350
personal assistant. *See* virtual assistant
personal information manager, 383
Personal Information Manager, 30, 37
personalized, 246, 255
personification, 245, 246, 247, 250, 255,
    365, 375, 383
phonetic recognition, 357, 376
phrase boundary, 47
pitch, 68, 69, 70, 104, 127, 128, 135, 138,
    139, 140, 141, 142, 282, 286, 371,
    376, 377
pitch contour. *See* prosody
plagal cadence, 140
point and speak, 113, 114, 115, 157, 160,
    161, 195
Poisson distribution, 320, 377
press or say, 190, 191
professional protocols, 249
progressive disclosure, 58, 117, 146, 148
prompt
    as speaking opportunity, 155
    data, 52
    feed forward, 201, 202, 203, 208, 209,
        210, 211, 212, 213, 214, 215, 304,
        305, 312
    natural language, 272, 374
    tone, 123, 128, 133, 134, 135, 136,
        137, 139

transitive, 52, 53
turnaround, 58, 123, 124, 125
verbatim, 51, 52
prosody, 38, 69, 70, 117, 244, 309, 344, 348, 352, 377, 381
provisioning
    hardware, 28, 31, 32, 187, 310, 313, 317, 319, 320, 321, 322, 324, 377
    recognition licenses, 318, 320, 321
pseudocode, 91

Q

quasi-menu, 162
    compound question, 48

R

rate of speech, 34, 41, 67, 377
rejection
    and confidence, 55, 90, 91, 103, 107, 140, 164, 165, 166, 209, 213, 214, 280, 283, 284, 287, 291
    correct rejection, 23, 188
    definition and discussion, 20–24
    inter-word, 24, 26, 56, 74, 75, 80, 82, 84, 87, 88, 89, 90, 92, 115, 159, 165, 166, 167, 168, 170, 173, 174, 180, 181, 193, 194, 195, 256, 285, 290, 377, 378
reusability, 6, 30, 59, 144, 179, 181, 367
rhythm, 12, 33, 41, 66, 67, 70, 100, 101, 111, 125, 126, 130, 139, 141, 359
runaway conditions. *See* error amplification

S

scale, 137, 140, 263
schwa, 84, 85
searching dialogues, 149, 150, 195
secondary conditioning, 131
segmentation, 74, 367, 379
sentience, 12, 172, 174
server, 32, 100, 141, 322, 323, 369
sheep, 371, 379
signal-to-noise ratio, 33
signature sound, 128, 129
silence

and endpointing, 105
    embedded, 75, 85
    window of, 77, 112, 161, 368, 384
SLM. *See* statistical language model
sound-alike words, 73, 75, 81, 82, 84
speaker verification, 7, 81, 361
speaking rate, 41
speech behavior, 12, 89, 139, 182, 236, 258, 300
speech detection, 71, 72, 106, 109, 174
speech recognition
    continuous, 24, 71, 72, 74, 76, 197, 198, 257, 284, 285, 365, 366, 367, 368, 370, 371, 373, 374, 379
    discrete, 24, 37, 39, 71, 72, 76, 151, 152, 173, 256, 257, 284, 300, 367, 368, 370, 374, 379
    grammar, 24, 42, 137, 272, 300, 314, 319, 321, 322, 323, 324, 365, 371, 374, 378
    speaker dependent, 55, 78, 81, 82, 379
    speaker independent, 379
    when to abandon, 175
speech recognition errors
    deletion, 23, 25, 54, 74, 367, 368, 370, 371, 377, 379, 381
    false acceptance, 73, 74, 102, 103, 106, 107, 108, 109, 112, 118, 120, 149, 256, 278, 283, 300, 366
    false rejection, 13, 23, 74, 77, 103, 107, 108, 112, 117, 189, 283, 306, 368, 370, 378, 380
    insertion, 74, 256, 380
    intrusion, 74
    spoke-too-soon. *See* spoke-too-soon
    substitution, 23, 25, 40, 54, 56, 74, 75, 76, 78, 80, 82, 84, 85, 86, 87, 88, 89, 138, 168, 273, 276, 278, 280, 283, 285, 300, 366, 367, 368, 370, 371, 377, 378, 379, 380, 381
    syllable deletion, 84, 85
speech synthesis. *See* synthesized speech
spoke-too-soon, 13, 25, 26, 45, 46, 113, 115, 121, 122, 125, 136, 158, 165, 169, 170, 172, 173, 174, 181, 272, 274, 275, 276, 282, 380
    recovery, 122
spurious errors, 26, 155, 311, 380
standards

HFES-200, 9, 363
HFES-HCI, 33, 35
ISO 9241, 8, 363
state
    definition and discussion, 12–14
    machines, 12, 13
    state errors, 13, 14, 15, 40, 118, 123,
        124, 153, 172, 185, 278, 351, 369,
        380, 381
    transition, 13, 380, 381, 382
statistical artifacts, 72, 78, 79, 80, 83
statistical language model, 218, 239–44,
    331, 342, 381
statistical noise. See background noise
stopping prompts
    energy detection, 107
    word detection, 108
stuttering. See turn taking
substitution. See speech recognition errors
sub-vocabulary, 171
super-numeric, 65, 66, 366, 368, 374,
    381. See digits
surface features, 253, 345
syllables
    dropping, 87, 88
    unstressed, 73, 84, 85, 87
synesthesia, 129
synonym, 88, 95, 167, 300, 383
syntactic, 40, 104, 110, 130
synthesized, 1, 36, 38, 39, 41, 111, 121,
    128, 360, 381
synthesized speech, 7, 381

T

T1, 99, 100
talent. See voice talent
talk ahead, 105, 106, 190, 372, 381
telephone as a computer terminal, 1
tempo, 139
temporal, 114
terminal, 199, 200, 201, 202, 203, 208,
    304, 305, 363, 372, 381, 382
text-to-speech. See synthesized speech
timbre, 128, 139
time
    and efficiency, 11, 23
    and memory, 11, 12, 16
    consuming, 11, 12

control over, 16, 26
extracting information from, 5, 11
long time scales, 139
wasting, 6, 11
time alignment, 72
timeout, 26, 156, 171, 172, 174, 181, 272,
    282
timing values, 39
toggle, 90, 91, 92
token, 106, 197, 200–215, 200, 305, 312,
    370, 372, 373, 382
token density, 304, 305, 306, 312, 372,
    373, 382
tone
    help. See help
    prompting. See prompt
tones
    as landmarks. See landmarks
    dominant, 137, 138, 140
    for menus, 140
    for waiting, 142
    multiple, 133
    pairs, 137, 138, 139
    tension/release, 139
    tonic, 137, 138, 140
touch to select, 160, 161, 195
training, 80, 83, 118
triad, 138
trigrams. See statistical language model
tritone, 138, 140
turn taking
    and false starts, 108, 368
    and stuttering, 104
    choosing a protocol, 110–15
    designing prompts for, 117–19
    example of errors, 101–2
    overview, 15–16
    with barge-in, 116–20
    without barge-in, 120–26
tutorials, 2, 58, 65, 142, 274
two-way branching, 48, 162, 163

U

unvoiced, 74, 80
usability lab. See usability testing
usability testing, 51, 76, 118, 138, 164,
    165, 206, 293, 294, 301, 303, 304,
    305, 343, 363, 382

questionnaires, 9, 306, 307, 348
user initiated. *See* user-driven
user interface overhead, 327
user-centered, 254
user-driven, 134, 145, 146, 147, 148, 151,
    155, 192, 203, 205, 257, 278, 279,
    280, 294, 372, 373, 382
users
    expert, 112, 136, 137, 155, 164, 186,
        196, 372, 381
    novice, 46, 137, 163, 164, 248

V

value-add. *See* business model
verbatim prompts. *See* prompts
virtual assistant, 30, 37, 154, 250, 259,
    262, 263, 264, 265, 290, 375, 383
vocabulary
    low-energy words, 81
    mutual funds, 190, 191, 211, 382
    start over, 43, 76, 77, 88, 93, 149, 279,
        280
vocal quality, 72, 260
vocal tract, 36, 85, 104, 366, 372, 376
voice
    coach, 343
    talent, 32, 34, 251, 343, 383
voice browser. *See* browser
voice portal, 29, 32, 325–42, 383
    and VRU, 329
    consumer, 18, 19, 331–32
    enterprise, 329–31
voice recording
    warmup, 349
Voice Response Unit, 3, 9, 77, 383
voice web, 32, 239
voice-activated dialing, 55, 79, 81, 95,
    120, 123, 147, 155, 180, 256
    phonebook, 81, 82, 83, 161
voiced, 74, 80, 81
voices
    dual, 190
    female, 35, 36, 37, 38, 114, 156, 157,
        158, 190, 191, 285, 287
    male, 35, 36, 37, 38, 62, 63, 114, 156,
        157, 158, 190, 191, 285, 287
    multiple, 36, 37, 63, 64, 65, 159, 206
VoiceXML, 328, 360, 384

W

web browser. *See* browser
Web-Lite, 331
windowing
    recognition, 77, 112, 158, 175, 192,
        281, 384
Wizard of Oz tests, 31, 73, 76, 89, 118,
    206, 244, 294–99, 307–9, 317–20, 384
word detection, 106, 108
word pair, 72, 86, 91, 378
    asymmetrical, 88
WoZ. *See* Wizard of Oz tests

Y

yes/no
    error recovery, 168
    for noise detection, 173
    implicit windows, 170
    interrogative, 47
    queries, 163, 166, 196, 282
    synonyms, 167
    to stabilize dialogues, 172